John Hervey Wheeler, Black Banking, and the Economic Struggle for Civil Rights

John Hervey Wheeler, Black Banking, and the Economic Struggle for Civil Rights

Brandon K. Winford

UNIVERSITY PRESS OF KENTUCKY

Paperback edition 2022

Scholarly publisher for the Commonwealth, serving Bellarmine University, Berea College, Centre College of Kentucky, Eastern Kentucky University, The Filson Historical Society, Georgetown College, Kentucky Historical Society, Kentucky State University, Morehead State University, Murray State University, Northern Kentucky University, Spalding University, Transylvania University, University of Kentucky, University of Louisville, and Western Kentucky University.

Editorial and Sales Offices: The University Press of Kentucky
663 South Limestone Street, Lexington, Kentucky 40508-4008
www.kentuckypress.com

Portions of chapter 5 were originally published as "'The Bright Sunshine of a New Day': John Hervey Wheeler, Black Business, and Civil Rights in North Carolina, 1929–1964," in the *North Carolina Historical Review* (July 2016): 235–78.

Library of Congress Cataloging-in-Publication Data

Names: Winford, Brandon K., author.
Title: John Hervey Wheeler, Black Banking, and the Economic Struggle for Civil Rights / Brandon K. Winford.
Description: Lexington : University Press of Kentucky, 2020. | Series: Civil Rights and the Struggle for Black Equality in the Twentieth Century | Includes bibliographical references and index.
Identifiers: LCCN 2019037387 | ISBN 9780813178257 (hardcover) | ISBN 9780813178271 (pdf) | ISBN 9780813178288 (epub)
Subjects: LCSH: Wheeler, John H. (John Hervey) | African American civil rights workers—North Carolina—Biography. | Civil rights workers—North Carolina—Biography. | African American bankers—North Carolina—Durham—Biography. | Bankers—North Carolina—Durham—Biography. | African Americans—Civil rights—North Carolina—History—20th century. | United States. President's Committee on Equal Employment Opportunity—Biography. | African Americans—North Carolina—Economic conditions. | Democratic Party (N.C.)—Biography. | North Carolina—Biography.
Classification: LCC E185.93.N6 W56 2020 | DDC 323.092 [B]—dc23

ISBN 978-0-8131-9609-1 (pbk. : alk. paper)

This book is printed on acid-free paper meeting the requirements of the American National Standard for Permanence in Paper for Printed Library Materials.

Manufactured in the United States of America.

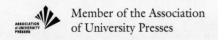

Member of the Association of University Presses

To my parents, Ray and Cynthia Winford
my sister, LaFonda Rae Griffin (1974–2007)
my grandmother, Annie Belle Winford Heaggans
(1924–2011)

Contents

Illustrations

Figures

Tables

Abbreviations

A&T	Agricultural and Technical College of North Carolina
AME	African Methodist Episcopal Church
CAP	Community Action Program
CMCHR	Charlotte-Mecklenburg Council on Human Relations
CORE	Congress of Racial Equality
CT	*Carolina Times*
DBPC	Durham Business and Professional Chain
DCNA	Durham Committee on Negro Affairs
DCSBMM	Durham City School Board Meeting Minutes
DHA	Durham Housing Authority
DHRC	Durham Human Relations Council
DIC	Durham Interim Committee
DMH	*Durham Morning Herald*
DMRRBML	David M. Rubenstein Rare Book and Manuscript Library, Duke University
DRC	Durham Redevelopment Commission
DS	*Durham Sun*
ESC	North Carolina Employment Security Commission
FDIC	Federal Deposit Insurance Corporation
FEPC	Fair Employment Practices Committee
FHA	Federal Housing Administration
HHFA	Housing and Home Finance Agency
HRC	Mayor's Human Relations Committee
HUD	Department of Housing and Urban Development
LDF	NAACP Legal Defense and Educational Fund
LIHDC	Low-Income Housing Development Corporation
L&M	Liggett and Myers Tobacco Company
M&F Bank	Mechanics and Farmers Bank
NAACP	National Association for the Advancement of Colored People

NC Fund	North Carolina Fund
NC Mutual	North Carolina Mutual Life Insurance Company
NCBA	North Carolina Bankers Association
NCC	North Carolina College
NCCHR	North Carolina Council on Human Relations
NCCN	North Carolina College for Negroes
NCTA	North Carolina Teachers Association
NCVEP	North Carolina Voter Education Project
NNBA	National Negro Bankers Association
NUL	National Urban League
OB	Operation Breakthrough
OEO	Office of Economic Opportunity
PCEEO	President's Committee on Equal Employment Opportunity
RAC	Recreation Advisory Committee
RTP	Research Triangle Park
SCLC	Southern Christian Leadership Conference
SNCC	Student Nonviolent Coordinating Committee
SRC	Southern Regional Council
TWIU	Tobacco Workers International Union
UNC	University of North Carolina
UNCF	United Negro College Fund
UOCI	United Organizations for Community Improvement
VBG	Voters for Better Government
VEP	Voter Education Project

Introduction

> The battle for freedom begins every morning.
>
> John Hervey Wheeler

In November 1945, Mechanics and Farmers Bank (M&F Bank) cashier and vice president John Hervey Wheeler penned an article for the *Tarheel Banker*, the voice of the North Carolina Bankers Association, writing "the South cannot hope to participate fully in the benefits of the approaching period without first committing itself to the full integration of its Negro population into all phases of its economy." As world war gave way to peace, he urged the state's white financial power brokers to steer the region toward an end to Jim Crow segregation for economic reasons. With statistical data on black buying power in hand, Wheeler pointed to civil rights as the precondition for growth while placing race, power, and citizenship at the crux of his appeal for economic justice. He posed a challenge while pointing to the South's greatest opportunity. His words were not meant only for white bankers in the Tar Heel State. He indeed spoke to the entire region, declaring that the South was at a crossroads where it had to "choose between preservation of many of its time-honored mores [or] taking its full place in the American economy. To have both would be like eating its cake and having it too." His article exemplified a lifelong mission. In the mid-twentieth-century South, Wheeler used his keen economic sense as a banker and his legal skills as a civil rights lawyer to break down discriminatory barriers that kept blacks in a perpetual state of economic inferiority.[1]

This work asks us to rethink the role of black business—often criticized as too conservative, largely absent, or nonsupportive—during the civil rights movement. This book explores the black freedom struggle through the lens of John Wheeler (1908–1978), one of the nation's savviest behind-the-scenes black power brokers, a political activist, civic leader, educator, statesman, and philanthropist. The book argues that if we are to fully understand how central economics was to the civil rights movement, we must consider black business. Black businesspeople had emphasized and promoted racial uplift through economic advancement since the turn of the twentieth century. Yet amid the Great Depression and following World War II, leaders such as Wheeler offered a new paradigm that in many ways rejected racial uplift. They held that economic advancement was simply impossible for black people unless they first obtained racial equality. Full citizenship would lead to black economic power and set the stage for widespread prosperity in the New South. As both black Americans and black capitalists, the creators of this paradigm had a dual stake in ensuring racial equality and economic justice. They also wanted to see whether the civil rights movement would achieve complete integration and freedom of movement—and if so, how those gains would impact the survival and expansion of black enterprise and black institutions.

Wheeler understood how powerful the white North Carolina bankers he was addressing would be in determining the economic course the region would follow in postwar American society. He recognized that these bankers, much like himself, would help usher the region into a new era of unparalleled prosperity. The black banker articulated a bold economic vision I call New South prosperity, ideals he believed were grounded in black economic power. Black southerners, Wheeler argued, represented a large portion of the population. For regional prosperity even to begin, black southerners had to contribute, and before they could improve their economic condition, they needed full citizenship. Wheeler reminded the white South that its future and survival was bound to the economic plight of black citizens. He made it clear that Jim Crow segregation hindered not only black people's social advancement but their economic possibilities. Unless Jim Crow ended, economic advancement and New South prosperity would be impossible because the region would not be able to maintain a competitive edge over other regions—at a time when the country as a whole was experiencing unprecedented prosperity because of World War II.

Wheeler believed the fervor of the immediate postwar period would lend itself to the transformation of southern society if only the South would finally grant African Americans full citizenship. When the region turned a pivotal corner away from a largely agricultural economy dependent on cheap labor, black southerners had to fit within the new economic vision. Wheeler also recognized that the South had to change the old economic system whereby other regions benefited from the labors of the South while the region itself benefited little. He operated from an integrationist framework, which would give African Americans complete "freedom of movement" in every area of American life and remove institutional forms of racism from all facets of American society. Wheeler believed freedom of movement could happen only if black people and black institutions were integrated into society in a fair and balanced way. Thus, he advocated more than access to physical spaces through direct action. In his vision, if a previously all-white institution hired a black American, it had to give him or her full access to the same resources that all other employees had, especially opportunities for merit-based promotion and advancement.

This book shows that Wheeler spent his entire career trying to fulfill the ideals of New South prosperity through his institutional and organizational affiliations, as part of his civil rights agenda. Though he was a central figure in North Carolina's civil rights movement, he has yet to receive scholarly attention. This work examines his involvement in black banking, law, education, employment, voting, housing, health care, public accommodations, antipoverty, and urban renewal—all of which he viewed through an economic lens. It explores what it meant to be a black power broker in the mid-twentieth-century South and what the goals and objectives of the civil rights movement looked like to a black banker with significant political and economic leverage. Ultimately, it traces how black business advanced black economic liberation in the postwar era.

Wheeler began his business career just before the Great Depression. After graduating from the all-black Morehouse College in Atlanta in 1929, he moved to Durham, North Carolina, and landed a bank teller job with M&F Bank, a twenty-one-year-old institution with resources of nearly eight hundred thousand dollars. It was one of five black-owned banks operating in the state at that time. Some of the bank's founders had earlier helped establish the North Carolina Mutual Life Insurance Company; and NC Mutual and M&F Bank became sister institutions and sources of pride for black Durham. Since the late nineteenth century, the city had been becoming a thriving black commercial center and one of the foremost New South cities.[2]

Wheeler became a banker just months before the stock market crash of October 1929. He came to Durham at the end of an era that historian Juliet E. K. Walker refers to as the "Golden Age of Black Business," the period from about 1900 to 1930 during which about 134 black-owned banks were founded in the United States. North Carolina would lose roughly 215 banks during the first half of the Great Depression, and of the many black-owned banks that existed at the crash, M&F Bank was one of only twelve that came through the Depression without collapsing. Only a handful of those banks survived World War II. In a 1925 essay, the noted black sociologist E. Franklin Frazier called Durham the "Capital of the Black Middle Class," where there was "promise of a transformed Negro." In 1927, the *Pittsburgh Courier* compared Durham to Harlem, writing that it had far surpassed that intellectual epicenter from an economic standpoint. An October 1929 article in the same newspaper outlined the depths of black business by pointing to Durham's "Second Line of Defense," which was prepared to take charge of black financial institutions when the current leadership moved on. During this Golden Age, black Durham became a training ground for what I call "black business activism," where Wheeler and others used their "economic independence" as a "launching pad into civil rights."[3]

In 1952, Wheeler became president of M&F Bank, and in the early 1950s he also served two terms as president of the National Negro Bankers Association (NNBA). As bank president, Wheeler carried the community bank banner while also expanding the bank's reach beyond Durham and Raleigh. M&F Bank opened its first Charlotte branch in 1962, on the cusp of the city's rise in the financial sector and just as the region was wrestling with the civil rights revolution. When Wheeler became M&F Bank's president, the financial institution's resources came to $5,910,890. They stood at $16,966,426 in 1964, $24,038,411 in 1970, and $41,405,000 in 1976. He supported the economic struggle for civil rights in postwar America through fair housing policies, increased black home ownership, and investments in low-income housing developments.[4]

During the Great Depression, Wheeler joined with black leaders to found the Durham Committee on Negro Affairs (DCNA) to provide broad community leadership on critical issues that African Americans faced in the city. He came into his own politically through increased involvement in the DCNA, which commanded a significant voting bloc in the city and was the most powerful black political organization in the state, if not the entire South.

In the late 1940s, blacks launched a massive battle for racial equality and economic justice, which culminated with huge legal victories under the leadership of the National Association for the Advancement of Colored People (NAACP). In 1947, Wheeler was among the first graduates of the North Carolina College School of Law, and, in cooperation with the DCNA, he embraced the NAACP's strategy and helped advance the legal phase of the civil rights movement. In his role as a civil rights lawyer, he demonstrated his strong commitment to black education. He spent the decade after World War II engaged in the battle for educational equality and became the lead attorney for black plaintiffs in *Blue v. Durham* (1951), a case that set an important legal precedent as the first successful school equalization suit in the state. By the early 1950s, the NAACP had won significant victories leading to the landmark US Supreme Court case *Brown v. Board of Education* (1954). After *Brown,* Wheeler gained widespread visibility when he warned political leaders in the South that a failure to adhere to the landmark decision was akin to "economic suicide." He navigated civil rights by continuously outlining their larger significance to New South prosperity. In 1956, he joined with several other local DCNA and NAACP attorneys, including future Congress of Racial Equality (CORE) chairman Floyd B. McKissick, to successfully argue the US Supreme Court case *Frasier v. Board of Trustees of the University of North Carolina* (1956), which led to the first three black undergraduates gaining admission to the state's flagship institution.[5]

During the 1960s, at the height of the modern civil rights movement, Wheeler was North Carolina's most influential black power broker and among the top civil rights figures in the South. Between 1957 and 1978, he served as DCNA's chairman. In 1964, he became the first black president of the Southern Regional Council (SRC), the Atlanta-based interracial research and publication civil rights organization, a national group that influenced policymakers in various ways. That same year Governor Terry Sanford appointed him as the first black delegate to represent North

Carolina at a Democratic National Convention. Wheeler also held several presidential appointments in the Kennedy and Johnson administrations, including an appointment to the President's Committee on Equal Employment Opportunity (PCEEO), an immediate forerunner to the Equal Employment Opportunity Commission (EEOC). Wheeler's civil rights activism defies traditional categories in very striking ways. The banker-lawyer might be described best as a black business activist—a suave tactician who skillfully demanded civil rights and full citizenship on behalf of black Americans. His personal motto and favorite refrain was, "The battle for freedom begins every morning," which meant the difficult fight against racial injustice was continuous and should never stop, and that freedom was part of a larger goal that could not be won overnight.[6]

Wheeler employed many tactics—including lawsuits and behind-the-scenes brokering—to press for equitable opportunities, and some of his tactics straddled the line between confrontation and negotiation. Moreover, when the direct-action phase of the movement was in full swing, he embraced the emergent student leadership and their organized civil disobedience as a tactic for obtaining racial equality and economic justice. He was more inclined than most black businessmen to not only operate behind the scenes but also to stand up publicly in the face of the white power structure. By the mid-1960s, he saw the battle for civil rights as having three distinct phases: the legal phase, the direct-action phase, and the implementation phase. He believed the latter phase was especially uncharted territory and perhaps the most difficult to accomplish, as it dealt with eliminating institutional forms of racism. Wheeler led in many arenas, and he brought the full weight of his extensive institutional and organizational affiliations to bear in all his civil rights activism.

Wheeler eventually learned harsh lessons: the goals of civil rights and black economic power did not always mesh with those of black capitalism, and he paid the price for believing that they could. This became most evident when Durham's urban renewal failed, and he was roundly criticized for his blanket support of the program. In the last decade of his life, Wheeler was more frustrated than ever with the Democratic Party because he felt that it had all but abandoned black Americans. In 1968, for example, he supported the outlier candidacy of black Charlotte dentist Reginald Hawkins for governor. Wheeler joined the board of the Nixon administration–backed Soul City, the black town and economic development project engineered by Floyd B. McKissick a year later. Then, in 1972, Wheeler broke ranks and supported black congresswoman Shirley Chisholm in her historic presidential campaign rather than former North Carolina governor and Duke University president Terry Sanford. Sanford, the supposed moderate, was highly disappointed. Later, faced with a lack of support among black voters and eventually a poor performance in the primary, he dropped out of the race.

Though Wheeler wielded considerable power, he was limited in what he could accomplish because he relied on institutional and organizational support. Some might view him as too beholden to these established structures. But throughout his life, he counseled, "the best tactics . . . are to work through the courts, become involved in politics, and use 'organized' pressure."[7]

In a career that spanned five decades, Wheeler also joined countless boards, commissions, and organizations, from local to national bodies, some of which were comprised of several businesses, financial institutions, and economic development partnerships. Moreover, he worked continuously with educational institutions, hospitals, churches, libraries, charitable organizations, fraternal societies, and professional associations. The banker-lawyer financially supported a myriad of institutions and organizations because he believed in the integrity of black people and black institutions in the same way that many of his elders had. Wheeler especially believed in continuing to build black-owned institutions and gave generously in this endeavor.[8]

This work draws on previously unexamined primary and secondary sources. It relies heavily on the extensive John Hervey Wheeler Collection, located at the Atlanta University Center Robert W. Woodruff Library in Atlanta, Georgia. In fact, it is the first scholarly contribution grounded mainly in the Wheeler Collection, and I am the first scholar to be granted unrestricted access to these materials. The rich collection informs a variety of topics related to the black experience from about 1897 until 1978. The book combines scholarship on black business and civil rights history to illustrate how economics helped achieve the goals and objectives of the modern civil rights movement. While any discussion about the centrality of economics to civil rights might seem to require a discussion of black business, nothing could be further from the truth. This study contributes to and draws from the extensive discourse on the broader civil rights movement and especially considers the framework of the long civil rights movement. This approach allows us to see and understand exactly how economic concerns factored into the entire spectrum of civil rights leadership. This book also builds on previous scholarship about civil rights lawyers, expanding our understanding of the crucial role that lesser-known attorneys played in the black freedom struggle. Moreover, it joins the growing scholarship on the civil rights and black power movements in North Carolina. Black Durham has received significant scholarly attention, but this book casts the city as a place struggling to redefine itself and its landscape amid the turmoil of the nascent civil rights movement.

Chapter 1 presents the Wheeler family in the decades after emancipation and highlights their educational accomplishments, which put them on a path toward middle-class respectability in the early part of the twentieth century. It underscores how, though the Wheeler children were subject to the limitations of the Jim Crow South, their middle-class status and economic independence provided them a more level playing field. Moreover, I argue that at the end of the nineteenth century the ideological underpinnings of the industrial New South offered black business leaders a vision of racial uplift through economic independence as a way to reclaim full citizenship. This first chapter emphasizes the close proximity Wheeler had to black business from an early age because his father became an executive with NC Mutual, and it explains why he chose a career in banking.

Chapter 2 examines M&F Bank's establishment and its survival amid the catastrophic collapse that precipitated the Great Depression. Because M&F Bank was deeply committed to the overall prosperity of the black community, it was in a much better position than most black-owned banks to advocate that the community return to political participation. In this way, Durham's black businesspeople served as stalwart community leaders, training a younger cadre of well-educated and ready activists. Moreover, they embraced a multidimensional strategy of reciprocity—complicated by gender, class, and intergenerational tensions. This chapter also traces the rise of the DCNA and its assertive, collective agitation for citizenship.

Chapter 3 explores how the legal phase of the civil rights movement came together as World War II ended. It considers the economic vision of New South prosperity that Wheeler articulated to bankers in the Tar Heel State in the postwar period. It also highlights Wheeler's postwar involvement in the battle for black educational equality in North Carolina and the South more broadly. His embrace of legal tactics helped challenge an unjust educational system that effectively prevented black schoolchildren from learning the skills needed to obtain jobs. While white local and state leaders devised creative laws to forestall desegregation, from the moment *Brown* came down Wheeler and other black leaders argued for immediate school desegregation and proactively publicized their desire for implementation.

Chapter 4 examines Wheeler's activism during the direct-action phase of the civil rights movement, the effort to implement *Brown* and other high court legal rulings. It considers how Wheeler, a black businessman, served as a steadfast advocate of alternative tactics during the 1960s. Despite the emergence of student-centered leadership with the 1960 sit-in movement, Wheeler continued to operate behind the scenes while publicly and privately lending his support to student activists. He rejected appeals from powerful white moderates that he and other traditional black leaders facilitate a quick end to sit-ins. White leaders considered Wheeler to be more radical than most, and his acceptance of young activists and his integrationist views set him apart from many of his black business contemporaries. While direct action represented a shift away from strict reliance on legal tactics and a generational shift in leadership, Wheeler recognized that ongoing civil disobedience put him in a much better position to fulfill the ideals of New South prosperity because he could become more involved in reform and policymaking at the local, state, and national levels. In other words, he built on previous legal victories through implementation and the removal of institutional forms of racism.

As direct-action protests opened up new possibilities for civil rights in the area of sweeping congressional legislation, Wheeler became a broker on a wider scale. Chapter 5 examines his efforts during the early 1960s, when he utilized his increasing political influence regionally and nationally to change policies related to discrimination in employment and voting rights for black Americans. Wheeler also vigorously championed the inclusion of blacks in high-level positions within local, state, and federal governments and condemned agencies for failing to implement new employment policies mandated by the federal government.

Chapter 6 demonstrates the limitations of black business activism during the 1960s. Durham's urban renewal program began in 1958, a consequence of the Housing Act of 1954 and the state's Research Triangle Park (RTP) initiative. Wheeler became the lone black member of the Durham Redevelopment Commission, the group responsible for administering the federally funded program. His support fit his own thinking on how best to implement the gains already being won by the civil rights movement. Wheeler believed that urban renewal was one step toward black enterprise's reentrance into the larger marketplace. The chapter also examines his involvement with the North Carolina Fund, an antipoverty agency Governor Terry Sanford created in 1963. The NC Fund became the model for President Lyndon B. Johnson's War on Poverty and Great Society national reform agenda. Wheeler was instrumental in getting philanthropic organizations such as the private Ford Foundation to financially back the program, and he served on the NC Fund's board of directors during its five years in existence. M&F Bank became the repository for its monies, and Wheeler strongly advocated economic investments in low-income housing. He considered M&F Bank's financing of such programs to have pushed white banks to extend their own lending policies to black borrowers.

1

From Slavery to Middle-Class Respectability

> *Trust God*—trust him for success, for support, for life. If in this way you will trust God, he by his word, by his Spirit and by his providence, will lead you into the highest usefulness of which, in your day and generation, you are capable.
>
> John G. Fee, founder of Berea College, 1891

The year 1908 represented new beginnings for the Wheelers. On New Year's Day, John Leonidas and Margaret Hervey Wheeler welcomed their second child into the world, a son they named John Hervey Wheeler. Across the country on that date, African Americans celebrated the annual Emancipation Day, gathering to rejoice in their freedom from enslavement and seeking full citizenship. In May, John Leonidas Wheeler resigned from his position as president of Kittrell College to take a job as an insurance agent with the North Carolina Mutual and Provident Association (later named North Carolina Mutual Life Insurance Company, or NC Mutual), the Durham enterprise founded a decade earlier. Both Wheelers had taught at Kittrell, a small college in Vance County, about thirty-seven miles north of Raleigh, from the time they arrived in North Carolina in 1898. Kittrell graduate John Moses Avery, a former student of John Leonidas and the company's assistant manager, convinced him to join the NC Mutual family.[1]

"It was an inducement of making much money," John Leonidas later explained. One generation removed from slavery, the Wheelers came to enjoy middle-class respectability through a post–Civil War vision of racial uplift alongside the hopes and aspirations of freedom rooted in educational attainment. The family's transition from education to business, and their move to Durham, underscored the economic opportunities available in the city with its growing black community. The industrialization that had taken place there in the late nineteenth century was making Durham "the quintessential city of the New South."[2]

Like John Leonidas, many black leaders delved into both education and business, and both black business and economic advancement are important for understanding black community development across the South. In the South in the 1890s, black business leaders had publicly articulated that the only path toward racial equality would be investments in black economic uplift. Shortly after the 1898 Wilmington Race Riot, NC Mutual president John Merrick asked, "What difference does it make to us who is elected[?] We got to serve in the same different capacities of life for a living." In the first half of the twentieth century, many black business leaders hoped to achieve equality through expanding black enterprise. Early on, John Hervey came to appreciate the importance of economics to the overall plight of black people and to the New South more broadly.[3]

The NC Mutual had a profound impact on John Hervey's early life in several ways. By 1912, the company promoted John Leonidas, and the Wheeler family moved to Atlanta. There, they regularly opened their home to company officials, including its founders, John Merrick and Dr. Aaron McDuffie Moore. The young boy would "listen carefully to the conversations" and observed: "Although he was a man of few words, Dr. Moore's brain appeared to be a constant beehive of activity and his personality indicated a constant searching for truth and for new and better ways of doing things. For a youngster ten years old, these experiences left upon me a lasting impression of the all-inclusive manner in which Mr. Merrick and Dr. Moore worked so hard to place the company on a firm footing." The two men, he said, "were in every sense of the word, social engineers, possessed with a oneness of purpose" and "exercised a strong influence upon my life as well as upon the lives of countless others."[4]

John Hervey's parents achieved economic success and middle-class respectability, which set them apart from the economic struggles of the black masses. They worked hard to place their children on a level playing field by building important community institutions and organizations. Nevertheless, their generation could not end Jim Crow segregation. John Hervey and his two sisters, Ruth and Margery, needed to carry their parents' legacy forward to ensure they would have equality commensurate with their skill, potential, and intellect.[5]

"To Be Helped to Places of Usefulness and Respectability"

The Wheeler family came from Nicholasville, Kentucky, the seat of Jessamine County in the central part of the Bluegrass State. John Leonidas was born to Phoebe Wheeler on July 8, 1869, four years after the American Civil War ended. Phoebe and her parents, Lucius and Winnie Wheeler, had been slaves in Jessamine County, and her son joined "freedom's first generation," black people born during the war or to their ex-slave parents in the postwar era. During this adjustment period, blacks asserted their claims to full citizenship for the first time. John Leonidas's father was white, reportedly his mother's former owner, whose surname was Willis. Although John Leonidas never knew his white father, the family's oral tradition held that he was a banker and one of Nicholasville's leading citizens. The family selected the Wheeler surname upon emancipation.[6]

In 1863, the Union army established Camp Nelson in the county, and the military outpost soon became a symbol of freedom for enslaved Kentuckians. "Here," writes historian Richard D. Sears, "the country's newest citizens heard their first news about voting and citizenship and equality." Margaret Hervey was another child born to ex-slaves in the Bluegrass Region. Born on April 12, 1877, at the end of Reconstruction, she was one of seven children born to John and Jennie Thomas Hervey. The senior Herveys may have been freed and bought farmland before the Civil War, though this is not documented. John Hervey estimated that his maternal grandparents owned about 150 acres where they grew tobacco and corn, putting them in a much better economic situation than most black families. Margaret Hervey took pride in having received her early education at a school that abolitionist John G. Fee built at Camp Nelson.[7]

Former slaves received emancipation in 1865, and once Reconstruction began, their hopes centered on education, land ownership, political rights, and control over their own labor. But only in February 1874 did the Kentucky state legislature finally establish a public school system for blacks. The new law unfairly taxed black Kentuckians, provided less state money for black education than white, and called for racially segregated schools. It also essentially withheld control over black education from black leaders, leaving white administrators to determine the direction of black education in the state.[8]

The Hervey-Wheeler family, showing the offspring of John and Jennie Thomas Hervey and their daughter Margaret Hervey, who married John Leonidas Wheeler on September 25, 1901. Their children, Ruth Hervey, John Hervey, and Margery Janice, are also pictured here. Three of Margaret's siblings are included, two brothers and sister Ida Hervey (later Smith). Reprinted by permission from Caroline Bond Day and Earnest A. Hooton, *A Study of Some Negro-White Families in the United States,* Harvard African Studies, v. 10, Peabody Museum of American Archaeology and Ethnology, Harvard University (Cambridge, Mass., 1932), plate 16.

Despite the challenges, John Leonidas attended public school, and he began teaching in Kentucky public schools in the late 1880s. Through determination and financial sacrifice, he saved up enough money to move to Xenia, Ohio, in 1889 and began attending Wilberforce University in 1890.[9]

Margaret Hervey also studied at Wilberforce, the AME Church's flagship institution and the embodiment of black aspirations for freedom during the post–Civil War era. Founded in 1856, it was the premier hub for Christian liberal arts education for blacks. The school emphasized

The Allen Building on the campus of Kittrell College housed the Industrial Department and doubled as a dormitory for male students until it burned to the ground on April 7, 1913. Reproduced from *An Era of Progress and Promise, 1863–1910: The Religious, Moral, and Educational Development of the American Negro since His Emancipation*, by William Newton Hartshorn (Boston: Priscilla, 1910). Courtesy of the State Library of North Carolina, Raleigh.

Christian values, piety, morality, and clean living, as well as the need for students to understand the extent to which they represented their race in everything they did. It is highly likely that John Leonidas and Margaret Hervey courted during their days at Wilberforce, and their courtship may have even had its origins in Kentucky, given that the two came from the same area. In college, they joined a rising postwar generation destined "to be helped to places of usefulness and respectability." John Leonidas demonstrated a strong work ethic, paying his way by working in hotels and as a cook. A year after he enrolled, he received a scholarship that "was

Kittrell College faculty. *Men, left to right:* Earle Finche, John R. Hawkins, George W. Adams (later M&F Bank cashier), Pinkney W. Dawkins, and John Leonidas Wheeler. The photograph's original description includes the names of only five women, pictured here in no particular order: Mrs. John R. Hawkins, Kate Telfare, Mrs. Hawkins, Lena Cheek, and Rosa Alexander. *Kittrell College Faculty,* Scrapbook 2, undated, John H. Wheeler Collection, Atlanta University Center Robert W. Woodruff Library.

of great assistance to him." Margaret Hervey's training would have primarily centered on the domestic arts, while John Leonidas studied classics. One of his professors was W. E. B. Du Bois. Having graduated at the head of his class, John Leonidas received an invitation in December 1897 to chair the new classics department at Kittrell College in Kittrell, North Carolina. He accepted and moved there in 1898.[10]

Kittrell College began in 1858 as a resort, the Kittrell's Springs Hotel, built exclusively for the use of wealthy white families. When the Civil War broke out, the Confederate army converted it into a Confederate general hospital. After the war, it briefly became a school for white women and then, again, a hotel. Just four days before the AME Church's North Carolina Conference took possession of the site, a mysterious fire broke out, probably at the hands of an arsonist angered that the formerly all-white edifice would now be used to educate and uplift blacks. The fire left the two largest buildings in shambles. But the AME Church continued its plans and opened the school's doors on February 7, 1886. A place built to serve whites and later used to protect the institution of slavery had become a place of black uplift and refuge, and its historical backdrop remained visible while the Wheelers lived at Kittrell.[11]

Margaret Hervey arrived after she graduated from Wilberforce in 1900, and the couple married in 1901. They would have expounded to their students the same principles they had learned at Wilberforce and through the AME Church. Kittrell's annual reports and catalogues for this period reveal that the school's primary objective was to foster in students "a spirit of self reliance and Christian manhood and womanhood." In 1901, John Leonidas became president of what by that time was Kittrell College.[12]

"Planted on a Firm Basis": The Industrial New South and the Rise of NC Mutual

By 1900, southern cities such as Durham, Atlanta, and Richmond had gained prominence because of industrialization in the latter half of the nineteenth century. In Durham, tobacco-manufacturing titans and other industrialists helped remake a region in shambles after the Civil War into what white southern newspaper editors deemed the "New South." The idea described the South's transition away from the "Old South" plantation society, which depended heavily on the slave economy. Southerners shifted gears to keep up with the North, which by that time outpaced the region industrially. The southern industrialists focused on the region's economic advancement, which supposedly precluded racial antagonism, and the development of communities and towns around factories. These industrial centers, or New South cities, became known for manufactured goods that fueled economic growth, prosperity, and commerce.[13]

In the first thirty years after the war, Durham gained a reputation as an important and prosperous manufacturing town. At the center of its economic boom stood the tobacco industry, closely followed by cotton textile manufacturing, which helped place Durham on the map in relation to the regional, national, and global economies. The tobacco industry spurred development of financial institutions such as banks and insurance companies.[14] The 1895 *Hand-Book of Durham, North Carolina: A Brief and Accurate Description of a Prosperous and Growing Southern Manufacturing Town,* a promotional publication implicitly for whites, described the city's assets this way:

> Durham has four lines of railroad; five tobacco factories, two of which are the largest in the world; four large cotton mills; four cigar factories; one fertilizer factory; one bag factory; one soap factory; two sash, door and blind factories; three banks; four tobacco warehouses for the sale of leaf tobacco; about 100 leaf tobacco brokers; two foundries; four machine shops; two carriage factories; four job painting offices; one book-bindery; one laundry; one marble yard; one cotton roller covering works; four insurance agencies; two daily papers; two weekly papers and two monthlies; four furniture stores; five drug stores; three hardware stores and about 100 other merchants representing various lines. Has twelve churches; one college; two graded schools and other industrial, educational and benevolent institutions.[15]

The list captured the mood of American industrial capitalism in the city, where world-renowned tobacco brands such as "Bull Durham" became synonymous with the Piedmont city. Black Durham's rise, also spawned by industrialization, began before 1877, by which time the city's largest black section was already referred to as "Hayti" (pronounced Hay-tī), a name some suggest derived from the early black republic of Haiti.[16]

In the 1898 elections, the North Carolina Democratic Party launched a deadly statewide white supremacy campaign that consisted largely of racist propaganda from white newspapers, often instilling fear of miscegenation, sensationalized threats of "Negro domination," racial violence, and the rape of white women by black men to garner widespread support. It effectively dismantled the populist moment in the Tar Heel State, drew racial dividing lines between blacks and poor whites, and suppressed black citizenship rights. During what the historian Rayford W. Logan termed "the nadir" in American race relations, black southerners turned inward toward racial uplift as a means of survival.[17]

The heightened racial violence and opposition resulted in the 1898 Wilmington Race Riot, which peaked when local Democrats—using race as a crucial element—planned and executed a deadly coup d'état against the large black community and the Fusion-controlled government in Wilmington in the days following the November election. The riot destroyed black businesses and homes, forced black and white officeholders to flee to other parts of the country or risk being murdered, and silenced the black press. The Wilmington Race Riot was the most visible consequence of the white supremacy campaign, but the campaign culminated with huge Democratic victories during the 1898 election and continued with the 1900 Suffrage Amendment, a devastating measure that led to black disenfranchisement in the state.[18]

Just a month before the Wilmington Race Riot, a group of black leaders from a cross section of professions founded the North Carolina Mutual and Provident Association in Durham. The NC Mutual received its articles of incorporation on February 28, 1899, and began operations soon thereafter. Some historians suggest its founders may have started NC Mutual in direct response to the racial violence of 1898. Just a year into its operations, the company struggled when insurance claims outpaced premium income and threatened its existence. At that point, all the founders except John Merrick and Aaron McDuffie Moore withdrew their investments, and the two reorganized the company with the addition of Moore's nephew, Charles Clinton Spaulding. The restructuring of the organization proved beneficial to the company's survival.[19]

The industrialization of the New South gave rise to black leaders who took up free enterprise and promoted racial uplift, grounded in economic advancement, as the way to racial equality. At the same time, places such as Durham with significant industry made enterprises like NC Mutual possible because black people increasingly worked in those industrial factories and represented the core clientele at the insurance company and other black-owned institutions. Black business leaders believed in racial uplift as much as white business leaders believed in the New South creed. They advocated economic independence, moral respectability, education, and cultural engagement. Nevertheless, economic progress was extremely difficult to achieve without civil rights, as the rollback in gains widened the racial and economic divide.[20]

Durham piqued the Wheelers' interest. In April 1906, John Leonidas had considered leaving the South and his position at Kittrell to accept a job as principal at the black high school in Evansville, Indiana. Although he ultimately declined, the couple was clearly open to a major move, perhaps spurred by the birth of their first child, Ruth Hervey Wheeler, in 1906. Then, on January 1, 1908, John Hervey was born and named after Margaret's father, John Hervey, and her husband, John Leonidas. His birth meant increased financial responsibility and accelerated John Leonidas's decision to resign from Kittrell in May and take the job NC Mutual offered, set to begin that summer.[21]

The strong relationship between Kittrell and Durham helped nudge the Wheelers in that direction. Connections between the college and Durham's leading industrialists and entrepreneurs, both black and white, may help explain John Leonidas's decision to shift careers from education to business and to do so in Durham. These leaders gave generously to Kittrell from its inception in the way of money, personal time, construction supplies, heading special committees, and serving on its board of trustees. Among them were John Leonidas's new employers and associates at NC Mutual.[22]

John Leonidas was also prepared to enter the field of business because he had limited involvement in other ventures before accepting the position with NC Mutual. Since 1903, he had held shares in two black-owned businesses in Kittrell: the American Union Industrial Company and the American Union Benefit Association. While at Kittrell, Wheeler became president and special agent for the Union Benefit Association, an insurance company that offered policies to blacks in Vance County. John R. Hawkins (by that time the AME Church's education secretary) also partnered with John Leonidas in the two enterprises and became an investor in several others. The recommendation letters supporting his candidacy for the Evansville job spoke to his standing as an accomplished and well-respected educator. Wilberforce president Joshua H. Jones called him "an exceptionally strong man intellectually, morally, and socially . . . thoroughly trustworthy" and "a Christian gentleman to the core." Charles H.

Johnson, a colleague at Kittrell, described him as "brilliant, conservative, refined and honorable . . . and a progressive educator." John R. Hawkins noted his "executive ability and an enviable tact." John Leonidas also had the self-proclaimed ability to "get along with people" and knew "how to concede to every man his right to his own opinion, and if at variance to anyone, try by word and deed, without antagonism, to convince him of his error and thus leave him without any cut to chew." The Kittrell-Durham nexus, and John Leonidas's entrée into business, reinforced the important link between education and business in racial advancement.[23]

The Wheelers arrived in Durham in July 1908, as NC Mutual prepared to celebrate its first decade in operation. After reorganization in 1900, it had overcome additional obstacles before experiencing unprecedented growth and becoming a successful black enterprise. It had by 1908 expanded operations within North Carolina and into South Carolina. It had purchased several lots in the heart of Durham's business district and erected its first home office building, and it had absorbed the Peoples Benevolent and Relief Association in Charlotte. It now offered whole life insurance policies, and it had provided for the establishment of M&F Bank by purchasing shares. The year John Leonidas joined the company, it absorbed the Capital Benevolent Association in Columbia, South Carolina, and deposited the required $10,000 with that state's insurance commission. A major test of its strength came that year with the first examination by the North Carolina Insurance Department. In 1909, the enterprise marked its tenth anniversary with a premium income of $220,100, admitted assets of $72,808.67, and insurance in force of $1,535,668. It officially became an old-line legal reserve insurance company in 1913, which mandated that "a portion of each premium paid by the policy-holder be set aside" to cover liabilities. According to several histories of the company, however, it had been functioning in this capacity as far back as December 1909. It was the second black-owned insurance concern to become a legal reserve company in the United States, after Mississippi Life Insurance Company.[24]

The success of NC Mutual and other black-owned businesses in Durham prompted Booker T. Washington to visit the city in 1910 and later dub it "the City of Negro Enterprises." During the time the Wheelers lived there, black Durham laid claim to nearly 160 businesses, from

Titled *Durham's First Negro Kindergarten,* this photo depicts middle-class black children (*front row, left to right*): C. C. Spaulding Jr., Haywood Townsend, Arnetta Glenn, Otelia Spaulding, Fannie Allen, Inez Bynum, Minnie Pearson, Sarah Yearby, Norma Bruce, Novella Spaulding, and Berta Mae Townsend; (*back row, left to right*): John Hervey, Marion Bailey, Ruth Hervey (older sister), Lina Russell, Dorothy Alston, Mattie Louise Moore (daughter of Dr. Aaron McDuffie Moore, who later married R. L. McDougald), Sam Whitted, J. C. Scarborough Jr., Samuel Green, Edgar Pratt, Janet Avery, Annie Smithey, and Amey Armistead. *Durham's First Negro Kindergarten,* Scrapbook 1, undated, John H. Wheeler Collection, Atlanta University Center Robert W. Woodruff Library.

drugstores to a cotton textile mill. In 1912, W. E. B. Du Bois visited Durham and praised the expanding black business community and the city's race relations, which he called a nonhostile environment where whites took a "hands off—give them a chance—don't interfere" approach.[25]

The Bull City offered the Wheelers better opportunities for upward mobility and economic independence and would have ensured their son and daughter had certain advantages as well. At the behest of the NC Mutual leadership, several important social institutions were established, among them Lincoln Hospital, built in 1901 with some financial backing from the Dukes and Carrs. In 1909, Dr. James E. Shepard launched the National Religious Training School and Chautauqua (now North Carolina Central University). The black community already had several religious institutions, including St. Joseph's AME Church and White Rock Baptist Church, which Durham's black middle class attended. In addition to its social and economic institutions, black Durham boasted an increasing labor force, which mostly consisted of black women who worked in the city's tobacco factories. Factory employment allowed Durham's working-class blacks to support black-owned institutions, and these community institutions created a black professional class that included nurses, teachers, and secretaries. The Wheelers lived in Hayti, Durham's Third Ward, where they attended religious services and taught Sunday school at St. Joseph's AME Church.

Margaret Hervey became a homemaker, and the Wheelers enrolled their son and daughter in what was called "Durham's First Negro Kindergarten," which they attended with other children from the black middle-class elite. The family remained in Durham from 1908 until 1912, when John Leonidas received a promotion and transferred to the company's Atlanta office. At the time, Margaret Hervey was pregnant with the couple's third child. John Leonidas later supervised the company's entire Georgia district.[26]

"With More Than He Started": The NC Mutual and Jim Crow Segregation in Atlanta

The NC Mutual had begun operations in Georgia a year before the Wheelers made their home there, and the company eventually had five branch offices in the state (Atlanta, Savannah, Macon, Americus, and Augusta). The Wheelers arrived in Atlanta just six years after that city's deadly 1906 race riot. Since that time, black Atlantans had been disenfranchised by a suffrage amendment the state legislature passed in 1908. Although Durham had an expanding black community, Atlanta outpaced the tobacco city several times over. As a New South city, Atlanta had a thriving black middle class with strong businesses, private schools, and religious institutions. It was home to the South's most prominent black churches, including "Big" Bethel AME Church, where the Wheelers attended and John Leonidas and Margaret

Hervey taught Sunday school. Morehouse, Morris Brown, and Spelman Colleges were among the five black institutions of higher learning alongside Clark and Atlanta Universities. "Sweet Auburn Avenue" became the central hub of black Atlanta's commercial district and home to NC Mutual's Atlanta office. John Leonidas helped the company maintain a competitive edge over their Atlanta counterparts, "keeping the Mutual prosperous in the face of a powerful challenge from a large black middle class that founded" the Atlanta Life and Standard Life Insurance Companies. At NC Mutual, John Leonidas enjoyed a very successful career. In 1922, he became the company's assistant agency director and a member of the board of directors. In 1927, the company promoted him to regional supervisor, and he became the institution's assistant agency director in 1933. He helped found the National Negro Insurance Association and held a membership in the National Negro Business League. In 1948, two years before retiring after forty-five years of service, John Leonidas became a vice president with the company.[27]

The Wheeler children, who now included Margery Janice (born in 1912), held an advantage over most black children reared in segregated Atlanta. They had a life of privilege that few blacks could claim. By this time, Atlanta had already made good on its efforts to implement Jim Crow segregation, as evidenced by the black Auburn Avenue and the white Peachtree Street. During John Hervey's childhood days in Atlanta, he and his sisters had a significant economic advantage over most black Americans. "I started off life even" is how John Hervey described his fortunate upbringing. His father, John Leonidas, "had to work his own way through school, [and] he came out of college with more than he started." Margaret Hervey, herself an educator, homeschooled their three children until third grade and then enrolled them in the Atlanta public schools. They attended Butler Street Elementary School through seventh grade. The Wheeler children had a comfortable childhood, reared under the best possible circumstances for blacks considering the limitations of the Jim Crow South. John Hervey told an interviewer some years later that since childhood he "never felt that [he] was outside of the American society." Instead, Wheeler "always felt [his] freedom to go anywhere [he] wanted to go, and participate in anything that [he] had a desire to participate in." At the same time, Wheeler admitted that he had to "develop some blind spots [in order to] believe this." By the time he came of age, the Wheeler family had middle-class status in black Atlanta, and his family had clearly advanced economically, owning real estate in Ohio, North Carolina, and New York.[28]

John Leonidas and Margaret Hervey raised their children in a Christian household where culture abounded. Ruth played the piano, and John Hervey played the violin; Margery Janice had a strong interest in art. The family lived on Johnson Avenue in Atlanta's Fourth Ward, not far from Auburn Avenue, where John Leonidas worked. The Wheeler children grew up alongside other children from Atlanta's black middle-class elite, a "substantial" group, according to one magazine. It included the White family, whose son Walter H. White eventually headed the NAACP, and the King and the Dobbs families.[29]

The Wheelers' economic standing helped both John Leonidas and Margaret Hervey become civic leaders. John Leonidas helped expand the black Butler Street Young Men's Christian Association (YMCA) and joined its board of directors. That role often included giving generously to help support various causes; he regularly paid memberships for children "not able to pay the fee." He also helped increase recreational opportunities for blacks, "popularizing the game of tennis in Atlanta." John Leonidas supported athletics in the black schools in the area, especially Booker T. Washington High School. Margaret Hervey became active in cultural and civic organizations such as the Carrie Steele-Pitts Orphans Home and the Atlanta Woman's Club.[30]

Despite John Hervey's assertion that he always felt part of the American society, Jim Crow segregation remained a constant barrier. Before the Wheelers moved to Atlanta, the city's Fourth Ward experienced years of increased tensions because whites feared black intrusion into adjoining, previously all-white neighborhoods. In 1913, Atlanta passed a restrictive covenant law that forbade residents from moving into neighborhoods already occupied by the other racial group. The Georgia Supreme Court rejected the law in a 1915 case, and the ruling caused tensions that reached a tipping point in Atlanta's Fourth Ward. White residents complained "the 'black tide' was crowding white people out of their homes, forcing the sale of property at greatly reduced prices."[31]

In response, a "representative" interracial committee formed with six whites and eight blacks, among them John Leonidas. The group decided on a two-point agreement, which also passed at a larger community meeting, stating that they would "use all moral influence to prevent any colored person from purchasing or renting any property in blocks [that were] predominantly owned by whites," and vice versa. A year later, the city council barred blacks from living as close as one block from largely white areas. In the 1917 case *Buchanan v. Warley,* blacks won a major victory when the US Supreme Court rejected a Louisville, Kentucky, ordinance because the order denied black citizens their Fourteenth Amendment rights. Despite *Buchanan,* Atlanta's housing problems persisted as city leaders passed further ordinances that allowed for residential segregation by race.[32]

Education, too, was segregated. In 1913, Atlanta's all-white school board voted to cut the seventh and eighth grades from black schools and shift the financial savings to white schools. The board failed to make those cutbacks at the time, but it did eliminate the eighth grade from black schools the following year. After that, black children could attend Atlanta's public schools only through seventh grade, whereas their white counterparts received free public education for another four years. By 1916, the board again attempted to do away with seventh-grade education for blacks to make room in the budget for "a junior high school for whites." Perhaps the board would have succeeded had it not been for the Atlanta NAACP, founded in 1917 and led by Walter White. The branch made the battle for educational equality a main priority and sought to mobilize African Americans by increasing membership and holding voter registration drives. John Leonidas described himself as a Republican "not active in politics." Nevertheless, he joined the Atlanta NAACP in its first year, a political act, and he and his wife would most certainly have helped in the organization's efforts to obtain better educational opportunities and improved facilities for blacks. Despite the NAACP's work, Booker T. Washington High School, the city's first public high school for blacks, was not built until 1924.[33]

"You Just Turned the Blind Side": Student Days at Morehouse College

John Hervey began high school in 1921 when his parents enrolled him in Morehouse Academy, the secondary department at Morehouse College, a

Baptist college for black men. After high school, he would continue with his collegiate studies at the institution. Benjamin Elijah Mays taught mathematics at Morehouse—in fact, he taught Wheeler high school algebra—and in his autobiography, *Born to Rebel,* Mays recalled, "It was in Atlanta that I was to find the cruel tentacles of race prejudice reached out to invade and distort every aspect of Southern life." Mays vividly described how deeply rooted Atlanta's system of segregation had become since the late nineteenth century, especially after the *Plessy v. Ferguson* (1896) decision. In Atlanta, black people encountered segregation in train stations, streetcars, buses, department stores, schools, and hotels. "The experience of one black man," Mays surmised, "was the experience of every black man whether he was a college professor, doctor, minister, janitor, or maid."[34]

Jim Crow segregation placed all blacks on the same level, and as John Hervey grew older and was able to venture off into the city by himself, or with others of his generation, he regularly faced difficult decisions about how to respond to it. "There were things," John Hervey asserted years later, "I just wouldn't do as a kid—I wouldn't give anyone a chance to Jim Crow me." At Morehouse, Wheeler learned important lessons about how to challenge and confront the unjust world to which he belonged. One of his college classmates, for example, was Martin Luther King Sr. (known as Michael King at the time), father of the celebrated civil rights leader. "One of the things about him [King Sr.]," Wheeler remembered, "was that he would never ride on the streetcars in Atlanta or [on] a bus." "I admit that I did," Wheeler continued, yet "there were some things that I wouldn't do. But you just turned the blind side to participation in anything that didn't leave you standing up as a man." John Hervey was able to attend high school and later college at a time when most black children could not. As a requirement, all historically black colleges and universities in the area had their own academy or high schools, including Spelman, Clark, Atlanta, and Morris Brown. The Wheelers could more easily afford to send their children to private school, but disparities in education stood as major barriers and destroyed the future for many other blacks during this period.[35]

Morehouse College began in 1867, when the American Baptist Home Mission Society (ABHM) of New York started the Augusta Institute in Augusta, Georgia. It got its new name in 1913. By the 1920s, the

A young John Hervey played violin in the Morehouse Glee Club and Orchestra as a high school student (1921–1925), then continued on as a college student at the institution (1925–1929). He became an accomplished violinist and "received great distinction in the musical world because of the training and development which he received by participating in the [Glee Club and] Orchestra. John Wheeler, in and out of Morehouse[, became] the recipient of many honors, favorable comments, and national applause, because of his skill and technique in playing the violin." *Young John H. Wheeler,* Scrapbook 1, undated, John H. Wheeler Collection, Atlanta University Center Robert W. Woodruff Library.

The Morehouse College Glee Club and Orchestra made an annual tour across the South, performing mainly for black audiences in local churches, high schools, colleges, and public halls. In 1927, the organization had performances in southern Georgia before traveling to Florida, where they made stops in Jacksonville, Palatka, Gainesville, Sanford, Orlando, Daytona Beach, and St. Augustine. John Hervey (*standing third row from the top, in the exact center*) and other students would have observed the similarities between Georgia and Florida's Jim Crow systems. Considering his family's background and social status, he probably would have been considered a "cosmopolite," a common student reference to "those who [had] been everywhere, seen everything, and [knew] everybody." *Morehouse College Band,* undated, John H. Wheeler Collection, Atlanta University Center Robert W. Woodruff Library.

Baptist school devoted itself solely to training young black men and ushering them into adulthood. By the time John Hervey entered Morehouse Academy, the venerable black leader Dr. John Hope had led the institution for over a decade while playing an influential role in improving black life in Atlanta. At Morehouse, Hope regularly pressed upon his students the value and necessity of their responsibility to community.[36]

As first violin with Morehouse's Glee Club and Orchestra, John Hervey learned responsibility and respectability. He later wrote his music professor Kemper Harreld: "As the years have gone by, the discipline which you instilled in me and your effort to impress upon me the great value of thoroughness have been among my most valued possessions. Although I have not always been able to live up to the high standards of perfection which you taught me to strive for, I have unconsciously found myself avoiding the pitfalls of doing things in a slipshod or casual manner." Performing with the Glee Club and Orchestra at Atlanta functions undoubtedly also taught John Hervey about pride in one's community.[37]

John Hervey's cultural sensibilities helped heighten his social consciousness and influenced his developing worldview. As an assistant editor with the Morehouse student newspaper, the *Maroon Tiger,* Wheeler wrote cultural and literary reviews and articulated his views on the Harlem Renaissance and the "New Negro" movement. The latter, he proclaimed, represented challenging circumstances and the desires of blacks to gain their "freedom." In an essay on religion, he suggests he saw his generation as integral to solving the problems caused by racial injustice. His generation could see things differently from previous generations, he wrote, and therefore had the responsibility to meet those challenges in more effective ways than ever before. The Wheeler family made their home in the South at a very critical moment for black southern life. John Leonidas and Margaret Hervey wanted better for their children in reaching their potential in a society where there were already limited possibilities for blacks. At the start of the Great Depression, black enterprise in Durham was built on a solid foundation, which had been tested and primed for decades ahead of new economic challenges.[38]

2

Black Business Activism in the Great Depression

> In the composite portrait of the New Negro must be put the sharp and forceful features of the Negro man of business. Through his effort and success, the Negro is becoming an integral part of the business life of America, and is sharing particularly in the economic development of the New South, which is perhaps the outstanding economic consequence of the World War on America.
>
> E. Franklin Frazier, *The New Negro: An Interpretation,* 1925

On October 26, 1929, amid the stock market crash, the *Pittsburgh Courier* asked: "Will 'The Town that Co-Operation Built' Hold Its Own? Will Durham Continue the Seat of Negro Business?" A decade after World War I and the death of John Merrick in 1919, the article pointed to the rising generation of black businesspeople to answer in the affirmative. Dr. Aaron McDuffie Moore had succeeded Merrick until his own death in 1923, and then Charles C. Spaulding became president of both NC Mutual and M&F Bank, becoming the new patriarch of black business in Durham and the New South. The article noted Durham had a "Second Line of Defense," a reserve "group of young men who could not only carry on the present businesses and make them bigger and better, but who would carry on the Durham tradition for business leadership as well." "It has been a cardinal part of the Durham leaders' program," the article continued, "to build an organization as well as a business—an organization that can and will carry the business on either with or without the presence of the chief executive." The article singled out Richard Lewis McDougald as "the man who [really] runs" M&F Bank:[1]

> Mr. McDougald has demonstrated that he is capable of not only handling the bank itself, but that he has the vision to foresee

> possibilities for sound development, and he had the courage to push in that direction. Much of the new activity in Durham in recent years is due to his initiative in advancing credit along safe and constructive lines. . . .[He] has been practically free to manage the bank as he sees fit. His methods, however, have been such that he has received the enthusiastic support of all the people of the community, high and low. He is perfectly at home with the humblest depositor, or with the largest depositor, and he knows the problems and possibilities of every type of endeavor that is in Durham. Although Mr. Spaulding is president, he rarely bothers with the bank, except to O.K. what Mr. McDougald does.[2]

McDougald not only shaped the everyday transactions of the bank, but he became the quintessence of "black business activism" in the late 1920s and 1930s. Though not included in the article, John Wheeler and his generation of inexperienced black businessmen were apprentices for the time being, a third line of defense.

This chapter captures how Durham's black businesspeople fostered the growth of their community during a period of transition. It follows the history of M&F Bank from a fledgling NC Mutual spin-off into a thriving institution, a front-runner among black banks in the United States, and the home of officers who helped launch the National Negro Bankers Association (NNBA). M&F Bank survived the Great Depression when many banks did not in part because it prioritized what McDougald referred to as taking care of the local community first before considering riskier investments elsewhere. "Wall Street call money," Spaulding declared after the stock market crash, "did not sweep" NC Mutual and by extension M&F Bank "off its balance because the company's investments of nearly two million dollars in first mortgages is on property owned by local, thrifty people. Furthermore, the company's investments are in states where it operates and insurance funds are not used in ruthless speculation."[3]

By the mid-1930s, black Durham residents embraced multilayered strategies in their quest for full citizenship. This demand was grounded in a desire for better education, an end to police brutality, increased job opportunities, and greater access to public accommodations. Moreover, the relationship between black capitalism and community became integral when the social, political, and economic marginalization of black people deepened. This age bore witness to the training of the third generation of black businesspeople who would one day take over black leadership in the city. This training in black business activism was twofold. First, black businesspeople were schooled in the racial etiquette that black and white power brokers in the Bull City depended on for what they deemed progressive southern race relations. This surface-level climate of racial togetherness, or what Spaulding called interracial "co-operation," lent itself to quiet, behind-the-scenes negotiations. Second, training in black business activism placed them at the center of community leadership during matters that threatened to unravel the perceived racial harmony. The added mix of gender, class, and intergenerational tensions pushed these business leaders to look inward for more aggressive means to solve problems facing black Durham. While the future of black business might have looked dimmer elsewhere across the New South, it seemed brighter and brighter for Durham's "Black Wall Street." This continued economic prosperity made it possible for black Durham to nurture successive generations of black businesspeople who helped sustain the black freedom struggle, with its emphasis on racial equality and economic justice, in the second half of the twentieth century.

"Durham Is Promise of a Transformed Negro"

In 1929, Wheeler moved to Durham after graduating summa cum laude from Morehouse College with an A.B. degree (fourth in a class of sixty-six students). He had landed a job as a bank teller for M&F Bank making sixty dollars a month. Though he considered a career as a professional violinist, having earned national honors during his senior year and having been asked to teach music at Tuskegee Institute in Alabama for $150 a month, he chose the bank and moved to the Bull City soon thereafter. He later found out that another Durham enterprise, NC Mutual, had planned to offer him a $110 monthly salary to work for them. His parents believed business was the better (and most logical) option, given his father's connections with Durham-based enterprises. In 1933, Wheeler would join the insurance company's five-member Securities Investments Committee.

In his new position, Wheeler succeeded Edward Decatur Pratt, a member of the second line of defense who had worked as an M&F Bank teller for the previous ten years. Pratt went on to become the secretary-manager for the Mortgage Company of Durham.[4]

In his seminal 1925 essay "Durham: The Capital of the Black Middle Class," sociologist E. Franklin Frazier concluded that black businesspeople best represented the black middle class because of their modern approaches to business and progressive outlook. He emphasized their "respectability" because of their shared traditional values, but he also noted their commitment to a proper work ethic. They had a philosophy grounded in the expansion of their business enterprises. Frazier referenced the similarities between black businessmen and their white counterparts across the New South, writing that the two groups in Durham were "brothers under the skin." Nevertheless, he noted, Jim Crow segregation persisted there and in other cities across the state, which denied black North Carolinians full citizenship. Frazier also pointed to Durham's "outstanding group of colored capitalists who have entered the second generation of business enterprise." "This younger generation," he continued, "is building upon the firm foundation of the work of the first generation." He hinted at Wheeler's generation of up-and-coming black business leaders when he recognized "Durham is promise of a transformed Negro." While Frazier applauded the progress of black businessmen in Durham, he minimized the significant class distinctions between the "capitalists" and the "workers," as historian Dolores Janiewski has noted.[5]

Durham was becoming "one of the most important Negro centers of the South" sociologist Hugh Penn Brinton wrote in his 1930 study, "The Negro in Durham: A Study of Adjustment to Town Life." Like Frazier before him, Brinton attributed Durham's growth to black middle-class professionals who built strong economic and educational institutions. He referenced the "talented tenth" in explaining "there are also professional men who, trained in the best universities, feel the obligations of the strong to the weak." He also detailed black Durham's striking class and gender dynamics, highlighting, for example, the significant difficulties many black residents had adjusting to town life, as most came from rural areas with relatively few or no job skills relevant in the urban setting. In fact, most blacks living and working in Durham held jobs as unskilled laborers—many in Durham's tobacco factories.[6]

By the time Wheeler arrived, black businesses were unlikely to hire individuals without advanced business training. "The type of men who are being picked as the future negro business leaders of Durham," Brinton surmised, were "college trained with a special emphasis on their particular kind of work." These were "capable men drawn from a considerable distance," and "there would seem to be but a slight chance that the unskilled Negro worker who migrates from the country to Durham will ever be able to hold a position of prominence in these businesses." In other words, for someone in Wheeler's position—a well-educated black person coming from Atlanta's black middle-class elite with arranged housing and employment—there was indeed "great promise of a transformed Negro," as well as certain comforts and advantages.[7]

Wheeler found himself in an ideal situation as he settled into the city's black Hayti section "where the best Negro homes in Durham [were] found." Wheeler boarded at the home of Mrs. Sarah McCotta "Cottie" Dancy Moore, the widow of late NC Mutual founder Dr. Aaron M. Moore. Cottie Moore not only opened her home at 606 Fayetteville Street to Wheeler, but she gave the Morehouse class historian instructive lessons about black Durham's past. She would have also helped ease his transition to the tobacco town where "new comers [were] made to feel they were just that." Moore was Richard L. McDougald's mother-in-law, and as the McDougalds lived at 609 Fayetteville Street, McDougald and Wheeler would have regularly crossed paths at home as well as at the bank's offices. Mattie Louise Moore McDougald, Richard's wife, had taught kindergarten to both Wheeler and his sister Ruth when the Wheeler family lived in Durham between 1908 and 1912. From the outset, McDougald took Wheeler "under his wing and prepared him to succeed himself as executive vice president and . . . C. C. Spaulding as president." The relationship between Wheeler and McDougald soon became that of mentor-mentee, as McDougald had twelve years over Wheeler.[8]

Besides social connections, Wheeler had secure, year-round employment, and his monthly salary would have covered his needs as a single person. In contrast, most blacks who came to Durham during this same time would have been assigned to the most labor-intensive, lowest-paid jobs available. Moreover, these migrant workers came without any guaranteed employment arrangements and had few, if any, contacts to rely on. The only housing available to them would have been in the city's most neglected, poorest, and oldest sections.

"Owned, Lock Stock and Barrel by Colored People"

The early part of the twentieth century marked an important turning point in the history of black banking in particular and black business in general. These institutions cropped up when they did because the US Supreme Court's *Plessy* decision (1896) led to segregated, parallel institutions. In February 1910, the black banker Henry A. Boyd of the One-Cent Savings Bank and Trust Company in Nashville, Tennessee, counted approximately fifty-three black banks across the United States. With the exception of the Binga Bank in Chicago, Illinois (1908), all the banks listed operated in the New South. Many of these black banks grew out of the success of black-owned insurance companies, and as sister institutions became the repositories for the insurance companies' reserves. At minimum, there were 134 black-owned banks founded in the United States between 1888 and 1935.[9]

The six North Carolina banks included in the tabulation were the Mutual Aid Banking Company (1897) in New Bern, the Dime Bank in Kinston (1898), the Holloway, Borden, Hicks and Company, Bankers in Kinston (1903), the Isaac Smith's Bank and Trust Company in New Bern (year of establishment unknown), the Forsyth Savings and Trust Company in Winston-Salem (1907), and the M&F Bank in Durham (1908). Surprisingly, Raleigh did not have a black bank until M&F Bank opened its branch there in 1923. The capital city had a branch of the Freedman's Savings Bank before it ceased to exist, which makes it even more perplexing that the city went without a black bank for as long as it did. Banks in the Tar Heel State and throughout the South struggled to regain their proper place after the Civil War. But by 1896, total deposits for all banks operating in the state—some 196 state-chartered banks and another 27 national banks chartered there—reached $19,958,763.36. Continued expansion brought about the North Carolina Bankers Association

(NCBA) in 1897, and in 1899 the state legislature created the North Carolina Corporation Commission to oversee state banking.[10]

In the Bull City, citizens relied on banking institutions in places such as Raleigh until about 1878. At that time Eugene Morehead, son of Governor John Morehead, established the Morehead Banking Company, followed by the short-lived Bank of Durham (1886–1888), then the First National Bank in November 1887, and the Fidelity Savings and Trust Company in January 1888. In 1904, the Home Savings Bank opened, followed by the Merchants Bank a year later. The M&F Bank owed its existence to several developments. In February 1907, Dr. Manassa Thomas Pope, a black doctor from Raleigh, and Shaw University professor Edward A. Johnson met with black businessmen in Durham. Both Pope and Johnson were prominent black leaders in the capital city at the time. The two men tried to convince the leaders to set up a building and loan association in the city. Once the group assembled, however, it became evident they had no interest in a loan association but wanted a bank instead. In fact, entrepreneurs Richard B. Fitzgerald and William G. Pearson had about two years earlier broached the idea of a bank to NC Mutual president John Merrick, but Merrick did not endorse the proposal. However, after meeting with Pope and Johnson, the black leaders quickly set about forming a bank.[11]

In the meantime, Fitzgerald and Dr. James E. Shepard drafted the bank's initial charter. After meeting on several other occasions, Merrick, Moore, Fitzgerald, Shepard, Pearson, Warren, and Dr. Jesse A. Dodson each put down an initial investment comprising the bank's stock. In all, they raised approximately $10,000 and then took steps toward official incorporation. On February 25, the North Carolina General Assembly approved the charter in House Bill 1342 and Senate Bill 673, incorporating the financial institution as a "body politic." On July 29, M&F Bank organizers came together again for the first stockholders meeting, held in the offices of the black fraternal order the Royal Knights of King David, located in the NC Mutual Building. At that meeting, Fitzgerald, Dodson, Pearson, Merrick, Shepard, Spaulding, Stevens, Moore, and Warren became the bank's inaugural board of directors. The board elected Fitzgerald as the institution's first president, alongside vice president John Merrick and William G. Pearson as cashier. Pearson received a salary

On December 17, 1921, NC Mutual dedicated its new six-story home office building on West Parrish Street. The M&F Bank occupied the building's first-floor quarters alongside the Mutual Building and Loan Association. When NC Mutual completed its first home office building in 1906, the company operated only in North and South Carolina. By the time it completed the structure pictured here, NC Mutual also had operations in Georgia, Washington, D.C., Virginia, Maryland, Tennessee, Florida, Mississippi, Arkansas, Alabama, and Oklahoma. Courtesy of the State Archives of North Carolina.

of forty dollars per month while the other officers received no compensation. Later, M&F Bank occupied its own quarters on the first floor of the NC Mutual Building. The emergence of financial institutions such as M&F Bank "were not only symbols of the increased financial holdings of blacks but also an expression of defiance to white attempts to impose a separate and subordinate status on America's citizens of African descent."[12]

On August 1, 1908, M&F Bank opened for business, one month after the Wheeler family moved to Durham. "The Mechanics and Farmers Bank for colored people" wrote the *Raleigh Times*, "has started off handsomely and the first day showed deposits of $2,000." Black and white newspapers across the state noted this was North Carolina's third bank "owned, lock stock and barrel by colored people." There may actually have been four other black banks, possibly five, already in operation. The Mutual Aid Banking Company, the Dime Bank, the Holloway, Borden, Hicks and Company, and the Forsyth Savings and Trust Company were all open by 1907, but the establishment date of Isaac Smith's Bank has been difficult to confirm. It was in operation in 1910, according to contemporary sources. During M&F Bank's first week in operation, it received assistance from managers at the city's white banks. James B. Mason, the cashier from the Citizens National Bank, "came over each day for a week . . . and showed them how to open and close the bank." Already bolstered by NC Mutual's success, the bank was destined to become another link in the chain of black economic achievement in Durham and the New South. In its first three months in operation, M&F Bank showed total resources of $20,869.10, which increased to $26,200.07 by November 1909.[13]

M&F Bank's officers and board members included the same individuals responsible for NC Mutual's growth and expansion. Fitzgerald, the wealthy brick maker, served as the bank's president until January 4, 1910, when he withdrew his name from reelection. He reported health concerns but continued on the board of directors until his death on March 24, 1918. The board elected Merrick as its second president. The bank's cashier, William G. Pearson, also helped start several other businesses associated with NC Mutual and M&F Bank, including the Bankers Fire Insurance Company and the Southern Fidelity and Surety Company. Despite this, the consummate black entrepreneur seemed to withdraw his commitment from new ventures fairly quickly once they survived their embryonic stages, and so Pearson did not remain cashier long. This was mostly because of his responsibilities as a school principal at the black Hillside Park High School. The Reverend Dr. George W. Adams replaced him just a year into his tenure, although Pearson remained integral to the bank's leadership as a member of the board of directors. A native of Danville, Virginia, Adams had graduated from Kittrell College and then became a teacher there; he was the college's chaplain when John Leonidas and Margaret Hervey taught at the school, and later a dean. Upon entering its second year in operation, M&F Bank was "found to be very satisfactory," and "white bankers say the men about it know the business thoroughly." In fact, "it represents largely the deposits of working people, but there are a few wealthy men of the race who put big sums into it and its safety stage has long since passed. It is one of the institutions of the city here for a permanency and its people are very proud of it. Its [new] president [John Merrick] will popularize it. His record and rise here have inspired his race and he is one of the best business men this city has developed among the many successful colored men."[14]

During M&F Bank's first decade of operation, it began its rise to prominence among the nation's black banks. It handed stockholders dividend payments on a regular basis, and resources reached $51,906.31 at the end of the fifth year, nearly double the amount after the bank's first year. In those five years, M&F Bank's capital stock increased from $5,000 to $15,000. The bank's newspaper advertisements promised "Safety in our armor plate deposit vault" and wanted to "assure [customers] that [their] business, regardless of size, will be fully appreciated, and [their] savings will be not only safe, but earning something at the same time." It welcomed potential depositors to "Come and Grow with Us." The Durham bank made gendered appeals to "Young men," because "now is your time to begin to save for a rainy day." Another advertisement commanded, "Young Men" to "STOP wasting your earnings," "LISTEN to wise counsel," and "look out for the rainy day." "There's danger ahead," the advertisement continued, "for the man who squanders all his money or time during his productive years, and faces an old age dependent upon others." The bank's growth was due in no small measure to the diligence of cashier George W. Adams. On March 23, 1914, for example, a fire broke out at the NC Mutual Building where the bank was housed, causing $10,978.04 in property damage—though an insurance policy covered the losses. The fire generated false rumors in several local newspapers, which compelled Adams to write a letter to the editor of the *Durham Morning Herald*. "The Report as printed . . . to the effect that the Mechanics and Farmers bank lost $10,000 in the fire Monday night is entirely wrong," Adams wrote in exasperation. In fact, "The bank was not damaged by the fire at all. All of the damage done was done by the water thrown into the building, not to stop the fire in the bank room, but in the room above it. Even this did but small damage to the fixtures. Otherwise the bank did not lose a cent, and is in as good condition now as it ever had been." Adams worried that the erroneous report would cause depositors to lose trust in the institution, causing a "run" on the bank, which never materialized. When M&F Bank celebrated its ten-year anniversary in August 1918, its resources had reached $95,631.08. Unfortunately, Adams died a month later, on September 19, 1918. Following his death, C. C. Spaulding became M&F Bank's new cashier and had an integral role in steering the bank into its next decade of operation.[15]

Between 1918 and 1923, M&F Bank experienced another transition period. On August 6, 1919, John Merrick died, leaving a void in black economic leadership. It was the first time since the founding of NC Mutual and M&F Bank that the institutions would be tested without their patriarch. Still, a local newspaper called 1919 a "banner year" for banking in Durham and "possibly the biggest business in their history" with total deposits up $3,065,753.63 from the previous year. That year, shareholders from Durham banks received $118,900 in dividends, and M&F Bank paid its shareholders 6 percent in dividends, or roughly $900. "The company will not suffer on account of the death of John Merrick," noted the *Raleigh News and Observer*, "because he had drawn around him a trained set of operators." William G. Pearson became the bank's interim president from 1919 to 1920 while C. C. Spaulding remained cashier. Dr. Stanford L. Warren then replaced Pearson, serving in that capacity from January 1920 to January 1922. By 1920, the economic success of black business in Durham, anchored by NC Mutual, yielded enough prosperity for the company to begin plans for the "erection of a seven-story, fire-proof home office building, to be built on Parrish street.

Table 2.1. Resources and officers of the Mechanics and Farmers Bank from November 27, 1908, to December 31, 1930

Year	Resources	Officers
As of November 27, 1908	$20,869.10	R. B. Fitzgerald, President W. G. Pearson, Cashier
As of November 16, 1909	$26,200.07	R. B. Fitzgerald, President G. W. Adams, Cashier
As of June 30, 1910	$32,058.31	J. Merrick, President G. W. Adams, Cashier
As of November 10, 1910	$39,153.40	J. Merrick, President G. W. Adams, Cashier
As of June 7, 1911	$37,663.83	J. Merrick, President G. W. Adams, Cashier
As of December 5, 1911	$44,754.65	J. Merrick, President G. W. Adams, Cashier
As of June 14, 1912	$43,357.01	J. Merrick, President G. W. Adams, Cashier
As of June 4, 1913	$47,550.45	J. Merrick, President G. W. Adams, Cashier
As of October 21, 1913	$51,906.31	J. Merrick, President G. W. Adams, Cashier
As of June 30, 1914	$50,298.64	J. Merrick, President G. W. Adams, Cashier
As of October 31, 1914	$52,258.75	J. Merrick, President G. W. Adams, Cashier
As of June 23, 1915	$48,617.13	J. Merrick, President G. W. Adams, Cashier
As of November 10, 1915	$55,212.82	J. Merrick, President G. W. Adams, Cashier
As of June 30, 1916	$56,209.67	J. Merrick, President G. W. Adams, Cashier
As of December 27, 1916	$67,143.39	J. Merrick, President G. W. Adams, Cashier
As of June 20, 1917	$57,428.11	J. Merrick, President G. W. Adams, Cashier
As of November 20, 1917	$62,479.77	J. Merrick, President G. W. Adams, Cashier
As of November 1, 1918	$95,631.08	J. Merrick, President C. C. Spaulding, Cashier

As of June 30, 1919	$129,621.22	J. Merrick, President C. C. Spaulding, Cashier
As of December 31, 1919	$236,413.89	W. G. Pearson, President C. C. Spaulding, Cashier
As of June 30, 1920	$252,111.55	Dr. S. L. Warren, President C. C. Spaulding, Cashier
As of December 29, 1920	$301,239.66	Dr. S. L. Warren, President C. C. Spaulding, Cashier
As of June 30, 1921	$318,225.38	Dr. S. L. Warren, President C. C. Spaulding, Cashier
As of December 31, 1921	$390,645.53	Dr. S. L. Warren, President C. C. Spaulding, Cashier
As of June 30, 1922	$563,709.01	C. C. Spaulding, President William H. Wilson, Cashier
As of September 15, 1922	$621,016.98	C. C. Spaulding, President William H. Wilson, Cashier
As of December 29, 1922	$584,746.46	C. C. Spaulding, President William H. Wilson, Cashier
As of June 30, 1923	$673,177.83	C. C. Spaulding, President William H. Wilson, Cashier
As of December 1923	$762,492.00	C. C. Spaulding, President William H. Wilson, Cashier
As of June 1924	$734,542.44	C. C. Spaulding, President William H. Wilson, Cashier
As of December 31, 1924	$798,175.85	C. C. Spaulding, President William H. Wilson, Cashier
As of June 30, 1925	$750,624.51	C. C. Spaulding, President William H. Wilson, Cashier
As of December 31, 1926	$831,891.24	C. C. Spaulding, President William H. Wilson, Cashier
As of December 31, 1927	$748,481.46	C. C. Spaulding, President William H. Wilson, Cashier
As of December 31, 1928	$758, 707.92	C. C. Spaulding, President R. L. McDougald, Cashier
As of December 31, 1929	$702,981.09	C. C. Spaulding, President R. L. McDougald, Cashier
As of December 31, 1930	$704,273.07	C. C. Spaulding, President R. L. McDougald, Cashier

Source: Reports of the *Condition of the State, Private and Savings Banks* (Raleigh: E. M. Uzzell and Company, State Printers and Binders for the Department of the North Carolina Corporation Commission, 1908–1930).

Table 2.2. Member banks, National Negro Bankers Association, 1934

Bank name	City	State	President	Established
Citizens and Southern Bank and Trust Company	Philadelphia	Pennsylvania	R. R. Wright Sr.	1920
Citizens Savings Bank and Trust Company	Nashville	Tennessee	H. A. Boyd	1904
Citizens Trust Bank	Atlanta	Georgia	A. T. Walden	1921
Consolidated Bank and Trust Company	Richmond	Virginia	E. C. Burke	1903
Crown Savings Bank	Newport News	Virginia	W. P. Dickerson	1909
Danville Savings Bank and Trust Company	Danville	Virginia	G. W. Goode	—
Mechanics and Farmers Bank	Durham	North Carolina	C. C. Spaulding	1908
Charleston Mutual and Savings Bank	Charleston	South Carolina	J. A. McFall	—

Sources: Pittsburgh Courier, January 6, 1934; Alexa Benson Henderson, "Richard R. Wright and the National Negro Bankers Association: Early Organizing Efforts among Black Bankers, 1924–1942," *Pennsylvania Magazine of History and Biography* 117 (January–April 1993): 74.

This building will have all modern equipment, and is to cost not less than $150,000." A year later, NC Mutual completed a six-story home office building for $250,000.[16]

The Raleigh Branch

During the 1920s, M&F Bank's economic rise became most evident when it moved into branch banking. The Raleigh Branch opened on January 1, 1923, about a year after M&F Bank merged with the Fraternal Bank and Trust Company. The Fraternal Bank, which William G. Pearson had organized in Durham in August 1920, did well during its short existence, but the leadership at both enterprises believed black Durham could not support two separately owned black banks. Thus, on January 6, 1922, the stockholders at both institutions held a joint meeting and voted to consolidate Fraternal Bank into the folds of M&F Bank. In a good-faith gesture, the presidents of each body resigned, and shareholders elected C. C. Spaulding as the new president of the greater M&F Bank. The well-respected Pearson withdrew his name from consideration to devote more time to the fledgling Bankers Fire Insurance Company, which he also headed. The consolidation positioned M&F Bank among the foremost black banks in North Carolina and among the most profitable in the country. When the Raleigh Branch opened, M&F Bank became the first black bank with a branch.[17]

During the interwar period, Spaulding became the most prominent black businessman in the country. Born to former slaves on August 1, 1874, in Columbus County, North Carolina, he gained the nickname "Mr. Co-Operation." As Spaulding himself explained, "co-operation brings organization, efficient organization brings success, and success alone inspires confidence and understanding." "I tell the young people," Spaulding continued, "that life has to be lived out, not with money, not with machines, but with people. And I mean not only with other people of our own race but with the members of the white race—in fact, here in the South. I mean especially that." Spaulding firmly believed it to be "foolish . . . to talk about granting equality, except equality of opportunity." He had no formal education beyond high school, yet he encouraged blacks interested in business to attend college so they could learn scientific business practices.[18]

In the meantime, M&F Bank purchased a new building in the heart of Raleigh's burgeoning black commercial district, at 13 East Hargett Street. Before the branch's official opening, M&F Bank not only faced renovation setbacks but had to raise the required capital stock stipulated by the North Carolina Corporation Commission. But when the Raleigh Branch opened, M&F Bank had approximately $115,749 in capital stock, bringing the bank's general resources to $650,000. The branch closed its first day of operations with $24,000 in deposits, including about $10,000 from NC Mutual, $1,000 from white Raleigh financier B. F. Montague, a former member of that city's school board, and another $1,000 from the white Durham Life Insurance Company. Though the young bank branch encountered racist resistance—for example, a local white bank official told a colleague, "they ought to close that damn Negro bank"—it became an expression of racial uplift for Raleigh's black people. "The Negroes of the city of Raleigh and Wake County," explained Charles R. Frazer, cashier and manager of the Raleigh branch, "were very proud of what they called 'our bank,' a demonstration of pride in and loyalty to this forward movement was shown in a remarkable way."[19]

The staff at the Raleigh Branch "had to build almost from the ground up," he recalled. An early goal entailed increasing assets by $10,000 a month until the branch reached $100,000, which it eventually did. "Our number one problem," noted Frazer, became "building and maintaining our reserve to the point where we could safely make loans." A few "substantial depositors" helped the branch stay afloat during its infancy. Frazer knew intuitively when to "leave the bank and call on friends of the institution for a substantial deposit, only to return in time to offset the debit with the credit just received."[20]

Other encounters with local white banks threatened the branch with insolvency. One day, Julian S. Hughson, the assistant cashier from the Durham office, was covering Frazer's duties in his absence. Hughson "told the runner from the Citizens' National Bank that he would have to give him a check on our correspondent, the Wachovia, for the exchange." But the cashier at Citizens', John P. Stedman, had told his runner to accept only cash. When he didn't get it, Stedman phoned the bank examiner. In the racial climate of the Jim Crow South, it is difficult to know whether Stedman would have done so if M&F Bank had been a white bank or whether he simply followed normal protocol. Hearing what had happened, Frazer reached out to the president of the Raleigh Banking and Trust Company "in whose bank we carried an account, and asked him to place to our credit $5,000.00," which Frazer vowed to cover when he returned to Raleigh. When he did, he found the bank examiner in the process of "writing something against the window," which he thought announced the bank's closure, but instead cut M&F Bank some slack. It simply instructed President C. C. Spaulding to send over money to satisfy the exchange. But Stedman's actions show that some white

The M&F Bank Raleigh Branch building was located at 13 East Hargett Street in downtown Raleigh. The building's renovations proved challenging in the lead-up to opening, which threatened delays. "At last," the branch manager Charles R. Frazer testified decades later, "fortune smiled upon us; the sun came out and dried up the land, so that the foundation could be laid." *The Mechanics and Farmers Bank Raleigh Branch,* Scrapbook 7, undated, John H. Wheeler Collection, Atlanta University Center Robert W. Woodruff Library.

banking officials wanted to see M&F Bank close its Raleigh Branch. Stedman later became the state treasurer during the early 1930s, and, interestingly enough, his bank did not survive the Depression.[21]

In August 1928, a year before Wheeler joined the company, M&F Bank celebrated its twentieth anniversary, and the bank's total resources were at $758,707.92. North Carolina's lieutenant governor, Jacob Elmer Long, told the celebrants that in Durham they "could not have any better leaders" and "the State of North Carolina [was] exceedingly proud of [their] institution." Despite the bank's success, Spaulding relayed that they "were not going to get the big head" but would "keep our feet on the ground." To mark the occasion, they raised $82,000 in deposits "for both the Durham bank and the Raleigh branch." And they even received a $10,000 check from a "local white business for deposits." By that time, M&F Bank had become a depository for the city and county of Durham. Most observers credited the bank's cautious banking practices for its strength. In December 1927, for example, the black *Pittsburgh Courier* newspaper attributed Durham's black business success to Spaulding for "preaching 'cooperation,' and not only in Durham, but all of North Carolina, telling Negroes to pull together and they can get somewhere." The experts considered M&F Bank "a safe and conservatively managed institution." The M&F Bank president C. C. Spaulding and active vice president Richard L. McDougald traveled to Harlem in September 1928, a month after celebrating the bank's twentieth-year anniversary, where they deposited a check for $7,500 at the opening of the white-owned Dunbar National Bank on behalf of M&F Bank. Though established by the famed New York Rockefeller family, the bank's name honored the black poet Paul Laurence Dunbar. The other bankers and businessmen from across the country who made similar sojourns included Richard R. Wright Sr., of the Citizen's and Southern Bank of Philadelphia, and Anthony Overton, president of the Victory Life Insurance Company of Chicago.[22]

Although Frazer had earlier kept the Raleigh Branch away from having to close its doors, his hands were tied, literally, on the evening of January 29, 1929. As he stood near the front window at the end of the day, two men came into the building and immediately killed the lights. From there, "the two men entered the banking room, one a tall, lean thug and the other a short, stumpy mut with a funny face." "I had just started to the door when the lights went out," said Frazer, "'don't move or say a word,' said the pistol man, 'I mean business, I'm no novice, I've done this before.'" The two thieves tied Frazer's hands with cord and planned to lock him in the vault. In a split-second decision, Frazer dashed toward the bank's entrance thinking he "would rather be shot to death than to suffocate in the vault." He made it to the streets yelling "thie[ve]s" and "robbers." The criminals left with $5,600. He then phoned the Raleigh police, who took him into custody believing he had something to do with the bank robbery. They didn't collect fingerprints, but instead the police chief aggressively interrogated Frazer and detained him for two hours. Angered at Frazer's arrest, Richard L. McDougald, C. C. Spaulding, and Berry O'Kelly demanded that authorities release him. Before he left, however, the police warned, "You know, you are going to have a run on your bank tomorrow morning, don't you?" Frazer rejected the insinuation. The Raleigh Branch was spared a bank run the next day; however, bank officials prepared for the worst. "The next morning," Frazer recalled, "McDougald, the active vice president, was on hand with an extra supply of cash [$52,000] spread upon the counter of the teller's cage and the display of a hundred thousand dollar note [$115,000 in bonds], but none of this was needed. There was not a ripple in the current of the day's business."[23]

As M&F Bank made considerable economic progress, the larger black banking world formed the National Negro Bankers Association (NNBA). The idea came from Richard R. Wright Sr., a prominent educator from Georgia who served as president at the Citizens and Southern Bank and Trust Company in Philadelphia. In 1920, Wright opened his bank because he was disappointed with the black community's dollars passing into white hands while "building up businesses" that "discriminate[d] against our people." In 1926, the NNBA organized a meeting in Philadelphia where M&F Bank president C. C. Spaulding gave the keynote address, urging cooperation among a reported seventy black banks across the country. Before the meeting ended, the bankers selected Wright to be president of the new organization; Wilson Lovett of First Standard Bank

Table 2.3. Resources of the Mechanics and Farmers Bank from December 31, 1930, to December 31, 1945

Year	Resources
1930	$704,273.07
1931	$695,671.13
1932	$704,273.07
1933	$647,798.60
1934	$1,350,278.36
1935	$1,500,954.46
1936	$1,464,207.47
1937	$1,490,566.62
1938	$1,354,082.70
1939	$1,303,717.46
1940	$1,349,181.63
1941	$1,545,301.88
1942	$2,112,017.25
1943	$2,709,439.55
1944	$4,033,265.86
1945	$5,162,930.00

Source: Reports of the *Condition of the State, Private and Savings Banks* (Raleigh: E. M. Uzzell and Company, State Printers and Binders for the Department of the North Carolina Corporation Commission, 1930–1945).

in Louisville, Kentucky, to be secretary; and Spaulding to be treasurer. The NNBA's formation coincided with the move by blacks in other fields to create their own organizations to strengthen professional standards. Since its inception, Spaulding and M&F Bank played a vital role in the NNBA's development and survival. In September 1927, M&F Bank hosted the inaugural NNBA convention, where the group defined its concern with the "economic advancement of our group" and "effective mobilization of the money-power of the race" to solve the problem of "the unorganized Negro money-power." At the Durham meeting, the organization increased to fifty-five member banks, and the bankers in attendance received a firsthand look at how Durham's black businesses operated. They also traveled to Raleigh to visit Shaw University and M&F Bank's branch there.[24]

"All Sickness Is Not Death"

Wheeler had yet to work at the bank a full year before the stock market crashed in October 1929, bringing the country to its knees. The "Golden Age" of black business between 1900 and 1930 now faced an almost insurmountable giant: the Great Depression. According to one newspaper: "The advice to John Hervey was to get out of the banking business. But Mr. McDougald persuaded John to stay and with the enthusiasm of youth both John and the bank survived the crisis that swept the Nation."[25]

By all accounts, McDougald had a special knack for business and reportedly had worked as a Wall Street "runner." He was born on April 11, 1896, in Whiteville, North Carolina, one of the ten children of Richard and Ida Virginia Moore McDougald. He spent his childhood in New York, where he completed a year of high school before enlisting in the US Army and serving in World War I. After the war, he graduated from the National Training School (now North Carolina Central University) and married the youngest daughter of Dr. Aaron M. Moore. In 1919, M&F Bank hired the twenty-three-year-old McDougald as its bookkeeper, and he became active vice president and cashier within a decade. During this same time, NC Mutual brought him onto their finance department's Investments Securities Committee. He soon won election to NC Mutual's board of directors and then became a vice president with the concern in 1923.[26]

The entrepreneur helped found other important financial institutions in Durham, all closely linked to M&F Bank and NC Mutual. Most notably, he helped establish the Mutual Building and Loan Association (MB&LA) and had a prominent role in the Southern Fidelity and Surety Company. He started the MB&LA to educate blacks about the necessity of home ownership. Moreover, the company "aimed for the [black] masses, selling its 'shares' at twenty-five cents each. These shares were converted into saving certificates akin to bonds, which matured in 333 weeks. McDougald calculated that such a program would enable the black worker to accumulate a down payment on a home and then, of course, borrow the balance from the Association." He also became an officer and board member at the Bankers Fire Insurance Company. In the early 1920s, he had a

This appears to be a meeting about M&F Bank's "Year-End Statement of Condition," ca. 1930s–1940s. Pictured here are E. R. Merrick (*third from left*), C. C. Spaulding (*fifth from left*), John Hervey (*second from right*), and R. L. McDougald (*first from right*). *Unidentified Event with John H. Wheeler and others,* undated, John H. Wheeler Collection, Atlanta University Center Robert W. Woodruff Library.

hand in expanding the Merrick-McDougald-Wilson Company—later named the Union Insurance and Realty Company—and in 1929 he started the Mortgage Company of Durham. Moreover, McDougald "contributed much of his time, energy and means toward the development of facilities in the community for improvement of the health, education and social consciousness of Negroes." The financier was "very fair[-skinned]; he was often mistaken for white," remembered Asa T. Spaulding. Yet McDougald was extremely proud of being black. "You couldn't tell him from being white," Spaulding continued, "And a lot of people in Durham didn't know he was not white." However, "he never would [try] to pass for white." In fact, "it was an insult to consider him as white," and "he made no bones about it any time, that he was a Negro."[27]

McDougald summed up his philosophy of black business activism when he addressed the fourth annual meeting of the NNBA in November 1929, just over a week after the country suffered the stock market crash. "If a community entrusts its funds to a given bank," he told the group, "then that bank owes a moral obligation to that community to in turn invest a substantial portion of the funds back into the community rather than send it out of town where the people who have accumulated the money cannot benefit from its accumulation." McDougald had a simple motto: "Take care of your community and the community will take care of you." Although he seemed to speak from a strictly economic standpoint, he also believed that taking care of the community had larger significance for men in his position. "Something higher should be the goal of a Negro bank," he reasoned. After all, "The banker is the key man of the community, and he should create a feeling in the community, that above everything else he intends to serve the community's best interests." McDougald had no problem meeting this challenge as a banker and a black business activist in Durham's black community. He and other black business leaders in Durham expected no less from themselves and their employees at M&F Bank and NC Mutual.[28]

The economic downturn was especially difficult in the banking field and even more distressing for black banks. Of the reported seventy black banks that sent representatives to the 1926 meeting in Philadelphia, the Depression forced all but twelve into collapse. Though an overwhelming majority of black banks were in the South, the collapse of the Binga State Bank in Chicago best exemplifies the Great Depression's effects on successful black banks. Jesse Binga had established his State Bank as a private institution in 1908, and during the 1920s it became the nation's top black bank. Nevertheless, Binga's shady dealings compromised the financial institution's future. According to Juliet E. K. Walker: "Binga borrowed from white banks, using mortgages held by his bank on black real estate as security. But in the late 1920s, with Chicago's housing market in a slump, the downtown banks were unwilling to accept his mortgages, which tied up $800,000 of Binga's resources." The bank took out approximately $267,612 in "dummy loans" that were "made ostensibly to

[bank] employees or others at the behest of Binga, without security." An investigation into the bank's records revealed that loans given to Binga actually amounted to $379,000. After Binga made several unsuccessful attempts to rectify the situation by trying to raise $430,000 to satisfy state auditors, the bank closed suddenly for good in August 1930, stunning black Chicagoans.[29]

Charles R. Frazer, cashier and manager at the M&F Bank Raleigh Branch, described the collapse of financial institutions in Raleigh at the start of the Great Depression as a deadly economic explosion. The Raleigh offices of the Mutual Building and Loan Association and Parker-Hunter Realty toppled. Next came the Commercial Bank and Trust Company, the Citizens National Bank, the Raleigh Bank and Trust Company, the Wake County Savings Bank, and the Morris Plan Bank. "Banks were cracking up all over the country," explained Frazer, "and people in Raleigh lost their heads and pulled down by their withdrawals the oldest and strongest institutions in the city." "The stampede began with a whisper, a rumor," Frazer continued, "and the withdrawals of a few who became alarmed at the condition of affairs and touched off a fuse, and the fireworks were on." The most surprising blow to financial institutions in the Capital City hit the Commercial National Bank, which could not recover from the "long time loans" it provided farmers, one of its mainstay policies: "Like a bunch of firecrackers touched off by a match, these fine institutions, manned by men of integrity and high standing, burst and fell in rapid succession, one by one."[30]

The M&F Bank and Wachovia Bank and Trust Company were the "only two banks . . . that did not close their doors." Nevertheless, people's declining confidence in banking institutions affected them too. Frazer said M&F Bank, especially its Raleigh Branch, avoided collapse because of sheer luck and because most of its deposits were "comparatively small denominations. . . . They were not investments; so that, even if many had withdrawn their accounts, the bank would not have been terribly embarrassed as was the case with some of the other banks when a depositor withdrew several thousand dollars with one check." Moreover, "Negroes of Raleigh, greatly to their credit, and to the credit of the officers and directors of the bank, had built up a pride in and loyalty to the bank that sustained their confidence in the crisis. In all of this excitement there was not the slightest movement toward a panic on the part of any customer. Strangely, too, this year was the best year the bank had had up to this time."[31]

About 215 North Carolina banks closed in the first half of the Depression decade. As Milton Ready noted, this meant that between 1930 and 1933 two North Carolina banks went under every week. The state's conservative political faction met Roosevelt's New Deal policies with resistance and skepticism, but when Roosevelt instituted a national banking holiday on March 4, 1933, North Carolina's governor, John C. B. Ehringhaus, followed suit two days later. "On the night of March 13, 1933," remembered Wheeler, M&F Bank officials led by bank president C. C. Spaulding and cashier Richard L. McDougald "filed into the office of [the] Honorable Gurney P. Hood," the North Carolina banking commissioner. "Like other bankers," Wheeler continued, they went to Hood's office "seeking permission to reopen their institution." "Although comparative strangers to each other," Wheeler explained "there seemed to be an instant meeting of the minds between the commissioner" and M&F Bank's "white-haired president." Moreover, "After a brief but intense discussion of the condition of the bank, a license was issued to reopen for business the next morning. There was little doubt, however, that the apparent sincerity and great interest of this small group of men in the progress of their own race of people had influenced the commissioner's decision in large measure." That night M&F Bank became the first bank in North Carolina—white or black—to reopen. The go-ahead showed the bank's economic soundness, as "the criteria for allowing banks to reopen included strength of management and soundness of assets." It also showed the black bankers' skills at behind-the-scenes negotiations. Wheeler's vivid recollections about what transpired that night suggest he accompanied his M&F Bank superiors to Raleigh and would have observed their shrewd brokering firsthand. On June 16, 1933, Roosevelt signed the Banking Act of 1933 into law, establishing the Federal Deposit Insurance Corporation (FDIC). A year later, the FDIC "purchased and paid $100,000 worth of preferred stock" from M&F Bank whereby it insured "each deposit up to $5,000." Both M&F Bank and Wachovia Bank had the responsibility to service the capital in Raleigh for a time, the only two banks given that responsibility.[32]

In 1935, M&F Bank gained, as Wheeler put it, "the distinction of holding the permanent registration No. 1 of the lending agencies authorized and approved by [the] FHA in the State of North Carolina." Being the first North Carolina bank permitted to administer Federal Housing Administration (FHA) home loans gave M&F Bank cashier Richard L. McDougald the leverage he needed to achieve his vision of increased black homeownership. The Housing Act of 1934, which established the FHA and its Title II loans, proved especially beneficial to M&F Bank because, as Wheeler maintained, "in the '30s's, when there was no market for any FHA loans under Title 2 to a Negro borrower, and such market as there was existed in one or two Negro insurance companies. The big [white] insurance companies and big institutional investors in the country would" not offer them. Most people considered McDougald to be a finance genius, and the banker spent much time and expertise "scrutinizing" local bond referendums, weighing the advantages and disadvantages for black Durham. After receiving FHA approval, McDougald, himself a real estate developer, pressed city leaders to clear and rezone land he had in mind to use for building homes in Durham's black sections "so that he and Wheeler could finance new housing for Negroes through low-cost FHA loans." While FHA home loans had potential benefits for black Durham, as a banker he had the power to authorize or turn down loan applications. Consequently, some blacks viewed McDougald, Wheeler, and M&F Bank with resentment. An anecdote told to Durham businessman Nathan Garrett by his father, York Garrett Jr., a druggist who also came to Durham during the 1930s, is very telling. A prospective borrower went to see McDougald for a loan, the story went. As the conversation progressed, McDougald fired away question after question, all the while sizing up any potential risks for the bank. Finally, the applicant turned the tables around. "Say Mr. McDougald," the man started, "you've got a toilet in your house?" "Yes," answered McDougald. "You probably have a bathtub in there?" the man continued. "Yes I do," replied McDougald, probably now puzzled at the line of questioning. "Did you take a bath this morning?" the man went on. "Yeah I took a bath this morning," said McDougald. "Well I'm sure glad to hear it," the applicant concluded "because apparently I'm gonna have to kiss your ass in order to get this loan."[33]

The NAACP, Black Business Activism, and *Hocutt v. Wilson* (1933)

In the first three decades of the twentieth century, black North Carolinians, like the majority of black southerners, continued to be excluded from the traditional political process. Despite the economic advancement of M&F Bank and other black enterprises, blacks in places such as Durham still faced racial segregation and economic oppression, which intensified during the Great Depression. Increasingly, black North Carolinians considered their reentry into politics as a way to overcome racial inequality in the state. In 1920, North Carolina rescinded its discriminatory poll tax, a clause from the 1900 Suffrage Amendment that required eligible voters to pay a fee in order to exercise their voting privileges. In 1922, black attorney-businessman Robert McCants Andrews alongside Louis E. Austin organized the Colored Voters League to help facilitate black voter registration in the state. In 1923, however, registration rolls in Durham had just twenty-five black people and increased to a mere fifty within the next five years. While small, the increase in black registration happened because the above-mentioned political activists made it possible. McDougald was part of the political vanguard in black Durham during this time. "Those Parrish Street Negroes," he told a black sociologist conducting research on black Durham in the late 1930s, "told me that we don't go in for politics. We aren't interested in anything like that because it [would] only mean trouble." In other words, Andrews, Austin, and McDougald "had to bootleg politics" and seek an end run around the older black leadership.[34]

Although earlier attempts at voter registration by Andrews and others came up short, the efforts "were persistent and as the years went by, many more joined [Andrews] in his efforts to make the Negro vote-conscious." As the poll tax became a distant memory for black North Carolinians, prospective black voters faced ongoing problems from white registrars and their high-handed tactics to thwart black voter registration. The registrars held the sole authority to determine whether someone satisfied literacy requirements by having them read and interpret sections of the US Constitution. Wheeler's introduction to North Carolina politics came in 1930 when he registered to vote for the first time. "There were barriers," he remembered, that "weren't openly practiced but they were there." These subtle obstacles meant prospective black voters "were forced to wait a long time or required to do a lot of reading by registrants." In black Durham, people such as Andrews, considered to be among the black radicals at the time, regularly accompanied potential black voters to the registrar's office to ensure their successful registration. C. C. Spaulding regularly accompanied his employees to the courthouse because his presence made it more likely that they would get registered without any problems. Nevertheless, most black Durhamites avoided this process altogether to escape the embarrassment that often came with the whole ordeal. While "sophisticated tactics" served as impediments during these years, explained Wheeler, in subsequent decades black Durham eventually accounted for a third of the city's registered voters.[35]

Although older M&F Bank officials such as Spaulding took a less public stance when it came to politics, the bank's younger generation—the second and third lines of defense represented by McDougald and Wheeler—joined Austin and Andrews in their voter registration efforts. McDougald explained that he came into his own political activism when Andrews "proposed that a few of us get together and advise the Negro that before he could enjoy his full citizenship, it was not sufficient to be thrifty, but that he must also exercise his right to vote." In other words, a reliance solely on economic uplift would not bring about racial equality for black Durham. The only solution was having access to full citizenship, which became the most reasonable step toward economic power. The black businesspeople in the first line of defense eventually questioned the inherent limitations placed on black people's ability to gain racial equality through economic advancement alone. "The future of our group," one such black business leader expressed regretfully, "lies in getting more political power. Somehow we have to teach our people to use the ballot intelligently."[36]

As Spaulding and M&F Bank leaders maneuvered their way out of the banking crisis in 1933, another development gained traction that would test the behind-the-scenes tactics of Durham's older black leadership in several important ways. Wheeler would have paid close attention to how his seniors, especially Spaulding, handled the resulting controversy.

In addition to voting access, black people were seeking educational equality as a necessary requirement for full citizenship. In February 1933, with the backing of the NAACP, two young attorneys, Cecil A. McCoy and Conrad O. Pearson, started the effort to seek admission for blacks in the state's all-white colleges and universities. When the attorneys first laid out their plans, M&F Bank's Spaulding pledged his support, and NAACP executive secretary Walter White seemed more than pleased with the effort's prospects, especially since he believed it to be "very unusual for black businessmen to support such a radical move," as historian Jerry B. Gershenhorn has noted.[37]

In early March, as the banking holiday took effect, McCoy, Pearson, and *Carolina Times* editor Louis E. Austin accompanied twenty-four-year-old Thomas Raymond Hocutt on a bold mission to the University of North Carolina (UNC) in nearby Chapel Hill. Once there, the determined foursome went to the office of university registrar Thomas J. Wilson to inquire about Hocutt's course schedule and housing assignment. Wilson provided no such information because the university had a whites-only admissions policy. The group's effort to get Hocutt admitted to the university's pharmacy school failed. Wilson had no plans to admit Hocutt that day or any other day, and as the group left, segregation at the state's flagship institution was intact for the time being.[38]

Spaulding called Pearson, McCoy, and Austin into his office for a private conference hours after their return from Chapel Hill. He hoped to persuade the young radicals to reverse course, but they rejected his pleas. The meeting became so intense that M&F Bank and NC Mutual board member Edward R. Merrick threatened (idly) to throw Pearson out a window after Pearson called him a "handkerchief head." On March 16, Pearson and McCoy filed a lawsuit on Hocutt's behalf against UNC to obtain a writ of mandamus, "commanding the University . . . to show cause why he should not be admitted as a student." In the court documents, the young attorneys charged the university with violating Hocutt's Fourteenth Amendment rights under the US Constitution and the state's own charter. Within a week, Judge Maurice Victor Barnhill notified the university that it had until month's end to defend its decision not to enroll Hocutt.[39]

The local newspapers described the lawsuit as a broad move by several "younger and more aggressive Durham Negroes." Despite Spaulding's support just a month before, by the time *Hocutt v. Wilson* rolled out, he changed his tune about publicly endorsing the suit. McCoy wrote to White about Spaulding's back-pedaling, saying, "undoubtedly you have encountered this position before on the part of southern Negro businessmen." Opposition from white leaders—individuals with whom Spaulding had cooperated on race relations—prompted his about-face. On some level, too, Spaulding feared a violent backlash—harking back to the 1898 Wilmington Race Riot.[40]

He may also have been influenced by an incident he had experienced shortly before. In 1931, Spaulding was drinking a Coca-Cola in Conyer's Cigar Store in Raleigh when a new, white store clerk named George Brown commanded the older gentleman to take his drink outside. When Spaulding questioned him, Brown pounced. According to newspapers, he "rushed from behind the counter and knocked the drink from [Spaulding's] hand." He then "shoved [Spaulding] out the door, brutally beating and kicking him as he fell." The attack left Spaulding with two missing teeth and "bruises all about the face." After the incident, angry Spaulding supporters, including Spaulding's son Charles Jr., rushed to the store. At Spaulding's request the group disbanded, but the attack shocked the black communities in Raleigh and Durham. It gave them a sober reminder about Jim Crow's brutality and disregard for respectability. Despite Spaulding's hesitancy to appear in court, Brown received a small fine. Wheeler would have witnessed Spaulding's bewilderment and received some important lessons in navigating the delicate parameters of race in the New South. He would have seen that black economic wherewithal did not mean full escape from racial injustice.[41]

The Durham NAACP branch had existed on paper since about March 1919, but according to Conrad O. Pearson, by 1930 it had done little else except acquire dues-paying members. The organization's national office tried desperately on several occasions to entice the Durham arm to become more active on racial injustice in the city. In 1929, when Wheeler came to Durham, Austin of the *Carolina Times* criticized the city's black businesspeople for not supporting the NAACP with their actions and financial resources. "Durham," Austin wrote, "with its gigantic business institutions, its progressive schools, hospitals and churches does not find time or place for a branch of the N.A.A.C.P." Not only did the city need a local NAACP branch, he wrote, but "it ought to make its contribution toward safeguarding the opportunity to operate big business institutions by becoming active in that particular phase of the struggle of the race." "We praise the work of the N.A.A.C.P," Austin concluded, "but praise won't pay lawyers' fees, and other expenses that go with such an organization. It takes money and a plenty of it, and we certainly have no right to claim any part of a victory that organization has won unless we produced some of the wherewithal." When it came time to collect membership dues for the local branch in August 1930, Wheeler joined alongside other M&F Bank employees and officers. He also paid for a subscription to the NAACP's *Crisis* magazine. Between late 1930 and early 1931, NAACP field secretary William Pickens and director of branches Robert W. Bagnall from the national office pressed local officers to sponsor mass meetings and membership drives to build up the Durham branch. The national office believed Durham could be an important asset to the organization because it had the financial resources and economic independence to strongly support the organization's work. Nevertheless, local branch president James T. Taylor, a professor at North Carolina College for Negroes (NCCN), moved at a snail's pace in the endeavor.[42]

Like C. C. Spaulding, NCCN president Dr. James E. Shepard refused to publicly support the *Hocutt* case, and like Spaulding, he pushed his own behind-the-scenes crusade. He even leaked Pearson and McCoy's plans to a newspaper reporter from Greensboro well before they officially filed suit against UNC. Shepard had his sights set on what he believed to be loftier goals. Thus, he viewed the *Hocutt* case as an opportunity to expand his institution's educational offerings. Nevertheless, in private deliberations and correspondence with white city and state leaders, most notably Nathan C. Newbold, director of the North Carolina Division of Negro Education, Shepard outlined his overall views on the actions taken by his younger brethren. He argued that the *Hocutt* case proved why the state legislature needed to establish graduate and professional programs for black North Carolinians, and he maintained that the opportunity to do so could begin at his school. At the same time, Shepard knew he could not publicly criticize the actions by the second line of defense or he would risk serious criticism from blacks in Durham and across the state. As a consummate politician, Shepard had the ability and skill to turn unfavorable circumstances into an advantage for his institution. Attorney Conrad Pearson reasoned that if the elder statesman had "been white, he would have been governor of [the] state."[43]

The *Hocutt* case quickly raised internal tensions and heightened generational conflict about strategy between the old guard leaders represented by Spaulding and Shepard and the up-and-coming activists. By virtue of his employment with the bank, it is doubtful that Wheeler came out directly against the M&F Bank president, but he would have no doubt identified with the younger activists of his generation and probably wanted Spaulding to side with them without hesitancy. Wheeler might have been more vocal on the issue during conversations he more than likely had with Richard L. McDougald, who was perhaps just as ambivalent as his younger employee. In the days leading to the scheduled court date, rumors surfaced in the local press that Hocutt and his lawyers planned to withdraw their case in order to "adopt other tactics." Black leaders were allegedly "drafting a bill for presentation in the legislature which would authorize the state to pay the tuition of North Carolina Negroes in out-of-state institutions when facilities are not available within their borders to provide the courses of study desired." The rumor grew out of a March 18 meeting among fifty black Durham businessmen, a group that reportedly favored the out-of-state tuition option over the legal challenge. It is unclear where Wheeler stood on the matter or whether he attended the meeting. Nevertheless, once word reached Pearson about dropping the case, he dismissed his own involvement in the efforts to obtain out-of-state tuition for blacks.[44]

When the first hearing in the *Hocutt* case began on March 24, Judge Barnhill issued a continuance until the following morning but called attorneys from both sides into his chambers "for more than an hour and a half." In their private conference, the group tossed around several possible ways to settle the case. By that time, attorney William H. Hastie from the NAACP's national office had taken over as Hocutt's lead attorney, alongside Pearson and McCoy. After their private conference, lawyers from each side conferred with their respective legal teams. During their deliberations, M. Hugh Thompson, a black Durham attorney sent to represent the fifty black business leaders, tried to convince Hocutt's lawyers to drop the suit once and for all in exchange for the out-of-state tuition bill. One newspaper reported a heated argument between Thompson and Pearson about the best steps to take. After behind-the-scenes negotiations between the lawsuit's opposing factions, Pearson "intimated that 'some sort of an agreement' had been attempted." However, he and Hocutt's other lawyers rejected the agreement because State Attorney General Dennis G. Brummitt—the lawyer representing UNC—could not guarantee the out-of-state tuition bill's passage in the state legislature. In subsequent hearings, Hocutt's academic record came into question. His former Hillside Park High School principal, J. W. Wilson, described Hocutt's grades as borderline passing, which contradicted his lawyers' statements in earlier court filings that he had an exceptional academic background.[45]

The *Hocutt* case ended in late March. Judge Barnhill "declined to place his signature on a preemptory writ of mandamus compelling the university to admit the Negro to its school of pharmacy." Hocutt lost his case, as Judge Barnhill wrote in his decision, "on the grounds that the writ of mandamus sought in the complaint was not the proper remedy for the relief of the alleged grievance of the plaintiff." Barnhill saw no valid reason why the university had to admit Hocutt based on his lawyers' discrimination claims. The only obligation the university had, the judge wrote, would have been to consider Hocutt's application on its own merits without regard to race. Barnhill also ruled in the university's favor partly "on technical grounds." The most damaging evidence against Hocutt came at the hands of NCCN president Dr. James E. Shepard, who refused to send Hocutt's college transcript to UNC, thereby making his admissions application incomplete.[46]

Just as *Hocutt* started, the Durham NAACP reorganized under a new, enthusiastic branch president, Miles Mark Fisher, pastor at White Rock Baptist Church, where M&F Bank president C. C. Spaulding and other members from the black middle class and business community attended. But the *Hocutt* case derailed Fisher's plans for a workable program for the local branch, and he had just taken the helm when he resigned due to tensions within the black community and the branch itself. The more radical elements favored moving the *Hocutt* case forward rather than compromising. Despite the reluctance of black business leaders in Durham to give their public support to the *Hocutt* case, in the months that followed they carried on a productive exchange with the

NAACP's national office. Both Spaulding and McDougald reached out to Walter White after the NAACP leader toured the state in May to drum up interest in the organization's programs. The NAACP had plans for a statewide conference, more branches, and a call for the equalization of teachers' salaries. White's visit provided an opportunity to capitalize on the momentum from *Hocutt* and other high-profile NAACP cases in states such as Virginia. In October, the national NAACP held a conference to organize a statewide NAACP, and McDougald had a central role in the meeting's success. He also gave one of the main speeches at the gathering. With its feet now planted on a firmer basis in North Carolina, the NAACP pressed for equity in teacher salaries.[47]

"To Otherwise Act in Behalf of the Negro Citizens"

The mid-1930s were a turning point for Wheeler. In January 1935, his professional responsibilities expanded when John Hope—past president of Morehouse College and at the time president of the Atlanta University System—appointed Wheeler to the boards of trustees at Morehouse College and Atlanta University. At twenty-seven, Wheeler became the youngest board member ever appointed to either school. Education was by then the profession of his older sister, Ruth Hervey, an instructor at Bennett College in Greensboro, and his younger sister, Margery Janice, an art teacher who during the 1934–1935 school year taught at Durham's black Hillside Park High School. The board appointments gave Wheeler an opportunity to effect change at black institutions of higher education in the New South. The *Hocutt* case would no doubt have focused his attention on the need to provide advanced training for southern blacks, and in his roles as a black banker and trustee, Wheeler could begin to think more deeply about the centrality of education to full citizenship, black economic power, and New South prosperity. In 1940, he would interview his former mathematics professor, Dr. Benjamin E. Mays, for the Morehouse presidency, a post Mays accepted. During the next twenty-seven years, with support and encouragement from board members like Wheeler, the "School Master of the Movement," as Mays's most recent biographer has described him, turned Morehouse's declining reputation around and built a lasting legacy.[48]

Selena Lucille Warren and John Hervey Wheeler married on December 25, 1935. Selena became the head librarian at the Colored Library in 1934 (which became the Stanford L. Warren Public Library in 1940) and remained there until 1945, when she went to work for the Durham City Public Schools. During her tenure at the Stanford L. Warren Library, Selena instituted "Saturday Morning Story Hour," "Bookmobile Services," and "Book Review Forums" with authors such as Durham native and civil rights activist Pauli Murray. In 1990, the former "Negro Collection" became the "Selena Warren Wheeler Collection." *Wheeler Family Photos,* undated, John H. Wheeler Collection, Atlanta University Center Robert W. Woodruff Library.

The Wheeler family home, a "period cottage," was built in 1935 and located at 302 Fermosa Avenue in the College View neighborhood directly across from what became Hillside High School after it was relocated to Concord Street around 1949. *Home of John Wheeler, Durham, NC,* undated, John H. Wheeler Collection, Atlanta University Center Robert W. Woodruff Library.

Meanwhile, on Christmas Day 1935, he married twenty-four-year-old Selena Lucille Warren. The only child of Dr. Stanford L. and Julia McCauley Warren, Selena had graduated from the all-black Howard University in Washington, D.C., in 1932. Her physician father was M&F Bank's board chairman. Her mother was the first black hairdresser in Durham and operated a beauty parlor for whites near Main Street. Every Sunday, the religious Warren family attended St. Joseph's AME Church, which the Wheelers had also attended before they left Durham for Atlanta.[49]

Selena attended Durham's West End School before graduating from Hillside Park High School. She thoroughly enjoyed her experience at

Howard, her first time away from home. When she met John Hervey, she planned to attend law school to avoid becoming a teacher, an idea she hated. Nevertheless, she put those plans on hold temporarily to fill a position at Durham's Colored Library after the librarian died. Selena enjoyed the work so much that she put her law school plans aside permanently to pursue a degree in library science at Hampton Institute in Virginia (now Hampton University). As John Hervey drove her to Hampton, they probably contemplated their future together, but according to Selena, marriage came up only as an afterthought. She graduated from Hampton Institute in 1934 and became head librarian at the Durham Colored Library, later named the Stanford L. Warren Library in her father's honor. Wheeler had previously joined the library's board, having worked as a young man as an assistant in the Atlanta Public Library System and managed the Morehouse library while its librarian was on leave. When Wheeler asked Selena's father for her hand in marriage, he explained that his daughter would not settle for being a homemaker, nor would she be the domestic type. She would rather be a career woman. They had their first child on April 4, 1937, a daughter they named Julia Margaret Wheeler. Their second child, Warren Hervey Wheeler, was born October 1, 1943.[50]

During this period, men like C. C. Spaulding and Richard L. McDougald schooled Wheeler on local community politics and black leadership, and his training included observational exercises on how black business activism functioned in the New South. Yet he had to wait patiently for his turn to put those lessons into practice. He also learned from his senior colleagues about the survival of black financial institutions like M&F Bank. During the Great Depression, the older generation of black business leaders groomed and prepared Wheeler and others to take on larger community responsibilities. Although he joined the local NAACP branch and continued to exercise his voting rights, not until the Durham Committee on Negro Affairs (DCNA) formed in 1935 did his role as a black business activist begin to materialize and take on greater meaning. The organization offered a new outlet for a generation of up-and-coming leaders to get involved in community affairs. Spaulding called the group's initial meeting on August 15 of that year at the Algonquian Tennis Club, the private country club for Durham's black middle class. Black leaders had previously tried to establish a stronger voice for racial equality and

Julia Margaret Wheeler, daughter of John Hervey Wheeler and Selena Warren Wheeler. This "charming" photograph, one of many taken of children in black Durham, was featured in the May 3, 1941, issue of the *Carolina Times* newspaper. *Unidentified Girl,* undated, John H. Wheeler Collection, Atlanta University Center Robert W. Woodruff Library.

Warren Hervey Wheeler and his father, John Hervey Wheeler, riding bicycles on what appears to be a boardwalk. This photograph reflects how seriously Wheeler took recreational and leisure activities among black people because he believed these kinds of activities were important to accessing "freedom of movement" and the fullest extent of citizenship in American society. *John H. and Warren H. Wheeler Riding Bicycles,* Scrapbook 5, undated, John H. Wheeler Collection, Atlanta University Center Robert W. Woodruff Library.

economic justice alongside Durham's white power brokers. In the previous two years, they had focused on forming an organization to confront widening disparities. The earlier attempts by the NAACP to establish an active presence in black Durham never came to fruition to the extent national leaders wanted. Instead, Durham's black business leaders preferred to deal with local circumstances on their own terms, and they believed that could be accomplished partly through group solidarity. The failed promises of Roosevelt's New Deal programs for black Americans also motivated leaders to form the DCNA.[51]

The widely held narrative credits Reverend George A. Fisher from Raleigh with bringing the idea to attorney Conrad O. Pearson and NCCN professor James T. Taylor. At the time, both Pearson and Taylor held positions with New Deal agencies, the Works Progress Administration (WPA) and the National Youth Administration (NYA) in Raleigh. Fisher and the black Raleigh Citizens Committee succeeded in getting city officials to build the Chavis Park Swimming Pool for African Americans. He envisioned similar citizens' groups in black communities like Durham throughout the state as a way to expand access to the levers of power that had for so long rested in the hands of the few, men like Spaulding, Shepard, and W. G. Pearson. Conrad Pearson and Taylor consulted McDougald, who gave them his blessing without hesitancy. McDougald aligned himself with businessmen such as Spaulding on certain approaches to handling community problems, but perhaps more than any single black Durham businessman at that time, he came across as "liberal minded," progressive, when it came to tactics for bringing about racial equality. Wheeler, who would be promoted to M&F Bank's assistant cashier by the end of the 1930s, had a front seat to how the veteran banker navigated race relations.[52]

At DCNA's initial meeting, Wheeler counted ballots for the leadership committee, though he was still "too junior," according to Asa T. Spaulding, to serve on the committee himself. Spaulding was elected chair, Dr. James E. Shepard vice president, James T. Taylor secretary, and McDougald treasurer. Louis E. Austin, Rencher N. Harris, and William Daniel Hill were also voted onto the executive committee. They later invited Hazel S. Knox and Cora Russell to join the executive committee meetings.[53]

Between 1935 and 1941, the DCNA's primary goal became strengthening its credibility in the black community by taking on several important community issues, including "requesting police protection in Negro sections; conferring with school authorities with a view toward improvement of the local school system; securing of donations for sowing [*sic*] room for Negroes; writing of letters and conducting conferences regarding injustices." The DCNA also wanted to "obtain for the Negroes of the Community more consideration in the matter of government employment, especially in the various government [New Deal] relief units." It saw the need for the "improvement of municipal recreation facilities for Negroes" as an effective agent for "good citizenship." In many ways, the

DCNA's establishment helped bridge the class divides, but as several authors have pointed out, this did not happen easily.[54]

During this time no single issue, aside from politics, garnered the DCNA's time and attention more so than the battle for black educational equality. The organization lobbied the Durham City School Board for improved educational facilities, black representation on the board, equitable distribution of city and county resources, programs and curriculums that met standards already in place at the city's white schools, and additional vocational education. In 1936, the DCNA pressed the board to purchase land near Whitted School for "recreational and playground purposes," but the board declined, citing a lack of funds. In January 1937, the DCNA wanted a twelfth grade added to the black Hillside Park High School to correspond with a twelfth-grade addition to the white Durham High School.[55]

The following May, the DCNA conducted its own investigation into black school conditions and demanded the board upgrade and build new facilities and employ a "Negro as Supervising Principal in charge of Negro schools" alongside "an advisory committee of interested and public spirited Negro citizens." In July, the Durham city and county school boards agreed on a four-room addition to Lyon Park School for $16,800 and a new seven-room school for blacks in East Durham for $21,000. At the same time, the boards agreed to build the white East Durham Junior High School with twenty rooms at a cost of $176,000, more than three times the combined estimated cost for black school improvements. The boards also used funds from the Works Progress Administration to maintain these inequalities.[56]

By the late 1930s, the DCNA was pressing city leaders to hire qualified blacks in previously all-white positions, for example, to manage Durham's Alcohol Beverage Control (ABC) liquor store in Hayti. Executive committee member Louis E. Austin called the group's negotiations in that matter a "moral victory," but he continued, "There are hundreds of other jobs which Negroes should have in Durham that they do not, merely because no effort has been made to obtain them for the race." When the ABC after much delay finally hired a black manager, they rejected the person the DCNA suggested, in the group's view to avoid being told what to do by a black organization.[57]

In 1938, James McNeal's murder brought tensions to a boiling point. On May 28, ABC police squad officers led by T. D. Wilkie barged into McNeal's Hayti residence without a warrant, according to eyewitness accounts. Wilkie allegedly struck the unsuspecting McNeal with his billy club and then shot him dead in one of the worst crimes perpetrated by the Durham police force. Yet it was also par for the course as the Durham police conducted regular, aggressive, brutal liquor raids against local bootlegging operations. The white officer who murdered McNeal had been hired to protect rather than victimize, and black Durham stood up and demanded justice. Wheeler recalled years later that "'police brutality was one of the major problems we had'" and that the McNeal murder "'was one of the major organizing incidents that spread the Durham Committee's support among the masses of Blacks.'" The DCNA continued to pressure the city council to hire black police officers, but the city would refuse until 1944. Two months after the McNeal murder, an all-white, all-male jury acquitted Wilkie, despite what the *Carolina Times* described as "the preponderance of evidence, presented by the prosecution." Most blacks were not surprised, as whites were rarely found guilty for crimes committed against blacks in the South.[58]

The DCNA was just as vocal with city leaders about public accommodations and used every instance to obtain improved access for blacks. In 1938, they threatened city officials with a court injunction after bathroom facilities were locked in the local Armory, which a black fraternity had rented for a dance. During the years leading to World War II, the DCNA had to raise the issue of unequal public facilities time and again.[59]

By the end of the 1930s, the DCNA became a bona fide civil rights organization. In April 1941, they asked the city council to appoint a black board member because "it has not been able to get a hearing before the board in matters concerning the Negro schools." Blacks then made up a third of the city's population, they pointed out, and they argued that black citizens understood the problems in their own neighborhoods better than white board members. Up against a defiant board, the DCNA achieved only minor concessions, but it was progress nonetheless.[60]

From the organization's beginning, Spaulding was DCNA chairman but more or less a figurehead, as was somewhat typical of the first line of defense. However, McDougald led an important voter registration effort in 1935 that yielded about one thousand registered black voters, and Wheeler, too, became politically active on the local level. At a black county Democratic convention in 1938, he announced the main speakers.[61]

The DCNA solidified its increasing political power by endorsing candidates for public office during and after World War II. Early on, it endorsed white political candidates and wrestled political control away from Durham's ward heelers. Once white candidates recognized the DCNA's effectiveness, they vied for the organization's endorsement and support. In every year following World War II, the DCNA also endorsed black candidates who, though unsuccessful, received increasing numbers of black votes. Postwar, the DCNA stepped into the forefront of North Carolina politics, which one writer called "the theme of the DCNA" from then on.[62]

As behind-the-scenes negotiations proved ineffective in bringing about large-scale change, black business leaders embraced more effective strategies. The relationship between black capitalism and community became important during a period that intensified the social, political, and economic marginalization of black people. Although M&F Bank and Durham's Black Wall Street continued to experience economic success throughout the Depression, black businesspeople had to come to terms with the broader challenges facing the Bull City in that period. In other words, black business was forced to take greater responsibility at a moment of uncertainty. Eventually, they worked collectively alongside other segments of black Durham to combat injustice.

3

The Battle for Educational Equality in the Postwar New South

> The South of the future . . . is a South freed of stultifying inheritances from the past. It is a South where the measure of a man will be his ability, not his race; where a common citizenship will work in democratic understanding for the common good; where all who labor will be rewarded in proportion to their skill and achievement; where all can feel confident of personal safety and equality before the law; where there will exist no double standard in housing, health, education, other public services.
>
> "The South of the Future," Southern Regional Council, 1951

In the November 1945 issue of the *Tarheel Banker*, John Wheeler wrote, "That the South's popular designation has quite recently been changed from 'America's Number 1 Problem' to 'America's Number 1 Opportunity' is the occasion for jubilation on the part of many, but careful scrutiny of our present situation presents a number of sobering considerations." As World War II ended and the South entered a pivotal moment in its economic growth, he warned, "Indeed such an opportunity may not appear again in this century." As a black banker, he tried to "interpret to the remainder of the banking profession not only the ambitions and latent abilities of colored people, but also the true meaning of the impact which full and unhampered developments of these abilities will make upon our economy." He articulated an economic vision for the postwar South, and he made clear that the path to New South prosperity included a moral imperative to bring forth a just society.[1]

Wheeler called on the South's business leaders to change their outdated "'colonial economy,'" which still "exported its wealth of raw materials or partly processed goods to other regions for fabrication and thereafter found itself unable to repossess the full benefits" because it relied on an "unskilled and low wage labor" system. The exploited workers, overwhelmingly black, found themselves in a perpetual state of economic inferiority due to discrimination. Thus, they could never expand their purchasing power or fully contribute to the South's economic advancement. Wheeler insisted that because blacks made up one-fourth of the region's 42 million citizens, the South had to improve their economic viability.[2]

Wheeler directed his essay at North Carolina's white bankers in a language they could understand. He presented raw data on how the white South missed out by restricting black citizenship rights. "In 1940," he reported, "750,000 Negro families owned their own homes valued at one billion dollars, and in the South alone, 700,000 Negroes owned 8,325,000 acres of farm land valued at $850,000,000 plus farm implements worth $40,000,000." Black businesses accounted for "approximately 32,000 retail stores having an annual sales volume of approximately $100,000,000. In all, about 60,000 business enterprises in over 200 different lines are conducted by Negroes, among which are 55 life insurance companies reporting total assets of more than $45,000,000 and total insurance in force of approximately $600,000,000." In addition, "the income of all Negroes in the United States should reach $8,500,000,000 in 1945 and out of this figure they may be expected to spend at least 6 billion dollars for goods and services."[3]

Despite limitations placed on their freedom, blacks had steadily improved their economic status since emancipation. Wheeler took pride in the accomplishments they had made with inadequate resources but believed if given equal opportunities, they could achieve much more. He wrote that if segregation prevented full citizenship, there would be no black economic power. He also said blacks deserved better opportunities in health, housing, employment, education, politics, and public accommodations. Unless artificial barriers collapsed, he argued, black Americans would never gain full citizenship or black economic power. If a large segment of society could not fully participate in the southern economy, then the South would suffer because it could not compete economically with other regions.[4]

This chapter examines Wheeler's perspective on the most significant opportunities that presented themselves to the South after World War II.

Historians have made clear that the total receipts of black enterprises across the United States never came close to meeting those of white enterprises, and this chapter pushes up against that assertion by examining why. It highlights Wheeler's efforts and those of others to remove the obstacles that he believed prevented black business from reaching its full potential. Wheeler well knew the deck was stacked against black capitalism and that consequently it was impossible for black businesses to establish the foundation that made the most lucrative white firms successful. He focused on the larger promise of black business, the widespread disparities in black economic life, and the limitations therein.

World War II represented a watershed moment for black Americans, as they intensified their battle for full citizenship during the war and sought to carry it on afterward. Wheeler supported the war effort through M&F Bank and the Durham Committee on Negro Affairs (DCNA), but he believed this support had to be reciprocated by removing discriminatory obstacles that locked black Americans out of the full promises of American democracy. Wheeler's vision of New South prosperity included education as a fundamental requirement in the expansion of economic rights. During the war, and with an eye toward the postwar period, black people had to embrace strategies to attack unjust segregationist laws, and public education seemed the most likely avenue of approach. As the postwar period advanced, Wheeler became a staunch critic of the negative economic consequences of the public education laws political leaders passed. Later still, he would welcome the NAACP's legal strategy and its 1954 victory in *Brown*.

"Preserving the Ideals of American Democracy"

On October 20, 1942, a group of prominent black leaders from the South convened on the campus of North Carolina College for Negroes (NCCN) in Durham. The Southern Conference on Race Relations, or the Durham Conference, as it became known, came about through efforts led by Gordon B. Hancock, a sociology and economics professor at the black Virginia Union University. They wanted "a New Charter of Race Relations in the South" because they saw "the old charter [as] paternalistic and traditional." The group asserted, "The Negro ha[d] paid the full price of citizenship in the South and nation, and the Negro want[ed] to enjoy the full exercise of this citizenship, no more and no less."[5]

As Hancock recalled, Wheeler was "one of those who met with [them] at Durham on that memorable morning when [they] set in motion the movement that eventuated into our now great Southern Regional Council," though Wheeler's name did not appear on the official list of attendees. These included prominent educators—Dr. James E. Shepard and James T. Taylor of NCCN and Drs. Rufus E. Clement and Benjamin E. Mays, presidents at Morehouse College and Atlanta University, respectively. M&F Bank president C. C. Spaulding attended the meeting as well. At the conference, working groups identified problems and proposed solutions in education, agriculture, military service, industry and labor, service occupations, political and civil rights, and social welfare and health. Sociologist Dr. Charles S. Johnson headed the subcommittee that prepared their formal statement, "A Basis for Inter-racial Cooperation and Development in the South: A Statement by Southern Negroes," which they issued to the press on December 15.[6]

The Durham Statement, or Durham Manifesto, tactfully insisted on full citizenship rights for blacks, noting, "We are fundamentally opposed to the principles and practices of compulsory segregation in our American society, whether of races or classes or creeds, however, we regard it as both sensible and timely to address ourselves now to the current problems of racial discrimination and neglect and to ways in which we may cooperate in the advancement of programs aimed at the sound improvement of race relations within the democratic framework."[7]

The manifesto's most daring demands came in political and civil rights, industry and labor, and education. It demanded abolition of the "poll tax," "white primary," and "all forms of discriminatory practices . . . and intimidation of citizens seeking to exercise their right of franchise." The statement called for equal employment opportunities for blacks because "the only tenable basis of economic survival and development for Negroes is inclusion in unskilled, semi-skilled and skilled branches of work in the industries or occupations of the region to the extent that they are equally capable." The group endorsed the Fair Employment Practices Committee (FEPC) as "sound and economically essential" to improving job opportunities for blacks. They demanded "the same pay for the same work" and fair participation for blacks in organized labor unions. The manifesto called for improvements in black education within the "separate but equal" framework and demanded equal salaries for black schoolteachers, better-equipped black schools, and identical school terms for black and white children. The group also wanted training for blacks in graduate and professional schools and black representation on school boards.[8]

As historian Raymond Gavins concluded: "Never before in Southern history had black people made such a comprehensive and lucid declaration of what they expected from white people. Despite its purposeful ambiguity on segregation, the statement indicated that Southern Negro leaders were not mere accommodationists. They were dead set against the status quo. As one variation on the theme of rising racial aspirations during World War II, the Durham statement projected a vision of equality and projected the changing mind of the black South." The Durham Conference proved consistent with Wheeler's belief that full citizenship in all areas would lead to economic advancement for blacks, the South, and nation. Together with follow-up meetings in Atlanta and Richmond, it laid the foundation for establishing the Southern Regional Council (SRC), an interracial civil rights organization, in 1944. The organization pledged itself to "the ideals and practices of equal opportunity for all peoples in the region; to reduce race tension, the basis of racial tension, racial misunderstanding, and racial distrust; to develop and integrate leadership in the South on new levels of regional development and fellowship." From the SRC's beginning Wheeler was a vice president, and in the next decades he became one of its most influential leaders.[9]

By then, Wheeler had worked his way up the ranks and achieved significant success and leadership in the banking field. During the annual M&F Bank stockholders meeting in January 1940, Wheeler received a promotion to cashier, and Richard L. McDougald became the executive vice president. "The elevation of both these two men," explained the *Carolina Times*, "to higher positions in the local bank is considered a tribute to the fine manner in which they have conducted the affairs of the nation[']s largest Negro bank," as the financial institution had over $1.3 million in assets at the time. Later that same month, Wheeler's father-in-law,

John Hervey Wheeler at M&F Bank. In October 1943, during World War II, he became chairman of the DCNA's education committee whereby he kept pressure on the Durham school board to make good on its promise to build a "Technical High School for [N]egroes in the City of Durham." During this same time, Wheeler enrolled in law school at the North Carolina College School of Law. He worked at the bank during the day and attended law classes at night, and his "rigorous schedule meant . . . four hours sleep a night." In a September 1944 report, Wheeler warned DCNA leaders that "'nothing short of legal action [would] change' the 'numerous inequities in the present [educational] system.'" *John H. Wheeler at Mechanics and Farmers Bank,* undated, John H. Wheeler Collection, Atlanta University Center Robert W. Woodruff Library.

Dr. Stanford L. Warren, died, a major loss for both the family and M&F Bank, where he chaired the board. In 1907, Warren had helped charter M&F Bank, and he held its presidency from 1920 to 1922.[10]

As M&F Bank's cashier, Wheeler hoped to move the bank forward in significant ways. In July 1940, he, Spaulding, and McDougald attended the

The most recognizable black businessman in the country during the interwar period was Wheeler's (*right*) predecessor, Charles Clinton Spaulding (*left*), M&F Bank president between 1922 and 1952. Spaulding doubled as NC Mutual president from 1923 to 1952. He represented an older generation and was far less aggressive than R. L. McDougald, and later Wheeler, in pushing for black political participation. He believed strictly in quiet, behind-the-scenes negotiations with the white power structure. "The Negro leadership," explained Wheeler, "had to be very skillful. And it didn't dare express itself except in rare instances. It played the white leadership for all it was worth, and being very careful and very skillful, knowing that they had no redress." *John H. Wheeler and C. C. Spaulding,* undated, John H. Wheeler Collection, Atlanta University Center Robert W. Woodruff Library.

white North Carolina Bankers Association's (NCBA) annual conference, the first interracial meeting for the organization. The M&F Bank delegation wanted to strengthen their cooperative relationship with the state's white bankers and discuss financial principles and North Carolina's economic future. They were the only black businesspeople at the weeklong conference, as M&F Bank remained the lone black bank in the entire state at the time.[11]

As the United States' involvement in the global conflict dovetailed into a declaration of war after the December 7, 1941, attack on Pearl Harbor, Wheeler and M&F Bank showed support in a number of ways. Black businessmen served on the Durham County Draft Board and purchased war bonds. M&F Bank held fund-raisers, and by December 1942, M&F Bank and NC Mutual had each purchased $100,000 in war bonds. Wheeler and the bank also responded to appeals from black business leaders from across the country to support wartime food production. In March 1943, they assisted black 4-H Club of North Carolina members in purchasing "a carload of high grade calves at a total cost of $2,400." By the end of that same year, M&F Bank issued a $300,000 check from NC Mutual's account to purchase more war bonds. The purchase, according to one newspaper, "brought forcibly to public attention the remarkable manner in which Negro capital is supporting the country's war effort." The check itself was "said not only to mark the largest single purchase of war bonds by a Negro business but is also the largest check ever to be issued against a Negro bank" up to that point. M&F Bank and NC Mutual purchased a total of $200,000 and $2,120,300 in war bonds, respectively.[12]

In October 1944, the nation's black banking community was stunned by the sudden death of Richard L. McDougald from an apparent heart attack at forty-eight years old. Wheeler became the bank's executive vice president and officially part of the second line of defense at M&F Bank much sooner than expected, given that McDougald would have most certainly succeeded C. C. Spaulding as president. Wheeler's first project was to establish a pension plan, a brainchild of McDougald's, as an incentive for M&F Bank employees to spend their careers at the bank. Especially following World War II, the employees were expected to complete their regularly assigned duties and yet find time to volunteer for community activities. Vivian Rogers Patterson, a native of Holly Springs, North Carolina, and graduate of NCCN, came to work at M&F Bank in 1944 as a teller. She held several positions ranging from teller to loan officer, and eventually became an assistant vice president with the company. Before coming to Durham, Patterson had worked for the Citizens Trust Bank in

Table 3.1. Resources and deposits of the Mechanics and Farmers Bank from December 31, 1945, to December 31, 1958

Year	Resources	Deposits
1945	$5,162,930	$4,840,781
1946	$5,018,973	$4,664,376
1947	$5,408,303	$5,048,732
1948	$5,336,328	$4,955,569
1949	$5,111,941	$4,732,942
1950	$5,258,218	$4,842,993
1951	$5,960,165	$5,508,002
1952	$5,910,890	$5,512,864
1953	$6,750,773	$6,315,036
1954	$6,750,773	$6,293,247
1955	$6,860,371	$6,395,629
1956	$7,556,520	$7,080,142
1957	$7,095,657	$6,532,220
1958	$7,728,384	$7,129,784

Source: Ilon Owen Funderburg, "An Analysis of Operating Problems of a Bank Serving a Predominantly Negro Market" (master's thesis, Rutgers University, 1959), 43.

Atlanta for about two years and then joined M&F Bank. At M&F Bank, Patterson remembered the leadership's "whole thing was that all of us [employees] should participate in outside activities." She vividly remembered being encouraged to become active in the DCNA. "When you get there [to the DCNA meetings] you found that you had been volunteered to do this or that." Patterson was part of a pioneering generation of black women in banking and finance.[13]

M&F Bank and the larger black banking world looked to take part in the affluence of the postwar economy. Once Congress passed the Veterans Readjustment Act of 1944 (otherwise known as the GI Bill), Wheeler helped to fulfill the needs of black veterans in accordance with the bill. In November 1946, for instance, he prided himself that M&F Bank had a role in granting approximately $600,000 in loans to about three thousand borrowers. He told his friend and business colleague Asa T. Spaulding, NC Mutual actuary and M&F Bank board member, "These loans have been for the purpose of financing almost every conceivable kind of

The National Negro Bankers Association (NNBA) held its 25th Annual Convention on the campus of Lemoyne College in Memphis, Tennessee, in 1952. (The organization removed "Negro" from its name in 1948.) Wheeler attended (*front row, fifth from right in the light suit*), along with other M&F Bank board members including Shag Stewart (*middle row, second from left*) and E. R. Merrick (*middle row, third from the left*). In 1927, the NNBA held its first annual convention in Durham, North Carolina. That year, M&F Bank's vice president and cashier, R. L. McDougald, made local arrangements for the gathering, which also included a tour of M&F Bank's Raleigh Branch. In September 1950, Wheeler was elected NNBA president and received a second term in 1951. *National Negro Bankers Association's 25th Annual Convention,* undated, John H. Wheeler Collection, Atlanta University Center Robert W. Woodruff Library.

operation including construction of numerous homes for returning war veterans and it is our hope that in the future we may find even greater means of contributing to the growth and development of Durham and its surrounding areas." As one chronicler of M&F Bank's history noted, the bank's home loan financing program for returning war veterans became "one of the great accomplishments of the bank" in the late 1940s. The bank's interest in lending to war veterans reflected the thinking of Richard L. McDougald, himself a World War I veteran, and Wheeler was eager to extend the bank's policies in this area.[14]

During this time Wheeler became president of the National Negro Bankers Association (NNBA) and then was reelected to a consecutive term. In August 1952, he would become M&F Bank president upon the death of Spaulding, but by all accounts, Wheeler started unofficially serving in this capacity much earlier. Between when he joined the bank as a teller and his election to its presidency, M&F Bank had become the "largest bank in the United States owned and operated exclusively by Negroes," with more than ten thousand customers in North Carolina. The bank's December 1948 year-end report claimed $5,336,328.64 in resources. In 1954, M&F Bank opened its Fayetteville Street Branch in the Hayti section of Durham, the city's largest black neighborhood.[15]

Wheeler and the DCNA remained committed to ensuring full citizenship rights for black North Carolinians. In 1944, he became the first black person appointed to the Durham Recreation Advisory Committee (RAC), which placed him in a strategic position to expand recreational opportunities for black Durham in spaces previously closed off to them. In early 1946, Wheeler was actively involved when the RAC bought the Fayetteville Street United Service Organizations (USO) building from the federal government to use as a youth center. Wheeler believed expanding recreational facilities in black Durham would go far in "preserving the ideals of American Democracy." In other words, recreation paved the way for "effective citizenship," as "one of the means by which many customs of the south which now deny equal opportunity to Negro citizens may be changed in order that everyone may have the same chance for achievement."[16]

Wheeler also played a critical role in advocating new political alliances in Durham alongside DCNA chairman John S. "Shag" Stewart and political chairman Davis Buchanan "Dan" Martin. The most influential political coalition in the city became the black-white Voters for Better Government (VBG) that formed in 1947. The VBG comprised the DCNA, organized labor groups, and white liberal factions. Wheeler's articulation of New South prosperity in his 1945 *Tarheel Banker* article had highlighted the

The M&F Bank Fayetteville Street Branch opened on January 15, 1954, with thousands in attendance. The "drive-in" branch—its first to open in Durham's Hayti section—was "erected, equipped and furnished at a cost of some $95,000" and was "among the most modern in the city, featuring bullet proof and bullet resistant windows." M&F Bank cashier I. Owen Funderburg supervised the branch's operations. *Mechanics and Farmers Bank, Durham, NC, 1957,* undated, John H. Wheeler Collection, Atlanta University Center Robert W. Woodruff Library.

central role of labor, and he maintained there that it would be "perhaps easier to integrate skilled Negro workers into any given industry now than it may be ten years hence." The VBG became a viable political coalition not only because of its influence during close elections but because it helped shift the power dynamics within the local Democratic Party, which a group of conservative local lawyers had been controlling. As labor leader Wilbur Hobby explained, "They had been filling out the precinct applications and running the [county] Democratic party from the law offices of . . . [Senator William B.] Umstead."[17]

The board of directors at M&F Bank in 1959. *Seated, left to right:* Asa T. Spaulding, E. R. Merrick, Rencher N. Harris, C. C. Spaulding Jr., Shag Stewart, Charles A. Haywood Sr. *Standing, left to right:* I. Owen Funderburg, J. C. Scarborough, Dr. Lewyn E. McCauley, Dr. Clyde Donnell, John H. Wheeler, William Jesse Kennedy Jr., T. D. Parham, and James E. Strickland. *M&F Bank Board of Directors,* Scrapbook 8, John H. Wheeler Collection, Atlanta University Center Robert W. Woodruff Library.

Moreover, the VBG succeeded in electing insurance agent Leslie Atkins, one of its leaders, to the chairmanship of the Durham County Democratic Party in 1948. That same year, the VBG and the broader labor movement in the state played an instrumental role in ousting Senator Umstead from the US Congress after he supported the Taft-Hartley Act (1947), which placed restrictions on labor unions and paved the way for "right to work" laws in the South. In 1949, the VBG helped elect Dan K. Edwards as Durham's mayor and labor organizer Ernest R. "Sparky" Williamson to the city council.[18]

Wheeler had begun chairing the DCNA's Education Committee in October 1943. In November 1946, he joined the school board's Committee on the Needs of the City Schools. The committee recognized the obvious disparities between the black Hillside High (which after 1941 no longer included "Park" in its name) and the white Durham High in curriculum, facilities, and equipment, and it stressed the immediate need to build technical vocational buildings at both schools. The school board had already completed plans for such a building at Durham High, and it agreed to build one at Hillside High on land already purchased. But it did not spell out a schedule.[19]

Wheeler and the DCNA's Education Committee also pressed city leaders to appoint a black person to the school board, suggesting NCCN professor James T. Taylor. "On previous occasions," Wheeler reminded them, "we were assured that it would be both desirable and expedient to place a Negro on the Board of Education when the next vacancy occurred." And he advocated for equal spending on black and white education. "Through the years," Wheeler reminded city leaders, "the inequality between facilities provided for Negro and White students has widened to such proportions that our city is or should be greatly embarrassed by the present differentials between these facilities." Despite the "separate but equal" mandate, the board spent $494 per white child and only $190 per black child. "The present inequalities in our educational system," Wheeler warned, "are such fertile ground for litigation which would be embarrassing to Durham and the entire South."[20]

Wheeler and the DCNA Education Committee followed up by attending the next city council meeting in April. It was a major turning point for black Durham. Wheeler, Dr. James E. Shepard, and James T. Taylor spoke in an overcrowded room filled with about fifty blacks. The three leaders gave what the white *Durham Morning Herald* called "eloquent" appeals. Moreover, Shepard, the seventy-one-year-old founder and president of NCCN, urged council members to appoint a black board member because "a Negro understands better what is best for his people," and "I am only asking that you give us one sixth representation for one third of the population." Both Taylor and Wheeler insisted that they did not come to the council meeting to "protest against the board of education" or to lobby for any one individual but only "for representation."

Despite these appeals, the city council bypassed adding a black board member and reappointed two white men.[21]

Shepard's public appearance in this instance and his death later in the year forecasted a shift in tactics. In May, Wheeler and other DCNA leaders went before the board again, pleading that it "appoint a supervising principal of Negro schools." Moreover, Wheeler contacted school board chairman Basil M. Watkins for a detailed summary of how a proposed $3 million school bond referendum would be spent. He wanted to know exactly how much would go toward black schools compared to the amount allotted to white schools.[22]

Dissatisfied with Watkins's response, Wheeler and the DCNA then arranged a meeting with the board before deciding whether to publicly support the scheduled vote on the bond referendum. At the meeting, Wheeler demanded that the board give him some "'definite commitment'" stipulating how much funding would go toward black schools.[23]

Although "there was no definite agreement reached as to any amount of money being appropriated for any project for either race," Wheeler and the DCNA pledged their support for the bond in good faith that the board would construct the technical building at Hillside High School. A year later, the city and county boards met secretly together to reconfigure how they would spend the bond money and refused to discuss the funding redistribution publicly, a move that suggests they may have decided to reduce the funding allocations for black schools. Wheeler and attorney M. Hugh Thompson met with the board about the bond issue one last time in December 1948. When they were unable to get a breakdown for how the money would be spent, they left Watkins with something to bear in mind: they told him they were now prepared for legal action.[24]

By then, Wheeler too was a lawyer. On June 2, 1947, he had graduated among the first class of law school students at NCC, and shortly thereafter he passed the North Carolina bar exam. His law degree ensured his readiness to take on larger and more significant civil rights battles. Although the time had not come for Wheeler and the DCNA to initiate a school equalization suit in Durham, other North Carolina cities were facing such action. In late 1946, the local NAACP's National Youth Council spearheaded a strike at the Lumberton City Schools, and hundreds of black students defiantly left class to protest deplorable school conditions. In July 1947, with support from the NAACP's national office, Wheeler's former law professor Herman L. Taylor filed a school equalization lawsuit on behalf of the students against the Lumberton City Schools, the Robeson County Board of Education, and other city leaders.[25]

Taylor resigned from NCC that summer to play an active role in the battle for civil rights unconstrained by Dr. Shepard's views on school litigation. He remained committed to fighting educational inequality in North Carolina, turning down a $6,000 yearly salary to teach at a law school in Texas. As a law student, Wheeler had probably held informal conversations with Taylor about the legal possibilities of bringing about changes to the educational system. As the first school equalization challenge in the state, the Lumberton case no doubt influenced Wheeler, but because of several legal obstacles and the NAACP's waning interest in the suit, by 1949 Taylor dropped it. Also, the Lumberton school board made significant improvements to its schools before litigation could move forward. Nevertheless, the Lumberton case "galvanized blacks across the state to pursue similar battles for equalization," as historian Sarah Caroline Thuesen has noted.[26]

Wheeler and Thompson considered pursuing a school equalization case against the Durham board, but they began litigation efforts away from the city. In November 1948, Mark Sharpe of the African American Men's Civic Club in Wilson County asked Wheeler to serve as their attorney in a potential lawsuit against the Wilson County School Board. Wheeler seized the opportunity, although C. C. Spaulding had continuously dissuaded Durham's next line of defense from using legal pressure in the battle for educational equality. Wheeler told Sharpe he believed they could win if they sued based on the "separate but equal" mandate, as opposed to directly challenging the larger issue of segregation. Their extended meeting ended with Wheeler accepting the case and being paid a one-thousand-dollar retainer. Wheeler suggested the Wilson group hire another lawyer to share the responsibilities, and he solicited M. Hugh Thompson's assistance. In January 1950, with substantial evidence to prove the county's inequalities, the two attorneys filed a lawsuit in district court, citing the need for two new black high schools. In response, Wilson County proposed to build the two high schools in exchange for withdrawal of the lawsuit. Wilson's black leaders agreed, and though the

Carolina Times newspaper editor Louis E. Austin (*center*) presents "golden plaques" to M. Hugh Thompson (*standing, left*) and John H. Wheeler (*standing, right*) in receiving the Durham Press Club's "Page One" awards at a banquet held on Monday, August 28, 1950. The ceremony recognized the two lawyers for their efforts in the *Blue v. Durham* trial a month earlier. *Unidentified Ceremony with John H. Wheeler,* undated, John H. Wheeler Collection, Atlanta University Center Robert W. Woodruff Library.

board stonewalled at first, by year's end the black community's ongoing legal threats forced it to plan to build the two high schools.[27]

Meanwhile, Wheeler, Thompson, and the DCNA were no longer attending Durham school board meetings month after month and requesting equal funding and black representation to no avail. Now their demands coincided with the NAACP's broader assault on school segregation, which the organization had carried into courtrooms across the country beginning in the 1930s. The NAACP's legal strategy gained considerable momentum during the 1940s and 1950s, when it would culminate with the US Supreme Court's landmark *Brown* decision in 1954. In the late 1940s, Wheeler and the DCNA continued their own legal push for school equalization, again making Durham and North Carolina battlegrounds in the struggle for educational equality, full citizenship, black economic power, and New South prosperity.[28]

"Such Fertile Ground for Litigation"

On May 18, 1949, Wheeler took legal action to follow up with the earlier warnings to the Durham mayor and city council. Assisted by Wheeler, M. Hugh Thompson, and the DCNA, sixty students and twenty-six parents filed a complaint against local and state school administrators in US Middle District Court in Greensboro, North Carolina. The Durham suit, formally *Blue v. Durham* (1951), argued those school officials violated students' Fourteenth Amendment rights under the US Constitution because educational facilities provided for black and white children were unequal. The bold, resolute action by Wheeler and the DCNA in the Durham suit signaled "a departure from the Spaulding-Shepard style of quiet, behind the scenes negotiations," as historian Christina Greene has noted. Wheeler stood at the forefront in this push and led the fight in the courts.[29]

The plaintiffs in *Blue* represented a cross section of African Americans. Many of them came from working-class families who believed strongly in community involvement. Margaret Blue, an active DCNA member, wanted better educational and economic opportunities for her three children, Carolyn, Donald, and Portia. Arthur Stanley worked for the American Tobacco Company when he allowed his name and that of his son, William Ernest, to be listed among the plaintiffs. At the time, Stanley was also president of the Tobacco Workers International Union's (TWIU) segregated black Local 204. John Lawrence Curtis depended on his job at the Liggett and Myers Tobacco Company (L&M) to support his family, which lived in the same neighborhood as the Stanleys. His daughter Omega Curtis Parker, another named plaintiff in the case, later remembered her father for his activism in the DCNA and local NAACP. Her father's labor organizing with the TWIU took him on frequent trips to Richmond, Virginia, to attend union meetings. Joseph Riley Sr. also worked in a tobacco factory and attached his name and the names of his children Nellie, Inez, Joseph Jr., and Clarence to the case. That tobacco workers were among the plaintiffs demonstrates their interest in providing their children with the best education possible in preparation for better job opportunities in the postwar period. They also risked possible economic sanctions from their white employers by participating in the case. In contrast, the plaintiffs from black business-owning families were not economically dependent on white employers and weren't threatened with economic reprisal. The DCNA's chairman, Shag Stewart, secretary-treasurer for the Mutual Building and Loan Association (MB&LA), and his daughter Ethel Marie were named plaintiffs. Junior high student J. C. Scarborough III and his father, J. C. Scarborough II, owner of the black Scarborough and Hargett Funeral Home, were plaintiffs, and so were NC Mutual executive Dan B. Martin and his children Carolyn, Joseph, and Winfred, as well as DCNA member and NC Mutual executive James J. "Babe" Henderson and his daughter Ann. DCNA Education Committee member and NC Mutual employee William A. Clement and his children Alexine and William rounded out the list.[30]

Attorney M. Hugh Thompson had been daringly confronting racism across North Carolina since the 1930s, when he was one of the few black lawyers in the state. Prior to the Durham suit, he had handled countless cases. Born on May 3, 1898, in Goldsboro, North Carolina, he finished high school in Newark, New Jersey, and then enrolled in Syracuse University after saving up money working as a bricklayer. After college, Thompson enlisted in the US Army, saw some action in Europe during World War I, and suffered a shrapnel injury to one leg. Perhaps motivated by discrimination he suffered as a soldier, he attended law school at the black Howard University after the war. He came to Durham in 1923, established his law office, and also joined the legal teams of NC Mutual, M&F Bank, and MB&LA. In one case during the early 1930s, Thompson barely escaped death while defending a black Henderson man for his alleged role in kidnapping and raping a white woman. As Thompson and his white cocounsel, Reuben O. Everett, traveled between Durham and Henderson, an unknown assailant fired on them. Governor John C. B. Ehringhaus dispatched state patrols to guard the lawyers until the case ended.[31]

Wheeler and Thompson filed the Durham lawsuit when—to no one's surprise—construction on the vocational building and gymnasium at the white Durham High proceeded before work began on the technical high school promised at the black Hillside High. Wheeler and Thompson notified the school board on May 7, 1949, about their intent to file a formal complaint. The lawyers reminded the board that DCNA and other black leaders had negotiated repeatedly in years past to improve school facilities for black children. They had decided to take matters beyond the local level because the board had yet again put black education on hold.[32]

Board chairman Basil M. Watkins dismissed the case as without merit. In a reply to the attorneys before they filed their complaint, he said he hoped they would reconsider. He noted that within thirty days, contract bids for the new black high school would begin, and he said the board had in the previous twenty years provided black children with more school facilities than white children. The board planned to stand its ground, Watkins announced, warning, "If the Negro pupils of Durham are delayed in their enjoyment, or ultimately deprived of their enjoyment of the Negro high school building . . . it will be the fault of some (not by all by any means) of the Negro citizens of Durham and not the fault of the Board of Education." "The Negroes responsible for bringing this suit," he maintained, "were fully advised and knew before its initiation that the Board of Education had been working for a long time upon plans for a new [technical] high school plant for Negroes that would include all necessary facilities for a modern and fine school."[33]

Wheeler and Thompson argued the case on economic grounds because ignoring vocational education meant delaying crucial job training for blacks, many of whom were unlikely to attend college or obtain advanced training beyond high school. Moreover, the child plaintiffs—mostly junior and high school students at Hillside—were only a few years away from graduating and entering the workforce. Had the board begun construction on the black vocational high school when it began construction on the white school, Wheeler, Thompson, and the DCNA might have decided against legal action. The attorneys placed the vocational high school issue and economic justice at center stage during the trial.[34]

With the earlier Lumberton case and later Wilson case, *Blue* joined a growing list of school equalization challenges that sprang up in the South. As the NAACP had in previous cases, it used Durham as a "test case" in a statewide effort to eliminate educational inequality. The state NAACP chairman, Kelly Alexander, told reporters, "We want equal schools on the elementary, secondary and college level," and "if necessary, there will be many suits in cities and towns of North Carolina." Despite claims that the NAACP was behind the Durham case, Thompson maintained that the actions were initiated by the local group and had no connection to the state NAACP. However, he did agree that the NAACP would be interested in the case as "the opening gun" in North Carolina. The Durham suit followed NAACP school equalization cases in states such as Virginia, and when the trial began the following year, Richmond, Virginia, lawyers Oliver W. Hill and Martin A. Martin (of the Hill, Martin and Robinson law firm) joined the case on behalf of the NAACP Legal Defense and Educational Fund (LDF). During the 1940s, their law firm had successfully litigated several school equalization cases in the Old Dominion. *Blue* was the first case in North Carolina to reach the final stages of full-scale litigation. The Durham school board hired attorneys R. P. Reade and William B. Umstead, the latter being the former senator and future governor, as their legal counsel. State education officials requested, unsuccessfully, that charges against them be dismissed because they had no control over decisions made by administrators at the local level.[35]

In the meantime, DCNA and NAACP attorney Conrad O. Pearson filed another lawsuit against UNC. In the previous decade, Pearson—the lead attorney for Thomas Hocutt in 1933—had gained a reputation as a radical and pioneer for his legal attacks aimed at Jim Crow. The new case had been in the works since March 1949, when NCC law school students picketed the state Capitol in Raleigh to publicize the unequal facilities between their law school and UNC's. Pearson and the NAACP took up the students' cause and filed a lawsuit against UNC for denying two NCC law students' applications. In October 1950, Judge Johnson J. Hayes ruled in UNC's favor, asserting that the NCC law school was "equal to and in some ways, surpassed, opportunities offered students at the University." On appeal, however, the law students won their case, and the courts ordered UNC to desegregate its law school. The reversal came on the heels of *Sweatt v. Painter* (1950), a similar case in Texas the US Supreme Court had decided that June. In the *Sweatt* case, the court ruled against the University of Texas Law School because the education available at the state's black law school in no way compared to that at the flagship institution. The *Sweatt* decision made Wheeler more determined than ever to pursue equal education, as he believed the victory proved "conclusively that Negroes must, by their own bootstraps, lift themselves to the level of total citizenship and that to depend on their so-called friends in other groups for that purpose is futile." A year later, Floyd B. McKissick, Harvey E. Beech, J. Kenneth Lee, James R. Walker Jr., and James Lassiter became the first black law students admitted to UNC. While the *Sweatt* decision affirmed the US Supreme Court's sincerity about enforcing its "separate but equal" doctrine, it also revealed that separate was not necessarily equal in law schools. Therefore, the ruling became a major step in the NAACP's eventual decision to attack the larger issue of racial segregation head-on.[36]

Nevertheless, the Durham case centered on school equalization within the segregated educational system. The trial took place between June 26 and July 13, 1950, just over a year after its initial filing. The plaintiffs wanted relief on the grounds that Durham schools discriminated against black children when it came to expenditures, courses of study, facilities, teachers, equipment, and furniture. The original complaint pointed to differences between Durham High and Hillside High, underscoring economic bias. Durham High had a "well-equipped science laboratory, sufficient vocational equipment, adequate space and facilities, gymnasium, swimming pool, football field, cafeteria, four tennis courts, outdoor track and a Home Economics cottage." In contrast, at Hillside "practically none of these advantages are offered to or provided for Negro school children. The vocational shop equipment is completely inadequate." Wheeler and his team asked the judge to grant a "permanent injunction forever restraining and enjoining the defendants . . . from denying, failing or refusing to provide for the Negro school children of the City of Durham . . . such courses of study, modern facilities and opportunities for physical and cultural developments as are provided for white school children . . . similarly situated."[37]

Understanding the steep obstacles they faced trying to convince a white judge in the South that school conditions in Durham were indisputably unequal, and to rule accordingly, Wheeler and the other attorneys meticulously compiled evidence that they hoped would speak for itself. They hired a photography company to produce more than six hundred photographs indicating educational inequality—buildings, classrooms, multipurpose facilities, equipment, furniture, and relevant miscellaneous items. In large storage trunks, Wheeler's group hauled into court thousands of documents comprising fifty years of official reports generated by the Durham school board, superintendents, school principals, and other school administrators. These documents included school board meeting minutes, statistical reports to the state Department of Public Instruction, capital outlay expenditure reports, and appraisal reports. The lawyers also submitted into evidence documents that detailed a history of attempts by the DCNA to get the board to improve school conditions for blacks. Wheeler's group hired a three-person committee of education experts, all African Americans with years of experience in education, to personally inspect every nook and cranny of every black and white school in the system. Using the documents provided by the school board, alongside their own observations, Drs. J. Rupert Picott, Stephen J. Wright, and Ellis O. Knox produced a 135-page statistical analysis that highlighted all major disparities. The committee focused on several areas—courses offered, curriculum, instruction, facilities (including libraries, art and music rooms, auditoriums, and cafeterias), as well as buildings—with the purpose of "looking at this thing from every possible angle, as objectively as possible."[38]

Picott wrote most of the 135-page report, and during the trial, Wheeler's team relied heavily on his evidence. The executive secretary for the black Virginia Teachers Association, Picott had had a critical role in the school equalization cases there. His report contradicted Watkins's insistence that in the previous twenty years the board had spent more money on black schools due to an increase in their student population, while the population at white schools had decreased. Picott reported that during the 1928–1929 school year, the Durham school board had spent $454,937.58 on white schools and $123,505.56 on black schools. During the 1948–1949 academic year, the board spent $901,914.44 on white schools compared to $575,326.13 on black schools. The black school population had increased from 2,801 in 1928–1929 to 4,187 in 1948–1949; meanwhile, the white school population had decreased from 5,684 in 1928–1929 to 5,073 in 1948–1949. Still, the overwhelming majority of funding was going to white schools.[39]

During the trial Wheeler's team shed light on the major disparities, a point the defense eventually had to concede. However, the defense

The plaintiffs' lawyers from *Blue v. Durham* (1951) in the summer of 1950. *Left to right:* M. Hugh Thompson, Oliver W. Hill, John H. Wheeler (*dark suit*), and Martin A. Martin. During the trial, the legal team meticulously compiled a mountain of evidence, which included thousands of official documents from several decades. They hauled these materials into the courtroom in a large, oversized storage trunk. Moreover, they hired a photography company to produce more than six hundred photographs that gave visual representation to the city's educational disparities. Courtesy of the Durham Historic Photographic Archives, Durham County Public Library.

countered by blaming school inequalities on rationing and construction halts during World War II. The defense claimed the war made it difficult for them to construct the much-needed facilities to accommodate a rapid increase in the black school population, which they said soared between 1930 and 1940. In his testimony, Chairman Watkins noted that before the war, the board met increased demands by building Whitted School in 1935, an addition to Lyon Park School in 1938, Burton School in 1939, as well as East End and Walltown Schools in 1940 (all black schools). Watkins maintained that during the same time, they only built a home economics building at the white Durham High School and, with insurance money, rebuilt the Fuller School because it burned down in 1937. They built the white East Durham Junior High School with bond money, but Watkins insisted that county commissioners initiated the move after being pressured by white citizens. Superintendent L. Stacy Weaver also testified that the rapid increase in the black school population, in addition to the economic challenges caused by World War II, made it difficult to build at the rate needed. Moreover, Weaver explained that the postwar period represented the first time when "intelligently planned schools could be built." The state's lawyers placed blame for the inequalities in Durham schools on local authorities, arguing that the state had responsibility only for enforcing the "minimum" standards.[40]

On January 26, 1951, six months after the Durham trial concluded, Judge Johnson J. Hayes ruled in the plaintiffs' favor. He dismissed all charges against the state, agreeing that state administrators had a responsibility only to ensure minimum standards were met. Hayes held the school board responsible, citing "unequal plant facilities." In dismissing the board's reasoning, he concluded that "these circumstances are plausible . . . [but] they do not afford a legal excuse or justification for not furnishing the negro school children substantially equal educational facilities to those furnished white children." He continued by pointing to the overcrowded conditions in black schools as well as the "advantages" that white students had "better supervision, greater extracurricular opportunities, better laboratory equipment and facilities, in music and art, lighter teacher load, better recreational facilities and better accommodations." Hayes cited the Virginia school equalization cases to support his opinion that "plaintiffs have been, and are, discriminated against on account of their race and that they are entitled to injunctive relief."[41]

The *Blue* decision is significant in many ways. While giving the plaintiffs victory, Judge Hayes offered no concrete plan for how injunctive relief should be achieved in the Durham schools. In addition, the board did not appeal Hayes's decision, which raises the question of what a higher court would have decided. Nevertheless, the outcome gave Wheeler and the DCNA the legal leverage to push the Durham school board to finally take corrective action and bring black schools up to par with white schools. If the board failed to comply with the court ruling, Wheeler and the

DCNA could bring contempt charges against them. The decision also gave black North Carolinians the confidence to continue the battle for full citizenship by shifting to legal tactics, especially when it came to educational equality. In December 1950, just as the school equalization movement gained momentum in North Carolina, LDF leaders had changed their litigation policies and resolved to focus their legal efforts on cases that directly challenged the Jim Crow system. One of the next cases the Virginia lawyers Hill and Martin handled was *Davis v. County School Board of Prince Edward County* (1952), which eventually became one of the five cases consolidated into *Brown*.[42]

Wheeler's experience and success in litigating the *Blue* case made him an expert on school segregation, particularly on the conditions that existed in Durham. When the city council seriously considered appointing a black school board member in April 1951, Wheeler's name surfaced as the most qualified applicant. The DCNA backed him and informed the city council that unless it appointed Wheeler, "no other Negro would serve" because the black community would "rather not have a Negro representative on the Board if any other person besides Wheeler is appointed." Wheeler also had support from the VBG labor coalition. Some city council members, such as Walter A. Biggs, came out in strong opposition to Wheeler's nomination because he and others feared he was too radical and aggressive. Given Wheeler's role as counsel for the plaintiffs in the recent school suit, a few council members translated Wheeler's potential membership as a way for him to represent only black interests rather than those of the entire city. The *Durham Sun* supported this contention, saying Wheeler "has not concealed the fact that he is a belligerent and militant worker for political power by the Committee on Negro Affairs and Parrish Street." Moreover, the newspaper reasoned, "however able he may be, he is not concerned for any of Durham's citizens except the Negro residents and . . . he would represent only them, rather than the whole of Durham." The council wanted someone whom they saw as less problematic in maintaining the status quo. With other black leaders, C. C. Spaulding objected to Biggs's claim that Wheeler would be biased against white children, calling his nomination a "forward step that would advance the educational program of the entire City of Durham." Spaulding clarified that Wheeler was unanimously supported above all other possible candidates "on the basis of his firsthand knowledge of school conditions." A day before the city council announced its decision, *Carolina Times* editor Louis E. Austin predicted, "We don't believe there is enough fairness on the City Council to elect any Negro who is not considered 'safe' by certain powers that-be in Durham." Austin also underscored why the black community unanimously wanted Wheeler on the board, stating, "Since the suit we are of the opinion that if one is appointed who is not familiar with all of the intricacies involving the educational machinery that it would be far better that no negro be given the appointment."[43]

The city council split on whether to appoint Wheeler. Despite Biggs's opposition, Councilmen M. F. Johnson and Sparky Williamson initially agreed to support Wheeler's appointment. But when the time came to vote, Johnson backpedaled after "talking with numerous people" who convinced him to switch his position. Williamson, on the other hand, maintained his support for Wheeler, regretting "a missed opportunity to promote race relations" four years earlier when the city council failed to appoint a black member to the board after an appeal by Wheeler and the DCNA. Williamson, a VBG leader whom Wheeler and the DCNA helped elect in 1949, believed "Durham is ready to support a Negro on the Board." He supported Wheeler in part because of the political alliance. He also dismissed the notion that Wheeler could not perform his duties objectively as a board member because of his role in the school suit. Bringing up old battle lines stemming from the VBG's 1948 takeover of the county Democratic Party leadership, Williamson reminded the council that despite Frank Fuller being a board member, his law firm, Fuller, Reade, Umstead, and Fuller, represented the board in the school equalization case without any grumblings about conflict of interest. Williamson saw "no more reason to object to Wheeler than to object to that law firm representing the Board." Although council members like Williamson supported him, Wheeler lost the appointment by one vote.[44]

The city council then voted unanimously to appoint Spaulding, though the M&F Bank and NC Mutual president had warned them he would not accept the appointment. Councilman Watts Carr Jr., who had opposed Wheeler from the beginning, nominated Spaulding, advising the city council to approach the issue with caution because "electing a Negro to a school board in the south is a serious thing. Some white people have prejudices which they just can't overcome." Prior to the council's vote, Carr went to the DCNA to try to convince the organization to reverse its endorsement of Wheeler and endorse someone who could get a unanimous vote. Carr also made a personal visit to Wheeler's office and asked him to withdraw his name, a request Wheeler firmly rebuffed.[45]

In the end, Spaulding respectfully declined the appointment, claiming it went against his doctor's advice. He also reflected on his fifty-two-year career as a black leader in Durham and his role in training the second line of defense, saying he had "tried to select and train several young persons [who were] qualified to serve in almost any capacity." In reality, Spaulding no longer handled the day-to-day operations at M&F Bank, NC Mutual, or any other business where he served as president. But his words here, and his decision to decline the appointment in favor of black solidarity, suggest that he understood the struggle for educational equality necessitated a level of aggressiveness that he couldn't provide. Furthermore, Spaulding recognized that the city council viewed him as far less troublesome than Wheeler. Although blacks failed to get one of their younger leaders on the school board, the city council's effort to suppress black Durham's desires also failed, and justly.[46]

"Skirting Around the [Real] Problem of Integration"

On May 17, 1954, the US Supreme Court handed down the *Brown* decision. It was a resounding deathblow to its 1896 *Plessy* decision, a ruling that had provided the legal justification for Jim Crow. The *Brown* decree stated: "In the field of public education the doctrine of 'separate but equal' has no place. Separate educational facilities are inherently unequal." Despite this monumental directive, the US Supreme Court withheld any ruling on how its decision should be implemented until the following year. In the interim, southern states like North Carolina took a more cautious and less hostile approach but avoided implementing the US Supreme Court's decision in favor of preserving separate public schools. In its opinion, the US Supreme Court had opened the door for attorneys general from individual states to appear amicus curiae and file briefs on the best way to implement the decision. North Carolina's attorney general, Harry McMullan, petitioned the US Supreme Court accordingly.[47]

Initially, North Carolina's state and local officials indicated they would fully comply with the *Brown* decision. Although displeased with the outcome, which he regarded as an infringement on states' rights, Governor William B. Umstead was not convinced that he should openly defy it. Lieutenant Governor Luther H. Hodges wanted North Carolina to take a levelheaded approach until they could more precisely understand the specifics of the decision. In Durham, Mayor Emanuel J. "Mutt" Evans expressed an interest in solving the problem in a way that would benefit all residents. In the interim, Umstead called on the Institute of Government at UNC to conduct a careful study and outline the state's options in response to *Brown*.[48]

Black leaders across North Carolina were very pleased with *Brown* and hoped it would compel state leaders to put their concern for the economic future above maintaining racial disparities. Wheeler commented that the judgment would "prove to be a social and economic bonanza for the southern states." He pointed out that southerners who wanted to continue racial segregation "have not realized that it looms as the greatest single barrier to lasting prosperity and to social maturity in the South." Not only that, but eliminating segregation would "do much to free the white south from the ever increasing burden of having to earn enough to support itself and an additional fourth of its population which, through segregation, has been denied the opportunity to become self-supporting." This was the "only path" for North Carolina and presented the South with another "golden opportunity to reach new social and economic heights—an opportunity which we must not fail to grasp."[49]

In Durham, black leaders saw the decision as promoting true democratic principles. DCNA chairman Shag Stewart said it laid "the ground work for the extension of democracy all over the world." Conrad O. Pearson was pleasantly surprised, saying "the clearness of this decision not only represents a step forward for Negro citizens alone; it also represents a trend toward unity of all American citizens in upholding the basic principles of our democratic form of government." Nathan B. White, DCNA Economic Committee chairman, commented: "Those who would seek to circumvent the decree may delay the God-given rights of freedom and equal opportunity for all, but they cannot stop this onward march to make real the [democratic] ideals set forth in the constitution by the founders of our great country."[50]

As a member of the North Carolina Council on Human Relations (NCCHR) executive committee, Wheeler made his perspective on *Brown* and the need for its rapid adoption clear to his fellow committee members. He expressed his concern that the NCCHR was "trying to skirt around the [real] problem of integration and that we are in danger of abdicating our responsibility. We need courage in this organization . . . and we need courage among ou[r] state officials at the top where policies are made." Wheeler pointed to states like New Jersey as "example[s] of what wisdom and courage can do in facilitating the process of integration." During the meeting, Wheeler also made a motion, which passed, that the NCCHR contact Governor Umstead regarding his plan to set up an advisory committee to counsel him on the necessary steps to take in North Carolina's response to *Brown*. They wanted the governor to pay attention "particularly [to] our concern that the committee should be composed so as to be truly representative of the best talents in North Carolina."[51]

In the early 1950s, Wheeler had helped revive the former North Carolina Commission on Interracial Cooperation in its transition into the newly created NCCHR, the state's Southern Regional Council (SRC) affiliate. He served as its treasurer from 1954 to 1961. He increased his involvement with the SRC's work in the 1950s and joined the at-large SRC executive committee in 1958. His growing participation in NCCHR and the SRC programs intensified because of their emphasis on school desegregation via active membership, academic research, and publications. As the SRC made a concerted effort to strengthen its base at the local and state levels, Wheeler willingly gave his time, financial resources, and expertise. As a civil rights lawyer, he regularly sat on panels at general meetings alongside educators and sociologists offering his insights on a range of issues including segregated schooling. In the years following *Brown,* the banker also volunteered as a consultant with the SRC's consultative services program, helping to mediate school desegregation crises. Wheeler worked with interracial organizations such as the NCCHR and the SRC because he saw them as useful tools in helping to convince North Carolina's state and local leaders that immediate school desegregation was the best path for the state and its economic well-being. He believed that to be an advocate, one needed reliable research.[52]

In August the Institute of Government at UNC completed its report to Governor Umstead. The report analyzed school desegregation from several angles and emphasized a number of directions that North Carolina could take. It considered the possibility of private schools supported by state funds but reasoned that the US Supreme Court would view it as an offshoot of public schools. The report viewed giving state grants to students to pay for private schools in that same light. The authors offered theoretical, but what it believed to be reasonable, arguments that North Carolina's attorney general could make to the US Supreme Court in amicus curiae hearings that had the potential to go over well with the justices. The report especially emphasized the idea of "gradual adjustment" to desegregation, which included a relatively flexible timetable for implementing the decision. The report proposed that if the US Supreme Court accepted a gradual approach, then North Carolina had to have a well-structured plan in place. That plan had to consider criteria such as assignment, redistricting, and school choice as ways to realistically desegregate schools. The document also called on the state to enact broad but consistent legislation to produce a desegregation plan that could be applied across the board. It neither pursued nor detailed what desegregation might look like. In addition to asking the Institute for this report, Umstead set up the Governor's Special Advisory Committee on Education on August 10, 1954. He selected Thomas J. Pearsall, a Rocky Mount attorney and former state legislator, as chair. The nineteen-person committee also had three African Americans: Drs. Ferdinand D. Bluford and James Ward Seabrook, presidents of the Agricultural and Technical College of North Carolina (A&T) and Fayetteville State Teacher's College, respectively; it also included Hazel S. Parker, an Edgecombe County home agent from Tarboro. Because of their positions as state employees, the three black leaders could go only so far in advocating immediate school desegregation. The Pearsall Committee had the responsibility to review the school issue in light of *Brown* and the recent UNC report. It also had the task to recommend specific actions for the governor to take.[53]

Wheeler continued to articulate why North Carolina and the South needed to meet the *Brown* decree for their general economic advancement. In September, he outlined his New South prosperity ideals in a speech to an audience attending a New Farmers of America Convention in Atlanta. Wheeler explained to the group that it was "an economic truth that with the rapid industrialization of the South, white workers cannot possibly earn enough money to support the remaining one-fourth of the population which a few years from now will be impoverished by the lack of opportunity unless the mandate of the Supreme Court is followed wholeheartedly. To my way of thinking, therefore, the South cannot prosper under segregation."[54]

"Formerly," Wheeler said, "we were concentrating upon the task of getting down in black and white in the Constitution—in the Statutes, and the mandates of the Supreme Court, the broad principles and machinery by which we may live above our prejudices." "Now," he continued, "we are concerned with the task of winning the battle for the minds of men that we may learn the secret of living together in brotherhood with mutual respect for one another." This meant letting the nation and world know "the American Negro wants no special trains, no special buses, no special schools, no special factories in which to work. He simply wants the same job opportunities in industry and other lines of employment with the right to be promoted and paid on the same basis as other Americans."[55]

As the Pearsall Committee prepared its final report that November, Governor Umstead died in office. Lieutenant Governor Luther H. Hodges took over as governor and pledged his continued support to the Pearsall Committee. On December 30, the committee issued its report to Hodges. They concluded that school integration in North Carolina could not be "accomplished and should not be attempted." The committee determined that racial customs precluded any likelihood that integrated public schools could operate effectively. The committee also recommended that the state find a way to comply with *Brown* within the segregated school structure. The committee suggested that state officials place authority solely in the hands of local school boards and urged the 1955 General Assembly to pass legislation accordingly. In January 1955, the state legislature worked to modify North Carolina's public school laws in accordance with *Brown* and the Pearsall Committee's December report.[56]

Once the proposed legislation was drafted, Wheeler and other black leaders from across the state hoped to convince the state's political leaders

The DCNA met with Governor Luther H. Hodges on February 22, 1955, to discuss impending public school legislation. John H. Wheeler is standing before Governor Hodges (*seated at desk*). Wheeler told Governor Hodges that integration was possible and could happen without any problems if state leaders took a "forthright position leading to integration of the schools." Afterward, Wheeler gave an important speech before the legislature's Joint Committee on Education. The other DCNA members seated are (*left to right*): Lyda Moore Merrick (*with glasses to Wheeler's left*), D. B. "Dan" Martin, M. Hugh Thompson, and Reverend George A. Fisher (a priest at St. Ambrose Episcopal Church in Raleigh credited with suggesting the DCNA in 1935). *John H. Wheeler Standing before Governor Luther H. Hodges (seated at desk)*, undated, John H. Wheeler Collection, Atlanta University Center Robert W. Woodruff Library.

not to pass it in its current form because, they said, it would have devastating consequences for the state's economic future. On February 22, Wheeler led a three-hundred-person delegation of the state's black leaders to Raleigh, where they appeared before the state legislature. He and a small contingent of DCNA leaders met face-to-face with Governor

Hodges. While not a formal organization, the group included leaders from several statewide organizations, such as the Prince Hall Masons, the North Carolina Teachers Association, the General Baptist State Convention, and the North Carolina Federation of Women's Clubs. During their meeting with Hodges, Wheeler told the governor they believed integration was possible and could happen without any problems if state leaders took a "forthright position leading to integration of the schools." Afterward, the entire group attended a public hearing held by the Joint Committee on Education of the North Carolina legislature, where they lobbied for immediate compliance with *Brown*. The proposed legislation had the potential to determine the direction and timetable that North Carolina's public schools would take in view of *Brown*. Three days earlier, Wheeler had told students attending his Morehouse College founder's day address that "more people must know the score." There could be "no prosperity here" in the South, he continued, "unless [the] negro has [an] opportunity to earn his way," because the "Dual System of Education is sapping the financial strength of our southland."[57]

On the delegation's behalf, Wheeler gave a speech before the Joint Committee to advocate for immediate integration to release the state from economic bondage. The "progress of all people in North Carolina," explained Wheeler, "has been seriously retarded by the shackles of segregation and that the removal of these shackles through a State policy on integration . . . will enable us to make great strides of progress, proudly and to the advantage of all citizens." He saw the proposed legislation as "a means to avoid the execution of the Supreme Court's decision and to slow down or retard the process of integration." He maintained that restricting black citizenship rights would "backfire" as usual because it "not only limited the opportunities of negroes but hampered the total progress of our State in industry, economics and education." Wheeler believed the most efficient way for North Carolina to desegregate its public schools successfully would be centralizing operating authority, meaning he wanted the State Board of Education to oversee the desegregation process with the assistance of local school boards. This would also eliminate fiscal waste as North Carolina struggled "to carry a burden which exceeds our [economic] ability." Wheeler referred the legislators to several school studies that indicated "North Carolina [put] forth great financial effort but [received] a disappointingly small return on its educational investment" since the state still produced low-performing white and black students when compared to other states. He worried that putting the issue solely in the hands of local school boards would be "perpetuating and encouraging educational inefficiency through legislative enactments that [instead] skirt the real problems of public education in North Carolina: small schools, small administrative units, and the dual education systems." In other words, North Carolina could save money on administrative expenditures and improve student performance by combining separate school systems, especially those with smaller populations.[58]

During Wheeler's presentation, he pounded his message that desegregation was economically beneficial to whites as well as blacks. The M&F Bank president argued that "racial segregation in the public schools and in employment [was] producing a burden which is becoming too heavy for the economy of our state." African Americans had "a deep and understandable yearning to prove its economic worth to our economy." In addition, "the tremendous tax burden which must be assumed by the remaining three-fourths of the population [which was white] also looms as a block to real prosperity for any segment of our population." Thus, Wheeler explained, "It is our considered opinion that if there is to be lasting prosperity in North Carolina, all of us must learn to work and live together in an atmosphere of mutual respect and understanding which cannot be attained as long as there are barriers which prevent us from knowing and understanding one another."[59]

In case Wheeler's economic reasoning failed to convince state lawmakers, he ended by reminding them that a failure to desegregate would also damage North Carolina's "progressive" reputation. The "enactment of the proposed legislation," Wheeler went on to say, "would not be in keeping with North Carolina's traditional respect for law and order and government in accordance with the ideals of our democracy." "Moreover," he said, "what we do in North Carolina has an important bearing on the position of the United States in the rest of the world." Wheeler warned them, "We feel assured that no one will be proud of what may happen if North Carolina's record of progressiveness and enlightenment is besmirched by a long period of bickering, litigation, and unpleasantness occasioned by efforts to avoid the decision of the Court."[60]

Wheeler's February 22 appearance before the Joint Committee placed him at the forefront of North Carolina's desegregation crisis. He made every effort to expose the state's citizens to the stakes of failing to desegregate. A month after the delegation's visit to the state legislature, the SRC's *New South* magazine followed up with an article asking, "Can North Carolina Lead the Way?" The essay included excerpts from Wheeler's speech. The potential exposure that his ideas would receive once leaders throughout the country read the *New South* article was immeasurable. By then, the SRC had active state and local branches in all eleven ex-Confederate states. This point was not lost on Wheeler as he moved to keep blacks' desire for immediate school desegregation, and improved economic conditions for whites and blacks, burning in the minds of North Carolinians. He attempted to use the March *New South* article and other publicity surrounding his February 22 appearance to pressure state and local school board officials. He personally ordered and paid for fifty copies of the March issue to distribute them to leaders he knew around the state. He also suggested that the NCCHR and the SRC send free copies to local school boards and city officials in select North Carolina cities.[61]

Some NCCHR and SRC leaders saw Wheeler as moving too swiftly and wanted instead to appeal to southern leaders' attitudes indirectly. Harry S. Jones, executive secretary for the NCCHR, felt that "while it would probably be a good move . . . my experience in talking with many business and civic leaders leaves me with some doubt as to whether the results would be what we would hope for." He saw circulating the March article as "'beating the drum' pretty loudly for integration, and this is what many of these people want to avoid or delay as long as possible." From Wheeler's perspective, if he could get whites to comprehend the potential economic consequences involved in continuing segregation, then he would succeed at achieving his overall objectives. Instead, Jones suggested they circulate NCCHR pamphlets, alongside pertinent information about the NCCHR, the SRC, and their "approach to the [school desegregation] problem." Jones concluded: "It is a matter of strategy of course. We all want the same thing." The SRC's executive director, George Mitchell, had no real objections to Wheeler's suggestion but stressed the SRC's importance over Wheeler's desire for continued emphasis on school desegregation. Mitchell thought that *New South* subscriptions would instead provide "continuity of the magazine to distinguished citizens." He ultimately left it up to the NCCHR's programming committee to make the final decision, but it is unclear whether the organization acted on Wheeler's suggestion.[62]

Wheeler's last maneuver came in response to the North Carolina General Assembly's March 30 passage of the Pupil Assignment Act, which implemented the Pearsall Committee's December recommendations. The act gave local school board administrators complete control over the desegregation process. It further stipulated that any parent or guardian could seek to enroll their child in any public school in their district by submitting a reassignment application. If a school board denied a reassignment request, the parent or guardian could then request a formal hearing with the local school board to reconsider their application. The final decision rested with the local school board, which had authority to accept or reject reassignment applications based on a number of criteria, supposedly without regard to race. If dissatisfied with the school board's final decision, and after exhausting all "administrative remedies," the parent or guardian had ten days to appeal the school board's verdict to a superior court. The Pupil Assignment Act placed individual responsibility on the parent or guardian, making the task of getting one's child reassigned to an integrated school a difficult procedure. Moreover, that summer the general assembly made provisions for a second Pearsall Committee to make further recommendations on school desegregation to the governor and other state leaders.[63]

Meanwhile, on May 31, the US Supreme Court provided its follow-up ruling with *Brown II,* instructing states to implement *Brown I* "with all deliberate speed" but leaving an ambiguous timeline for compliance. The Court made its decision after hearing arguments from attorneys general from North Carolina, Arkansas, Oklahoma, Maryland, Texas, and Florida. North Carolina's assistant attorney general, I. Beverly Lake, made the most convincing argument and was very instrumental in the court's final decision on implementing *Brown*. Lake, a firm segregationist, hinted at voluntary segregation as a solution by arguing that the court's ruling failed to explicitly require integration. Although Lake made no objections to the decision outlawing segregation, he strongly warned the court that if immediate forced integration happened, there would be violent reprisals that would spell the end of public education in North Carolina. He wiped his hands of any violent repercussions North Carolina could suffer if the court failed to grant states complete authority in handling desegregation.[64]

The Pupil Assignment Act and *Brown II* put implementation squarely in the hands of local school administrators. At their next meeting, on June 13, the Durham school board selected members Frank L. Fuller Jr. and Herman Rhinehart as a two-man desegregation subcommittee with the responsibility to consider the *Brown II* ruling and the Pupil Assignment Act and make recommendations to the full board. At that meeting, DCNA and NAACP leaders asked for a special meeting with the board to discuss *Brown II* and the board's plans for desegregation. That meeting came on July 11, and the DCNA submitted a petition signed by 740 black Durhamites, the result of their work in conjunction with the local NAACP, the Durham Ministerial Alliance, the DBPC, the PTA Council, the East End Betterment League, and the black AFL union local. Wheeler read the petition to the board, maintaining, "We are convinced that implementation of the [*Brown*] decision in the Durham public schools will be a progressive step designed to improve the moral, economic, and religious fiber of our community." He called on the board to "take immediate steps to reorganize the public schools under your jurisdiction on a non-discriminatory basis." The group believed that "the May 31 decision of the Supreme Court, to us, means that the time for delay, evasion or procrastination is past," and "as we interpret the decision you are duty bound to take immediate concrete steps leading to early elimination of segregation in the public schools." It became clear that black and white leaders held very different views about *Brown II*'s meaning. Whereas white leaders believed it gave them more time to avoid desegregation, black leaders believed it required local school leaders to produce some "good faith" tangible actions.[65]

Wheeler argued against I. Beverly Lake's contention that immediate forced integration would bring about turmoil. He especially dismissed "predictions of violence, strikes, and racial disturbances which may occur if integration of the schools is attempted in North Carolina." Instead, he pointed to good examples of successful school integration that had already occurred in Washington, D.C., Baltimore, Maryland, and St. Louis, Missouri. This would likely happen in North Carolina "as similar predictions have failed to materialize in the cities which have set out with determination to follow the mandate of the court." Wheeler also pointed to school desegregation that took place at North Carolina's military bases "to see that right here in our midst, the pattern of integration, at work and in school, is operating smoothly." He called again for black economic empowerment, saying, "We are sure, however, that you will recognize how difficult it is for any group of people to carry its share of the economic burden if it does not have an equal and unrestricted opportunity to earn its way." Hoping school board members would comprehend how continued school segregation had a negative impact on whites, Wheeler drew contrasts between the plight of white and black workers. Since 1930, white workers "gained 2,700,000 jobs in southern industry" while "Negro workers have lost 900,000 jobs." "These figures," Wheeler noted, "are alarming to us and should be alarming to every citizen of our State."[66]

Wheeler again warned white leaders what they could expect if they failed to heed blacks' call for desegregation: "In spite of the best efforts of leading negro citizens living in communities throughout the South, very few of these gains have been achieved by conference and mutual understanding; instead, most of the gains referred to have been achieved against the backdrop of coercive action of the courts." Once Wheeler and others finished their comments, school board officials thanked the delegation and left it at that. The school board's unwillingness to offer an immediate response gave Wheeler and his group a harsh indicator about the challenges that lay ahead.[67]

One potential setback happened later in the month when Rencher N. Harris, who became Durham's first black city councilman in 1953, said he believed "'if Negro children of the [black] Walltown section of the city were given their own choice in the matter they would walk past [the white] Durham High School to attend [the black] Hillside High School.'" Harris's comments landed him in hot water with other members of Durham's black leadership since he implied most black children would choose voluntary segregation and unequal education. Leroy B. Frasier Sr., a DCNA executive committee member and PTA Council president, expressed his disappointment to Harris saying, "You can imagine with how much contempt and skepticism I read your recent statement in the local press concerning the problem of desegregation in our public schools." Wheeler went a step further and made a personal visit to Harris's office to caution him against making such statements, despite their veracity. In explaining why Harris's statements could potentially hurt blacks' appeals for immediate desegregation and full citizenship, Wheeler reminded him that whites would construe Harris's words as a concession and acceptance of a continued segregated school arrangement. In August, the school board's desegregation subcommittee advised it to operate the schools on a segregated basis since their assessment would not be finished before the start of the 1955–1956 school year.[68]

On August 8, Governor Hodges gave a radio and television address to North Carolina citizens that called for voluntary segregation and provided little hope for groups pointing to the economic drawbacks of segregation for North Carolinians. Hodges directed his remarks at white moderates and blacks by arguing that the independent cultures of both races would be jeopardized "unless we can . . . continue our separate schools voluntarily." Hodges maintained that a failure to continue segregation on a voluntary basis would prematurely force the state to choose between desegregation and an end to public education altogether. He made specific reference to the NAACP and similar organizations like the DCNA by advising blacks not to let any "militant" groups dissuade them from accepting voluntary segregation. On August 26, he addressed an audience of black teachers representing the North Carolina Teachers Association (NCTA) and asked them to support his call for voluntary segregation. The next day, the NCTA denounced Hodges's plea, stating: "We do not now, nor have we ever ascribed to voluntary segregation, but as good citizens we have abided by segregation because it was the law of our state. Now that the Supreme Court has ruled that this state law is in conflict with the Constitution of the United States it is our conviction that it is inconsistent with our obligations as good citizens for us to advocate voluntary segregation."[69]

The prospects looked bleak for school desegregation in North Carolina's primary and secondary schools, but Wheeler and other lawyers made progress on other fronts. On June 20, he and fellow DCNA and NAACP lawyers Conrad O. Pearson, Floyd B. McKissick, and William A. Marsh Jr. filed a lawsuit on behalf of three recent graduates of Hillside

Lawyers for the plaintiffs in *Frasier v. UNC* (1956) outside of the US Supreme Court Building. *Left to right:* Conrad O. Pearson, Floyd B. McKissick, George E. C. Hayes, John H. Wheeler, and Selena Warren Wheeler. *Supreme Court Steps with John H. Wheeler and Others,* undated, John H. Wheeler Collection, Atlanta University Center Robert W. Woodruff Library.

High School against UNC to seek admission to its undergraduate program. In early April, the university had rejected their applications for admission, citing the school's long-standing segregation policy. On September 16, a three-judge panel from the Fourth Circuit Court ruled in the plaintiffs' favor in the case *Frasier v. Board of Trustees of the University of North Carolina* (1956) and ordered the university to admit its first black undergraduates that fall. Following the September verdict, Leroy B. Frasier Jr., Ralph K. Frasier, and John Lewis Brandon became the first black undergraduates to desegregate UNC. The university appealed the decision, which made it all the way to the US Supreme Court. On November 16, George E. C. Hayes, one of the LDF lawyers who helped argue the *Brown* case, introduced Wheeler, McKissick, and Pearson, and the three civil rights lawyers were admitted to the bar of the US Supreme Court. The high court ultimately upheld the lower court's ruling in its judgment on March 5, 1956.[70]

The "Penalties of Segregation"

In the years following *Brown,* North Carolina made little progress toward school desegregation. While Wheeler's fundamental ideas about desegregation, full citizenship, and New South prosperity remained intact, he had to consider other approaches to solving the real problem of integration. In fact, in March 1956 he attended a strategy conference in Capahosic, Virginia, sponsored by the Phelps-Stokes Fund and its executive director, Frederick D. Patterson. As Patterson told Wheeler, the purpose of the conference would be to "examine critically the serious tensions which have arisen incident to the several decisions of the Supreme Court" and to brainstorm about realistic solutions to bring about school desegregation, better employment, and housing opportunities for blacks. Other well-known black leaders (notably all male) at the conference included Ralph Bunche, Rufus E. Clement, Lester Granger, William Hastie, Thurgood Marshall, Benjamin E. Mays, Robert C. Weaver, and Roy Wilkins. Wheeler wanted the conference to focus also on "the desires of southern Negroes for full citizenship and for unrestricted movement," as "little is being said by white or Negro southerners concerning the necessity of preserving the ideals of democracy and creating a favorable climate in which to implement the mandate of the Supreme Court." After attending the conference, Wheeler felt it had "provided an excellent medium for the exchange of ideas."[71]

In April 1956, the second Pearsall Committee issued its report, offering additional desegregation recommendations to the state legislature. The overarching theme of the committee's new report was that North Carolina could preserve its public school system only through continued segregation. As for desegregation advocates like Wheeler, the committee confidently stated, "The Negro leaders from outside the State, and those who are now vocal within the State, appear to be totally indifferent to the fact that their belligerence, their attempt to use the threat of Federal punishment to achieve complete integration, will prevent Negro children from getting a public school education in North Carolina." Although the committee held tightly to the idea of segregated schools, they agreed with Wheeler on one central issue. As stated in its report: "If the State of North Carolina is to go forward, if the white race in North Carolina is to go forward, the Negro must go forward also. The advancement of our economy and the preservation of our democracy depend in large part upon the education, the understanding, and the morality of the Negro as well as the white. If there prevails ignorance in either race, servitude in either race, hatred in either race, our economy will stall, our society will seethe, and our democracy will degenerate." Despite the Pearsall Committee's assessment about the economic future of North Carolina and the South, they made only passing reference to the inherent possibilities of eliminating segregation and the impact integration stood to have in meeting the above reality.[72]

The second Pearsall Committee suggested that the General Assembly reconvene for a special summer session to pass immediate legislation. First, they recommended the General Assembly make public funds available through private tuition grants to any parents opposed to racial mixing, if space in a segregated school could not be made available. Second, the committee suggested that the General Assembly introduce a constitutional amendment to give local communities the option to suspend public schools in favor of private schools with a referendum vote. In a special session during the summer, the General Assembly deliberated on the suggested legislation. Soon after the Pearsall Committee issued its report,

Wheeler compiled research material on industrial development in the South in preparation for the summer's special legislative session. He contacted Julius A. Thomas, director of the Department of Industrial Relations for the National Urban League (NUL), who relayed some confidential information to Wheeler. Thomas told Wheeler about many "northern-based industries that are reconsidering plans to set up operations in the South." Thomas received the information from Sylvia Porter, a white news reporter, who suggested some of the companies were the largest "'blue-chip' corporations" in the country. Porter could not divulge the names of individual companies because "the information was given to her in confidence." Thomas went on to tell Wheeler that "it looks as though I am not able to deliver what I thought I might be able to get from Miss Porter," but "I think she is perfectly honest in her statement, just as I will have to be when we release the results of our [industrial] survey." Like Porter, Thomas also "promised a good many multi-plant corporations" that he would "not mention their names in the final report, except with their permission." Yet Thomas gave assurances that Wheeler would "certainly be safe in saying [to the legislature] that a good many important industries are now delaying their plans to expand further in the South because of the disturbed race relations picture."[73]

In another appearance before the North Carolina legislature in July, Wheeler represented a group opposed to the Pearsall Plan called the Negro Committee of One Hundred Counties. The committee was a collective of black civic organizations from around the state spearheaded by Louis E. Austin. The state NAACP and other organizations also came out strongly against the Pearsall Plan and vowed to challenge it at every turn. Governor Hodges later explained that the Pearsall Plan was "designed [specifically] to discourage attempts by the NAACP and other groups to force integration." In his speech, Wheeler presented more details about what continued segregation would ultimately mean to North Carolina's economic future. While white leaders saw the Pearsall Plan as a surefire way to preserve public education, Wheeler denounced it because it would "actually undermine and destroy the public school system." He called the proposed amendment "unsound, [and] impractical" because it failed to "comply with the Mandate of the U.S. Supreme Court with reference to segregation in the public schools."[74]

This time, Wheeler gave his argument more substance by pointing to specific obstacles to North Carolina's industrial development. He argued that the "publicity given racial conflict in the school controversy was driving prospective industry away [because companies were] deeply concerned over the economic condition of our state which last year ranked 48th among the states in average weekly earnings paid to manufacturing employees." Wheeler again asserted that the economic status of North Carolina's one million blacks was "key to prosperity and further industrial growth in our state." He also cited Thomas's survey of twenty of the country's top industrial companies, who "stated frankly their reluctance to construct additional plant facilities in those Southern States where local conditions prevent them from following the same non-discriminatory employment policies followed by their plants elsewhere in the United States." Wheeler used one example of a company that had plans for a huge facility in North Carolina that would employ some four thousand people but changed its mind and built the facility in Omaha, Nebraska, because of North Carolina's continued racial strife. Wheeler said this was evidence that the "pattern which we follow in respect to our schools leads also to economic suicide for the entire state. Not only are our prospects poor for obtaining new industries, but we stand to lose some of the industry that has already located in our state but whose management is already dissatisfied with the present employment pattern and is also fearful that the children of its key personnel may not be able to obtain satisfactory schooling within our state." Wheeler also explained that "hysteria generated by certain forces within the state has not blinded the vision of many industrial leaders and thoughtful citizens of our State who do not favor enactment of the proposed bills and who are deeply concerned lest our extreme reluctance to adhere to the democratic principles shall surely lead us to economic ruin." However credible, legislators ignored his appeal again and approved the measure, sending it to voters in a constitutional amendment that fall.[75]

In a statewide election in September, voters made the Pearsall Plan official. It passed overwhelmingly across North Carolina, but votes cast in Durham represented tighter margins. The people registered in the city's all-black precincts voted against the amendment in line with Wheeler and the DCNA's recommendations. With the Pearsall Plan just around the corner, Durham's black leadership fell short of persuading the school board to work out an immediate plan for school desegregation. As early as June 1956, the DCNA had contacted the school board, warning them that if the board did not take steps to end racial segregation in its schools, black parents would take matters into their own hands by submitting reassignment applications on their children's behalf. On October 12, the DCNA and affiliated organizations sent another petition to the school board with 740 signatures from blacks asking for a school desegregation plan. As expected, the school board rejected the appeal at its November meeting because, it said, its desegregation committee wanted more time to study the issue and work out a plan that would provide Durham students with the best educational opportunities. With the passage of the constitutional amendment, North Carolina effectively completed its resistance to *Brown*. In the meantime, Wheeler and the DCNA laid out an overall strategy to provide parents in the black community with information about the Pupil Assignment Act and the school reassignment process. They set up a responsible ad-hoc committee, independent from the direct influence of DCNA and NAACP lawyers so as to avoid breaking North Carolina's solicitation laws. The special committee provided powers-of-attorney forms to all parents who wanted to request reassignment of their children to white schools. Although parents had to take the lead in filing reassignment applications, in the event the board denied their request the attorneys would already have the authority to attend appeal hearings and initiate court proceedings on their behalf. Between the fall of 1956 and summer of 1957, sixty-five parents granted powers-of-attorney to Wheeler, Pearson, Marsh, Thompson, and McKissick.[76]

Just as Wheeler considered any effort to forestall school desegregation an obstacle to North Carolina's economic progress, he understood that the state's progressive image depended significantly on how it reacted to *Brown*. White leaders on the local and state levels often used the same reasoning he did but to justify very different actions. Trying to avoid interfering with North Carolina's economic development led state leaders to choose a path that on its face complied with *Brown* but forestalled school desegregation more effectively than more blatant defiance would have done. State leaders believed passing the Pupil Assignment Act (1955) and Pearsall Plan (1956) protected their economic relationships with various industries. Wheeler reminded them that North Carolina's new school laws did the opposite of what they hoped because running away from integration also jeopardized the future for white North Carolinians. In Wheeler's eyes, the new laws did nothing to remove segregation. White leaders had implemented moderate measures to avoid bringing negative attention to North Carolina, but they failed to see that integration was more important to the state's economic prosperity.

On May 17, 1957, Wheeler spoke at the eighth annual North Carolina Editorial Writers Conference in Greensboro, North Carolina. He detailed blacks' disappointment at the slow process of school desegregation in a talk he called the "Penalties of Segregation." His presentation was part of a panel titled "Three Years after the May 17 Supreme Court Decision, What Next in N.C?," and the other participants were two white state leaders, Winston-Salem attorney Irving Carlyle and William T. Joyner, a state legislator and cochair of the second Pearsall Committee. Wheeler tried to convince the audience of North Carolina newspaper editors, a vital group in the state's progress, that segregation hurt North Carolina economically. He expressed frustration that white North Carolinians seemed to be satisfied with what he described as the same backwardness. As he put it, while the South has "been busily engaged in waving the confederate flag and giving rebel yells, the rest of the country had moved on ahead of us in every phase of social, economic, and intellectual development." He gave a critical and unapologetic indictment of the legislative acts, arguing again that North Carolina's economy "cannot possibly grow as it should if the earning power of one-fourth of the population is held down because of enforced racial segregation" and that racial segregation was a barrier to equal education for blacks. "Without question," he asserted, "employment and training barriers set in motion by segregated schools have operated to retard the development of manpower skills of the Negro population." He blamed North Carolina's attempts to avert school desegregation in the years following *Brown* on "pro-segregationist forces in North Carolina [who] have worked with determination, and with some degree of success, to create a number of mechanisms or devices which may be used to slow down, or prevent entirely, integration of the races in our public schools."[77]

Wheeler concluded by articulating blacks' immediate desire for full citizenship, not just school integration. He reminded the group: "It is increasingly difficult if not impossible to convince a Negro citizen who has served in an integrated army, and who has experienced the genuine fraternity and respect of his fellow soldiers, that he is anything less than a full blown American citizen entitled to freedom of movement into every area of American life. To him, his immediate family, and his uncles, his aunts and cousins, holding back the process of integration would be like trying to hold back the dawn." Wheeler applauded mass, direct-action protests and made specific reference to the 1955 Montgomery bus boycott and other "mass movements for greater freedom" that had taken place in the previous two years. He told the audience that it was "commendable" that blacks had been willing to bypass violence in favor of seeking justice through the prescribed legal methods set forth in the US Constitution, despite violent reprisals "practiced against [them] by various hate groups throughout the South."[78]

As demonstrated in his talk to the editorial writers, Wheeler still believed that desegregation was a step toward North Carolina and the South's economic prosperity. He argued that the public schools would continue to suffer because the state spent far too much money on a dual educational system. Despite North Carolina's large expenditures on education, it did not produce black or white students who, on the whole, achieved at or above the national standards; as such, there was little return on this investment. He drew the audience's attention to the 1950 census figures, which indicated that "North Carolina's 1,000,000 Negroes [had] an annual median family income which [was] approximately one-half of the annual median income of white families in the state." This severely limited black spending power. Moreover, Wheeler explained that to "those who would brush aside this [economic] argument by pointing to the rapid growth and industrial development of the South within recent years, it should be sobering to learn that the movement of major industries into our region may have already begun to run its course[.] [Additionally,] many [of the] large corporations are now fully aware of the tremendous burden which racial barriers impose upon the tax structure thereby making it necessary for a relatively small number of persons and corporations to support this structure." Wheeler also criticized the editorial writers in attendance, urging them to approach the school desegregation issue more objectively. While many southern newspapers reported the racial strife accompanying school desegregation in places such as Clinton, Tennessee, complained Wheeler, those same newspapers reported the successes only in small print, in the backs of their newspapers. By way of an implied threat before he concluded his talk, Wheeler remarked, "in my humble opinion, North Carolina's legislative attempts have not been subjected to a full court test of their constitutionality."[79]

Wheeler's talk was effective, as white and black newspapers across the state reprinted significant excerpts from his speech. He had tried in earnest to get whites to understand the frustrations and disappointments of blacks. He presented an intellectual argument about why blacks wanted desegregation and their full citizenship rights: so they could shoulder the burden of their economic responsibilities in North Carolina and the South. After the conference, Wheeler wrote to his fellow panelists saying he had enjoyed his participation on the panel. In his letter to Joyner, Wheeler acknowledged, "Although our views are not the same on some of [the school desegregation] matters, I was impressed by the fact that whenever we have an opportunity for discussion, the atmosphere of courtesy and mutual respect invariably makes it possible for us to get closer together." Joyner's response to Wheeler was brief but cordial, as he noted, "I think that discussion of these matters in an atmosphere of calm and mutual respect is always helpful." Carlyle, on the other hand, promised Wheeler he would take his comments a bit further. He planned to address the Charlotte-Mecklenburg Council on Human Relations (CMCHR) and would "try to help out the situation in Charlotte some by saying some of the things [Wheeler had outlined] with a little different approach."[80]

Wheeler's May talk was also effective because of the way he outlined blacks' desire for full citizenship and freedom of movement. He articulated blacks' willingness to use mass, direct-action protests to obtain these rights. Wheeler reminded the editorial writers that blacks were not interested in obtaining some of their citizenship rights but all of them—immediately. He emphasized this point to William Snider, associate editor of the *Greensboro Daily News* and the conference chairman, when Snider wrote to Wheeler about possible school desegregation in several North Carolina cities beginning in the fall. Snider also said he was "much disturbed" by what he described as "the NAACP's decision to press for mixing in swimming pools as part of its Summer campaign." He wrote, "This will certainly raise emotional issues that should not be raised at this time, and I sincerely hope there can be some understanding between the races on such matters." Wheeler dismissed evidence that hinted at the NAACP's involvement in such a program, although it was true that the NAACP had endorsed actions that summer to integrate swimming pools in North Carolina. Wheeler told Snider he had no problems with mass, direct-action protests and stated:

> These efforts are just another indication of the widespread changes in the thinking of the masses of Negro people. As indicated in my talk to the Editorial Writers Association, the southern Negro's image of himself is changing rapidly and has reached the point where he sees himself as a full blown American citizen whose movements must not be restricted in any manner. This may be shocking to many white southerners who as yet have not come to the point of understanding that it is reasonable for a Negro citizen to expect the same freedom of movement here (in the South) as he has enjoyed in the Armed Forces and in other states which are more liberal and have, within recent years, enacted legislation which guards effectively the Negro citizens' rights to education, housing, employment, travel, hotel accommodations, etc. on a non-segregated basis.[81]

Snider said he sympathized with the position of blacks but he was also disturbed "considerably that the best efforts of many moderate whites may go for naught in this critical time simply because some individual Negroes may try to move too rapidly." He continued: "I am aware of the fact that white Southerners have been negligent about trying to understand the Negro's dilemma but at the same time any effort to move far beyond what is acceptable to at least part of the white majority, it seems to me, will be futile and foolish. Even the courts realize the potential tragedy for a people which could foolishly decide to destroy their school systems and their public recreation facilities rather than submit to radical change."[82]

In the same letter to Wheeler, Snider also shared with him confidential information about informal desegregation meetings among the Charlotte, Winston-Salem, and Greensboro school boards: "I have been sitting on several meetings of the school boards of some of the larger Piedmont cities, and I believe there may be some pupil assignments across racial lines this Fall." In June, following the Editorial Writers Conference, the boards met and agreed to desegregate their public schools and planned to make simultaneous announcements later that July. Snider, alongside other news editors from Charlotte and Winston-Salem, participated in the informal talks and all agreed to withhold reports about the meetings until after the desegregation announcement. Snider and the other newspaper editors probably relayed Wheeler's warnings from the May 17 Editorial Writers Conference to the three school boards, particularly his emphasis that the Pupil Assignment Act and Pearsall Plan had not been subjected to constitutional scrutiny in federal courts. The city school boards in Charlotte, Greensboro, and Winston-Salem resolved to desegregate their schools on a "token" basis, allowing a small number of black students to attend all-white schools beginning in August.[83]

After *Brown,* Wheeler and other black leaders in the Tar Heel State pointed to the need for the state to implement the decision immediately or else risk economic stability. On the local level, Wheeler and the DCNA's Education Committee shifted their battle from one that firmly argued for school equalization based on the separate but equal doctrine, to one that pushed for complete and immediate school desegregation. In their unrelenting efforts to obtain educational equality in accordance with the new public school laws in North Carolina, Durham's black community agitated for change through private negotiations, public appeals to state and local leaders, petitions, and community mobilization. They realized school desegregation, as mandated by the Pupil Assignment Act and the Pearsall Plan, would most likely never happen if left to local and state officials. Thus, they again resorted to more aggressive legal measures to get the local school board to desegregate once and for all.

Through the DCNA, NAACP, black PTA Council, and affiliated organizations, Wheeler battled with the Durham school board for the next two years to obtain compliance with *Brown*. They called on the Durham school board and other civic leaders to outline a specific plan for school desegregation and offered their collaboration to make this a reality. Nevertheless, the Durham school board, in contrast to comparable Piedmont city school boards in Charlotte, Winston-Salem, and Greensboro, served as a direct obstacle to desegregation, full citizenship, and New South prosperity. Thus, the Durham school board did not desegregate its schools until August 1959, when it approved the reassignment applications of eight students in the face of a pending lawsuit, *McKissick v. Durham City Board of Education* (1959). In *McKissick,* a judge ruled in favor of the school board but gave one student an opportunity to exhaust all administrative remedies, at which point the board approved the reassignment application of its ninth student that year.

4

Direct Action and the Search for "Freedom of Movement"

> And I said to the man who stood at the gate of the year: "Give me a light that I may tread safely into the unknown." And he replied: "Go out into the darkness and put your hand into the Hand of God. That shall be to you better than light and safer than a known way." So I went forth and finding the Hand of God, trod gladly into the night. And He led me towards the hills and the breaking of day in the lone East.
>
> Minnie Louise Haskins, 1908

The Montgomery bus boycott that began in December 1955 made a deep and lasting impression on John Wheeler. At an Emancipation Day program in Durham in January 1956, just a month after the boycott began, he asked the audience a piercing question: "Will we have the courage and discipline to do what Montgomery has done[?]" Wheeler had earlier displayed ambivalence about direct action and had focused instead on lawsuits and negotiation. But as his question indicates, he was open to other strategies, including direct action, long before blacks in Durham and throughout North Carolina took up new tactics. In the audience that day was Douglas Elaine Moore, a young minister from Hickory, North Carolina, who had recently moved to Durham. Shortly after hearing Wheeler speak, Moore traveled to Atlanta to attend a leadership conference on nonviolence at Wheat Street Baptist Church. Very late one night, he wrote what in retrospect can be viewed as a pivotal letter to Wheeler. Moore explained that at the conference, Wheeler's earlier "question became more haunting." Earlier that night, Moore had "heard the leader of the Atlanta Movement" discuss Atlanta activists' focus on "law liberty and love." He wrote that because black Durham had "so many resources at [their] disposal," they "ought to do something for in so doing [they could] give encouragement to those who fought the tough trials." Moreover, he pointed out that the city's black community needed to make an "impact upon the economic and social institutions in [their] communities." "If Durham could make a witness in these areas," the preacher believed, it would "aid the people in the deep south" in places such as Mississippi and Alabama. Moore concluded by thanking the activist banker "for causing" him to "think about these matters." Moore's letter reveals that Wheeler had become inclined toward direct action and demonstrates that Moore saw him as a potential ally in such activism. Throughout the rest of the decade, Wheeler made the argument that mass, direct-action protests would at some point become an ever-present tool for blacks to assert their rights to "full blown citizenship."[1]

This chapter examines efforts in Durham after 1955 to remove physical barriers to integration in education and other areas. Histories of direct-action demonstrations tend to view the Montgomery bus boycott as a prelude and pay more attention to the period after the sit-in movement began on February 1, 1960, in Greensboro, North Carolina. But efforts to implement the *Brown* decision led to fierce and, in many instances, violent, resistance in cities and towns across the South, including North Carolina. The period right after the *Brown* decision chipped at Wheeler's—and other activists'—belief that civil rights could be achieved solely through a continued legal assault against Jim Crow.

Since the end of World War II, Wheeler had argued for unrestricted freedom of movement by cautioning whites that if segregation did not end in North Carolina, the state and region would be doomed economically. By the time he addressed the North Carolina Editorial Writers Conference in May 1957, he was predicting that blacks would no longer be willing to wait as patiently as they had in years past for their concerns to be addressed. He had become frustrated and disappointed at the slow pace of change after *Brown*, as implementation in North Carolina's public schools had proven extremely difficult. And change was also slow to come in other areas. Demands for immediate change were surfacing in Durham and other places, and Wheeler had begun to embrace, at least from an ideological standpoint, the notion of nonviolent direct action as a viable and realistic strategy for the black freedom struggle and as an added tool to help blacks achieve their full citizenship rights.

Wheeler believed blacks needed only to wait for the right opportunity to move forward with direct-action tactics. He believed the legal battle for educational equality had put them a step closer to ending segregation and that this "first phase" had laid the groundwork by removing significant legal barriers in "'black and white' [and] on the printed page." But he came to champion direct action as the "second phase" of the black freedom struggle, a tactic to help blacks obtain the necessary physical access in housing, transportation, employment, and public accommodations. When the 1960 sit-in movement spread to Durham, he defended and legitimized the student actions to state and local leaders, and though he was a member of the traditional black leadership, he refused to dissuade student leaders from demonstrations. He also pointed to the "spontaneous" and grassroots nature of the movement, which expanded black leadership. As direct action proved an increasingly effective strategy in the black freedom movement, Wheeler did not stay on the sidelines. As a 1964 *Business Week* article explained, he "received calls from whites and from some negroes, assuming he would help quell the demonstrators." However, he "drafted a statement of support. Then he went on the picket line one morning to make his position unmistakable." Wheeler welcomed student sit-ins as a good thing, a necessary step, because he realized that city leaders had to take more concrete actions to solve the serious problems confronting blacks. Moreover, the white power structure had to agree to real, substantial changes. Wheeler became entirely committed to the student activists, supporting their efforts publicly, privately, and financially. He saw the sit-in movement and the direct-action strategy as critical to his own civil rights and economic objectives.[2]

"Will We Have the Courage to Do What Montgomery Has Done[?]"

On June 23, 1957, six African Americans left a meeting at Durham's Asbury Temple Methodist Church and followed their twenty-eight-year-old minister, Douglas E. Moore, to the Royal Ice Cream Parlor on the corner of Roxboro and Dowd Streets. It had been a little over a year since Reverend Moore's emotional midnight letter to Wheeler, in which he credited the banker with again awakening his conscience to take more aggressive action. Moore had graduated from North Carolina College (NCC) a few years earlier. Before coming back to Durham in 1956, he attended divinity school at Boston University alongside Dr. Martin Luther King Jr., who a year earlier had underscored the power of nonviolent direct-action protests with the successful Montgomery bus boycott. While in Boston, Moore participated in student demonstrations that regularly confronted the country's unequal social conditions. Once settled in Durham, he had staged several one-man protests related to municipal facilities throughout the city. He publicly pleaded with the city council to remove racial barriers in the city-owned Durham Public Library and Carolina Theater, and the city later granted Moore a card to its white library. A few weeks before the group walked from the church to the Royal Ice Cream Parlor, he had unsuccessfully attempted to gain admission for himself and his family at an all-white swimming pool in Long Meadow Park.[3]

Aside from Reverend Moore, the six activists were students at NCC: Mary Elizabeth Clyburn (20), Vivian Jones (19), Virginia Williams (20), Claude Glenn (24), Jesse W. Gray (34), and Melvin Willis (32). Upon entering the ice cream parlor, they went to the white section and sat down, occupying four booths. The owner, Louis A. Coletta, approached them and requested that they move to the adjacent section set aside for blacks. They refused, and Moore invoked his rights as a Christian and an American. He also referenced examples of persecution throughout the world, to which Coletta responded, "That don't concern this place—this place is not owned by the city or the state, this place is private property." The group continued in its refusal to leave, and Coletta proceeded to call the police. When they arrived, they arrested the seven for trespassing. The next day, the activists were convicted and each received a ten-dollar fine in addition to court costs.[4]

The Royal Ice Cream sit-in fit squarely with Wheeler's beliefs about the necessity of complete freedom of movement for blacks as it sought to remove the physical barriers of segregation; it also related to black access to employment, as the shop employed only whites. In Wheeler's mind, complete freedom of movement entailed equal access to the same, not separate, resources and opportunities available to whites. That access meant that blacks could reach their full potential and societal responsibilities. While the courtroom battle for educational equality had succeeded in getting the US Supreme Court to strike down segregation as fundamentally unconstitutional, the *Brown* decision dealt only with educational access, just one area of the larger civil rights spectrum. The Montgomery bus boycott and the Royal Ice Cream sit-in shed light on the additional restrictions that Jim Crow segregation imposed on the freedom of blacks. In the years following these actions, Wheeler would continue to point out the devastating economic consequences that segregation restrictions had for blacks, particularly on their ability to obtain employment. As he explained: "Accessibility to a job depend[ed] on [things such as] free access to housing. Negroes are restricted. They don't have freedom of movement. Put a Negro on the road; how would he fare? Could he get a room? Could he do business? People are not just used to seeing Negro traveling businessmen, to seeing Negroes in hotels and restaurants. Put yourself in the Negro's place. You can't go looking for a job if you haven't got a place to stay or a place to eat. When a person's freedom of movement is restricted, it cuts down his access to jobs."[5]

Before their sit-in at Royal Ice Cream in Durham's predominantly black East End, the protesters had discussed a number of issues, including the difficulties young blacks had finding employment in Durham stores. Virginia Williams noted years later that Moore and her fellow student activists belonged to an organization known as ACTION, "whose purpose was to integrate public places including tennis courts, swimming pools and theaters." The group originated during Bible study sessions at Asbury Temple, which often turned to conversations about ways to obtain social equality for blacks and to remove the badge of second-class citizenship. ACTION, according to Williams, saw mass, direct-action demonstrations as necessary and believed organizations such as the NAACP and the DCNA moved too cautiously. The group's meeting just before the sit-in dealt with black access and economic inequality, but they insisted that their actions that day were not prearranged or planned as "an attempt to crack the color line at the place." Rather, because the ice cream bar was close to the church, they decided "to get some ice cream and milk shakes." Nevertheless, by refusing to leave the shop, the group signaled their view that while blacks brought the Royal Ice Cream Parlor and other local enterprises most of their business, they were continuously denied the same privileges as whites and could not gain employment at those same

The DCNA was founded by a group of black leaders during the Great Depression. It structured itself into five subcommittees: Political, Education, Economic, Civic Affairs, and Social Welfare. Those subcommittees eventually expanded or merged with the addition of committees that addressed legal redress, health, housing, religious matters, and youth-related issues. No membership dues were required, as everyone in the black community, regardless of class status or educational background, was considered a member. In this meeting from the 1950s, Wheeler is seated closest to the front, on the far left next to the wall near the first window. Attorney M. Hugh Thompson is seated in the first row on the left with arms and legs folded, and Reverend Ruben L. Speaks of St. Mark AME Zion Church is to his left. The woman at the end of the first row is Ellen Lee Warren, the niece of Dr. Stanford L. Warren and cousin of Selena Warren Wheeler and John Hervey Wheeler. A few other identifiable attendees in the second row include Robert C. Perry (*third from right, with mustache*), W. G. Pearson II (*second from right*), and Reverend Emmett T. Brown (*first from right*). Attorney Lisbon Berry can be seen back, left center, in a light suit with bowtie. Courtesy of the Durham Historic Photographic Archives, Durham County Public Library.

businesses. Thus, they had restricted freedom of movement even in their own neighborhoods.[6]

The Royal Ice Cream sit-in came on the heels of other incidents. In April 1957, more than one hundred black people showed up at the Durham Athletic Park to attend the home opener for the Durham Bulls minor league baseball team, which had recently broken the color line by hiring its first black player. Told they had to enter through a side gate and watch the game from segregated seating, the group declined. Afterward, they hired attorneys Floyd B. McKissick and M. Hugh Thompson to press city leaders on freedom of movement and equal access to city-owned recreation facilities. They also demanded clarification on official Durham Recreation Department policy. Some blacks sought more widespread desegregation in municipal facilities, while others called for a new strategy to obtain freedom of movement on a larger scale. In June 1957, *Carolina Times* editor Louis E. Austin criticized what he considered to be the "lethargy" of the DCNA's efforts to improve the economic and other opportunities available to blacks in the city. He particularly challenged the DCNA for its failure to seek desegregation more broadly with a "determined campaign to open up new venues of employment for Negroes in Durham" and "the promotion of integration in the public of municipally owned theaters and the municipally owned Durham Athletic Park." Moreover, Austin also charged the Durham Ministerial Alliance, another influential organization, with dragging its feet on important issues. Finally, he chided what he deemed the "old-guard" leaders in both organizations who "smothered efforts of the younger and progressive members to push the segregation question to the front." Austin called the leaders "'dead ducks' on the all-important question of civil rights." "There comes a time in the life of an organization," he wrote, "when it needs new blood, new faces and some new ideas." "Certainly," he continued, "this is no hour to be at ease but an hour for positive action. The struggle for freedom and human dignity for all must go on." The Royal Ice Cream sit-in was in many ways the activists' response to Austin's challenge toward a direct-action strategy.[7]

Shortly before Austin's editorial charged the organization with inactivity, the DCNA had begun a period of transition. In May 1957, with the DCNA's endorsement, its chairman, Shag Stewart, won a seat on the city council. He resigned as DCNA head and Wheeler succeeded him as the organization's new chairman. Whites may have deemed Wheeler a black radical, but his elevation to the DCNA's chairmanship came as no surprise as he had consistently proven himself as a skilled banker, a civil rights lawyer, the organization's longtime Education Committee chairman, and a leading spokesman for blacks across North Carolina. According to historian Walter B. Weare, the DCNA never pressed Wheeler to run for public office because he "perhaps better served the Committee as dean of its brain trust, its ablest tactician and toughest negotiator." Despite Austin's criticism, Wheeler and the DCNA continued with its plans to attack school segregation by utilizing the state laws established in the aftermath of *Brown*. Additionally, the DCNA had already begun to ponder a legal challenge to force the Durham school board to desegregate schools.[8]

Events in his personal life earlier in 1957 underscored Wheeler's dedication to effecting change. With the death of his father, John Leonidas Wheeler, on March 30, he became the family's official patriarch, a role that he took very seriously and had already assumed some time earlier. He moved his mother and disabled sister, Ruth Hervey, to a home near him in Durham, and he continued to financially support Ruth's two sons, David and Richard Lowe, while they attended school. For Wheeler, civil rights activism was also about ensuring freedom of movement for the next generation of Wheelers.[9]

A month after the Royal Ice Cream sit-in, Wheeler and the DCNA deliberated on the "desirability of a [direct-action] Boycott." DCNA's Economic Committee, chaired by Floyd B. McKissick and businessman Nathan White, met with Reverend Moore at Asbury Temple to discuss the possibility of a formal demonstration. Views expressed at the meeting indicated the black community's mixed reactions. While some blacks saw the sit-in as "premature," others were willing to give their support for a mass boycott. Reverend Moore believed that a formal demonstration was necessary but warned against boycotting the Royal Ice Cream Parlor because the owner, Louis Coletta, was Greek and thus considered a member of a minority group. DCNA and NAACP lawyers Conrad O. Pearson, M. Hugh Thompson, William A. Marsh Jr., and Floyd B. McKissick would represent Moore and the student activists in court and were ultimately unsuccessful at getting their convictions for the sit-in overturned.

The Hervey-Wheeler family at the funeral of John Leonidas Wheeler, who died on March 30, 1957. *Front row, left to right:* David L. Lowe, Richard C. Lowe, Margery Janice Wheeler Brown. *Middle row, left to right:* Margaret Hervey Wheeler, Janie Smith Myers (niece of Margaret Hervey), Joan Myers (great-niece of Margaret Hervey and daughter of Janie S. Myers), Ida Hervey Smith (sister of Margaret Hervey). *Back row, left to right:* John W. Smith (nephew of Margaret Hervey), John Hervey, Selena Warren Wheeler, and Morton W. Smith (husband of Ida H. Smith and brother-in-law of Margaret Hervey). *Inset:* Ruth Hervey Wheeler Lowe with sons David L. and Richard C. Lowe. *Wheeler Family, John Leonidas Funeral,* Scrapbook 2, John H. Wheeler Collection, Atlanta University Center Robert W. Woodruff Library.

This legal representation would be the only formal support the traditional black leadership, represented by Wheeler and the DCNA, the NAACP, and the Durham Ministerial Alliance, seemed willing to provide the young activists. At that time, Durham's black leaders typically handled tense problems facing blacks by negotiating with the white power structure, finding some type of middle ground, and turning to legal approaches only if a compromise could not be reached.[10]

Yet Wheeler's challenge a year earlier to a Durham audience to follow the lead of the Montgomery movement, a challenge that moved Reverend Moore to reembrace direct action, seemed to indicate Wheeler was poised to accept the tactics represented by the Royal Ice Cream sit-in. Still, he wrestled with the idea of moving forward with direct action in that case, probably believing the group had not exhausted all their options and that freedom of movement could still be achieved through less aggressive means. He was well aware school desegregation was possible in other North Carolina cities and perhaps worried that any attempts by Durham's black community to use direct-action methods, even on an issue other than schools, would further jeopardize desegregation in the Durham schools. Other reasons also help explain Wheeler and the black community's nonsupport of the Royal Ice Cream sit-in. Moore had failed to obtain the influence and backing of Wheeler and other leaders, and as Moore was a newcomer to Durham, critics viewed him as an impatient outsider, "irresponsible, opportunistic, and dangerous." Attorney William A. Marsh Jr. recalled that Moore was "an out-of-towner who moved fast—too fast for Durham, North Carolina." While evidence is lacking about how Wheeler felt about Reverend Moore's actions, because he longed to be informed about any events affecting the entire black community, he probably took some issue with Moore as well. Had Moore asked Wheeler and the other black leaders, they would have most certainly outlined concerns about how a sit-in would affect their ongoing desegregation efforts. Other historians have pointed out that Moore also failed to obtain widespread community support beforehand, particularly among black women whose "rich history of civic involvement could have provided the broader community backing the sit-in lacked."[11]

"I Just Came to Play Tennis"

If the Royal Ice Cream sit-in did not warrant support for a mass demonstration, events later that summer proved it would be challenging to get Durham to desegregate without direct action. On Thursday, July 11, twenty-three-year-old NCC student Joseph Gilbert Riley and fifteen-year-old Joe Williams, a rising junior tennis star, decided to play at the

John Hervey Wheeler (*left*) and tennis standout Joe Williams on the lawn of the Wheeler family home at 302 Fermosa Avenue in Durham, North Carolina. *John H. Wheeler and Joe Williams,* Scrapbook 3a, undated, John H. Wheeler Collection, Atlanta University Center Robert W. Woodruff Library.

Forest Hills tennis courts in an exclusive white Durham neighborhood. While they played, someone alerted the city recreation director, Clarence R. Wood, who called police and had Riley and Williams arrested for trespassing. However, their most serious offense was disobeying the recreation department's segregation policy. On that charge, Williams received probation from juvenile court. As an adult, Riley faced an upcoming trial and possibly more severe penalties if convicted. When later asked why he chose to play at Forest Hills, Riley pointed to the inferior facilities at the black tennis courts. They "were crowded and not kept up as well as the Forest Hills courts," and he "just came to play tennis." The Riley tennis case, too, showed that blacks wanted unrestricted freedom of movement and were willing to break Jim Crow laws to obtain that access. The actions by Riley and Williams also demonstrated that young black students would continue to test their rights to freedom of movement in the years to come.[12]

Wheeler and other DCNA leaders objected to the confusion the city's inconsistent segregation policies caused and the fact that black tax dollars supported recreational facilities blacks usually could not lawfully use. Blacks had begun playing in an annual citywide tournament at Forest Hills three years earlier, and just a week before they were arrested, Riley and Williams had played in the predominantly black Southeastern Open Tennis Championship, held at Forest Hills with permission from the city council and the recreation department. Riley had been spotted playing tennis at Forest Hills on at least two other occasions before that tournament, and a week before the arrests, police had warned teenagers Cardoza McCullom and Vincent Moore to stay away from the Forest Hills tennis courts after they wrapped up a game of their own. In the championship, Joe Williams had won the junior division in a surprise upset victory over top-seed and future Wimbledon champion Arthur Ashe. Riley competed in the men's doubles but lost. Wheeler, a tennis enthusiast and an executive officer in the black American Tennis Association (ATA), had played in the tournament's men's senior doubles and strongly supported young black tennis players like Williams and Ashe financially. In fact, Wheeler regularly directed national funding campaigns for the ATA, which sponsored the country's most talented young black tennis players, including tennis great Althea Gibson.[13]

Coming less than a month after the Royal Ice Cream sit-in, the Riley tennis case presented the first opportunity for Wheeler and the DCNA to seek freedom of movement for blacks in recreational facilities. It was also a chance to use negotiation rather than direct action, as Wheeler and other leaders still had some hope that white city leaders would make concessions toward desegregation. After the arrests, Wheeler requested a meeting with city attorney Claude V. Jones, city manager Robert W. Flack, recreation department director Clarence R. Wood, and Police Chief William W. Pleasants. In anticipation of their meeting, Flack was able to get Riley's case postponed by a week. William A. Marsh Jr., M. Hugh Thompson, Conrad O. Pearson, and Floyd B. McKissick joined Wheeler at the meeting. They wanted to set the record straight on

The Southeastern Open Championships were regularly held at the Algonquin Tennis Club in Durham, North Carolina, after World War II. The Durham-based Merrick-Moore Memorial Park Association (with Wheeler as secretary) hosted the tournament between June 29 and July 4, 1950. *Left to right:* Dr. Lewyn E. McCauley, John Hervey, R. D. Russell, Dr. R. Walter Johnson, tennis great Althea Gibson, Nathaniel Jackson, Dr. Richard Cohen, Dr. Hubert Eaton, and W. L. Cook. *Unidentified Group with John H. Wheeler and Althea Gibson,* Scrapbook 3a, undated, John H. Wheeler Collection, Atlanta University Center Robert W. Woodruff Library.

"certain unclarified" matters regarding the city's recreational policy. During the two-hour closed-door session, Wheeler stressed to city officials that blacks had used the Forest Hills courts during most of the tennis season that year without incident, and many were specifically invited by whites to play. When city officials suggested that blacks and whites have designated days for accessing the courts, Wheeler reminded them that blacks had the right to use *all* publicly owned tennis courts at any time. On several previous occasions, city attorney Claude V. Jones had advised the city council and recreation department officials that they had no legal authority to prohibit blacks from accessing city-owned facilities since North Carolina had no official laws sanctioning segregation in public facilities. While Wheeler did not completely object to designated times, he doubted that either race would use the tennis courts only on their assigned days.[14]

It appears both parties came to the meeting set on finding an agreeable solution. After the session, Wheeler told reporters that he arranged the meeting "to try to avoid litigation" and maintained that the tennis court matter was "no test case" as Riley "had not anticipated his arrest." Wheeler also noted that none of the lawyers representing Durham's black community were there on the NAACP's behalf. City manager Robert W. Flack also made sure that the police refrained from arresting any blacks who used the Forest Hills tennis courts until after the private meeting and ensured all parties that administrators would give the tennis issue careful consideration. Nevertheless, Flack's comments during the meeting and to the press afterward made clear where the city stood. With Wheeler and other attorneys present, Flack told reporters that "the law is one thing and asserting all rights guaranteed under the law is another."[15]

Initially, the private talks yielded few changes. City officials reaffirmed their position by upholding the charges against Joseph Riley and continued to operate recreational facilities on a segregated basis. Flack and Jones decided that future policies regarding these facilities needed to be left to the judicial system and the city council. The failure to come to some type of agreement did not imply powerlessness on the part of black leaders but standing policy: they were unwilling to capitulate to the white power structure by conceding their right to the freedom of movement they believed already belonged to the black community. On July 23, Judge A. R. Wilson dismissed the case against Riley after defense attorney William A. Marsh Jr. requested a non-suit for lack of evidence. The arresting officer failed to show up in court, and no other witnesses could confirm whether he had asked Riley to leave the tennis court before making his arrest.[16]

The Royal Ice Cream sit-in and the Riley tennis case signaled the need for a mass movement and shift toward a more effective strategy. When Durham's white leadership failed to desegregate Durham's schools in August, the stage was set for direct-action protests. Riley's defense had "deliberately sought to settle the issue around the conference table rather than the court room," and though his case was dismissed, it became evident to blacks that city officials got what they wanted in the end: "[Their] wish [is] to continue to circumvent the issue . . . which . . . leaves the situation as regards [to] segregation pretty much as it was before." The dismissal also meant that blacks could not move forward with using Riley's case as a test. As Louis E. Austin mulled things over, he concluded that in the future blacks had to "carefully plan and consolidate efforts to attack Durham's extra legal jim crow if the benefits of the Supreme Court's [*Brown*] ruling against segregation are not to be entirely nullified." In the end, additional private talks succeeded in changing the city's segregation policy when it came to the tennis courts and other recreational facilities. The city agreed to allow blacks to use the tennis courts without penalties in the future as long as they did so in small crowds. In exchange, black leaders agreed to prevent any large-scale community actions that sought to integrate other white-only facilities, including swimming pools. As he often had, Wheeler skillfully walked a delicate line when it came to the Royal Ice Cream sit-in and the Riley tennis case, pushing hard enough to put city leaders on notice while avoiding dropping the ball on school desegregation.[17]

Nevertheless, black leaders perceived white leaders' overall resistance to any desegregation as an insult. In October 1957, Wheeler and the DCNA sent the mayor a resolution stating that the organization "is not willing to take the position that all is lost. It is not willing to throw in the towel at the feet of the demagogic conqueror." "Unfortunately," the resolution continued, pointing to failed negotiations that summer, "of late the lines of communication between these men and women of good will have been severed. Particularly is this true in Durham and Durham County. Where formerly there was trust—there is now mistrust—where formerly there was a candid discussion of problems on which there were differences of opinion—there is now silence." The document urged white and black community leaders to reaffirm their commitment to working together to end the city's racial discord. The resolution ended by requesting Mayor Emmanuel J. "Mutt" Evans and city council members to appoint a "committee of outstanding citizens of both racial groups to consider many of the problems that now confront[ed] [them]." This group eventually became the Mayor's Human Relations Committee (HRC).[18]

Between 1957 and 1960, Wheeler and the DCNA continued to expose vast inequalities, especially when it came to job opportunities for blacks in the city. The DCNA's Economic Committee took an active lead in addressing employment concerns and used the findings of their December 1956 economic survey to draft the report "Where the Durham Negro Spends His Money." The report strove to show the importance of black buying power and to provide the "total economic picture . . . to show the value of full employment opportunities for Negroes." The Economic Committee also attempted to secure employment for black high school and college students during the 1956 Christmas holiday season and targeted local dime stores in that particular effort. After the DCNA's decision not to push for an economic boycott following the Royal Ice Cream sit-in, during the remainder of that year the Economic Committee focused mainly on "collecting data, adopting procedure[s] for future action, and generally a year of organization."[19]

The DCNA also made inroads with several local and state research-oriented organizations. The DCNA joined with the American Friends Service Committee in Greensboro to get assistance in gathering "information and tactics for securing jobs." Through Wheeler's acquaintance with Julius A. Thomas of the National Urban League (NUL), the DCNA's Economic Committee established a working relationship with that organization to obtain "pressure assistance with [the] Larger [National] Corporations from the top level." It also worked cooperatively with NCC's Social Sciences Department, utilizing faculty expertise and student resources to carry out its programs. The Economic Committee met with several department and dime store managers in Durham in the hope that they would consider hiring black employees, and the committee continued to discuss procedures for future economic boycotts. In 1958, the Economic Committee expanded its outreach and direct-action programs significantly by seeking to secure "additional jobs for Negroes in areas where they have been heretofore denied employment on the basis of merit, devoid of segregational practices." The Economic Committee also teamed with the North Carolina Council on Human Relations (NCCHR), an organization Wheeler served as an executive committee member and state treasurer, using a five-thousand-dollar grant from that organization "for the purpose of studying problems related to employment of Negro

Youth in North Carolina." During the summer of 1959, the DCNA's Economic Committee, in conjunction with the American Friends Service Committee, conducted a merit employment survey "to determine what training [was] needed by Negroes to be able to secure jobs which [were] presently withheld from [them], to determine what businesses [would be] willing to attempt to employ Negroes, and to be generally appraised as to what [was] being done in the Durham Community as it applie[d] to the employment of Negroes."[20]

Freedom of Movement on the Horizon

Although the 1957 Royal Ice Cream sit-in did not generate the response needed to sustain further direct action, it was the first of its kind in North Carolina. On February 1, 1960, four black students at the Agricultural & Technical College of North Carolina (A&T), now North Carolina A&T State University, in Greensboro decided to embark on a similar attempt, with the opposite effect. That Monday, the four freshmen—Joseph McNeil, Ezell Blair Jr. (Jibreel Khazan), Franklin McCain, and David Richmond—walked into the local Woolworth's store and staged a formal sit-in. Having arranged for someone to contact the local press at an agreed-upon time, the foursome paid for a few school necessities and other personal items and then made a beeline for the lunch counter. They were immediately refused service, and, given that they had just been served in another area of the store, the students questioned why. They decided to remain seated until they received the same service as their white counterparts at the lunch counter. Moreover, they vowed to return the next day and did so with twenty-five additional students from A&T. On each subsequent day, their numbers swelled significantly. By week's end, students from Greensboro's local high schools and colleges, including the all-black Bennett College for women and the all-white Woman's College of the University of North Carolina, joined in the sit-ins that also targeted the S. H. Kress and Company store. The stores were forced to close down that Saturday when someone phoned in a bomb threat. The demonstrations prompted Greensboro mayor George Roach to appeal to A&T students to end their actions temporarily to avoid violence. Recognizing their short-term victory, the students agreed to halt their demonstrations for two weeks to allow for negotiations.[21]

Their actions had already made a major impact on students throughout North Carolina. On February 8, exactly a week after the Greensboro sit-ins began, black student leaders in Durham and Winston-Salem began similar lunch counter protests. The events soon spread to Charlotte and the state capital in Raleigh. In Durham, students from NCC and a few white Duke University students participated in that day's protests at the downtown Woolworth store. When Woolworth's manager closed the store's lunch counter after a bomb threat, the students quickly proceeded to the Durham Kress, and when that closed they moved on to Walgreen's, which promptly followed suit. Later that night, the student protesters received legal counsel from attorney Floyd B. McKissick and "learned then that they had the moral backing of the Durham Ministerial Alliance, the NAACP, and the Durham Committee on Negro Affairs." The next day, Durham's Mayor Evans sought an immediate solution to the sit-ins through negotiations. He assigned the task to the Mayor's HRC, the interracial group set up in 1957 to help convince the Durham school board to allow black city leaders to assist with a reasonable school desegregation plan. The Reverend Warren Carr, a white civic leader and minister at Watts Street Baptist Church, headed the HRC. Days after the initial sit-ins in Durham, Woolworth's and Kress reopened their stores but kept their lunch counters closed-off, citing "the interest of public safety." Meanwhile, Walgreen's reopened as normal while Rose's removed its lunch counter stools and thereafter served white and black customers standing up.[22]

North Carolina officials reacted to the statewide demonstrations by pointing out violations to state laws. Governor Hodges, who oversaw the state's school desegregation crisis after *Brown,* was doubtful that the sit-ins would achieve any significant gains. William H. Murdock, solicitor for North Carolina's Tenth Judicial District, called on dime store operators to utilize the state's trespassing laws to their advantage. He specifically referred to the North Carolina Supreme Court's verdict in the Royal Ice Cream sit-in (1957), which held that state statutes "place[d] no limitation on the right of the person in possession to object to a disturbance of his actual or constructive possession. The possessor [could] accept or reject whomsoever he please[d] and for whatsoever whim suit[ed] his fancy . . . [and] race confer[ed] no prerogative on the intruder; nor [did] it impair his defense." State Attorney General Malcolm B. Seawell agreed that business managers had the right to demand that trespassers leave or risk being arrested for failure to do so. Seawell clarified that potential customers had the right to seek services from retailers but "private retail establishments ha[d] a legal right to operate their businesses without being interfered with, and to sell or not to sell to customers as they [saw] fit." Seawell also blamed sit-in disturbances on outside agitators, "persons coming into North Carolina from other states" whom he saw as "troublemakers . . . whose actions [could] only result in irreparable harm being done to racial relations . . . in North Carolina." Noting that the state's hands were tied, Seawell acknowledged that no state laws sanctioned segregation at lunch counters. But he also reminded the parties involved that local officials in cities and towns affected by sit-ins had the responsibility to maintain peace and order, particularly through initiating municipal ordinances to prevent further disruptions. Finally, he added that college and university administrators also had the responsibility to ensure that their students refrained from causing strife in the community. In his disdain for "outside agitators," he told the New York–based American Civil Liberties Union, which had criticized his public statements regarding the sit-ins as an affront to students' Fourteenth Amendment rights, that his statements "[were] none of [their] business." He very bluntly told them that "[if they didn't] like it, [they] could lump it."[23]

In response to state leaders' appeal for college and university administrators to act responsibly, NCC president Dr. Alfonso Elder held a meeting that Wednesday between faculty members and leaders from the Student Welfare Committee and Student Government. The group urged students and store operators to try negotiations mediated by the HRC. The school designated the faculty-student group of campus representatives to enter into negotiations on behalf of student demonstrators, and that group released a statement to the press detailing its willingness to negotiate while also maintaining its belief in "the principles of democracy." Although the NCC negotiating committee recommended talks, it also sided with students because "to deny an individual because of his racial identity the privilege of enjoying services and courtesies that are extended to the general public [was] an act that [was] undemocratic, un-Christian and morally indefensible." None of the student demonstration leaders were on the student-faculty committee, and many of those involved in the sit-ins were "disappoint[ed]" to learn about the decision to negotiate so early and saw the move "as settling for less than the desired goal." Nevertheless, the student-faculty committee went into negotiations while the student demonstrators temporarily halted their protests for the first time on Friday, February 12.[24]

Durham city leaders—both black and white—were accustomed to hashing out their differences through behind-the-scenes negotiations. Indeed, the white power structure called on the traditional black leadership to help quickly end the disturbances. Yet a carefully crafted public statement Wheeler put out as DCNA chairman on Thursday, February 11, three days after the Bull City sit-ins began, marked a departure from the way things typically played out. It expressed Wheeler and the DCNA's strong support for the student demonstrators, a departure from just three years earlier when the same group did not heartily endorse the Royal Ice Cream sit-in but only provided legal counsel. This public support came during the initial week of sit-ins, before Dr. Martin Luther King Jr. gave an uplifting speech a week later to black Durham at White Rock Baptist Church. In representing the DCNA as its chairman, Wheeler praised the "orderly and dignified manner in which these students have sought to make [the] state and nation fully aware of a pattern of discrimination which hinder[ed] the development of wholesome relations between the various racial groups which compose[d] the American citizenry." He rejected calls from "portions of the daily press, certain public officials and other highly placed persons within the state" that wanted "the responsible Negro Leadership (including college presidents) to use its influence to halt activities of Negro students and their white counterparts." Highlighting the ideals of New South prosperity, Wheeler remained adamant about the DCNA's "obligation to support any peaceful movement which [sought] to remove from the customs of [their] beloved Southland; those unfair practices based upon race and color [which continued to be] a stumbling block to moral and economic progress of the region." He also affirmed how "necessary" and crucial direct-action protests were in achieving the overall goals and objectives of the black freedom movement, noting that "Approximately two years [prior], the Durham Committee on Negro Affairs conducted a survey of the 5 and 10 cent stores located in Durham," which "indicated that between 50 and 60 percent of the persons entering the Kress, Silvers, and Woolworth Stores, were colored people." "Obviously," Wheeler continued, making the connection between equal employment and freedom of movement, "the students' protest [was] against a system which solicit[ed] and accept[ed] the trade of Negro patrons while denying them employment opportunities and the use of dining facilities which [were] usually offered for the exclusive convenience of white and foreign patrons." In directing his comments at white moderates, Wheeler clarified that while "many thoughtful Southerners believe[d] such practices to be morally wrong and economically unsound, the South as a whole, [had] not moved voluntarily toward eradicating such injustices as long as any vocal segment of the white population express[ed] its opposition." He further explained why direct-action protests now took precedence over past strategies, saying the "protest also recognize[d] the historic failures and frustrations of numerous efforts by Negro groups [such as the DCNA] to negotiate changes in the present pattern through persuasion and conference." And that "the [most] important advances . . . in the field of civil rights" happened "against the backdrop of litigation and mass protest."[25]

Acknowledging the shared mantle of leadership, Wheeler explained that the students "now emerge[d] as a vital and strong group of stalwart citizens whose image of themselves is such that they are determined to accept no longer the inferior status which the South still [sought] to thrust upon them." He also made it clear that this was a student-led movement wherein students, and no one else, held the leverage to negotiate. He "hope[d] for successful negotiations between student leaders and representatives of the various stores affected." Making a final appeal to New South prosperity, Wheeler noted, "indeed, it is urgently necessary that we shall prove ourselves to be, in fact, what we have been saying we are when talking to those corporations which we have invited to establish new factories within [state] borders on grounds that there [was] in North Carolina a climate of racial tolerance and understanding which [would] enable personnel coming from other sections of the country to live in an atmosphere consistent with American ideals of freedom and equality for all." Wheeler commended the students' courage in the face of "being cursed, showered with eggs, and threatened with physical violence by irresponsible elements of . . . various N.C. communities."[26]

Wheeler's open support of direct action in 1960 was connected to his vision of freedom of movement for blacks. He had viewed direct action positively since at least 1955, but he was now willing to put himself, his reputation, and his relationship with white leaders to the test in the fight for full citizenship. It was the next logical step for blacks because they had exhausted all other tactics. It was an opportunity to work toward many of the same civil rights and economic objectives but from a different angle. Direct action became the best way for blacks to fulfill his idea of unrestricted freedom of movement, which ultimately centered on their ability to achieve integration. Direct action interrupted southern customs because it dramatized the presence of blacks in previously restricted public spaces. When it came to white businesses, direct action also highlighted the economic impact that demonstrations could have. By disrupting the operations of those establishments, activists demonstrated the extent to which they depended on black dollars. Then too, whites avoided patronizing businesses where there were ongoing civil rights protests. As historian Charles Payne has pointed out, this was also significant because "the sit-ins, like other forms of direct-action politics that were developed around them, also meant directly interfering with the life of a community so that it had to respond. If the powers-that-be would not respond to moral suasion, they would have to do something about disruption."[27]

Wheeler's idea of freedom of movement was not simply about physical access but also about what happened once blacks gained initial access. They needed "maximum," not "minimal," access in all areas, he said. In the area of employment opportunities, for instance, could a black doctor expect the same staff privileges at a white hospital as a white doctor? Would that black doctor be allowed to treat white patients? Could a black banker employed by a white institution expect to rise through that company's ranks? Could they be president of that institution, or would their advancement be capped at a certain level? Would an industrial worker have "the same open invitation to industry and to industrial employment or training or to promotion advantages that a white person would have[?]" For Wheeler, this went beyond token representation because freedom of movement and a completely integrated society were necessary components in the larger equation of democracy, equality, and full citizenship. Wheeler's activism during the 1960s increasingly reflected his concerns about the overall impact that integration would have from an institutional perspective. This new role included both unwavering support for student-led direct action and pressing for civil rights through behind-the-scenes brokering at the local, state, and national levels.[28]

Dr. King and Reverend Ralph D. Abernathy's arrival in Durham a week after its sit-ins began inspired the students and gave them a strong push. Douglas E. Moore, King's former Boston University classmate, invited the pair, having tried unsuccessfully on several previous occasions to get King to speak in Durham. Wheeler also had strong connections to King and his family, and alongside Shag Stewart, Conrad O. Pearson, Asa T. Spaulding, and Louis E. Austin, he met King and Abernathy at the airport when they arrived. Wheeler had attended Morehouse with King's father, Reverend Martin Luther King Sr., in the late 1920s, and when the younger King became a Morehouse student, Wheeler had already served nearly nine years on the college's board, which the elder King had been on since the early 1950s. Already acquainted through their two families, in December 1956 Wheeler and King sat on a United Negro College Fund (UNCF) panel called "The Negro Southerner Speaks." They continued to run into each other at annual UNCF-sponsored events. Furthermore, when in 1959 Dr. King and his wife, Coretta Scott King, moved from Montgomery, Alabama back to Atlanta where the Southern Christian Leadership Conference (SCLC) headquarters was located, the Kings moved into the home owned and formerly occupied by Wheeler's parents, John Leonidas and Margaret Hervey Wheeler, located at 563 Johnson Avenue.[29]

Upon his arrival in Durham, King told reporters that continued segregation could potentially have even more severe economic consequences than lunch counter protests if states like North Carolina continued discrimination. That evening King and Abernathy spoke to between 1,200 and 1,500 audience members at a rally at Durham's White Rock Baptist Church. Abernathy addressed the audience first. He had succeeded King as president of the Montgomery Improvement Association, the organization responsible for the 1955 Montgomery bus boycott. At one point in his speech, Abernathy turned directly to the news cameras and reporters. Taking aim at State Attorney General Seawell, he said, "Write this down, and get it straight . . . I'm no outside agitator, America is my home."[30]

In his speech, Dr. King, like Wheeler the week before, recognized the sit-ins as a student-led movement. He explained that the students had "taken the undying and passionate yearning for freedom and filtered it in [their] own soul and fashioned it into a creative protest that [was] destined to be one glowing epic of [their] time." He also reminded the audience that tokenism was not the desired outcome because it was "nothing but a new form of discrimination covered up with certain niceties of complexity." The preacher assured the students that, morally, they were doing the right thing and urged them not to "fear going to jail." "If the officials threaten[ed] to arrest [them] for standing up for [their] rights," he continued, "[they] must answer by saying that [they were] willing and prepared to fill up the jails of the souls." "Maybe," King went on, "it [would] take this willingness to stay in jail to arouse the dozing conscious of [the] nation." He reassured students that they had the full support of the SCLC and urged both black and white "people of goodwill" to lend the students their support. After King's speech, Reverend Moore asked the overflow audience to rise if they were willing to give their unwavering support to an all-out boycott of segregated stores. Everyone in the crowd stood up, and during the church offering they eagerly flashed their dollars before dropping them in the donation buckets, saying their goal was "freedom, freedom, freedom." King was there not just to support the students but to strategize about how his national civil rights organization, the SCLC, could effectively organize and help sustain these kinds of direct-action protests.[31]

Though the Durham college students agreed to halt demonstrations temporarily to allow for negotiations with downtown businesses, by late February it was clear that negotiations were going nowhere. Students saw NCC officials and the HRC as stepping over their bounds by pushing student leaders to the margins during talks. An editorial in the *Carolina Times* shed some light on the student point of view on the arrangement. "Since no school official had any hand in initiating the sit-down protests, [the newspaper saw] no sensible reason why any of them should assume

A United Negro College Fund (UNCF) symposium on public education, "The Negro Southerner Speaks," was held in New York City in December 1956. The panelists pictured here are (*left to right*): John Hervey, Dr. Martin Luther King Jr., August Heckscher (director of the Twentieth Century Fund), Quincy Howe (ABC commentator), Carl Rowan (writer for the *Minneapolis Tribune*), and Dr. Rufus E. Clement (Atlanta University president). *United Negro College Fund with John H. Wheeler and Martin Luther King, Jr.*, undated, John H. Wheeler Collection, Atlanta University Center Robert W. Woodruff Library.

the role as the sole representative of students in any future program pertaining to them." "If and when it [became] necessary to negotiate with the stores," the newsweekly continued, "it [was their] feeling that only in the presence and with the approval of the student leaders should any attempt at settlement be made." Lacy Streeter, a junior at NCC and the main demonstration leader, also expressed his concern that adult leaders from NCC and the HRC disregarded student protesters' goals and demands in their efforts to reach a compromise. He also maintained that students were "not hopeful that [they could] obtain satisfaction through [that particular negotiation] process." This was especially true since "several meetings [were] held between the two groups, but there [was] no official statement as to the progress of talks." Streeter went on to tell the local press that "none of the parties involved in the original protest were a part of the negotiations nor any of the representatives of stores hit by the protesters were on the committee." The HRC seemed to singlehandedly take over the talks. Thus, student protesters "believe[d] the main purpose of the talks would be to squash the whole thing rather than reach a genuine solution." The HRC went as far as "authoriz[ing] the Rev. Warren Carr . . . to issue a statement" detailing an agreement. No such statement was ever issued, however, and a lack of an agreement prompted students to resume demonstrations through early March.[32]

Wheeler's stance during such an intense period was important to the new student movement. One morning he went on the picket line to finally put his own words into action, a *Business Week* article reported, but it is hard to determine when this occurred. Though Wheeler didn't march with student activists in every single direct-action demonstration, or most of them for that matter, he always made his support for their efforts clear. Additionally, when there was a question about his views on a given protest, he made his position unmistakably clear with his physical presence. During the 1960s, Wheeler's unquestionable loyalty to the student activists struck politicians like Terry Sanford, who later told an interviewer that quite often during that time "John Wheeler was more inclined to be caught up in the activists' point of view [to the extent] that sometimes [it] would have been detrimental [for Sanford politically] if [they] had followed what [Wheeler] wanted."[33]

Wheeler's activism shifted that day in 1960 when he joined the picket line. He began using a different weapon in his battle for freedom, and his actions proved how far he was now willing to go in the quest for New South prosperity. As attorney Floyd B. McKissick said: "Direct action require[d] a greater risk. You are out there when you take a direct action. You are totally exposed." Wheeler was exposed when he let student demonstrators use the M&F Bank lobby in downtown Durham to warm up, rest, and drink hot chocolate on cold winter days during demonstrations.

The same could be said when he and others provided financial assistance to help bail student activists out of jail for their civil disobedience. Wheeler took an even greater risk when white leaders in Durham begged him for his help in shutting down the sit-in movement.[34]

"Some Very Real Dangers"

"You, of all people, must realize that there are some very real dangers in widening the gap which already exists between the two racial groups," explained Watts Hill Jr. in a five-page letter to Wheeler on March 17, 1960. Hill, a prominent white state legislator, as well as a banking and insurance executive in Durham, wrote to Wheeler just days after a meeting that Hill called "disquieting." On Tuesday, March 15, around thirty of Durham's white and black community leaders gathered for a "secret" meeting Hill arranged, summoning the white leaders himself. NC Mutual president Asa T. Spaulding had the responsibility to gather black leaders, who included Wheeler. They met in the familiar behind-the-scenes manner to discuss the increasing conflict arising from the February 8 sit-ins, and according to Hill, the meeting ended disastrously. Responding to Hill's fears, Wheeler scribbled in the letter's right-hand margins: "This is a dangerous age. Danger cannot be avoided." Wheeler responded line by line in the margins of Hill's letter, defending himself against Hill's accusations that he and other black leaders had known about the plans for sit-ins for quite some time. "CORE," Hill argued, "as represented by Mr. [Gordon] Carey was in Durham at North Carolina College discussing this very situation which faces us all today as long ago as June 1958." Wheeler wrote that during the late 1950s, sit-ins "were not on the horizon at that time! Evidence please!"[35]

As the sit-in movement in Durham reached an impasse, the situation exacerbated racial anxieties among the city's white leadership. The HRC headed by Reverend Carr called for negotiations once more. Whereas earlier attempts at negotiations included student leaders to some degree, this time Carr only invited members from the traditional black leadership alongside white leaders. Although there is no official list of the meeting's attendees, in addition to Spaulding and Wheeler (who was not a member of the HRC) other black leaders included school board member Rencher

N. Harris and NCC president Dr. Alfonso Elder, both in attendance as members of the HRC. Carr made sure white attendees were moderates on the race issue rather than extreme segregationists. This meeting was a significant tipping point in negotiations because Wheeler again made clear his firm support of the sit-in demonstrations and his unwillingness to serve as a broker in the absence of the students themselves.[36]

Wheeler's outright refusal to negotiate on behalf of the students, whom he felt were perfectly capable of negotiating for themselves, infuriated white leaders in attendance, especially Hill. Hill was the most vocal about Wheeler's position, and he made his disappointment at how the meeting unfolded clear to Wheeler in this confidential letter. In outlining his personal feelings as a self-proclaimed "moderate," Hill indicated that he felt slighted by Wheeler since the two had "had numerous extremely pleasant and productive conversations" throughout the years. This gave Hill "a rare opportunity to gain a very real understanding of the problems and the objectives of the Negro citizens." Hill confessed that he wanted to provide Wheeler with his most "honest and blunt reactions with the hope that they would give [Wheeler] pause to stop and consider whether [he was] defeating the very goal which [he] attempt[ed] to achieve." Hill believed that the recent disturbances in Durham were completely "out of hand." "Not only [were they] out of hand," Hill insisted, "but there [were] elements in the Negro community, perhaps including [Wheeler], who believe[d] that this may [have] even be[en] desirable." Hill also thought that the sit-ins happened because blacks felt "progress by legal means . . . through the courts . . . [and] legislative bodies . . . [came] too slow and that adequate progress [could] only be obtained by applying economic sanctions."[37]

It also became obvious that Wheeler was the main source of Hill's discontent. Writing about the meeting, Hill pointed out that he was "troubled greatly by what seemed to [him] to be the first evidence of a breakdown in integrity [on Wheeler's part], a willingness to employ almost any means to achieve the end goal." This gave Hill the "impression that the Negro race . . . throughout the South if not throughout the Nation [would be] willing to suffer temporarily in order to achieve [their] long range goals." In response, Wheeler wrote in the margins, "Isn't this to be commended?" Hill pointed to one particular instance during the

March 15 meeting when Wheeler "took issue with the implied comments of, [as Hill] believe[d], both Dr. Elder and Rencher Harris by stating that the current sit-down situation [was] truly a 'grass roots, spontaneous' movement," a point that Hill strongly disagreed with. "Please do not misunderstand me," Hill wrote. "I am not saying that you are not telling the truth. I am saying that I find it difficult to understand how you can be so uniformed on this matter when you are so magnificently well-informed in every other area." In the margins Wheeler scribbled that he saw "no evidence to substantiate said information." Acknowledging past battles with Wheeler, Hill said he "realize[d] that [Wheeler had] not been treated with complete candor by the white community in recent months much less during the many past years, but . . . mistakes of one group [did] not justify similar mistakes on the part of the other." "Two wrongs," Hill reminded Wheeler, "still [did] not make a right." To Wheeler, the dangers seemed well worth facing, and he was not surprised that white leaders had sought him out with the idea of negotiating their way out of the student protests, but these demonstrations would not die in the face of white reaction. In some ways, Hill and other white leaders were at Wheeler's mercy because during past squabbles, they could always depend on him to bring an objective and calming voice to the discussion. At the same time, Wheeler had plenty of past experience with whites who resisted compromise.[38]

The first of the "very real dangers" that Hill warned Wheeler about was political backlash—the impact that the sit-in movement would have on the increasingly tense 1960 gubernatorial campaign. In North Carolina and the rest of the one-party South, the Democratic primary mattered most and would surely determine who the state's governor would be. As that year's primary heated-up, with candidates adding their names to the contest, the sit-in movement heightened the issue of race. On February 4, just days after the Greensboro sit-ins started, Terry Sanford threw his hat in the ring, making a "New Day" in North Carolina the motto of his campaign. A politically savvy Fayetteville lawyer and former state senator, Sanford was considered to be a racial moderate. During the school desegregation crisis following *Brown,* he became a vocal proponent of the Pearsall Plan, a directive that Wheeler condemned time and again because he saw it as "economic suicide" for the state. By March, John Larkins,

I. Beverly Lake, and state attorney general Malcolm B. Seawell had all launched their bids for governor. Lake, a devout racist and former assistant state attorney general, had argued for continued segregation before the US Supreme Court in *Brown's* aftermath. Hill explained to Wheeler that after talking with some of his closest associates, whom he described as politically astute, he thought there was a strong possibility that Lake could become governor. According to Hill, even Lake's entrance into the race came in direct response to the student sit-ins as the timing could not have been worse. On this point, Wheeler conceded, acknowledging that "this is true—or it would have been wise not to push the sit-ins until after the 2nd [Democratic] primary." Though Wheeler agreed that the sit-ins had potentially disastrous political implications for blacks, he refused to back down from his stance that the new student movement had merit. Hill reminded Wheeler that although many whites publicly supported the other more moderate Democratic candidates (Sanford, Larkins, and Seawell) they would nevertheless "vote for Lake when they [got] in the voting booths" and split the anti-Lake vote three ways. In Wheeler's opinion, it was "not unusual" for whites to publicly support moderate candidates while casting their actual ballots for pro-segregationists.[39]

The second danger that Hill urged Wheeler to consider was that the sit-ins would further alienate white moderates like him. Hill provided an example of a conversation he had with one of the other white leaders in attendance at the March 15 meeting. The white leader presented Hill with a laundry list of questions: "What [were they] facing? A rule or ruin proposition? By saying that there are not even temporary limitations to the aspirations of the Negro community, is this to be interpreted that every forward step will, in turn, immediately bring on four or five more demands on the basis that success has come once and that proves that what is needed is more of the same? Will there be no time allowed in the future for the white community to assimilate the forward steps?" Wheeler quipped in the margins, "Isn't turn about fair play?" His more serious response acknowledged that "No this [was] probably not the idea. Of the Negro." Hill also pointed to the concerns of a moderate white minister who approached him, worried about black protesters showing up at white churches demanding they desegregate. Hill maintained that actions like these were "causing many a previous moderate to say, 'what are [blacks] trying to do, destroy their friends?'" Hill again pointed to the potential consequences, reminding Wheeler that "the knife cuts both ways. . . . It is one thing to solidify the minority. It is quite something else to solidify the majority" because "the majority will win out." "And," Hill continued in a threatening tone, "in North Carolina, don't forget that the majority also writes the laws."[40]

Hill concluded his letter by asking, "Where [does] one go from here[?]" He offered Wheeler a solution and made a request: "The Negro community has made its point and if the demonstrations were to be called off for six months, then [he thought] it would be possible to go to top management outside of the Southeast and get them, as a matter of national policy, to feed white and Negro alike and, if that did not work, then to just close the lunch counters and stop serving food entirely. Hill asked a question similar to his previous one, but slightly rephrased, "how much, how soon?" "Too much, too soon," he warned, "then the Negro community [would] suffer major reverses because they [were], after all, still the minority. The climate in this community was improving. Look how public school desegregation, token though it may be, has been accepted. But the way the Negro community is proceeding now, at least as interpreted by the white community, would indicate that you are in danger of losing what you have fought for for so long. I ask whether this is what you want?"[41]

The existing channel between white and black leaders in Durham, as far as Wheeler was concerned, was closed off temporarily. Moreover, since white leaders were so used to negotiating with black business leaders like Wheeler, and with Asa T. Spaulding to a lesser extent when it came to community matters, the white leadership was now at somewhat of a disadvantage. The only option left in front of them was to establish direct talks with the young, brazen, uncompromising risk takers. In understanding the role that Wheeler played in defending the sit-ins, one might consider whether the sit-in movement would have succeeded on the level it did and with the same momentum had the traditional black leadership not supported it. Wheeler could have used his economic sway over the black community, which he often did, in order to get blacks to side with him. In short, Wheeler probably had more say when it came to the sit-ins than he might have let on. Hill's assumptions about Wheeler's possible involvement were probably correct. Wheeler held leverage with NCC students; they knew who he was, they knew about his black business activism, and they understood his views when it came to civil rights. He frequently spoke to the NCC students on campus. In January 1960, shortly before the sit-ins began, Wheeler gave a lecture at NCC regarding his recent trip to apartheid South Africa and told the students about his refusal to participate in the United States–South Africa Leader Exchange Program (US-SALEP) on a second-class basis.[42]

The HRC and the thirty community leaders met once more in March and came up with a proposal that called for desegregation at the three main lunch counters at an agreed-upon date. According to their proposal, desegregation would take place after a temporary halt in lunch counter demonstrations and then proceed on a small scale before being completely implemented. The student protestors subsequently accepted the proposal, but the chain stores that ran the lunch counters rejected it; thereafter, the Durham sit-ins continued through the spring and summer. By the end of April, students from across the South met at the historically black Shaw University in Raleigh to determine how they wanted to proceed with the momentum ushered in by sit-in demonstrations. In the Capital City they organized the Student Nonviolent Coordinating Committee (SNCC, pronounced Snick) to manage the new student movement. Throughout the next decade SNCC activists became the heartbeat of the black freedom movement.[43]

In April, a month before the May 28 Democratic primary, Hill contacted Wheeler again, this time to talk straight politics. Hill's March letter to Wheeler had failed to convince the latter to help squash the sit-ins. Now, running out of time before the primary, Hill called on Wheeler for his political support. He attempted to persuade Wheeler to pledge his allegiance to Malcolm B. Seawell, the state attorney general who only a few months earlier had called the sit-in movement a ploy by "outside agitators." Hill worried that Wheeler and the DCNA had already decided to back Sanford before Seawell's Durham campaign committee could make its pitch for black Durhamites' votes. Hill reasoned that "John Larkins [did not meet the DCNA's] standards," and "Beverly Lake [was] so obviously not the candidate [for black North Carolinians]." Hill said Sanford was "the 'leading' candidate historically in that his machine [had] been organized longer—some [people said] since the fifth grade." However, Hill said if Sanford was pitted against Lake in the second Democratic primary runoff, Wheeler would not "be able to tell who [was] speaking on the question of desegregation" since "Sanford want[ed] to win too badly to oppose Lake's position." "The real danger," Hill explained was "that Lake may be elected." Hill reminded Wheeler about the contentious Frank Graham–Willis Smith Senate race (1950), where race-baiting played a key factor in helping Smith defeat Graham; Smith's camp also highlighted Graham's liberal politics as a threat to North Carolina.[44]

Hill also tried to explain why Seawell had yet to take a clear position on desegregation, saying, "If Seawell were to speak more strongly on the question of desegregation . . . it might well [have] elect[ed] Lake by excluding Seawell from the second primary." Seawell's "great struggle," wrote Hill, would be "get[ting] into the second primary and the key vote [was] going to be the vote of the negro community." Therefore, Hill advised Wheeler that "the time for drawing the [battle] lines [was] in the second primary not the first primary." "John, I am worried about the future of the South," said Hill, "and the future of all citizens of the State and I do mean most specifically the negro community." However, "the timing of the sit-down demonstrations has made this a terribly different time for any statewide political candidate to speak his true feelings." By that June, after Sanford and Lake were the only two Democratic candidates left standing, Wheeler and the DCNA endorsed Sanford for governor and collected financial contributions from the black community toward his gubernatorial campaign.[45]

In the midst of the Durham sit-ins that summer, representatives from the national chain stores contacted the HRC and black leaders about reconsidering the earlier three-point proposal. Once they renewed negotiations, the parties reached a settlement that included desegregating the lunch counters even earlier than they had previously discussed. On July 27, direct-action demonstrations aimed at lunch counters in Durham came to an end. As part of the new agreement, lunch counters were to desegregate beginning August 1. Durham joined other North Carolina cities such as Winston-Salem, Charlotte, Greensboro, and High Point in desegregating its lunch counters. Hill's prediction about the May 28 Democratic primary was not off by much in the end. Sanford came in first place with 44 percent of the vote, and his nearest rival was I. Beverly Lake with 28 percent. Lake's second-place victory came as a surprise considering Larkins held strong party support and Seawell came from the Hodges administration. In the weeks leading to the June 25 Democratic primary runoff between Sanford and Lake, the latter continued to run on a segregationist platform. Sanford defeated him for the Democratic gubernatorial nomination, having skillfully avoided getting into a political tug-of-war on the race issue and having deflected his opponent's attempts at "injecting a false issue on race," by letting North Carolina voters know he would give it "prayerful consideration." In the general election that November, Sanford won his race for governor without difficulty, defeating Republican candidate Robert Gavin.[46]

The 1963 Durham Agreement

At the beginning of the 1960s, direct action allowed the civil rights movement to make significant strides and sustain the national attention it had garnered. In Durham, the economic limitations that resulted from unequal access to employment were at the center of renewed direct-action protests that began on May 18, 1963. Vivian McCoy, a student activist from NCC, maintained that the demonstration intended "to start with employment first because we felt that employment was the essence of it all, to get blacks out of these menial jobs at department stores since we were spending all of our money there.'" That Saturday afternoon, hundreds of students from NCC and Hillside High School picketed several segregated restaurants before police arrested 130 of them for trespassing. Hundreds of people swarmed city hall and the county courthouse in solidarity with those arrested. The protesters vowed to continue until their demands to end all forms of segregation were met. That day's demonstration overlapped with citywide elections. On Friday, the DCNA endorsed Reverend Ruben L. Speaks, pastor at the black St. Mark AME Zion Church, in a one-shot voting tactic where they pledged support for a single candidate in the at-large city council race. The DCNA endorsed R. Wensell "Wense" Grabarek, a white accountant and city councilman, for mayor over Watts Carr Jr. With wide support from the majority-black precincts, Grabarek won the seat, while Speaks lost his bid for a council seat.[47]

On Sunday May 19, demonstrations continued as planned. This time the numbers swelled, as approximately five hundred demonstrators swarmed the Howard Johnson's Restaurant. The police arrested more than four hundred protestors and carried them off to jail. The remaining demonstrators made their way to the county courthouse, where they again convened on the steps to support the jailed protesters. As events unfolded that evening, huge crowds of white teenagers gathered directly across the street from the courthouse. A few fights broke out between blacks and whites before police ended hostilities. With further violence possible, some forty police officers formed a dividing line between the two groups. The next few moments were extremely tense, as Mayor-elect Grabarek tried to convince both sides to remain peaceful. However, it was attorney M. Hugh Thompson who later received credit for his role in easing that evening's tensions; he called on black demonstrators to disperse after he was able to obtain a few concessions such as cigarettes for those jailed.[48]

The next day, the NAACP and CORE Youth and College chapter representatives (the protest organizers) met with Grabarek, who failed to persuade them to halt demonstrations. The NAACP-CORE group soon attended a city council meeting where student leaders Walter Riley and Quinton Baker, alongside other members from the key organizations, submitted a petition outlining their requirements for ending protests. The group's demands came from its own twelve-member negotiating committee, which included attorney Floyd B. McKissick and NCC student leader Joyce Ware as cochairpersons. Again signaling the need to increase job opportunities for blacks, they first called for a local fair employment practices act to ensure that businesses, unions, and educational institutions no longer discriminated against people based on race, color, religion, or national origin. Next, they wanted a public ordinance law to forbid "discrimination in public places, public accommodations in any Hotel, Motel, Restaurant, Theatre, [and] Hospital licensed by the City of Durham because of race, color or religion and making a violation of said ordinance a misdemeanor punishable by fine." They requested an investigation into possible police harassment against female demonstrators and wanted those officers found guilty to be disciplined accordingly. They asked for all charges against student protesters to be dropped. Finally, the group insisted that an investigation be made into continued school segregation and specifically demanded that local school officials come up with a workable school desegregation plan. At the end of the meeting, Grabarek appointed city council members Luther Barbour, Sam Riley, and Shag Stewart (the only black city council member) to a committee to review the petition. Stewart became chair as the other committee members declined the chairmanship.[49]

That evening, students moved forward with mass demonstrations intended to integrate Durham businesses. They poured into several retail stores, city theaters, motels, and restaurants, at which point many of them were arrested. As protests dragged on, two Durham restaurants, Honey's and Tops Drive-In, agreed to integrate their dining facilities. Nevertheless, the Durham Restaurant Association decided as a body to continue segregation policies. As the weekend confrontations spilled over into the workweek, so did threats of physical violence as black activists and resentful white onlookers descended once more on city hall. With center-city streets in front of the courthouse serving as a buffer zone between both groups, the potential for violence grew closer as fireworks were thrown at black demonstrators. Police Chief William Pleasants called in the fire department to connect fire hoses to city hydrants and threatened to spray the swelling crowds, a move that served as a stark reminder of similar tactics used by police commissioner Eugene "Bull" Connor in Birmingham, Alabama, in the preceding weeks. Indeed, the Durham situation happened as an outgrowth of demonstrations in the Deep South. The crowds retreated once Pleasants called in the North Carolina State Highway Patrol as reserve backup for the Durham police.[50]

On Tuesday, May 21, students met with Grabarek in daylong conferences where they eventually reached an agreement to temporarily halt demonstrations. The good-faith measure happened in part because Grabarek obtained commitments from an additional five restaurants that agreed to integrate. The restaurants were the Rebel Drive-In, the Oh-Boy! Drive-In, Turnage's Barbeque Place, Blue Light Café, and McDonald's Hamburger Drive-In. Grabarek then gave them his word to work diligently on the grievances demonstrators had outlined. Grabarek announced the agreement that evening at a rally of one thousand people at St. Joseph's AME Church. He told the audience of mostly students, "The fact that you have agreed with me to forego demonstrations at this point proves to me that you deserve the rank of first-rate citizens," at which point the audience gave approval with a standing ovation.[51]

At midweek, Grabarek met with about fifty white and black businessmen and told them he would appoint a formal committee. It became clear that white leaders in attendance had no intention of sitting down with the NAACP-CORE negotiating committee but preferred negotiating with what they viewed as the more responsible black leadership. The Reverend Warren Carr, past HRC chairman, suggested that black leaders appoint one contingent to represent them so that meaningful compromise could be achieved. Watts Hill Jr. voiced his own desire to see that the issues were dealt with privately behind the scenes, noting that the few restaurants that desegregated earlier in the week had done so through private meetings outside Durham. Floyd Patton, the manager at Sears, Roebuck and Company, alongside others in attendance, stressed their willingness to hire more blacks. At the same time, Patton believed negotiations to be worthless because he thought black leaders could not negotiate effectively and the NAACP-CORE negotiating committee would never agree on conditions. Patton relayed that in early 1962, for example, his store hired a black salesperson on a permanent basis and the company considered hiring another black employee until he received demands from a group of student activists to hire at least four more blacks in exchange for ending their pickets. He also noted that after going into negotiations, black leaders came back wanting him to hire thirty-five more black people before they would stop. "I can't have this organization [NAACP-CORE]," explained Patton, "or any other organization telling me who to hire but negotiations [could] be opened with responsible Negro leadership such as the [Asa] Spauldings, [John] Stewarts and [the John] Wheelers." The NAACP-CORE group thanked Grabarek in a letter for his efforts to find a reasonable solution, but they also made it clear that they had ultimate authority in determining whether negotiations satisfied their objectives. "Unless noticeable progress is made on a daily basis," they warned, "we cannot promise that mass demonstrations will not resume at any time." The NAACP-CORE group realized the "dire necessity of an excellent advisory committee and [were] certainly pleased with its formation, [but] it must advise you that since our objectives were outlined to you (Grabarek) in our first meeting we will not be bound by any decision the committee recommends if it does not correlate with our outlined objectives which you have in your possession." "Please understand," the letter went on to say, "that we are a distinct group, with distinct leaders and will not subordinate ourselves."[52]

By week's end, Grabarek appointed the Durham Interim Committee (DIC). The eleven-member negotiating committee of mostly white businessmen was headed by Watts Carr Jr., Grabarek's rival in the recent mayoral election. Unsurprisingly, Wheeler and Asa T. Spaulding were the only black leaders on the committee because whites were unwilling to negotiate directly with the NAACP-CORE leaders. Wheeler and Spaulding did voice their concerns about being the only two black leaders on the DIC. By most accounts, Spaulding had been somewhat aloof when it came to his involvement in direct action, aside from serving as an intermediary selected by white power brokers who relied on him when they wanted to end disturbances. When sit-ins took place in 1960, for example, Spaulding attended meetings as part of the group of about thirty community leaders who met behind the scenes to consider ways to end them peacefully. On the other hand, Wheeler was more outwardly involved as an activist businessman, as his record demonstrated. Regardless, unlike the 1960 sit-ins, the students affirmed that no group or individual would speak on their behalf without first consulting its twelve-member negotiating committee, which held an advantage given its power to resume direct-action demonstrations at a moment's notice. That Thursday, NAACP executive secretary Roy Wilkins addressed another rally, this time held at St. Mark AME Zion Church. During his speech, Wilkins referenced President Kennedy's move toward finally pushing civil rights legislation through Congress but reminded the audience that the problems sweeping the South could have been avoided had blacks received their citizenship rights one hundred years earlier.[53]

At the DIC's first meeting, Floyd B. McKissick again presented the objectives of the NAACP-CORE contingent with other negotiating committee members in attendance. At that meeting, the DIC appointed four subcommittees: "Hotels, Motels and Restaurants," "Employment," "City and County Schools," and "Miscellaneous Grievances." Wheeler was appointed to the Miscellaneous Grievances Committee, which planned to consider the public accommodations ordinance included in the list of demands. As DIC chairman, Carr assured McKissick that the DIC would be strictly about finding an agreeable solution rather than serving as an obstacle to compromise. In the next few weeks, the DIC and its subcommittees held several meetings with various Durham businesses and the NAACP-CORE negotiating committee. Along the way, the city recreation department recommended desegregating city swimming pools immediately. During negotiations, Wheeler played an integral role by keeping student concerns in the forefront, in contrast to Spaulding, whom many student leaders saw as an obstacle to their objectives. Carr, the DIC chair, later explained that Spaulding "did not represent the [civil rights and political] power-structure of the black community," but Wheeler "had a tight rein." Student activist Vivian McCoy remembered that Wheeler was sure to seek guidance from Floyd B. McKissick and that he also attended NAACP Youth meetings in order to get a sense of what the NAACP-CORE leaders wanted discussed during DIC meetings. Grabarek supported this assessment, agreeing that Wheeler was beneficial in negotiations as an intermediary between the DIC and demonstration leaders, and as a mediator between the mayor and the black community in general. During DIC meetings, Wheeler's astute opinions and observations most often represented student perspectives, and he made sure that any agreements reached between the DIC and businesses were completely aligned with the students' goals. Carr also explained that Wheeler "voiced the views of the students to the DIC." Jocelyn McKissick, Floyd B. McKissick's daughter and herself a student activist, recalled that "John Wheeler was always cooperative . . . [and] always responsive" to student angst.[54]

In early June, the DIC announced the Durham Agreement, which it touted as a "voluntary" desegregation plan, though it was far from that. The most significant compromise in the Durham Agreement focused on public accommodations, as many local businesses agreed to desegregate. These businesses included the Jack Tar Hotel, alongside the city's eleven motels. At least fifty-five of Durham's 103 restaurants desegregated while another eight restaurants agreed to consider desegregation; another six restaurants refused outright to desegregate their facilities. In reality, however, all of them still had full discretion over whether to serve individuals. Carr characterized the Durham Agreement as plain "economics. That's the first thing you threw at 'em. If you don't do this thing . . . we['re] just going to be ruined. The town can't [survive] it [otherwise]." With regard to education, very little was accomplished in the way of any progressive school desegregation plan. Additionally, the Durham City Schools claimed it needed to wait for the anticipated outcome of a pending school desegregation ruling in federal court before determining the actions it could take.[55]

In the area of equal employment, the Durham Agreement promised little progress in increased jobs for blacks right away. No major retail businesses, for instance, targeted during the May demonstrations agreed to immediately hire a specified number of black employees. Instead, the employment section included in the Durham Agreement revealed the employers' contentions that there were just not enough qualified black applicants to fill needed positions with their companies. The DIC reported that some thirty retailers agreed to eliminate race-based hiring practices as outlined by President Kennedy's Executive Order #10925. They also planned to work with Durham's relatively new Industrial Education Center to institute job-training programs to increase the number of qualified black applicants. The DIC also noted that other private companies pledged to hire skilled applicants without regard to race; however, the companies said that there were few qualified applicants and that, as a result, they could not immediately increase the number of black employees. Durham's six commercial banks planned to adhere to nondiscriminatory policies. The three insurance companies headquartered in Durham agreed to hire on the basis of merit rather than race. There was a general voluntary agreement to the principle of fair employment practices. However, there was no agreement to pass any fair employment ordinance as student demonstrators had initially wanted. "We eliminated some of the job discrimination," Vivian McCoy recalled, and "we opened the door for accommodations in motels. But we didn't get all the jobs that we should have gotten for blacks. [But] it was effective in that time." The DIC examined the employment practices of Durham's city government, which previously placed blacks in restricted (or menial) positions, something that Wheeler had strongly objected to for quite some time. The DIC concluded that blacks deserved better and more frequent job opportunities within local government agencies, including opportunities for promotion. The DIC praised Durham for having already begun employing blacks in government jobs, and the city agreed to continue their efforts in this area. As evidence, city administrators pointed to their job application forms, from which they had removed the requirement for job applicants to provide their race.[56]

The Durham Agreement received national attention and press coverage for its sweeping desegregation measures. In the days immediately following the agreement, Mayor Grabarek and other DIC members asked Wheeler to contact Vice President Lyndon B. Johnson to ask him to send a positive public response. In a brief note to Johnson's assistant George E. Reedy, Wheeler mentioned "some Comment by the Vice President will be extremely useful in supporting the proprietors of the private businesses who have integrated." On June 7, Reedy prepared a Western Union telegram from Johnson that read: "My warm congratulations for the action that has been taken to solve the problems of Durham by community action. I have heard an excellent report from my good friend John Wheeler on the efficient and effective steps that have been taken, and my best wishes are with you." Vice President Johnson had reservations about sending the wire, but Reedy explained to him: "It would be well to call Wheeler directly and tell him why [a public response might not be such a good idea]. His regard for you is very high." On June 11, Wheeler phoned Reedy, and the two probably discussed the vice president's hesitancy about sending the wire. In the end, Durham city leaders were given one better, as President Kennedy publicly acknowledged the Durham Agreement in a congratulatory message to Grabarek. That evening, too, Kennedy delivered a powerful televised speech to the nation and announced his plans to send a major civil rights bill to Congress. But just hours after the president's hopeful promise, NAACP field secretary Medgar Evers was gunned down outside his home in Jackson, Mississippi. Evers's murder highlighted the country's continued inclination toward violence and the serious risks involved in the battle for freedom. It might have also served as a reminder to those living in Durham of how close the city had come to violence just a month earlier.[57]

The 1960 sit-in movement held larger implications as one of the most recognizable moments in North Carolina history. It was also one of the more defining turning points in the history of the United States and the civil rights movement. It placed the state in the national spotlight and brought civil rights back into the national conversation at the start of a new decade. The sit-in movement had an impact on state politics amid that year's heated gubernatorial primary race and the presidential election. It gave rise to a national student movement, which marked a decided shift in civil rights leadership by directly challenging the traditional black leadership, as direct action became another means by which blacks could agitate for change. The Greensboro sit-ins caused a chain reaction, ushered in a new generation, and served as the catalyst for protests led by student activists in town after town and city after city across the South. In all, this included fifty-four cities and towns from Atlanta, Georgia, to Nashville, Tennessee. The student leaders were on the verge of one of the most significant social revolutions, one focused on obtaining civil rights for blacks. In a much broader context, the sit-in movement underscored that this was indeed a "dangerous age" because blacks were now willing to literally risk their lives by disrupting community operations in order to secure the full citizenship rights that democracy supposedly guaranteed. Wheeler and the DCNA leadership stood relentlessly and unapologetically firm behind student activists in that effort. The most important role, then, that Wheeler played during this time was speaking up on behalf of the students when their voices were unfairly marginalized during the behind-the-scenes negotiations that had become so representative of how both black and white leaders in Durham attempted to handle racial discord. By rejecting the idea of negotiating an end to the sit-ins without the presence of students who had put their bodies on the line, Wheeler gave voice and even more legitimacy to the new student movement. And he drew a hard line that he refused to cross. While the sit-in movement succeeded in part because it spread like wildfire, the hard-line positions taken by individual leaders like Wheeler in favor of mass, nonviolent, direct-action protests proved extremely effective as well.

5

Equal Employment, Voting Rights, and Public Policy at the National Level

> The American Negro wants no special trains, no special buses, no special schools, no special factories in which to work. He simply wants the same job opportunities in industry and other lines of employment with the right to be promoted and paid on the same basis as other Americans.
>
> John Hervey Wheeler, 1954

In April 1961, John Wheeler sent North Carolina's new governor, Terry Sanford, a rather bold fifteen-page letter. The memorandum, which can more accurately be described as a jobs blueprint, detailed how Sanford could make his "New Day" proclamation more meaningful to black North Carolinians. In his January 5, 1961, inaugural address, Sanford echoed his campaign slogan when he declared, "There is a new day in North Carolina!" The state had to "give our children the *quality* of education which they need to keep up in this rapidly advancing, scientific, complex world." "No group of our citizens," Sanford concluded, "can be denied the opportunities of first-class citizenship."[1]

"North Carolina cannot," Wheeler argued, "enjoy the bright sunshine of a New Day in industry, agriculture, education, and democratic living unless it frees each one of its citizens to develop to the maximum of his capabilities." Sanford's hard-fought gubernatorial campaign had begun amid the 1960 sit-in movement led by student activists. Sanford's success during the Democratic primary leading to his nomination happened in large measure because he cleverly sidestepped race-baiting from his opponent, former Wake Forest University law professor I. Beverly Lake, in favor of broad appeals to moving the state forward.[2]

Once he became governor, Sanford moved in the opposite direction than did most of his southern counterparts. The optimistic tone of his speech concerning North Carolina's future fit within the broader context of the "New Frontier" ushered in with the vibrant presidency of John F. Kennedy. The governor's declaration emphasized new beginnings in education and represented a fresh outlook on the state's economic future. He believed that improvements in education provided the best path for all North Carolinians because better education would help prepare the citizenry for modern job opportunities. In his letter, Wheeler applauded the governor's forthrightness in his inaugural address and said he believed the possibilities were endless, but he called for specific actions to back up the enthusiastic rhetoric. He saw equal employment as one important way Sanford could make his declaration a reality for black North Carolinians. Wheeler was pleased that the governor wanted to remove some of the racial barriers through what became his signature "Quality Public Education Program," but he said the onus was also on Sanford to open up job opportunities to blacks in local and state government. The state had to serve as an effective example in employment equality. If one could not get the state government to change its own employment policies right away, then how could one expect private businesses to change theirs? From Wheeler's perspective, the status of black employment continued to determine how far the state could move ahead economically.[3]

The jobs blueprint Wheeler sent Sanford painted a disturbing picture of black employment in state government. This remained so even after President Kennedy signed an executive order in March to address employment discrimination in federal agencies. Black North Carolinians "held only menial positions among the 9,000 employees of the State Highway Commission, the 1,500 employees of the Department of Motor Vehicles, the 670 employees of the Department of Conservation and Development . . . [and] the 600 members of the State Highway Patrol." The North Carolina Employment Security Commission (ESC) received the most criticism because "in the State Offices . . . there were only ten Negro employees . . . one maid, two elevator operators, five janitors, and the two janitor-messengers. There were no Negro employees above the rank of janitor-messenger." Overall, the ESC had a total of 945 white and 51 nonwhite employees. There were "no Negro Directors" in the ESC's fifty-four local bureaus. "Our failure or refusal," explained Wheeler, "to make use of the qualified Negro labor market is indeed a costly economic error." Therefore, he "urged" the governor to launch a "positive" plan to remove discriminatory employment barriers.[4]

Though Wheeler recognized that his recommendations would not solve all these problems, the document represented a fresh starting point in the battle for equality of opportunity in employment. Wheeler suggested several steps. First, the local, state, and federal government had to increase the representation of qualified black professionals. Second, changes to employment policies needed to begin across the board and on a much broader level in state agencies. Third, qualified blacks had to receive administrative positions on boards and commissions so they could be actively involved in policymaking decisions. This would ensure that once policy changes were made, they would be implemented and maintained permanently. Finally, blacks deserved a chance at merit-based advancement through the ranks of a given agency, which meant increased recruitment and training to guarantee there would be no glass ceiling restricting how far blacks could advance. Wheeler targeted local and state governments because he believed realistic changes could begin in state-level hiring rather swiftly and then spread outward to all employment sectors. Wheeler also wanted to hold Sanford accountable for moving the ideals of a New Day forward.[5]

This chapter considers Wheeler's work on equal employment in the 1960s in the context of his broader civil rights activism on both the state and the national levels. The US Supreme Court case *Griggs v. Duke Power* (1971) was a pivotal moment in the equal employment battle in North Carolina, but well before *Griggs,* Wheeler was working to address employment discrimination in North Carolina outside the industrial sector. It is also noteworthy that North Carolina had one of its own civil rights leaders—a banker no less—serving on the President's Committee on Equal Employment Opportunity (PCEEO), an immediate forerunner to the Equal Employment Opportunity Commission (EEOC). Wheeler helped draft portions of the Civil Rights Act of 1964, which "was accepted by Congress virtually as the committee wrote it" and signed into law by President Lyndon B. Johnson on July 2, 1964. Wheeler's efforts on this milestone legislation illuminate the relationship between racial equality and economic justice for black Americans in the mid-twentieth-century South.[6]

This chapter also examines how Wheeler used his connections on the regional and national levels to obtain voting rights for black southerners. He did so through the Southern Regional Council (SRC), the national, Atlanta-based interracial civil rights organization engaged in research and publication that grew out of the 1942 Durham Conference and influenced policymakers in various ways. Wheeler had been active in the SRC and its very active affiliate branch, the NCCHR, since their establishment. He was an SRC vice president during its early work on school desegregation, and he served the group as a consultant during the school desegregation crisis in the latter half of the 1950s. Direct action in the mid- to late 1950s compelled the organization to become more oriented toward activism than it had ever been, and in 1964, Wheeler became the SRC's first black president. A hallmark of the SRC's involvement in voting rights became the Voter Education Project (VEP), which helped pave the way for increased black voter registration before the Voting Rights Act of 1965. With his position as a political insider, Wheeler's efforts in these areas helped determine public policy during the Kennedy and Johnson administrations.

The Kennedy Administration and the President's Committee on Equal Employment Opportunity (PCEEO)

On March 6, 1961, President Kennedy signed Executive Order #10925 establishing the President's Committee on Equal Employment Opportunity to "ensure that Americans of all colors and beliefs [would] have equal access to employment within the government, and with those who [did] business with the government." Kennedy appointed two black members to the PCEEO—Wheeler and *St. Louis Argus* newspaper editor Howard B. Woods. (Another African American, Hobart Taylor Jr., served as legal counsel.) The PCEEO had twenty-eight members: fourteen administrators from several federal agencies, including members of Kennedy's cabinet, and fourteen prominent civic leaders from around the country. The latter included organized labor union officials, such as George Meany, the president of the American Federation of Labor and Congress of Industrial

Organizations (AFL-CIO), and Walter Reuther, president of the United Automobile Workers (UAW).[7]

The PCEEO was not a new concept, nor did African Americans begin their equal employment battle with the Kennedy administration in 1961. The surge in defense industry production during World War II increased job opportunities for many American workers and lowered the unemployment rate. Yet while there was a need for more workers, black Americans had difficulty obtaining jobs because of discrimination by government contractors. By January 1941, blacks raised serious objections about the lack of job opportunities available to them. Thus, under the guidance of labor leader A. Philip Randolph, president of the all-black Brotherhood of Sleeping Car Porters (BSCP), the March on Washington Movement (MOWM) emerged. The MOWM represented a loose coalition of national labor and civil rights organizations whose leaders hoped to end the unfair bias and gross neglect that restricted black job opportunities.[8]

The movement worked to focus both national and international attention on problems ranging from discrimination in the military to unequal jobs in war-related production. The organization's most important goal was to highlight America's contradictory message: its political leaders decried fascism and totalitarianism abroad and ignored democracy at home by depriving blacks of their full citizenship rights. To ward off potential protests, President Roosevelt signed Executive Order #8802 on June 25, 1941, establishing the Fair Employment Practices Committee (FEPC), which enforced the order and monitored race-based discrimination in defense industry employment during the war. The initial executive order and the policies established by Roosevelt ended once the war was over, and the campaign to pass a permanent FEPC under President Truman failed in the late 1940s. Nevertheless, both Presidents Truman and Eisenhower passed their own executive orders to address equal employment within federal agencies and private contractors that did business with the government. These included establishing committees that were similar in scope to the FEPC. Although they had very limited enforcement powers, the committees took on similar work as the original FEPC. During President Harry S. Truman's administration, a similar agency became the Committee on Government Contract Compliance (CCC) and then the United States Committee on Government Contracts (CGC) under President Dwight D. Eisenhower.[9]

Throughout the committee's postwar existence, the NAACP, the National Urban League (NUL), and most other civil rights organizations viewed it as ineffective because it was unwilling to enforce policies or significantly alter discriminatory practices by government agencies and contractors. But at least in principle Wheeler embraced the existence of such a committee. In 1958, he wrote to then CGC chairman Vice President Richard M. Nixon about the Conference on Minority Community Resources the CGC was sponsoring. Wheeler told Nixon that "the Conference was ample evidence to the nation and world observers that the Government of the United States through its duly elected officials is firmly committed to implementation of the broad principle of equality of opportunity in employment for all citizens regardless of race." Wheeler appreciated these gestures, but in reality, the CGC relied heavily on a program of voluntary compliance rather than mandatory enforcement of the federal policies regarding racial discrimination in employment. The PCEEO appointment came at an opportune time, more than a year after the 1960 sit-in movement began in Wheeler's home state, bringing civil rights back into the national spotlight during the presidential election between Senator Kennedy and Vice President Nixon.[10]

The presidential contenders looked to civil rights organizations to meet the challenges posed by direct-action protests. Kennedy expressed an interest in working with the SRC in some capacity. As early as October 1960, the SRC commissioned University of North Carolina law professor Daniel H. Pollitt to study ways the president could address civil rights using his executive authority, given the difficulties and challenges he would face trying to push legislation through a Congress ruled by conservative southern Democrats. Wheeler served on the SRC's executive committee, which meant he read and commented on early drafts of the report that ultimately influenced national public policy related to black freedom. Wheeler became the SRC's executive committee chairman in February 1961, giving him an expanded role in the organization and more involvement in policymaking at the national level, as the council became a central component of the Kennedy administration's plans to promote civil rights. Kennedy campaigned on the promise to address civil rights "with the stroke of the presidential pen," through executive action, but he did so very cautiously.[11]

President John F. Kennedy speaking at the White House to the members of the PCEEO with John H. Wheeler (*middle of front row, seated*). In his work with the PCEEO, Wheeler said he "got to work a great deal with [Lyndon B.] Johnson," and the two became good friends. During his tenure on the PCEEO, Wheeler was extremely vocal in expressing his opinions to the mostly white PCEEO. As Wheeler himself pointed out, "I never had hesitancy about expressing strong views, to which Mr. Johnson was usually receptive." *John F. Kennedy Speaking to the President's Committee on Equal Employment Opportunity with John H. Wheeler* (*seated middle of front row*), undated, John H. Wheeler Collection, Atlanta University Center Robert W. Woodruff Library.

In January 1961, the SRC published its report, *The Federal Executive and Civil Rights,* and submitted it to the president. The report highlighted needed improvements in voting, housing, employment, and education for black people. The document recommended that "a national [voter] registration drive, under the personal sponsorship of the President, should be launched." This became the VEP, which sponsored countless voter registration initiatives that local and national civil rights organizations conducted in the years before the Voting Rights Act of 1965. During the summer of 1961, Wheeler played a central role in planning for the VEP during meetings with the private Taconic Foundation. As the SRC's executive committee chairman, Wheeler remained adamant during talks that the SRC would not be "a mere conduit" for the national civil rights organizations and "reserved [its] rights to distribute money to other groups." In other areas, *The Federal Executive and Civil Rights* recommended tighter restrictions on federal employment practices, including "effective enforcement of the bar against discriminatory employment by government contractors," the "aim of immediate compliance [by government agencies] with the policy of non-discrimination," and "the appointment of some Negroes to top regional or district positions in the South." The document stressed the role government agencies needed to play in setting examples of nondiscrimination for private employers to follow. After Kennedy's inauguration, the SRC seemed confident his administration would play a positive role in advancing civil rights.[12]

During the spring of 1961, the Kennedy administration confirmed the SRC's confidence to some degree by following the policies that *The Federal Executive and Civil Rights* outlined. That is, the report provided the administration with ways to act on various issues without introducing legislation to Congress. Though other civil rights organizations such as the NAACP and NUL also submitted similar proposals to the new administration, the Kennedy administration steered toward the SRC's emphasis on equal employment and voter registration. Kennedy appointed Vice President Lyndon B. Johnson as the PCEEO's chairman. Luther H. Hodges, Sanford's predecessor in the North Carolina executive mansion and now US secretary of commerce, was also a member. The presence of Wheeler, Woods, and Taylor on the committee represented a significant opportunity for blacks to directly influence public policy on the national level. Moreover, Wheeler exemplified what he demanded from white power brokers: black involvement in high-level decision-making.[13]

The PCEEO had a professional staff and the authority to investigate the employment practices of government agencies. The executive order that established the committee specifically prohibited employment discrimination in the federal government based on "race, color, religion, or national origin." It also included mandates for contractors doing business with the government to agree to nondiscriminatory clauses concerning hiring, pay rates, layoffs, recruitment, and training. The PCEEO had the authority to investigate all government contractors or subcontractors to determine whether they violated any aspects of the executive order. If a government contractor failed to comply, the committee recommended penalties to the Justice Department. The PCEEO also had the latitude to terminate or recommend termination of an agreement if a government contractor failed to comply with the provisions outlined in the executive order.[14]

The North Carolina Democratic Party strongly supported Wheeler's appointment to the PCEEO. These endorsements included state executive committee chairman Bert L. Bennett, former governor and commerce secretary Luther H. Hodges, and the state's two US senators, Samuel J. Ervin and B. Everett Jordan. The state party's support for Wheeler came in large measure because of the power he wielded as DCNA chairman. The DCNA by this time was a statewide clearinghouse that not only held black political leverage in Durham but also enjoyed significant sway in other cities across North Carolina with sizeable numbers of black voters. Wheeler garnered the DCNA's support (both financially and otherwise) on behalf of Sanford during the general election. He reminded Sanford of this in the April 1961 jobs blueprint, saying, "North Carolina Negro voters have not only demonstrated deep interest in good, clean, progressive government, but also they have been the margin of survival of the Democratic Party in the State." "In Durham County," he continued, "approximately 6,200 of 10,151 votes received by the present Governor in the June 27[25], 1960 run-off [election] were cast by Negro voters, and for the state as a whole [he] received at least 90,000 Negro voters, which could have caused his defeat by approximately 102,600 votes if they had been cast for his opponent." During the 1960 presidential campaign, Wheeler also served on Kennedy's "National Committee of Business and Professional Men and Women for Kennedy-Johnson," headed by Hodges. Sanford, who also had great standing with Kennedy, recognized Wheeler's political influence and supported his appointment. The endorsements aside, Wheeler's firm grasp on the economics of civil rights and its role in the well-being of North Carolina, the South, and the nation led to his appointment. Moreover, Wheeler's longer track record and commitment of working within the state Democratic Party might have been more favorable to the party's leadership given his reputation for diplomacy. Though Wheeler's appointment might have been viewed by some as tokenism, the banker believed that "somebody has got to get in" on the inside to better understand the requirements. If that person had their "thinking straight," they would pave the way for others.[15]

Dr. John R. Larkins also had an important role in Wheeler's appointment to the PCEEO. Not to be confused with the 1960 gubernatorial candidate, Larkins was a black social worker and trained sociologist who worked as a consultant for the state Department of Public Welfare. In 1962, Sanford appointed him as coordinator for civil rights for that department, and he went on to serve in various capacities under subsequent governors. Larkins was "elated" that Wheeler received the appointment. He had lobbied for a black North Carolinian to receive a key appointment in the Kennedy administration and suggested Wheeler's name, alongside city councilman Shag Stewart, as potential candidates. Larkins recommended Wheeler, he told the banker, because Kennedy "has not made any appointment of Negroes from the South," which "should be called to his attention." Like Wheeler, Larkins believed it was important to promote employment opportunities for blacks in state and federal government, particularly if the Democratic Party wanted to maintain black voter support.[16]

Wheeler and Larkins were a political tag team of sorts who worked with one another strategically to increase employment opportunities for black North Carolinians in government, using their positions effectively in behind-the-scenes brokering. They clearly understood the urgency of increasing black representation and had already begun laying out a year-long plan to obtain certain gubernatorial appointments during the Sanford administration. Larkins and Wheeler agreed to capitalize on the access the state had with the Kennedy administration as well. The two compared notes, drafted lists of potential appointments for Sanford and Kennedy to consider, and met with black national Democratic Party leaders such as Louis E. Martin in Washington, D.C., where they lobbied for other milestone concessions. In turn, Wheeler also recommended Larkins and others for gubernatorial appointments on state boards and commissions because "it is urgently necessary that the State of North

Carolina shall make a show of good faith in its intentions to provide equal employment opportunities for its Negro citizens."[17]

Wheeler's appointment to the PCEEO also reflected his previous record and interest in equitable jobs and better economic policies for blacks in North Carolina. In the 1950s, he connected this need with his education agenda and came out strongly against the state Employment Security Commission (ESC). He charged the agency with discrimination, pointing out that its official policy perpetuated "discriminat[ion] against Negroes in [the] listing of jobs." The practice in the ESC offices across the state was to refer certain jobs to white applicants only. Moreover, the ESC had its own internal problems with employment discrimination. "In general," Wheeler explained, "when we get a new industry . . . there are certain jobs that are not even referred to the Negro side of the office. [T]hat is not in keeping with the purpose of the commission." In the mid-to late 1950s, Wheeler was also involved in the activities of the DCNA's Economic Committee headed by black businessman Nathan White and attorney Floyd B. McKissick, future chairman of CORE, which was deeply concerned with matters related to equal employment. Convinced the PCEEO had more overarching authority, Wheeler attended the inaugural meeting on April 11 in the White House Cabinet Room.[18]

Initially, Wheeler viewed the committee as having the potential to correct past and present job discrimination by government agencies. He believed the PCEEO could be more effective than past committees because "President Kennedy's order seems to be broader and have more teeth in it than previous [executive] orders." He believed his presence on the committee would also benefit North Carolina and help move the state toward economic prosperity, as the state needed "only to establish a reputation for nondiscrimination in hiring to 'really expand industrially.'" North Carolina's economic growth, Wheeler believed, depended on expanding equal employment opportunities for black people, which in turn was essential in attracting potential industries to the state, one of his broader objectives. In his opinion, the Tar Heel State held an advantage because it did not replicate the kind of violence or hostile resistance exhibited by its Deep South counterparts, even though the school desegregation crisis revealed North Carolina to be as effective as Deep South states in forestalling *Brown*. North Carolina had another advantage over other

The inaugural meeting of the PCEEO, April 11, 1961, in the Cabinet Room of the White House. John H. Wheeler is standing in second row, far left, directly behind those seated. *Seated, left to right:* former North Carolina governor and then Commerce Secretary Luther H. Hodges, Labor Secretary Arthur Goldberg, President John F. Kennedy, and Vice President Lyndon B. Johnson. Courtesy of the John F. Kennedy Presidential Library and Museum, Boston, Massachusetts.

southern states in that white leaders there were willing to talk with black leaders about improving employment opportunities for blacks. Moreover, Wheeler believed individual government agencies and contractors needed to take a greater responsibility because "the burden of proof regarding job equality should fall on the agency or firm rather than on the complaining individual." Wheeler told Livingstone College president Dr. Sam E. Duncan and others who congratulated him on the appointment that it was an opportunity "to bring new hope to every citizen who has the ambition and desire to develop and make full use of his talents for the purpose of strengthening our society and the democratic way of life."[19]

Wheeler witnessed Kennedy sign the executive order establishing the PCEEO in Washington, D.C. The same day he, alongside Leslie Dunbar, the SRC's new executive director, met with top administration officials and civil rights advisers in an off-the-record luncheon. The meeting placed Wheeler at the bargaining table with the country's top power brokers, a position with which he was quite comfortable. Several representatives of philanthropic foundations also participated in the meeting. As the only black leader in attendance, Wheeler joined Attorney General Robert F. Kennedy, Assistant Attorney General Burke Marshall, and *Atlanta Constitution* newspaper editor Ralph McGill (an early SRC incorporator who had orchestrated the meeting). Another attendee was Harold Fleming, Dunbar's predecessor at the SRC and now executive vice president at the Potomac Institute, which philanthropist Stephen Currier had established earlier in the year as a private organization closely associated with the Kennedy administration. This meeting, and others held with different cabinet members that day, pushed Wheeler fully into the position of national public policy advocate.[20]

During the luncheon, those present expressed their ideas about civil rights to the attorney general. Although it is impossible to determine what each person said, Wheeler likely directed Bobby Kennedy's attention to the need to appoint blacks in the US Department of Justice. In the weeks leading to and following his visit to Washington, he contacted government officials about hiring blacks in that department. Wheeler also wanted an African American appointed as an assistant US attorney for the Middle District of North Carolina, and he might have said as much to Kennedy during the meeting. Once his term on the PCEEO began, he suggested the names of several potential black appointees. Wheeler possibly discussed other economic disparities facing blacks in the South. Afterward, he wrote to the PCEEO's chairman, Vice President Johnson, and expressed his gratitude to him for also meeting with the SRC group to discuss the executive order. Wheeler promised Johnson that the SRC's executive committee would work with the US Department of Labor to ensure the executive order was properly followed. "This action," conveyed Wheeler, "indicates clearly that we have an opportunity to move forward rapidly toward the goal of making maximum use of all of the manpower resources of our nation."[21]

Such off-the-record meetings typified the Kennedy administration's approach to civil rights. It relied on backdoor channels and executive orders to address specific problems while being careful not to openly confront the southern social order. The South's politicians had a tight rule over Congress and were part of Kennedy's Democratic Party coalition, which the president relied on to support his foreign policy agenda. But Kennedy's unwillingness to risk losing southern political support by seeking advances on racial issues made many civil rights activists and organizations wary. Yet Wheeler remained willing to work through various channels, including the Democratic Party establishment, to obtain concessions for black Americans. This meant being prepared to meet the Kennedy administration on its own terms and accommodating the administration's preference for less direct ways of handling civil rights. Wheeler chose to accept this arrangement because it offered close proximity to the president and vice president. He believed that even within the established framework one could be in a strategic position to critique policy. While he was convinced that the PCEEO could help initiate changes, he believed it would ultimately take comprehensive government legislation to deal with past and present failures. The PCEEO did not achieve a massive overhaul because it rarely exercised its broad enforcement powers to the fullest extent Executive Order #10925 outlined. By 1962, for example, the committee had issued only two cancellation notices to two companies, although it had received hundreds of complaints. In addition, most increases in black employment came directly through government agencies rather than private contractors. The PCEEO had received 1,413 grievances submitted against federal agencies, which resulted in 908 inquiries, and the committee moved on 665 of them. From there, 231 cases were deemed worthy of "corrective actions," and complaints were twice as likely to result in meaningful steps being taken compared to the previous decade. Before the committee started its work, blacks made up 12.6 percent of the federal workforce, though in low-paying jobs. Despite these positions being disproportionately semiprofessional, blacks represented 18 percent of "new federal hires." This number remained at 19 percent during Kennedy's presidency.[22]

One of Wheeler's primary goals was to improve employment practices of federal and state agencies, and he effectively used his position on the PCEEO to increase qualified black representation among the professional ranks. Soon after Kennedy created the committee, Wheeler sent letters to North Carolina senators Ervin and Jordan asking that they endorse an African American as an assistant US attorney for the Middle District, where William H. Murdock had been nominated as the US attorney. He also held conversations with John Seigenthaler, an administrative assistant to the attorney general, telling him it was his "understanding that Mr. Murdock has reacted favorably to the suggestion that a Negro be appointed as one of his assistants." Both Ervin and Jordan hesitated to endorse a candidate outright, a decision they couched in trite language about the attorney general having "absolute power" and discretion to appoint whomever he pleased to the position without consulting them. While this was true in a sense, Wheeler recognized that the state's two most powerful politicians were nervous about a backlash. He reminded them about the political mileage and "national prestige" they could get by supporting a black assistant US attorney, as their counterparts from neighboring Tennessee had. None of the names Wheeler initially put forward received the appointment, but another recommendation gained political traction. Henry E. Frye, a young black attorney from Greensboro, North Carolina, had graduated from the UNC Law School and founded a successful law practice. When Wheeler recommended him for assistant US attorney, he also submitted the name of Joseph C. Biggers for a deputy US marshal's position in Greensboro. Biggers had applied for the vacancy even before Wheeler recommended him. Wheeler believed that hiring blacks for such positions could potentially improve the judicial system and its treatment of blacks more generally.[23]

Both appointments remained in political stalemate for well over a year, into the fall of 1962, though state party officials had unofficially assured Frye and Biggers that their appointments were imminent. Wheeler had asked for an immediate announcement in spring 1961 because he and others were "convinced that a new and significant move in this direction will draw much less fire if the announcement of the appointment of Negro Assistant United States Attorney can be made" at the same time as all other assistant US attorney appointments, but to no end. While the official announcements lay in suspension, Wheeler worked tirelessly behind the scenes politically. Looking ahead to the November 7, 1961 election, he calculated the political impact that appointing African Americans would have on the Democratic Party's relationship with black voters in North Carolina and the South more broadly. He pleaded with the state and national Democratic Party establishment, including state chairman Bert Bennett, Senators Jordan and Ervin, Sanford, and Louis E. Martin, to make a swift announcement. Bennett was especially crucial behind the scenes in keeping the matter in the forefront politically. "It was going to be the one who pushes the hardest," he reminded Wheeler, "that gets the action here."[24]

While certainly pleased with these potential appointments, Wheeler was very critical of the snail's pace at which the Sanford administration moved on equal employment in the state. "Frankly," Wheeler told Sanford aide Hugh Cannon, "I find myself in the group of persons who feel the urgency for having the Governor demonstrate the kind of strong and positive leadership of which he is capable with considerably less concern for what the forces of reaction may think and do." He wrote to Louis E. Martin in confidence about his concerns and even considered taking the matter before the PCEEO. He worried that "Sanford's unusual fear of any progressive step and his lack of both courage and conviction concerning the need for aggressive action in order to insure fair play in matters of race [is] causing us [Democrats] to loose [*sic*] white as well as Negro votes."[25]

In the run-up to the 1962 election, Wheeler urged Attorney General Kennedy to make the Frye announcement because the "Democratic Party in North Carolina simply must have benefit of the prestige to be gained by prompt announcement." To this end, Wheeler believed the announcement had to be "dramatic" and come before the November 6 election. The political timing was critical because there had never been African Americans in these positions. But because the Kennedy administration had to deal with the Cuban Missile Crisis that October, all other considerations were temporarily sidelined. Thus, the official announcement that Henry E. Frye would be North Carolina's first black assistant US attorney did not come until late November. Frye was the sixth black assistant US attorney to be appointed in the South. After more political maneuvering, Joseph C. Biggers received his appointment as the first black assistant US marshal in North Carolina on February 18, 1963, nearly two years after the process began. Though Wheeler did not get the announcements before the elections, he succeeded in getting the persons he wanted for the positions. However, he was beginning to understand that despite his persistence, it was difficult and time-consuming to promote effective change in equal employment.[26]

He also wanted to ensure that the PCEEO was more forceful in getting government contractors to adhere to the executive order. He believed the white South, in particular, could not be left alone to implement policies effectively and that qualified black southerners had to be hired in administrative positions at all levels. During the PCEEO's first two years in existence, it was marred by the controversial Plans for Progress, an agreement fifty-two of the largest government contractors signed, volunteering to eliminate segregated facilities and train, recruit, and hire minority workers. Plans for Progress, which eventually maintained a separate office in Atlanta, morphed into a program in which companies submitted superficial compliance reports while escaping the full weight of compulsory compliance, in effect derailing the PCEEO's enforcement power.[27]

Wheeler's main contributions to the PCEEO came during its regular meetings, where he kept civil rights in the forefront of the committee's thinking. In at least two meetings early on, Wheeler voiced strong concerns that Plans for Progress was an attempt to hijack the PCEEO's intended objectives. After a December 1961 meeting, he told Secretary of Labor Arthur Goldberg that the program, directed by segregationist and Kennedy confidante Robert Batty Troutman, was "typical of the [delay] technique being used to nullify any serious effort to enforce the compliance features of [Executive] Order #10925." He also warned Goldberg that if the Committee showed too much leniency, they "may find [themselves] subject to public criticism while not being able to explain the reasons for failure." In a pivotal meeting about Plans for Progress in February 1962, Wheeler told those in attendance he feared it could "go off on a flier" and cautioned them that civil rights organizations would step up their opposition to Plans for Progress.[28]

In the following months, Wheeler's predictions came true as the NAACP's labor secretary, Herbert Hill, and executive secretary Roy Wilkins publicly criticized the PCEEO and its Plans for Progress. They both believed Troutman and his program gave businesses a free pass by allowing them to continue their lucrative relationship with the federal government while not taking any serious measures to deal swiftly with their discriminatory employment practices. In light of continued public criticism by the NAACP and other groups, Troutman became a political hindrance for Johnson, Kennedy, and the PCEEO. The developments further fueled the public debate over voluntary versus compulsory compliance, and they took attention away from where Vice President Johnson wanted it focused: on the PCEEO's entire program. A final straw came in June when the *New York Times* published a series of articles about the PCEEO's internal dispute and Troutman's firm support for voluntary compliance. The unwelcome public attention forced Troutman to resign by August 1962, at which point the PCEEO reorganized its day-to-day operations, with Hobart Taylor Jr., the group's legal counsel, now serving as the executive vice chairman. The PCEEO had received 819 individual complaints related to private contractors within a year, almost as many as its predecessor had received (1,042) in nearly eight years in existence. The PCEEO tossed 105 cases because the committee had no authority over them, and it had fully investigated some 291 cases against federal contractors by the first half of 1962, 108 of which the committee decided were "without cause." The committee required the offenders to take "corrective action" in the other 183 cases, and it had another 423 cases in need of investigation. The Plans for Progress report that Troutman shared with the PCEEO before his departure told a more positive narrative about the committee's work in this area. He had earlier projected a conservative figure of 1,200 jobs that he believed the program would help obtain. Thus, when the numbers revealed that participating Plans for Progress companies had hired 4,900 African Americans, it made the program seem more effective than it had actually been. The report said black employees were earning $20 million from these 4,900 jobs.[29]

Despite the changes the PCEEO made to its policies by 1963, reaffirming its "We Mean Business" stance regarding enforcement of Executive Order #10925, civil rights organizations continued to criticize Plans for Progress for its failures. In January 1963, for example, the SRC (with Wheeler as chairman of the executive committee) published a scathing special report titled *Plans for Progress: Atlanta Survey.* The exposé detailed the lack of progress being made in the city by companies that had signed

Plans for Progress pledges. The SRC report asked, "*Has employment of Negroes (and other minorities) increased, and have they been placed in non-traditional job categories?*" To answer the question, the SRC conducted field research and surveyed twenty-four of the original fifty-two companies that signed Plans for Progress pledges. The twenty-four companies surveyed had operations in Atlanta, where the SRC was based. The survey concluded that Plans for Progress did not translate into increased employment opportunities for blacks and other nonwhites in the South. Only three out of the twenty-four companies targeted "produced evidence of affirmative compliance with their pledges," and most companies had made little to no headway in dealing with employment discrimination. Although some companies had increased job opportunities, most were manufacturing rather than salaried or professional positions. Most of these companies saw Plans for Progress as a company-wide pledge with little relevance to operations in cities such as Atlanta or the South more broadly. Some managers of the Atlanta companies had made no attempts to address their pledges at all. Therefore, the report said, "indications are that the interpretation of the voluntary and affirmative provisions of the program is being left to the individual signers themselves."[30]

The public SRC report (written in part as a response to Troutman's report) alarmed the PCEEO's new executive vice chairman, Hobart Taylor Jr., who had no idea Wheeler was not only "a member of the Board of the Southern Regional Council" but the chairman of that board. Taylor also didn't know Wheeler had worked very closely with the SRC's executive director, Leslie Dunbar, on the organization's public policy agenda. It is extremely telling here that despite his position with the PCEEO, Wheeler did not keep the SRC from publishing its report. Clearly, his main objective was equal employment for blacks, and he understood that to achieve that goal it was necessary to put pressure on the PCEEO from all angles. As a result, Wheeler remained critical of the PCEEO and especially the employment situation in his home state. In one 1963 PCEEO meeting, Wheeler told a colleague that North Carolina would not be the best place to hold a PCEEO regional conference, which that colleague was organizing, because the state "may not be clean in many of its [employment] practices" and was "at present vastly overrated." While the SRC had its own limitations because it was never an "action-oriented" organization, as dictated by its constitution and bylaws, its research findings contributed significantly to public policy in the area of civil rights. Wheeler's involvement in the organization came precisely because it provided useful data (particularly on black education and employment), which he believed to be essential for the civil rights movement. At the same time, the SRC's *Atlanta Survey* compelled President Kennedy to demand that the PCEEO and several federal agencies look into the matters the report raised, which ultimately halted the rapid pace of Plans for Progress.[31]

The Battle for Equal Employment Opportunity in North Carolina

Inasmuch as Wheeler sought equal employment throughout the country through his membership on the PCEEO, he also used the appointment to seek better job opportunities for black North Carolinians. On April 29, 1961, shortly after being appointed to the PCEEO, Wheeler and the DCNA submitted their jobs blueprint to Sanford, imploring the governor to fulfill his New Day campaign promise by adding more black employees to state government. Wheeler led a delegation of DCNA members to Raleigh, where he personally delivered the jobs blueprint to the governor and met in a conference with other state Democratic Party leaders. Aside from the points previously mentioned, the blueprint also included better recruitment strategies in the North Carolina National Guard and a special appeal for state-operated hospitals to admit black patients and extend full staff privileges to black physicians. It also pointed to the "130 state administrative boards and commissions" where blacks had no representation. There were 1,100 such positions, 800 of which were gubernatorial appointments, yet the governor had only appointed eighteen African Americans.[32]

Wheeler's handiwork and views about economic rights could also be seen in a similar memorandum that the NCCHR sent to Sanford. Wheeler continued to serve on the NCCHR's executive committee, which drafted the memorandum. It reinforced the DCNA jobs blueprint by focusing on the state's need to compete with other regions for new industries and other areas of economic growth. The NCCHR asked the governor to immediately embark on a drastic overhaul of state-level employment because continued racial segregation would otherwise be an ongoing hindrance to the state's "economic health." The committee also urged the governor to reexamine the state's employment policies so as to set a positive example for private employers and major industries to follow. The memorandum pointed to the lack of black appointments, including black businesspeople such as Wheeler, to all-important bodies such as the Board of Conservation and Development. The NCCHR warned the governor if he didn't act, companies would be unwilling to expand into a state that did not extend first-class citizenship rights to everyone. The state had two alternatives, the memorandum concluded: "STAGNATION OF ITS ECONOMY . . . versus a state ON THE GO and fully competitive with the more progressive states of the Nation."[33]

In the meantime, by virtue of his new position on the PCEEO, Wheeler received countless requests from individuals in North Carolina and in other parts of the country to help them obtain federal employment or file complaints. "By your being appointed to the President's Committee," wrote Bert L. Bennett, "everyone in North Carolina expects you to push the button with immediate results." Carolyn Patricia Martin, a black graduate of the University of North Carolina and an employee at the black Stanford L. Warren Library in Durham, wrote to Wheeler in May for help in landing a job with the Library of Congress "because [she] read of [his] interest in helping qualified Negroes to secure employment in federal agencies." Wheeler promptly wrote a letter to Frank Reeves, special assistant to President Kennedy. Wheeler was more than willing to help Martin, especially considering her late father Dan B. Martin's "pioneering effort to stimulate voting activity among Negroes throughout the State of North Carolina."[34]

Although in this instance Wheeler was helping a friend's daughter, he responded similarly to persons with whom he had no personal connections, and his recommendations often proved effective. In August, Clarestene T. Stewart, whom Wheeler had also assisted, sent him an update on her position with the Internal Revenue Service in Greensboro. In September, David Stephens thanked Wheeler for his "kind recommendation" to the US Justice Department, which had trained Stephens to handle police brutality cases. "Those who [were] in the Civil Rights

Division," wrote Stephens, "particularly Mr. [Burke] Marshall and Mr. [Douglas H.] Hubbard [had] a great deal of respect for [Wheeler] as an individual and as [a] man of sound judgment." "It is this type of thing," continued Stephens, "that strikes the core of my heart and makes me proud to be a Carolinian."[35]

Other requests for Wheeler's help included complaints about discrimination from blacks already working in the federal government. For example, in July, Alonzo Eubanks outlined the treatment he faced from the human resources department as an employee at Durham's Veterans Affairs Hospital. Eubanks had accepted a low-grade post as a janitor, despite his qualifications as an electrician and military veteran. He followed the advice a human resources administrator gave him that "it would be better for [him] to try to get on in the housekeeping department or food service[,] though they were low paying jobs[,] so as to be on the campus when they got an opening in the electrical department." Then Eubanks "would have a better chance of being hired." The hiring agent also told Eubanks, "They did not call in people from the street when there was a person on campus that could do the job." Once a position opened in the electrical department, Eubanks interviewed for it but "never hear[d] any more about the job until Monday July 17 when [human resources] brought a man through showing him all the departments of the hospital." To Eubanks's disappointment, "They had hired a [white] man that was not on the campus and not in federal employment [already]." Eubanks felt overlooked unfairly since he was "a ten point preference veteran with a 90.5 rating for [work as an] electrician." Wheeler immediately forwarded Eubanks's complaint to the PCEEO's executive director, John Field. Field told Wheeler that once Eubanks confirmed that he had been discriminated against based on "race, creed, color, or national origin[,]" the committee would "take immediate action to have an investigation made." While Eubanks's concerns were taken seriously, it is not clear whether he ever received any remedy in the way of a better-paid position.[36]

Well into Sanford's term as governor, Wheeler continued to push him on equal employment in North Carolina by pointing to the same problems he had raised when the governor began his term in office. However, Wheeler recognized that he could not depend on the state alone to increase black employment. He believed southern states would take corrective action only if the president and Congress passed sweeping federal legislation. Even then, it would take constant pressure on local, state, and national leaders to enforce those changes. He also directed these renewed concerns at the National Guard. "We feel strong support," Wheeler told Sanford, with his patience worn thin, "for something more than mere token Negro membership in the North Carolina Guard." Wheeler also contacted the National Guard's Adj. Gen. Claude Bowers and expressed his frustration and disappointment with how few "Negro Personnel" were recruited to guard units across the state. He hoped Bowers and Sanford would do everything in their power "to remove one of the glaring sources of misunderstanding between the races of this State." Then, in the spring of 1963, Alonzo Reid, a black employee with ten years' experience working for the ESC's High Point office, filed a complaint with the Merit System Council (MSC) against the High Point office, claiming race-based discrimination when supervisors failed to promote him to an open management position after restructuring the division on an integrated basis in March. The MSC handled internal employment complaints against the ESC, and Reid appealed to Wheeler for legal assistance. Reid applied for two management positions with the Highpoint ESC, which required him to take two written examinations. He passed the exams with higher scores than did the two white men eventually promoted to the positions. Reid claimed his supervisors purposely snubbed him due to racial discrimination. Wheeler and attorney M. Hugh Thompson represented Reid at a July hearing. His supervisors stated that Reid did not receive a promotion because he was reprimanded in February and placed on six months' probation for breaking office rules by eating lunch at his desk, even though no one else was in the office. Wheeler later said the reprimand was based on "a trivial charge for violating a non-existent rule," which was "obviously open to serious question." Nevertheless, the Council met in closed-door deliberations and ruled in favor of the Highpoint ESC, citing a lack of evidence necessary for them to believe Reid was discriminated against on the basis of race.[37]

Wheeler was highly disappointed with the appeals process and complained to his colleagues at the PCEEO, which prompted an official investigation of the Highpoint ESC. Reid appealed to Wheeler again and noted that after the investigation, the Highpoint ESC "reverted [back] to [a] 'business as usual' procedure regarding the routing of nonwhite applicants for job referrals since [the investigators] have left the office." Reid wanted to find out from Wheeler if there would be disciplinary actions taken against the Highpoint ESC. "The office manager here," Reid Relayed to Wheeler, "was so upset by the investigation that it made him sick and he had to go back home this morning." As far as can be determined, no disciplinary actions were taken against the Highpoint ESC officials. As Reid explained to Jack Howard, assistant to the undersecretary at the Department of Labor, his own job situation improved, but many trainee positions were still not advertised to the general public. The person interviewing applicants for these positions continued to refer the best openings to white applicants. In mid-October, Howard traveled to North Carolina for a one-on-one meeting with Sanford and offered to meet with Wheeler and Reid to discuss in more detail the ESC situation in the Tar Heel State so he could hopefully "render a service that will result in greater opportunity for all people in North Carolina." Despite the Highpoint ESC investigation the previous year, in July 1964, just weeks after President Johnson signed the Civil Rights Act, Reid apparently gave up on getting fair treatment in the Highpoint office. He wrote to Wheeler stating his interest in finding employment elsewhere, at which point Wheeler pointed him to possible job openings with employment security in Washington, D.C. In this and similar matters, Wheeler's efforts yielded minor concessions but did not produce the kind of substantial changes that he deemed necessary to achieve equal employment in North Carolina. It ultimately took mass direct-action demonstrations in Durham and elsewhere in the spring of 1963, following sweeping protests in cities such as Birmingham, Alabama, before President Kennedy finally introduced civil rights legislation to Congress, which he did before his assassination on November 22.[38]

The High Point case underscored an even broader problem with eliminating equal employment barriers in the state. In adjacent Greensboro, for example, another experienced black ESC employee faced suspension because he did not inform his supervisors when he fell behind in processing employment applications for the black side of the office. The black side of the office did not have enough manpower to keep up with processing paperwork, as new hires in the previous decade had primarily been assigned to the white side. "The procedure adopted at High Point and at Greensboro," Wheeler believed, "represent a pattern for which it appears that the commission, in desegregating several of its North Carolina offices, seeks to avoid the promotion of qualified Negro employees to positions in which they will exercise supervision over both Negro and [w]hite personnel." In the Fayetteville ESC office, according to Wheeler, a black employee was transferred to the state ESC staff to keep him from receiving a management position in the local office, which would have otherwise made the individual a supervisor over an integrated staff.[39]

Similar examples occurred in Durham's municipal government. In 1964, city leaders refused to appoint NC Mutual executive James J. "Babe" Henderson, a vice president and treasurer of the company, as chairman of the Durham Housing Authority. As an inaugural member of the housing authority, Henderson had served since 1949 and in the field of public housing was "unquestionably the most competent and most experienced member of the organization." Louis E. Austin, the no-holds-barred editor of the black newsweekly the *Carolina Times,* declared, "Durham's greatest need" was to have the "type of leadership that [would] realize that Negroes no longer appreciate[d] nor [would] they accept or follow the kind of leadership that has only a master-slave or paternalistic attitude to offer." "Unless the white leadership," Austin continued "is willing to sit down on a man to man basis and talk in a spirit of equality [then] there is little hope that Durham [would] ever move forward in the direction of a better understanding between the races." To add insult to injury, during this same time the city's white power structure bypassed hiring its longtime black assistant recreation director (a twenty-year veteran) in favor of a younger, less experienced white man "fresh out of college" to head the city's entire recreation department. In these instances, there was no disputing the qualifications and experience of the black candidates.[40]

Between 1961 and 1964, Sanford made some strides toward the "Bright Sunshine of a New Day" for black North Carolinians, and Wheeler became a trusted adviser throughout the governor's term. Sanford appointed several black Americans to various boards, agencies, and commissions across the state during his first year in office. In July 1961, the governor appointed former Fayetteville State Teachers College president Dr. J. Ward Seabrook to the North Carolina ESC. By the end of September, there were another half dozen or so black appointments to the Welfare Board, Atomic Energy Commission, Prison Board, Board of Education, High School Drop-Out Committee, Commission on Post-High School Education, and on boards of trustees at several state colleges. Previously, only a few African Americans were serving in the latter capacity at several historically black colleges and universities across the state.[41]

Throughout 1962, Wheeler and other black leaders kept pressure on Sanford to deliver on his promises. Finally, as he entered his third year in office in a state where the chief executive was allowed only one term, Sanford took a bold step toward fulfilling his earlier promises. On January 18, 1963, he stood at the podium in the packed ballroom at the Carolina Inn on the campus of his alma mater, UNC. In a speech to the North Carolina Press Association's annual luncheon, he reflected on the one-hundredth anniversary of the Emancipation Proclamation. At a time when the civil rights movement daringly confronted the deeply rooted problems stemming from decades of racial and economic oppression, Sanford told the audience "now is the time in this hundredth year not merely to look back to freedom, but forward to the fulfillment of its meaning." "Despite this great progress," Sanford continued, "the Negro's opportunity to obtain a good job has not been achieved in most places across the nation. Reluctance to accept the Negro in employment is the greatest single block to his continued progress and to the full use of the human potential of the nation and its states."[42]

The speech pointed to the failures of states like North Carolina to live up to the principles of freedom, particularly the right to work for fair wages, outlined in the Emancipation Proclamation, and it announced Sanford's creation of the Good Neighbor Council to address issues of employment and education in local communities. He had appointed Wheeler and several other black leaders to serve on the council, and during a private breakfast meeting at the governor's mansion, Wheeler had insisted that the governor unveil his plan on the Emancipation Proclamation's anniversary because it had the potential to make freedom a reality for black North Carolinians. Sanford spoke along economic lines, declaring that "the time has come for American citizens . . . to give the Negro a full chance to earn a decent living for his family and to contribute to higher standards for himself and all men." He seemed more determined than ever to meet those principles and the ideals of a new generation because it "would be adding new economic growth for everybody." Sanford ended his daring speech by saying: "We can do this. We should do this. We will do this because we are concerned with the problems and the welfare of our neighbors." In addition to creating the Good Neighbor Council, Sanford later signed a bill aimed at eliminating racial barriers in the National Guard. The state still had a long way to go before it could claim victory on equal employment. Sanford did not drastically alter the state employment policies or do so in ways black leaders such as Wheeler imagined, and only a minority of blacks benefited from these actions. However, Sanford's actions represented a step in the right direction.[43]

Kennedy, Johnson, and the Southern Regional Council

Wheeler's efforts and influence at the national level regarding public policy developments did not stop with the PCEEO or the issue of equal employment. While he wasted little time beginning his work with the PCEEO, he simultaneously received an opportunity to address voting rights with the Kennedy administration's backing. On July 28, 1961, Wheeler and Leslie Dunbar attended a monumental meeting hosted by Audrey and Stephen Currier's Taconic Foundation, which had decided to fund a special program to increase voter registration, particularly among blacks in the South. The idea to focus specifically on voter registration came from the Justice Department, another example of the Kennedy administration following the SRC's *Federal Executive and Civil Rights* report. A discussion about voting rights may have also been the subject of the earlier off-the-record meeting with the administration in early March 1961 around the passage of Executive Order #10925. The Taconic meeting proved to be a circuitous way for the Kennedy administration to demonstrate its seriousness about civil rights. The Kennedy administration also wanted to avoid further Freedom Rides because the violence around them looked disastrous for the president from an international perspective. The administration may have been trying to sideline the Freedom Riders by focusing attention on voting, which was seen as less confrontational. Alongside Dunbar and Wheeler, the Taconic Foundation invited leaders from the major national civil rights organizations to attend the meeting in New York at the Foundation's offices.[44]

Wheeler's participation in the Taconic meeting reflected his high standing among the national civil rights leadership. He and Dunbar sat in a room alongside key figures of the national civil rights movement: Marion Barry and Charles McDew represented SNCC; Dr. Martin Luther King Jr. and Wyatt T. Walker represented SCLC; Roy Wilkins represented the NAACP; Lester Granger and Whitney M. Young Jr. represented NUL; James Farmer represented CORE; Timothy Jenkins represented the National Students Association (NSA); and Thurgood Marshall and Robert L. Carter represented the LDF. Other attendees included Stephen Currier, Burke Marshall, Harold Fleming, and Kennedy's civil rights advisor, Harris Wofford. Wheeler's attendance pleased Dunbar because the banker was an "enormous help to [him] in that [Dunbar] was a new boy, and [he'd] never met most of these people . . . and it just made life bearable that John Wheeler sat beside [him]" as "John had a lot of stature with the civil rights leadership at that time in New York." However, unlike many leaders representing their respective national organizations, Wheeler's closely rooted involvement in issues at the local and state levels, through his DCNA chairmanship as well as other civic responsibilities, helped guide his commitment to provide a voice to local organizations at meetings like this one.[45]

Wheeler told the group about the SRC's willingness to help as "the executive committee regard[ed] [the] matter as urgent." He noted the "SRC used consultants with great success in school desegregation; wisdom and value of their use in voting drives [needed] to be considered." Dunbar added to Wheeler's comments and offered the SRC's research resources and, more importantly, its administrative support. A few spokespersons detailed their own expertise when it came to voter registration, which they believed gave them a greater advantage over the others. NAACP executive secretary Roy Wilkins spoke most directly to the latter point, saying that the "NAACP [was] more active in this field than any other organization. Since January, 1958 it has had established a Southwide [voter registration] Campaign."[46]

The group also discussed the most efficient way for the Taconic Foundation to distribute funds to assist all organizations with major voter registration drives across the South. Toward the end of the daylong meeting, Dr. King suggested "entrusting the SRC with the central project role." The organizations agreed that the SRC would oversee the program, and, according to Dunbar, he and Wheeler "both sensed that this agreement was genuine. Indeed, [Dunbar] was deeply impressed by the amiability and harmony of the gathering." At a second meeting on August 23, the group asked the SRC to draft a comprehensive plan for cooperative action. Afterward, the SRC promptly sent a memorandum to the organizations explaining how it would administer the voter registration project. The plan outlined that each organization would request funding through a formal application to the SRC. The SRC would then approve or reject applications based on predetermined criteria.[47]

During all subsequent meetings Wheeler and Dunbar emphasized that the SRC's involvement with the project depended on their understanding that the SRC would not be "a mere conduit" and "reserved [their] rights to distribute money to other groups" beyond the six who had attended the Taconic meetings. Dunbar explained that giving money to local groups "was not what Wilkins, King, Young, [and others] had in mind. They resisted that very strongly." "They had in mind," Dunbar remembered, "that VEP [the Voter Education Project, as it came to be known] would get a chunk of money, and [the SRC] would then meet and decide how [they] could divide it up among them, and that was it. [But the SRC] didn't do that." In its written plan, the SRC reiterated that "effective registration work [might] depend not only on the work of [the national civil rights] agencies, but on that of local voters' leagues, churches, Urban Leagues, local ad hoc groups, etc. Consequently, such local groups should be eligible to receive funds and services from the Project." This meant that even Wheeler's local organization, the DCNA, could apply for funding, and it eventually did. In this instance, Wheeler maneuvered to achieve certain objectives and made calculated decisions to ensure that these initiatives trickled down to local communities, all the while helping to influence local interests.[48]

Even as he devoted himself to the PCEEO and toward increased voter registration in the South, Wheeler used his rising political clout with the Kennedy and Sanford administrations to confront discriminatory policies in North Carolina's segregated public facilities. In October 1961, as

President Kennedy was set to deliver the UNC's Founder's Day address (in part because Sanford had supported him during the presidential election), Wheeler contacted Sanford with major concerns. Did Kennedy know, he asked, that the airport where he would soon arrive still had segregated restroom facilities? Simultaneously, a group of NCC students contacted Kennedy directly and urged him not to come. Sanford quickly understood Wheeler's position and assigned a top aide to handle the matter before it escalated. Kennedy's assistant John Seigenthaler suggested that unless Sanford and his people found an agreeable solution, the president would have to pass on the visit. By the time the president arrived, the airport had reluctantly agreed to take down the restroom doors to avoid the "black" and "white" sign designations. As Wheeler sat in the audience as an invited guest to hear Kennedy's October 12 speech, he undoubtedly celebrated these minor steps toward civil rights.[49]

In late October, a month after the SRC sent out its memorandum about the voter registration project, it had received only one or two responses from civil rights groups. As a result, Stephen Currier expressed "unhappiness" at the delay and considered abandoning the idea. The slow responses also received criticism from Louis Lomax, the earliest black television journalist. In 1959, Lomax had given America its first look at the Nation of Islam and its outspoken representative, Malcolm X, in a five-part documentary he coproduced with Mike Wallace, *The Hate That Hate Produced*. Lomax had a reputation for being very critical of the traditional black leadership who, he explained, after the 1960 sit-ins, were "not too pleased to see young Negro students sit down at the conference table with Southern white city officials." Lomax described the student sit-in movement as "the Negro Revolt" but also argued that it was "more than a revolt against the white world. It [was] also a revolt of the Negro masses against their own leadership and goals." In recognizing the urgency of the voter registration project, Lomax attacked these organizations and their leaders in a radio address for their failure to "proceed with all speed and clarity to examine and ratify an offer that [would] aid the Negro in his eternal battle against bigotry." A full transcript of the address found in Wheeler's personal papers suggests that Wheeler might have tipped Lomax off with details of the voter registration project months in advance. Perhaps Wheeler was making a subtle attempt to pressure civil rights organizations into moving forward with the voter registration project before it was too late. Wheeler saw the voter registration project as an important opportunity for black Americans. Lomax pointed to organizational competition as a major barrier, saying that once organizations succeeded in doing a good job in one area, "somehow they become drunk with the wine of their own being."[50]

Lomax shed light on the biggest holdup for Wilkins and the NAACP, the last organization to respond to the SRC memorandum. Wilkins explained that the NAACP's experience in voter registration far exceeded that of the other organizations, "some of which . . . have little more than good intentions to offer" and would "be taken to imply equality as regards their relative importance and potential in the work to be done." Wilkins especially described the NAACP's experience in working with local organizations and "found that funds advanced to them are not uncommonly of little value unless their projects are closely supervised." Wilkins explained that the SRC should instead allocate all the funds to national civil rights organizations and none to local organizations. This would be better because, "in [their] opinion[,] these agencies [would] be in a better position than the SRC to evaluate particular local groups." Dunbar warned Joseph Haas, the SRC's legal counsel, that they "must keep an eye on the long haul, not chiefly on the preliminaries. The N.A.A.C.P. is being sticky now; over the long period [Dunbar] expect[ed] it will be the least of [their] headaches." Although Wilkins provided a long list stipulating his organization's terms in participating in the voter registration project, Dunbar believed that disagreements over local organizations could cause "real difficulty." However, he "hope[ed] [they] could, at least, agree to disagree." When Dunbar and the SRC sent in their official funding request to the Taconic Foundation for $250,000 for the "Citizenship Education Project," they noted the importance of having the full cooperation of the NAACP because they could not move forward without it. By the end of October, all of the organizations, with the exception of the NSA, responded to the earlier SRC memorandum and agreed to the guidelines.[51]

Despite the rival politics of the national civil rights organizations, the voter registration project was set. In January 1962, Dr. King, Wilkins, Young, Farmer, and McDew announced in a combined press conference their cooperation in a major two-year national voter registration drive. The SRC hired Wiley A. Branton, a civil rights lawyer who gained recognition in 1957 as legal counsel for the Little Rock Nine, as the first VEP director. Despite the competition among them, the organizations had ultimately found common ground in cooperation with President Kennedy, the Justice Department, and a philanthropic foundation and had agreed to work toward the major goal of increased voter registration. Wheeler had again played a prominent role in bringing about a development that brought closer his objective of New South prosperity. Administering VEP became the single largest and most important role the SRC played during the 1960s. It also crystallized the SRC's impact on the civil rights movement.[52]

When the SRC received its first round of funds for VEP in March 1962, one of the first local civil rights organizations to submit a proposal was the DCNA, another clear outcome of Wheeler's public policy influence and negotiations at the national level. As chairman of the SRC's executive committee, Wheeler worked closely with Leslie Dunbar as the SRC prepared itself to oversee VEP. In this position, Wheeler had the leverage to ensure that his organization received funding from VEP in May 1962, just in time for Durham's citywide elections. The DCNA received $2,500 for programs designed to meet registration deadlines. That same year, Durham also had a major bond issue on the ballot, which, if passed, would provide funding for the city's part of a $12 million urban renewal project that had been in the planning stages since 1958 (see chapter 6). Wheeler was also the only black member on the Durham Redevelopment Commission, the group formed by the city to manage the urban renewal program. Without support from most of the city's black community, the bond referendum stood to fail. The DCNA had many of its members on volunteer committees whose main roles were to help garner support for the urban renewal bond referendum. The bond issue had larger implications related to increased black economic empowerment with the added possibility of reopening the entire marketplace for black business as well. Throughout VEP's existence, Wheeler and the DCNA could always count on receiving grants for voter registration drives.[53]

Wheeler had worked from various angles and through several organizations (including the DCNA, the NCCHR, and the SRC) to press the issue of equal employment and voting rights both inside and outside the Tar Heel State. He directly influenced how Sanford responded to calls to hire more African Americans in state government. If Wheeler and others had not pressed the Sanford administration early on to improve employment opportunities for blacks, it is doubtful whether Sanford would have tackled these issues seriously prior to 1964. Because Wheeler relied on institutional and organizational support, he was limited in what he could accomplish. Some might view him as too beholden to these established structures. But Wheeler "liked the Southern Regional Council," explained former VEP executive director Vernon E. Jordan Jr., because it was "an organization based in research and the research that it did, it dispensed throughout the South and it helped people think about the issues in ways that they had not thought about issues before." If one "were going to be an advocate," continued Jordan, "you had to have information, and your information had to be accurate and right . . . [and] this advocacy and research by the Council had impact."[54]

On August 28, 1963, civil rights activists and their respective organizations gathered in the nation's capital for the March on Washington for Jobs and Freedom, which was a key turning point in the ongoing battle for civil rights. They came to pressure Congress to finally pass sweeping civil rights legislation. It was not until a year later that President Johnson, former PCEEO chairman, signed into law the Civil Rights Act of 1964, which rendered employment discrimination illegal on the basis of "race, color, religion, sex, or national origin." Wheeler served on the newly formed EEOC on a transitional basis (as a holdover from the PCEEO) until it began officially on July 2, 1965. While the Civil Rights Act placed African Americans at the threshold of freedom, democracy, and full citizenship, black business leaders like Wheeler also had a role, providing unheralded leadership at a transformative moment in the history of North Carolina and the South. Such leaders kept economic concerns at the center of their civil rights activism and recognized the relevance of economic issues to the success and advancement of the postwar New South. In 1964, Wheeler became the first black delegate to represent North Carolina at the Democratic National Convention (DNC). The official delegates and alternates—about 120 African Americans overall—came from twenty-two states in what newspapers around the country reported as the largest group of blacks to attend a major party convention. In civil rights history, the 1964 DNC is remembered not so much for President Johnson's nomination alongside running mate Hubert H. Humphrey, but for the controversy over state political representation in Deep South states such as Mississippi. Conversely, Wheeler's appointment represented black political power coming full circle in his home state.[55]

6

Urban Renewal and the Prospects of a Free and Open Society

> Southern cities which have not already begun, through adequate planning, to provide the means for developing a completely open housing market may find within a relatively short period that their efforts to eliminate bias and discrimination in the housing field will be too little and too late to prevent the eruption of massive protests by Negroes whose opportunities for better schooling and upgraded employment are stymied by customs and practices which prevent their escape from slums and ghettos.
>
> John Hervey Wheeler, 1964

Urban renewal came to the "Capital of the Black Middle Class" in the mid-1960s, and many Durham residents still blame Wheeler and other influential black business leaders for "selling out the black community" and causing the demise of the once-thriving Hayti neighborhood. Once the dust settled and the smoke cleared after the bulldozers demolished homes and businesses, activist Rubye Gattis noted many years later, the two remaining landmarks were the St. Joseph's AME Church and the local M&F Bank Branch, both located on Fayetteville Street and both dear to Wheeler. In her mind it was no coincidence that while most black residents could not escape being displaced from urban renewal areas, black power brokers like Wheeler could pick and choose what they considered worth preserving. Wheeler was treasurer of St. Joseph's, a member of its board of trustees, and even sang in the choir; he had also been a lay member on the AME Church's national body. In other words, Gattis said, not everyone paid a price for urban renewal.[1]

She is not alone in her assessment. During the mid-1960s, Gattis was the president of the newly formed black United Organizations for Community Improvement (UOCI), a coalition among Durham public housing councils that strove to confront housing discrimination, among other issues. Today—over a half century later—any mention of urban renewal to most of Durham's black residents old enough to remember "How Hayti Lived and Played" would be like rubbing salt into still unhealed wounds—ultimately the tragic loss of community. Others besides Gattis considered the city's black leaders to have sold them a "'bill of goods.'" From this perspective, Wheeler and other leaders misled black Durham about what urban renewal would offer Hayti and may have been motivated by greed and financial gain. The city's urban renewal program was promoted as "a chance to bloom," one longtime resident said. In practice, however, it became a farce and an unfortunate reality dubbed "Negro Removal."[2]

This chapter examines urban renewal in Durham during the 1960s as an example of the shortcomings of black business activism. Wheeler continually asserted that black business could expand within the framework of urban renewal, which he said offered an opportunity for "reentrance" into the mainstream American economy. He supported and worked for urban renewal because he believed the black community could benefit from it, and he promoted it as a remedy for public policy that had for so long neglected the community and caused such widespread suffering. The chapter also looks at how urban renewal in Durham was connected with development of the state's Research Triangle Park (RTP). The East-West Expressway (known today as Highway 147 or the Durham Freeway), built to connect RTP to the University of North Carolina, Duke University, and North Carolina State University, plowed through the heart of Hayti and other areas in its path. Urban renewal in black Durham was thus entwined with economic agendas well beyond the affected neighborhoods. Before his death in 1978, Wheeler himself came to doubt whether urban renewal had created an open society unhampered by racial and economic inequality.

The blame placed on Wheeler—during the 1960s and now—for his role in Durham's urban renewal is understandable given the level of his involvement. He held an appointment on the Durham Redevelopment Commission (DRC), the body tasked with overseeing Durham's urban renewal program, and became its chairman during the 1970s. He attended countless behind-the-scenes planning sessions about urban renewal in

Hayti. In the black community, Wheeler was urban renewal's number-one champion. When urban renewal began, the DCNA wielded significant power over the local black vote and was very active on the civil rights front as well. The organization, which Wheeler chaired, gave overwhelming political support to Durham's urban renewal program. By 1960, 68 percent of eligible blacks (more than 58,000 people) were registered to vote, and the DCNA's political bloc included more than 13,000 votes, or roughly 22 percent of the total black registration. Between 1949 and 1967, the DCNA's endorsees had received 85 percent of black voter support at the all-black precincts in all but two contested two-man elections. The black electorate proved instrumental when city leaders needed a bond referendum passed to pay for the federally backed urban renewal program. By the late 1950s, the direct-action phase of the civil rights movement was in full swing and black business and political leaders such as Wheeler found themselves in a position to demand more from the white power structure, or so it seemed.[3]

As Durham's urban renewal program continued and its lopsided outcome became evident, Wheeler became somewhat disillusioned. Vivian Rogers Patterson, M&F Bank's former corporate secretary, remembered "a lot of people were upset with Mr. Wheeler about [how] urban renewal [turned out]." Wheeler expressed some misgivings when Chapel Hill mayor Howard N. Lee contemplated that city's version of an urban renewal program. In 1969, Lee became the first black mayor elected in a predominantly white southern town and came to know Wheeler through state Democratic Party channels. Lee explained that "I did go to Wheeler . . . and I tried to learn from the Durham experience. . . . I think in fairness, as [Wheeler] looked back, he recognized that the urban renewal project was not serving the future of Durham's black community well."[4] Furthermore:

> When [Wheeler] was making those decisions [he] thought that the black businesses both on Parrish Street and on the other streets in and around Durham . . . would benefit. And I think he really believed that there would be a new crop of housing, affordable housing that would be developed. And when it turned out, the city just didn't move it in that direction. I think he felt [that] some people had actually hung him out to dry and then he

> became the target of black criticism, of destroying the black community in part. So when I was thinking about urban renewal versus redevelopment [for Chapel Hill], he suggested that I not follow the Durham model, and I didn't.[5]

In cities throughout the South, local and state leaders took advantage of federal funding and planned redevelopment programs that left similar marks of devastation in black communities in the name of New South prosperity. In most instances, major interstates replaced the once-proud and thriving black urban centers with little, if any, revitalization. In North Carolina, black communities in Charlotte, Winston-Salem, Greensboro, Salisbury, Greenville, and Highpoint faced ruin at the hands of urban renewal. In other states, long-standing black communities in the largest cities suffered significant losses as well, including Norfolk, Atlanta, Savannah, Miami, Birmingham, Louisville, Lubbock, Nashville, Memphis, Knoxville, Chattanooga, Little Rock, and New Orleans.[6]

"Outlook for Durham": Planning for Urban Renewal

The early stages of Durham's urban renewal program began with federal legislation enacted a few years after World War II. The passage of the Housing Act of 1949 by the US Congress "marked another milestone," explained Wheeler, "in our effort to meet the present and future needs of our cities, many of which found themselves still unable to cope successfully with rapidly spreading blight, congestion, and fiscal problems occasioned by stagnation of the center-city." The new housing legislation addressed problems spawned by overcrowded living conditions and unleashed government resources to assist local authorities in redeveloping decayed slums in urban areas. These resources included financing for low-cost housing developments, and cities around the nation submitted applications for federal dollars for those purposes. That same year Dan K. Edwards won Durham's mayoral election after an endorsement by the Voters for Better Government (VBG)—the labor coalition that included the DCNA—and he soon submitted a request to take part in the new government subsidies. The city then established the Durham Housing Authority (DHA) to oversee low-income public housing developments approved by the city council. The council appointed DCNA treasurer Babe Henderson, the NC Mutual treasurer and founder of the black Durham Business and Professional Chain (DBPC), as the only black member on the agency's board. Henderson, a native of Bristol, Tennessee, came to Durham in 1932 and worked for the Bankers Fire Insurance Company until 1937, when he took a position with the NC Mutual.[7]

During the early 1950s, Durham completed its first crop of public housing projects. In 1953, the city finished construction on a low-income housing complex it called Few Gardens. A year later, the housing authority opened the McDougald Terrace Public Housing Development for blacks, which it named in honor of the late M&F Bank cashier Richard L. McDougald. As previously discussed, McDougald had pushed for affordable housing for blacks in Durham and became the motivating force behind the bank's home loan program for returning World War II veterans. After the war, the FHA and other New Deal–era lending institutions were reorganized under the Housing and Home Finance Agency (HHFA), the predecessor of the Department of Housing and Urban Development (HUD). Wheeler took pride in M&F Bank's role in financing affordable housing for blacks, and he carried that ideal forward when he took the helm of the institution in 1952. During the 1960s, Congress continued to pass legislative measures to bolster housing policies, and the idea of community restoration gained significant traction as well. The major problem became enforcement, as with other laws passed by the federal government during this time.[8]

Wheeler consistently linked issues of unfair housing for blacks to employment and educational rights. In late 1956, he accepted an appointment to the national Commission on Race and Housing, where he replaced the deceased Dr. Charles S. Johnson, Fisk University president and SRC executive committee member since 1944. Robert C. Weaver, the first HUD secretary and first black cabinet member, served on the commission alongside Wheeler. The Commission on Race and Housing was an independent citizens' group created in 1955, financially supported by the Fund for the Republic, to examine racial discrimination in housing affecting minorities in the United States. In 1958, having completed a three-year study, the commission made extensive recommendations to housing agencies at the federal, state, and local levels. It advised the federal government to enact legislation and policies to make housing more accessible to middle- and low-income minorities and to create a nonsegregated "free housing market."[9]

Wheeler considered open housing fundamental to achieving freedom of movement, an essential component of his vision of New South prosperity. He told the SRC's president, James McBride Dabbs, that fair housing practices were "especially desirable because [open] housing is more often than not, the key to equal job opportunities." In 1959, Wheeler spoke to a group of real estate brokers in Cleveland, Ohio, about his work with the Commission on Race and Housing, saying: "We have developed a new consciousness and concept that the right to a job is a legal right. . . . It appears that we are now on the threshold of adopting a new concept that free and unrestricted access to the total housing market is also a legal right." To Wheeler, these connections were clear, and his service on the commission further exposed him to the broader problems related to fair housing throughout the country. By this time, he was more convinced than ever of the role fair housing would have on an open society, and he carried these considerations into his thoughts on urban renewal.[10]

Throughout the 1950s, Durham made further plans to improve the city's infrastructure and to make itself a more desirable place to live in the face of suburbanization. As an article in the *Durham Morning Herald* noted, suburbanization was siphoning city taxpayers and consumers from the downtown commercial district. In August 1954, while Americans focused on the recent *Brown* decision, Congress passed a new Housing Act to supplement the measure passed in 1949. The new act stated in part that "major emphasis [would be on] urban renewal—embracing the eradication and prevention of slums and urban blight—and coordinated application of federal aid. To further this new emphasis, local communities, as a condition for receiving federal assistance for slum clearance and urban renewal, low-rent public housing, and certain new FHA-insured mortgage programs, are required to develop and put into operation a workable program, approved by the Housing Administrator, utilizing all means available to eliminate and prevent slums and urban blight." The additional housing legislation not only dealt with "renewal" and "development" but also promoted "conservation" and "rehabilitation" in blighted areas. The measure allowed for commercial zoning alongside residential development and included provisions to do away with discrimination in public housing. In 1957, the North Carolina General Assembly passed a bill to allow cities to pursue federal funding for urban renewal programs. In response, Durham's city planner, Paul Brooks, commissioned UNC's City and Regional Planning Department to investigate the prospects for an urban renewal program. The group released a written report that spring, highlighting several major areas it believed to be most suitable for urban renewal. The report, *Outlook for Durham,* targeted the city's central areas adjacent to downtown. It identified the Hayti neighborhood because of dilapidated housing, poor infrastructure, and other problems that strained city resources while contributing little to its tax base. The *Outlook for Durham* authors subsequently participated in several public presentations regarding their study. In February 1958, for example, the black DBPC sponsored a meeting with the group so the "[black] business men and citizens of Hayti may become acquainted with the aims and purpose of Urban Renewal." At the meeting, attendees also discussed "the ways in which this city's urban renewal program . . . can and should be used to end segregation in housing."[11]

By December 1958, Durham's leaders formed the Durham Redevelopment Commission (DRC) to manage the city's urban renewal process. Wheeler received an appointment to the five-member committee, which also included Duke University law professor Robinson Oscar Everett (chairman), J. E. Irvine (vice chairman), R. G. Hurst, and J. G. Glass, all of whom were white. Without question, Wheeler's appointment to the DRC provided a semblance of racial inclusion among the decision-makers, and his appointment also assured the DRC of the DCNA's political support, as the targeted urban renewal area was Durham's Hayti section. But Wheeler's housing and public policy credentials meant his appointment went beyond simple tokenism. In a few cities throughout the state—Raleigh, Greensboro, Winston-Salem, and Charlotte—leaders had already received about $4 million in federal funds to help with their urban renewal plans. As the DRC took steps toward obtaining federal funds, urban renewal gained traction in black Durham. In a January 1959 poll of the *Carolina Times* newspaper staff about the top twenty-five events from the previous year, urban renewal came in second only to the pending school desegregation suit, *McKissick v. Durham* (1959). "If the plan for redeveloping sections of the Pettigrew street–Fayetteville street sector materializes," the newspaper forecasted, "a vast and dramatic change will come to the section and its thousands of residents. It would relocate most of the businesses and destroy the slums in the area, a change whose side effects could possibl[y] bring about a change in the community's mores."[12]

In the meantime, the DRC submitted its urban renewal application to the Federal Urban Redevelopment Commission based in Atlanta. In addition to an initial $1 million for its first project, the Durham group asked for $42,000 in start-up costs to devise a detailed and comprehensive urban renewal proposal. With the *Outlook for Durham* study as the blueprint, and city planner Paul Brooks as the DRC's acting executive director, Durham seemed confident about its plans for the future. (Ben T. Perry III, a housing administrator with the HHFA, would accept the executive director's post on a permanent basis in 1961.) In October 1959, after the DRC had been awaiting approval for most of the year, Paul Brooks asked for Wheeler's help getting "an early approval" under the Republican-led Eisenhower administration. Wheeler immediately contacted NC Mutual president Asa T. Spaulding, saying, "Whatever you do toward having Mr. [Val J.] Washington push this matter for us will be appreciated." In turn, Spaulding sent word to Val Washington, the black director of minorities for the Republican National Committee, asking for his help and pointing out that the urban renewal funds would go toward "improving a black neighborhood." Spaulding, himself a lifelong Republican and president of the NC Mutual since 1958, held significant influence nationally. By month's end, Durham's urban renewal application was approved. The approval came at an opportune time, as the federal government had made changes to its overall urban renewal policies in September, dropping a clause that stipulated families displaced by urban renewal had to be relocated to specific housing areas according to race.[13]

The DRC made its plans for urban renewal public in the spring of 1961. In the context of the sit-in movement and freedom rides that had recently taken place, blacks had been demanding a greater share of public resources, and urban renewal came as a possible solution to conditions made worse by racial discrimination. The proposed "Hayti–Elizabeth Street Renewal Area" plan was an ambitious ten-year urban renewal program to

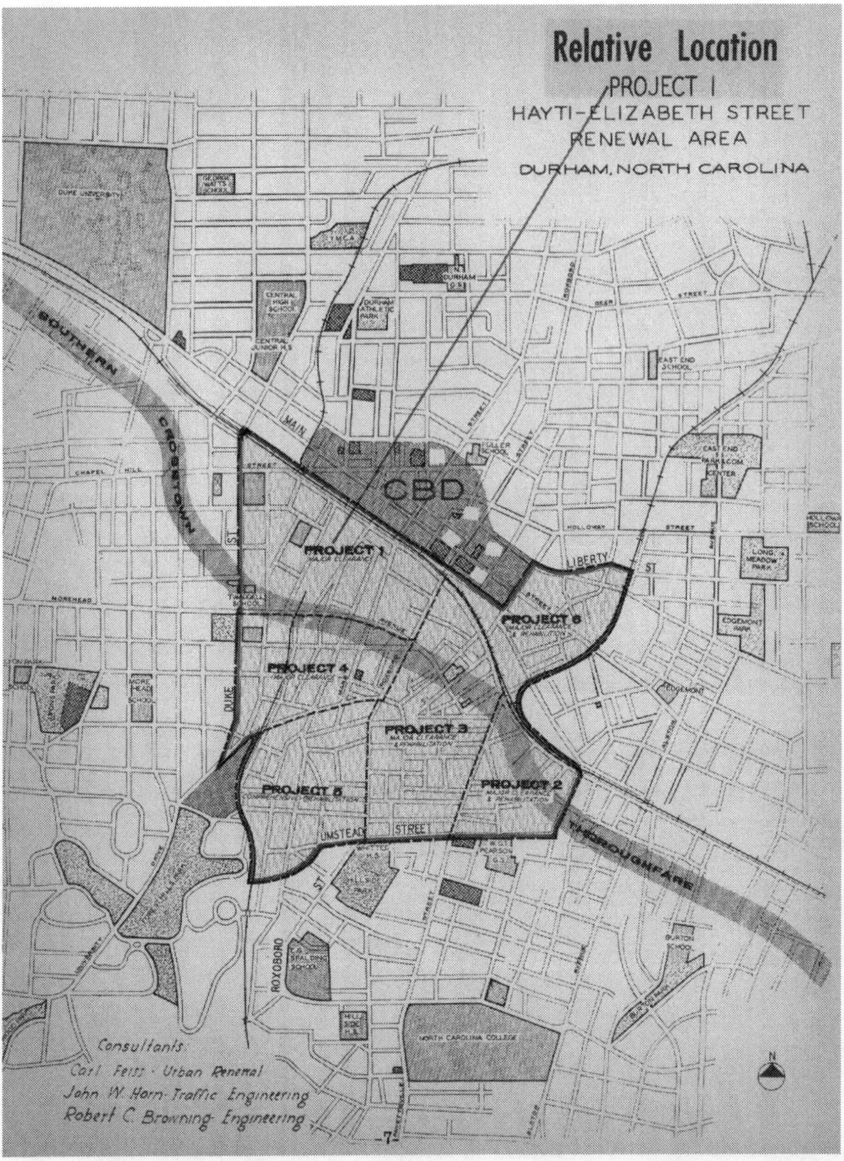

The image highlights "Project I" of the proposed Hayti–Elizabeth Street Renewal Area. The ambitious ten-year urban renewal program was to be completed in six separate projects comprising five hundred acres. It included provisions for the construction of a major $6.5 million thoroughfare, the "East-West Expressway," directly through the center of the designated Hayti clearance area. Durham had the responsibility to pay $1 million of that figure. Courtesy of the Durham Urban Renewal Records, Durham County Public Library.

be completed in six separate projects comprising five hundred acres. It included provisions for the construction of a major $6.5 million thoroughfare, the "East-West Expressway," directly through the center of the designated Hayti clearance area. Durham had the responsibility to pay $1 million of that figure. The projected expenditures for the entire urban renewal program came to approximately $18 million, two-thirds to be covered by the federal government and the other third ($4.5 million) by Durham.

The city leaders decided to ask voters to approve an $8.6 million bond issue to cover its share of urban renewal costs and improvements to the city's overall infrastructure. From an economic standpoint, the city's black financial institutions stood to conduct a good portion of business related to virtually every aspect of the urban renewal process.[14]

As the DRC moved forward with its agenda, it embarked on an aggressive citywide publicity campaign. In March 1961, for example, Wheeler and the DRC's executive director, Ben Perry, attended a meeting in Hayti alongside forty black leaders to organize citizen advisory committees. At the meeting, two subcommittees formed with the idea they would have some input when it came to planning and developing the Hayti–Elizabeth Street Renewal Area. More importantly, advisory committees had the responsibility to provide the citizens most affected by urban renewal with up-to-date information about various aspects of the process. At that meeting, twenty-eight DCNA members were appointed to advise on the first two projects of the six slated for the Hayti–Elizabeth Street Renewal Area. Similar advisory committees would be appointed later for the remaining four projects. Additionally, Durham mayor Mutt Evans established a forty-eight-member citywide advisory committee. The DRC and other city leaders used the citywide committee and the local subcommittees to inform Durham's general public, especially black Durham, about the advantages of the urban renewal program and to field questions from concerned citizens. An educational pamphlet that detailed the entire urban renewal program aided the advisory committees in explaining the program, but little was shared about its potential drawbacks. On the whole, the publicity campaign proved effective in helping the urban renewal program receive favorable backing from Durham's black community in the beginning. At this early juncture, there was very little pushback, if any, in Hayti.[15]

DURHAM'S first step - - -

Durham's first Urban Renewal action is in the *Hayti-Elizabeth Street Area* which covers about 500 acres and contains almost 10,000 people. A plan called the General Neighborhood Renewal Plan has been prepared for this area. This plan shows new streets and land uses and divides the area into six projects. It is estimated that all of the projects will be completed in ten years.

The total cost of the renewal action will be about $18 million. Sale of the land will bring approximately $6 million, leaving a net project cost of $12 million. Durham's share of this net cost is about $4 million.

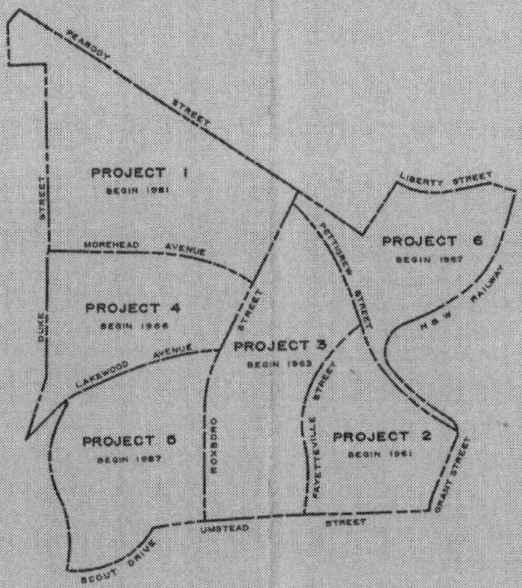

An educational pamphlet that detailed the entire urban renewal program aided the advisory committees in explaining the program in its entirety to citizens. Courtesy of the Durham Urban Renewal Records, Durham County Public Library.

It was not until a controversial commercial zoning order surfaced in the spring of 1961 that organized opposition arose. In April, the City Planning and Zoning Commission passed a proposed four-acre shopping center in a section of Hayti scheduled for clearance. Abe Greenberg, a wealthy white real estate developer, had proposed the shopping center and planned to ask the zoning commission to expand his initial four-acre request to twenty-two acres. In June, the DBPC raised serious objections about the new zoning request, noting it was in direct conflict with a similar proposal that the DRC itself had made for the same area. The DRC planned to sell about twenty-five acres in the renewal area to private developers with the contractual obligation that they use the land for a shopping center. Moreover, under the DRC's deal black businesses already in Hayti, including those that would be uprooted temporarily as a result of urban renewal, would have first priority for retail space in the center. It was probable, too, that the DRC would sell to an investment group formed through the DBPC, which had organized the Chain Investment Corporation in anticipation of the DRC's shopping center.[16]

The DBPC not only questioned Greenberg's shopping center but also balked at his new acreage request. In a letter to the local newspapers, DBPC president Floyd B. McKissick explained, "Survival of our membership businesses that will be forced to relocate under the urban renewal program is at stake." The DBPC worried that the Hayti community would be unable to support two shopping centers and that the proposed Greenberg shopping center would deter future economic development. The DBPC petitioned the city council to "delay or deny rezoning requests" so that a market analysis could be completed to predict with more accuracy whether two proposed shopping centers serving the same area could enjoy profitability. They said the Greenberg deal raised the issue of "fair play," and they asked whether black merchants who had for years nurtured their businesses in Hayti could succeed in reestablishing those same businesses once clearance ended. The DBPC wanted assurance that their members—some 135 merchants—would have an opportunity to benefit economically once urban renewal was complete. Wheeler and the DRC agreed with the DBPC and advised the city council to hold off voting on the recommended rezoning until they received the results of a market analysis study. The report validated the DBPC's claim that the buying power in the Hayti area could support either two smaller shopping centers or one large shopping center but not a large and small shopping center simultaneously.[17]

In light of the market analysis, Greenberg and his lawyers met with the DBPC in a private two-hour conference and reached a compromise whereby he would ask the zoning commission for just over seven acres for a shopping center, not the twenty acres he had initially wanted. At no point did the DBPC question whether urban renewal should move forward; instead they raised concern about who would benefit from the potential economic revitalization. The dispute had little to do with whether urban renewal should occur, as the organization believed that its members would ultimately benefit from the process. In August 1962, Greenberg completed the College Plaza and its first tenant was a bowling center that opened for business "to thousands" who "converged on the College Plaza lanes." The DRC shopping center never came to fruition, foreshadowing a recurring pattern in Durham's urban renewal.[18]

In order to fully grasp the economic implications of urban renewal in Durham, one has to consider its relationship to another venture that gained momentum during the mid-1950s. The initial planning for what became known as the Research Triangle Park had been in the works for several years. Leaders across the state had expressed concern about the employment opportunities for North Carolina's workforce, especially college graduates who left the state after being trained in its best universities. The noted UNC sociologist Howard Odum, the first president of the SRC, and others recognized the potential of the concentration of major research universities in Chapel Hill (UNC), Durham (Duke University), and Raleigh (North Carolina State College). He believed the area could replicate research centers already in existence around the country, such as the four-hundred-acre parcel comprising the Stanford Research Institute in California. While Odum is generally credited with conceptualizing RTP, the idea did not move forward until Greensboro businessman Romeo Guest became involved. Guest coined the phrase "Research Triangle," but both men envisioned the three research universities working cooperatively as a kind of consortium. Interestingly, no considerations were given to the possible role of NCC in the endeavor, even as plans for urban renewal targeted Hayti, near the historically black college.[19]

In 1954, Guest published a brochure called "Conditioned for Research," which laid out a major economic endeavor grounded in the possibilities of groundbreaking research. He then presented the idea to Governor Luther H. Hodges. The proposal immediately struck a chord with Hodges, himself a businessman, and he pledged his support but could not commit the state's financial resources at that point. In the meantime, Robert M. Hanes, the prominent president of Wachovia Bank in Winston-Salem, became chairman of the newly formed Governor's Research Triangle Committee, which organized in the spring of 1955 and gained incorporation in September 1956. One of the committee's chief concerns became enhancing the interconnectedness between industry and universities. The administrators at the three campuses took a favorable position on the Research Triangle concept. The first executive director of the Research Triangle Committee became George Simpson, a protégé of Howard Odum. In January 1957, in one of his first reports, Simpson outlined three primary objectives: publicizing the kind of work to be done in the RTP with leaders in industry and government; establishing a physical park where research industries would relocate; and launching a research institute. Within the first year of the Research Triangle Committee's operations, they contacted about two hundred companies to "sell" the idea of the RTP with the hope of enticing research-oriented corporations to relocate to the fledgling area.[20]

To help jump-start the initiative, private funds came in beginning with a $1 million investment from retired North Carolina textile executive Karl Robbins to be used for buying land near the Raleigh-Durham Airport. At a press conference on September 10, 1957, with the funds from Robbins secured, Governor Hodges officially announced plans for the RTP, which stood to rival the best research centers across the United States. Moreover, Robbins gave authorization to Romeo Guest to purchase land in the identified area under the company Pinelands, Incorporated. Meanwhile, the Tar Heel State was contending with its ongoing racial strife, which proved problematic when industries decided whether to relocate there. By 1958, Pinelands had purchased or optioned some four thousand acres of land at $175 per acre across Wake and Durham Counties. By that summer, however, the initiative nearly collapsed until Archie K. Davis, the new chairman of Wachovia Bank, came to the rescue and dedicated his time to selling stock in Pinelands. Davis became the economic force behind the RTP from that point on. He reasoned that the project needed to be placed on a nonprofit basis and suggested a $1.25 million fund-raising goal in order to get things off the ground. He targeted donors across the state rather than investors by appealing to New South prosperity and emphasizing the overall benefit to North Carolina, while ensuring that individual private investors would not benefit economically from the RTP. Davis's fund-raising campaign obtained 850 donors and raised $1.425 million, surpassing the initial fund-raising goal by the end of December. In January 1959, the Research Triangle Committee became the Research Triangle Foundation. The Durham banker George Watts Hill Sr., the father of Watts Hill Jr., became chairman of the newly created Research Triangle Institute, the research arm of the conglomerate.[21]

As leaders rolled out plans for the RTP, the newly formed DRC began planning in earnest for the Bull City's urban renewal program. It became unmistakably clear that the recruitment of major corporations was one driving force behind urban renewal. In 1955, local leaders had already organized the Committee of 100 to strategize about how to recruit innovative commerce to the city. The Committee of 100 eventually focused on what Durham leaders needed to do to support the RTP expansion. They wanted southern Durham to be the location for the statewide economic windfall. In the early stages of the RTP's expansion, as it transitioned from concept to reality, city leaders in Durham were pressed to ensure that the city fulfilled its obligations by providing adequate roads and infrastructure, a water supply, and necessary zoning approvals. The earlier *Outlook for Durham* report had explained that Durham had to alleviate the central city's traffic congestion to lure the kind of businesses included in the RTP plans. In other words, urban renewal helped facilitate the success of the RTP in southern Durham. In 1965, construction began on the East-West Expressway, the artery that would connect parts of Chapel Hill (UNC) and Durham (especially Duke University and the downtown district) to the RTP through the heart of Hayti. In explicit and implicit ways, then, the RTP initiative had racial overtones from the very beginning. While black residents and businesses had to vacate, room was being made to accommodate newcomers, many of whom were white.[22]

In early 1962, the major focus for city leaders was getting the voting public to pass the bond issue that would pay the city's share of urban renewal costs. In the months leading to the bond vote, Wheeler and the DCNA used $2,500 the organization received from the newly created VEP for a wave of voter registration efforts that supported the bond referendum. They presented the bond as placing the community's future in the hands of black voters, and Wheeler's chairmanship of the SRC's executive committee and his behind-the-scenes influence ensured that the referendum had a chance to succeed. Nevertheless, as the city moved closer to the vote, the black community feared white voters would defeat the bond since most taxpayer funds would go toward redevelopment in Hayti. Louis E. Austin (an ardent supporter of the urban renewal plan from the very beginning) articulated the underlying tensions a month before the vote, saying, "The mass of white voters of this city will not respond favorably to any movement that means the betterment of the Negro's lot." Furthermore, "the mere fact that the urban renewal bond issue has been isolated in an election where it is the only question before the voters is further evidence that there is no honest support for its passage in corners occupied by the political quarterbacks of Durham." Despite apprehension on the part of blacks, the bond issue narrowly passed in October and the DCNA's bloc vote provided the margin of victory with 92 percent of black voter support.[23]

By this time, the Research Triangle Foundation had succeeded in getting companies to consider relocating to the area. The Chemstrand Corporation committed to moving in May 1958, an important turning point for the RTP. The Chemstrand Corporation opened its research laboratory in the latter part of 1960, which helped the Research Triangle Institute operate profitably for the first time. In January 1965, after lobbying efforts from Governor Terry Sanford and Luther H. Hodges (now US commerce secretary), the US Environmental Health Sciences Center (now the National Institute of Health Sciences) arrived, choosing North Carolina over forty-five other states that had placed bids. A year later, IBM decided to relocate to the RTP after seven years of secret negotiations, and it acquired four hundred acres for a multiplex campus that opened in 1967. The Research Triangle Foundation paid off its mortgage with the IBM funds. In 1970, the pharmaceutical giant Burroughs

Wellcome and Company (now GlaxoSmithKline) opened a research laboratory in the RTP as well as a manufacturing facility in Greenville, North Carolina. That same year, the Environmental Protection Agency opened a campus in the RTP, its largest research laboratory in the country.[24]

"Unfinished Business": The NC Fund, the SRC, and the War on Poverty

In the months after Governor Terry Sanford's 1963 Emancipation Day speech (see chapter 5), he moved with swiftness toward achieving the ideals he preached that day. In fact, as early as November 1962, he and his aides met with several philanthropic foundations to pitch their ideas about addressing the problem of poverty. The Sanford administration hoped to obtain private financial support for a broad and radical reform program, and the Ford Foundation seemed the most eager to help. By meeting with private foundations, the governor sidestepped a resistant state legislature that he believed would never approve of spending tax dollars on the kind of action-oriented program that he put forward. The problem of poverty had weighed on Sanford's heart since his term began, as he pushed an agenda that looked to improve the state's educational system. Along the way, he could not help but connect the state's most pressing problems, especially when it came to the most underrepresented citizens, to the problem of poverty in the New South. By July 1963, Sanford's intentions were clear as he set up what became the North Carolina Fund (NC Fund).[25]

Wheeler proved extremely helpful in getting the Ford Foundation to commit to the proposed poverty program. In January and again that summer, the foundation sent representatives to tour the state at the invitation of Governor Sanford so they could determine whether to approve a major grant to assist him in bringing his ideas to life. Before Ford officials approved the funding, however, they went directly to Wheeler to see if the banker had any serious concerns related to the governor's proposal. In February, Sanford and his advisors brokered an initial meeting with Wheeler, the NC Mutual's William Jesse Kennedy Jr. (president of the insurance company from 1952 to 1958), Shag Stewart, and others to discuss the plans for a statewide organization, which had to include black involvement. Although Wheeler and others were "cautious," they saw it as a good opportunity nonetheless. Wheeler raised concerns later in the summer when the Ford Foundation and the Sanford administration began detailing specifics. Included in Sanford's proposal was the "Comprehensive School Improvement Project," where some funds would go toward enhancing the quality of poor public schools in the state. Given Wheeler's hard-fought battles in the previous two decades for educational equality, it was important to him that schools primarily serving black children received their fair share of funding, something not regularly practiced in North Carolina. The Ford Foundation also wanted to know if funds advanced to schools would be made available on an equal basis at both black and white schools. After reaching an agreement so that funds would be dispersed more equitably, Wheeler raised no objections to Sanford's program. Ford Foundation public affairs director Paul Ylvisaker recalled that when they sought Wheeler's endorsement it was "the first time anybody from the foundation's top echelon had gone to a black man." NC Fund executive director George H. Esser confirmed that, without Wheeler's endorsement, the Ford Foundation would have packed their bags and bypassed funding Sanford's poverty initiative. With Wheeler's endorsement, in no time the Ford Foundation pledged $7 million to be used in tandem with contributions from the Z. Smith Reynolds and Mary Reynolds Babcock Foundations.[26]

Once the NC Fund received its official incorporation on July 18, 1963, Wheeler's name appeared alongside those of Governor Sanford, *Charlotte Observer* newspaper editor C. A. McKnight, and Charles Babcock as the new organization's incorporators. The new agency's board members included Gerald Cowan, Anne Forsyth, Tom Pearsall (of the Pearsall Committee), Sam Duncan (president of the all-black Livingstone College and a close friend of Wheeler's), James A. Gray Jr., Hollis Edens, Rosa Parker, Wallace Murchison, Hargrove "Skipper" Bowles, and W. Dallas Herring. Robinson O. Everett, the DRC chairman, became the agency's attorney. "This was the first step," noted Korstad and Leloudis, "in building a relationship that within a year's time would involve Fund leaders in drafting the Economic Opportunity Act of 1964, establishing the federal Office of Economic Opportunity (OEO), and launching President Lyndon Johnson's national War on Poverty."[27]

The NC Fund was another resource for Wheeler to broker additional concessions on behalf of blacks as well as a realistic way to implement the gains the civil rights movement was making. NC Fund board members decided on Durham as the central location for its headquarters, a direct result both of Wheeler's reach within the new organization and the fact the NC Fund's lawyer was Durhamite Robinson O. Everett. The fund set up shop on Parrish Street, long recognized as the primary hub of Durham's black financial institutions, in close proximity to M&F Bank's headquarters. M&F Bank also benefited from the new antipoverty agency, as it became the official depository of NC Fund dollars. Wheeler also became treasurer of the NC Fund's board. The NC Fund gave a grant to Durham's Operation Breakthrough (OB), one of the first Community Action Programs (CAP). With the NC Fund and the urban renewal program headed in the right direction, Durham had significant resources to implement Wheeler's ideas of New South prosperity. In March, he served as the official US delegate at the international trade fair in Tripoli, Libya, on behalf of Commerce Secretary Luther H. Hodges. Later in the year, President Kennedy considered Wheeler for an ambassadorship to Nigeria, but the latter declined, citing his expanding banking responsibilities. In 1962, Wheeler and M&F Bank opened its third bank branch in North Carolina, located in Charlotte (the state's largest city) near Johnson C. Smith University (JCSU) and the city's largest black section. At JCSU's spring commencement a year later, in recognizing the economic impact the bank had in that community, the institution awarded Wheeler an honorary doctorate.[28]

In 1964, when the time came for George Esser to hire a comptroller for the NC Fund, Wheeler suggested Nathan Garrett, a black Durham native and certified public accountant. Garrett's father, York Garrett Jr., owned a successful drugstore in Hayti, and the young Nathan had taken a real interest in learning the business—everything from operating costs to bookkeeping. The elder Garrett later sold his drugstore to the DRC in cooperation with the city's urban renewal program. In 1952, Nathan Garrett had graduated from Yale University—said to have been the first African American from Durham to attend an Ivy League school. He went on to receive additional training from Wayne State University. Garrett lived and worked in Detroit for a few years before returning to Durham, where

Table 6.1. Resources and deposits of the Mechanics and Farmers Bank from December 31, 1958, to December 31, 1976

Year	Resources	Deposits
1958	$7,728,384	$7,129,784
1959	$7,996,390	$7,288,418
1960	$8,800,396	$8,040,041
1961	$10,112,362	$9,170,651
1962	$12,218,090	$11,222,895
1963	$13,112,958	$12,047,547
1964	$16,966,426	$15,942,254
1965	$15,369,220	$14,173,996
1966	$16,687,844	$15,253,683
1967	$19,373,423	$17,855,842
1968	$20,595,849	$19,106,180
1969	$21,554,817	$19,455,304
1970	$24,038,411	$21,632,193
1971	$34,161,473	$31,480,837
1972	$37,694,158	$34,166,230
1973	$39,141,484	$35,232,134
1974	$38,921,922	$35,016,495
1975	$41,199,351	$36,835,716
1976	$41,405,000	$37,381,000

Source: Vivian R. Patterson, "A Black Bank Revisited: An Update of 'Analysis of Operating Problems of Bank Serving a Predominantly Negro Market [1959]'" (master's thesis, Rutgers University, 1978), table 16, following p. 89.

he opened his own accounting firm. Wheeler had followed Garrett's career trajectory and, in keeping with the banker's objectives to seek employment for qualified black professionals in top-level positions, handpicked him as the NC Fund's comptroller and pressed Sanford to support his choice. As a member on the PCEEO, Wheeler would have had no opposition from NC Fund officials when they considered hiring Garrett.[29]

The assassination of President Kennedy in November 1963 left the nation without direction, and the civil rights movement was without a powerful force to advance legislation. In the months that followed, however, Vice President Lyndon B. Johnson stepped into his new role with determination. Wheeler and Johnson were born in the same year and had become good friends through their work with the PCEEO. While fond of President Kennedy, Wheeler had great confidence in Johnson's leadership and ability to get the country back on track. In his first State of the Union address on January 8, 1964, Johnson outlined a broad legislative agenda. "This administration today," Johnson proclaimed, "here and now, declares unconditional war on poverty in America." Within a few months, President Johnson embarked on his Appalachian tour and also made a trip to Rocky Mount, North Carolina, to evaluate an NC Fund CAP in May. Wheeler was part of the North Carolina delegation that accompanied Johnson across the state.[30] A *Business Week* magazine article described the racial tensions that Wheeler faced as a black power broker in the South with frequent contact with his white counterparts:

> At times, the irony of his position is striking. Wheeler recently went with a small group from the North Carolina Fund to 11 towns that had applied for assistance. At many meetings he presided over discussions that included mayors, city managers, other officials, and prominent businessmen. Yet, careful arrangements were necessary to insure that Wheeler could be served meals without incident. In one strictly segregated town a newspaper reporter, watching Wheeler talk to city officials, observed: "Look at the way he handles those people. And that man couldn't even buy a cup of coffee across the street."[31]

Wheeler wanted all black Americans to receive such concessions without any special arrangements. In October 1964, when the Lady Bird "Victory" Special brought the First Lady through North Carolina on a whistle-stop campaign tour for President Johnson, Wheeler received an invitation to board the train in Richmond and ride all the way through North Carolina, making stops in Greensboro and Charlotte. In May, in the same month that President Johnson toured Rocky Mount, he gave the commencement address at the University of Michigan and expounded on his vision for the country. He brought with him a promising message for ambitious young Americans, stating: "Your imagination and your initiative, and your indignation will determine whether we build a society where progress is the servant of our needs, or a society where old values and new visions are buried under unbridled growth. For in your time we have the opportunity to move not only toward the rich society and the powerful society, but upward to the Great Society." Johnson ended his speech by asking the students: "Will you join in the battle to give every citizen the full equality which God enjoins and the law requires, whatever his belief, or race, or the color of his skin? . . . Will you join in the battle to give every citizen an escape from the crushing weight of poverty? . . . Will you join in the battle to build the Great Society, to prove that our material progress is only the foundation on which we will build a richer life of mind and spirit?"[32]

While President Johnson was formulating his ideas about the Great Society, Wheeler officially began his tenure as the SRC president, declaring in his acceptance speech that "We have been able to sift out the ills and establish the morals in the South, and in many ways point the way to the techniques that have been helpful. We plan to continue to point the way in some fields which we have not yet touched." Responding to congratulatory letters about his election to the SRC's presidency, Wheeler told one well-wisher: "Those of us who have been associated with the Council for a long period are more than pleased at the manner in which it has been able to expand the range and quality of its services. We have also come closer to the point of realizing the full extent of our own commitment to the task of stimulating courses of thought and action which point the way to new heights of cultural and economic achievement in our Region." Wheeler used the organization's annual meeting in November to speak directly to Johnson's ideas about the Great Society and the War on Poverty, especially the relationship between civil rights and poverty. His speech stressed that poverty had always been an important area within the economic struggle for civil rights and that the SRC's agenda of "unfinished business" included addressing poverty. He pointed to the civil rights movement's emphasis on direct action at the beginning of the decade, which "signaled the point at which we have now formalized another and more enlightened effort to achieve an open society in which freedom of movement, equal opportunity in employment, equal justice under the law, and full voting rights are the goals of a South whose battle scars and whose frequent rendezvous with conscience should enable it to achieve the Great Society before other regions of the country are able to do so." The language of the War on Poverty and the Great Society perfectly captured the ideals of New South prosperity and put them on a practical basis. As always, Wheeler pointed to the importance of opening up more job opportunities to blacks in government and eliminating institutional forms of discrimination from government agencies. Thus, he pointed to the SRC's responsibility to define the next steps in their battle for freedom, as "we find a challenge for renewed efforts on our part to give life and substance to what is now only the framework of an open society."[33]

The SRC had become an effective and bona fide civil rights organization. As the SRC president, Wheeler wasted little time trying to shore up resources from philanthropic foundations to help the SRC continue its mission and pave the way for new endeavors. In March, for example, he and the SRC's executive director, Leslie Dunbar, met with Arthur Hollis Edens, an NC Fund board member and executive director of the Mary Reynolds Babcock Foundation, to discuss future SRC programming. Moreover, Wheeler and the SRC made a concerted effort that year to convince President Johnson not to appoint segregationists to federal judgeships in the South. In this regard, Wheeler sent a letter to Johnson on the SRC's behalf. Dunbar also wrote to other civil rights leaders to have them make similar appeals. In a letter to Dr. Martin Luther King Jr., Dunbar explained: "It would be most helpful, I think, if you could find an early opportunity to say, even more emphatically than does John Wheeler in his letter to the President, that no segregationist should be appointed or promoted to any vacancy. . . . With a probable six places to fill, I think the pressure on President Johnson to give one to a designee of Senator [James O.] Eastland and [John C.] Stennis [both of Mississippi] will increase, and should be strongly counteracted." In December, Wheeler, Dunbar, and Nat Welsh met with Vice President Hubert Humphrey's administrative aides to discuss a special resolution passed at the SRC's annual meeting related to judicial appointments in the Fifth US Judicial Circuit Bench. The previous year, Wheeler had successfully gotten Henry Frye appointed as an assistant US attorney for the Middle District of North Carolina. The judicial system's treatment as well as the level of injustice exacted upon black southerners was a matter of importance to

Wheeler and the SRC. As SRC president, he continued to recommend individuals for federal judicial appointments in the South. In 1966, for example, he recommended civil rights lawyers Donald L. Hollowell (Georgia) and Wiley A. Branton (former lawyer for the Little Rock Nine and the first VEP director) for appointments to the federal bench.[34]

Wheeler also made every effort to link the SRC's activities to urban renewal, housing, and poverty. In 1966, when his friend Robert C. Weaver became the first black cabinet member with his appointment as the secretary of the newly created HUD, Wheeler contacted Weaver about the SRC's new housing initiative, the urban planning project. In 1965, the SRC, under Wheeler's signature, also sent the important memorandum "New Federal Programs in the South" to national leaders, including members from the president's cabinet and virtually every federal agency, in an effort to lobby for equal employment opportunities during the implementation phase of the civil rights movement. He sent the memorandum to President Johnson, who forwarded it directly to Sargent Shriver, the head of OEO, which eventually oversaw federal funding for the War on Poverty. Wheeler also offered to come to Washington to sit down with Shriver and discuss the memorandum more fully. The memorandum speaks to Wheeler and the SRC's concern that blacks be involved in implementing new federal policies and that they be given a role on the local governing bodies for CAPs like those supported by the NC Fund. In his reply to Wheeler, Shriver pointed to one of the banker activist's main concerns. "We, too," Shriver explained, "are concerned with the need to appoint Negroes to top level jobs in Federal programs in the South. Staffing in our Southern (Atlanta) and Southwestern (Austin) Regional Offices had not been completed; however, the appointments we have made thus far indicate that minorities will share in top-level assignments in these offices. Of the 10 professionals thus far assigned in Atlanta, for example, two are Negroes. And in Austin, one of the six professionals thus far assigned is a Negro." Shriver assured Wheeler that his office would adhere to a strict policy to ensure that local communities "complied with our requirements for fair representation of minorities and the poor."[35]

In North Carolina, a moderate governor had laid the groundwork for the state's War on Poverty, which in its application helped shape the political discourse more forcefully toward the rights of poor Americans, aiding them in their growing activism. Yet other challenges loomed as the movement renewed its attention to voting discrimination in the South, especially after the violent battle of Edmund Pettis Bridge in Selma, Alabama, that March. On August 6, the president signed into law the Voting Rights Act of 1965, an unprecedented bill with powerful implications on New South politics. The SRC's VEP had played an integral role in helping to increase black voter registration in the South. Nevertheless, Leslie Dunbar cried foul when his organization failed to receive a formal invitation to the signing ceremony. In a stinging letter to the president's special assistant Lee C. White, Dunbar pointed out: "The Council is composed of white and Negro Southerners who believe not merely in civil rights but bi-racial cooperation toward a truly integrated political and economic order. No other organization has longer or more constructively worked to end voter discrimination and to encourage Negro voter registration in the South." In the previous three years, noted Dunbar, the SRC administered VEP, and the organization's research and field reports related to voter registration were used as evidence in support of the bill. Moreover, "The Council's long involvement in this field has been climaxed, for the present, by our administration during 1962–64 of the Voter Education Project, through which at least 700,000 new voters were enrolled in the eleven southern states."[36] Dunbar bitterly complained that not one SRC official received an invitation to witness the signing. Therefore:

> We find it strange that although a horde of people were invited to the August 6 signing of the Voting Rights Act, representation of the Council was not requested. Our president, Mr. John H. Wheeler of Durham, was invited, but as an individual, and he was not among the score or so selected to witness the signing. Ironically, on that same day he was one of a small group meeting to form realistic plans for making the new Act a success. In devotion to that end, a devotion certainly not recognized by the White House planners, and despite fatigue, he flew back South to rejoin the conference by 4:00 p.m. As far as I can note, invitations to the affair of August 6 excluded Negro and white Southerners unequivocally committed to a bi-racial approach to an integrated

> society, and as retiring staff head of the Council I want to express my chagrin and regret.[37]

Despite the gross oversight related to the signing ceremony and a half-hearted apology from White, Wheeler, Dunbar, and the SRC continued to force policymakers at the federal level to seek greater implementation of the gains already won.

The Hayti–Elizabeth Street Urban Renewal Area

In April 1963, $4.3 million in guaranteed federal funds arrived from the HHFA. These funds, coupled with the money from the bond referendum the previous fall, allowed Durham to begin executing its urban renewal program in earnest. The funds would be used for clearance in the first of six projects in the Hayti–Elizabeth Street Urban Renewal Area, which had a projected two-year timeframe. On a rather somber July 28, just over a week after the incorporation of the NC Fund, the "Old Boys Club," a "relic of [a] bygone era," became the first building leveled under the DRC's urban renewal program. The Old Boys Club had some historical significance. At one point it had been the home of barber John Wright, the business partner to John Merrick when the two made their way to Durham in the late nineteenth century to open up their first barbershop. The building, located on the corner of Pettigrew and Fayetteville Streets, later became the residence of notable black leaders such as P. B. Young, the editor of the black *Norfolk Journal and Guide,* and Dr. James E. Shepard, founder and president of NCC. The structure became integral to community life in Hayti as it housed the Harriet Tubman YWCA and then the John M. Avery Boys Club, where Wheeler had served as a board member since the organization began in 1939.[38]

A few weeks later, the first among many housing issues related to urban renewal surfaced in Hayti, revealing how the implementation of urban renewal further complicated the city's already tense housing situation. Demolitions created the need for additional housing for hundreds of displaced residents. They also unleashed class resentment in both whites and blacks critical of the city for introducing apartment-style housing in certain areas, which residents believed would bring down their property values.

Finally, the clearances compelled black Hayti residents to ask whether racism had prompted the city to approve concentrating new apartments close to existing public housing developments. In August 1963, in a nine-to-one vote, the city council approved a rezoning recommendation for an area in the Burton School community for a 150-unit housing development proposed by the newly formed Lincoln Hospital Foundation for Urban Renewal, a nonprofit investment group formed by Asa T. Spaulding and several other black businesspeople. The previous February, the Lincoln Hospital Foundation had acquired a ten-acre tract of land near NCC and McDougald Terrace and planned to construct a housing development to accommodate Hayti residents being uprooted because of urban renewal. Both the Lincoln Hospital Foundation and the DRC pressed the city council to approve the apartments for this very reason. City councilman Shag Stewart, president of the Mutual Savings and Loan Association (formerly the Mutual Building and Loan Association), abstained from the city council zoning vote because of his membership on the foundation.[39]

The Lincoln Hospital Foundation's venture was under the direct control and sponsorship of the Lincoln Hospital board of directors, which included Wheeler, so there was no question why the organization embraced this kind of economic investment. They expected the proceeds from the apartment rentals to go directly to the hospital. Wheeler would have played an important role in getting the DRC and Lincoln Hospital Foundation to press city officials. He would have been especially influential when it came to Stewart's impact on the decision, even if the councilman abstained from the actual vote. Stewart, the previous DCNA chairman, would have been in a position to explain to his colleagues on the city council what he believed to be the positive aspects of the zoning approval. In the months leading to the rezoning vote, there was immediate opposition from blacks who lived in the Burton School area because the section was originally zoned for individual family homes, and they believed any new housing needed to adhere to those guidelines. In accordance with their expressed opposition, the Burton School community submitted a petition to the city council with signatures from about 150 homeowners. Critics believed a new subdivision next to the McDougald Terrace would "result in 'intolerable congested' conditions and would overburden already crowded education and recreational facilities in the area." Blacks in the area believed the building plans would create a ghetto and concentrate them in one area of the city as opposed to opening up space in previously all-white residential neighborhoods. These critics also believed that there was little transparency because the city council held private sessions about the issue to the chagrin of those who would be affected most by the proposed changes. "We have not liked too well," explained a spokesman for the Burton School community residents, "the several executive sessions held by the City Council on the Lincoln Hospital apartment project." Despite protests from hundreds of homeowners in the community, the city council moved forward with the zoning change.[40]

Although it is impossible to provide details about the many ways urban renewal impacted the lives of Hayti residents, examples like the Brookstown community illustrate the dilemma of urban renewal. Areas deemed "blighted," and thus slated for demolition and clearance by the DRC, were strong and upstanding communities. There were roughly eighty families in Brookstown, which included two churches affiliated with the foremost black Christian denominations in the country. Nevertheless, the DRC and the city planning department deemed 73 percent of the area blighted, and Brookstown became an early example of what would be lost indefinitely. Moreover, the area attracted Duke University, which wanted to acquire the land in this urban renewal area to possibly expand its campus. Although it took time before the full ramifications of urban renewal became apparent, outside experts gave black Durham other warnings. In March 1964, for example, almost a year after the first structure was bulldozed, NCC brought Northwestern University professor Dr. Scott Greer to campus to discuss urban renewal. The director of Northwestern's Center for Metropolitan Studies and himself an urban renewal expert, Greer outlined some of the inherent challenges in a speech to an audience comprised of NCC students, faculty, and community members. He pointed to the ways urban renewal might "deprive many citizens of standard housing," especially in the event subsidized public housing was unavailable. Greer also "discussed the sociology of trends and discounted the efforts of planners to renew old business districts." The changes caused by urban renewal would indeed be "vast" and "dramatic," as the *Carolina Times* newspaper had predicted in January 1959. But they would not be as positive as the paper anticipated.[41]

The problems stemming from urban renewal in Durham, in housing among other issues, inched closer to the surface beginning in the middle of the 1960s. Concerns arose about the Durham Housing Authority (DHA), an agency that became more important to citizens as the city's intensified housing woes continued through the rest of the decade. In October 1964, NC Mutual executive Babe Henderson, the only black member on the authority, was not made chairman despite being the most qualified and experienced member. Henderson's leadership would certainly have inspired trust in the DHA and would have been crucial during an intense period in the city's history. On August 11, 1965, as the nation's civil rights leaders and their respective organizations celebrated the new voting act, a violent disturbance erupted in the Watts neighborhood of Los Angeles. The Watts Uprising was triggered by the arrest of a black resident suspected of being intoxicated. Nevertheless, the actions taken by the city's black residents in the aftermath centered on police brutality, high unemployment, poor schools, and substandard housing. After five days of violence, including the deaths of thirty-four people, the uprising left the city with millions of dollars in property damage and the destruction of hundreds of buildings. Although Durham seemed to be worlds apart from Watts, a similar powder keg of ingredients was nevertheless present. The day before the Watts Uprising, a group of Durham public housing residents organized the McDougald Terrace Mothers Club. On the same day as the uprising, the DHA sent an eviction notice to Joyce C. Thorpe, a single mother and McDougald Terrace tenant since November 1964. Thorpe had until the end of August to vacate, and, interestingly enough, her eviction came just a day after she was elected president of the Mothers Club. Moreover, Thorpe was not given an official explanation of why she was being evicted. But when sheriff's deputies arrived at her apartment to remove her from the premises, she made it clear she would not leave and warned the deputies that they would have to dodge bullets from the loaded shotgun she held if they wanted her gone. After unsuccessful attempts to learn why she was being evicted, Thorpe's attorneys filed suit on the grounds that eviction violated her First Amendment rights. Thorpe's case brought the policies of the DHA under intense public scrutiny in black Durham and set the stage for an eventual US Supreme Court challenge.[42]

As Wheeler explained in a speech at the SRC's annual convention in November, "Frequently the question has been raised as to whether a concentrated attack upon conditions of poverty could have prevented the devastating riots which have swept the Watts section of Los Angeles twice within recent months. . . . Based upon results obtained in other parts of the country, it appears that an adequately-financed community action program, properly staffed and operated within [OEO] guidelines, could have done much to change the feeling of hopelessness and despair which triggered the riots." An urban crisis had clearly taken shape, and in his speech to the annual SRC convention, Wheeler tried to make sense of it all by delineating the role that he believed the War on Poverty could have played in helping to solve the dilemma. In doing so, he reminded the audience that, while the uprisings were seemingly spontaneous, the level of discontent in urban America had festered for decades. These challenges were not completely on the radar of the southern civil rights movement, but the events in Watts forecasted a pivotal shift in the economic struggle for freedom. Wheeler did not explicitly mention urban renewal in this speech, but he believed it fit within the broader framework of the War on Poverty and the Great Society in achieving New South prosperity.[43]

The urban renewal program in Durham continued to take a disappointing downward spiral. In September 1965, two years after the first buildings were torn down as part of the Hayti–Elizabeth Street Renewal Area, Louis E. Austin raised questions about the slow pace of urban renewal and captured the sentiments of Hayti residents. He placed congested living conditions at the forefront and called on the DRC to build new public housing for displaced residents. Otherwise, it would continue to make an already depressed housing situation worse. By this time, it was clear to blacks that fulfillment of earlier promises made to them was slow in coming. Austin highlighted the quickness with which the DRC carried out the clearance part of the program, while at the same time dragging its feet in replacing demolished residential areas. Moreover, homeowners criticized the DRC for purchase offers that seemed below market value. "So far as the Hayti section of Durham is concerned," the editorial went, "urban renewal is not only a farce but just another scheme to relieve Negroes of property they own too close to the downtown business section of the city." There was a serious question about whether the low-cost housing developments would ever come. The answer came by way of a grandfather living in Hayti when he said, "I have already put it in my will that when my great-grandson moves into one of the apartments erected under the Urban Renewal program to not forget that his old great great grandpappy dreamed of such a day."[44]

While the Hayti grandfather waited for new public housing to go up, perhaps in vain, long overdue concerns about the city and the DHA's existing policies persisted. In October, McDougald Terrace residents were up in arms against the DHA and especially its executive director, Carvie S. Oldham. The residents had a laundry list of grievances ranging from deceitful leasing agreements, of which residents never received official copies, to unexplained charges on rent and utility bills. The McDougald Terrace residents again received assistance from OB staff that helped them present their grievances before city leaders. If the DHA failed to address the problem, explained another newspaper article, "McDougald Terrace [would persist as] a veritable seething cauldron which [might] erupt at any moment into an explosion of a more devastating nature." By December, the DHA announced changes to its policies, which included new rental agreements, a new requirement that all tenants be given an explanation for eviction, and the elimination of excessive water bills. Yet in other ways the DHA continued to ignore black demands. In February 1966, the DRC sold land to the DHA to build new public housing in an already overcrowded area. That same month the housing body bypassed another opportunity to appoint Babe Henderson to the DHA chairmanship, voting instead to appoint its newest member, Carl R. Harris, to the chairmanship, against the wishes of black Durham. By that time, Henderson was the ranking member and the only original appointee left in the group. The DHA's continued rejection of Henderson's chairmanship said as much about its views on race as did the actions of its executive director, Carvie S. Oldham. Their refusal to appoint Henderson was frustrating at a time when someone like him could have helped mitigate the city's deteriorating housing situation.[45]

The housing crisis in Durham reached a boiling point during the summer of 1966. As things became worse, black people collectively organized to push city leaders toward finding a reasonable solution to improve conditions. Black women from poor and working-class backgrounds, Rubye Gattis among them, succeeded in establishing an association they called United Organizations for Community Improvement (UOCI). The UOCI was a collective from several active neighborhood councils from across the city, including the one at McDougald Terrance formed the previous August. The group wanted local slumlords, especially white real estate developer Abe Greenberg, to improve the living conditions at their rental properties. In February 1966, Durham's Edgemont Community Council charged Greenberg with maintaining houses that were below standard. After investigating the charges against him, city housing code inspectors agreed that the homes were "below city building code standards." The Edgemont Community Council followed up on their complaints by "picketing Greenberg's offices, [and] City Hall." Moreover, when black businessman David Stith defended Greenberg, the group targeted his home as well. The Edgemont Community Council provided city leaders with a fact sheet based on inspections from twenty-one homes, which detailed significant violations such as "holes in the ceiling, no bath tubs, plaster falling down inside of houses, bad wiring conditions, no hot water, no screen doors, air condition without air condition, no paint on outside, broken down porches, holes in the floor, roaches, rats, snakes, bugs, etc." Despite the public outcry, Greenberg made only minimal attempts to repair the homes. On top of that, he charged exorbitant rents for properties that had been previously rented to all-white tenants, raising rents when blacks displaced by urban renewal, who had very few options for affordable housing, moved into the neighborhoods. Although Greenberg was by far the worst offender, black slumlords also owned rental properties in the same condition as Greenberg's. Additionally, many black property owners unloaded real estate in the Hayti–Elizabeth Street Urban Renewal area by cashing in with the DRC.[46]

In the meantime, the US Supreme Court decided it would hear oral arguments on the Joyce C. Thorpe eviction case against the DHA. The LDF represented Thorpe in the proceedings. Her case had large implications because it related to due process and became "the first time the nation's highest court has agreed to review the 'rights of a tenant' in public housing to be free from arbitrary eviction." Thorpe went on to win her case, setting a legal precedent, while the circumstances surrounding her eviction forced HUD to make major changes to its national housing policies. The decision stated that local housing authorities had to notify tenants in writing about the reasons for their evictions and also had to give the tenants an opportunity to appeal the decision to local governing bodies.[47]

In 1966, the civil rights movement turned another corner with the decisive shift to "Black Power" consciousness. It transpired in dramatic fashion as Stokely Carmichael (who later changed his name to Kwame Ture), the new SNCC chairman, captured black frustrations in a fiery speech during the Meredith March. The SNCC election that Carmichael won against John Lewis, Dr. King's protégé, represented a departure from the strict adherence to the philosophy of nonviolence and integration. James Meredith envisioned his "March Against Fear" as a one-man crusade in which he planned to trek from Memphis, Tennessee to Jackson, Mississippi. But he was shot just days into his journey. The national civil rights leadership rallied behind Meredith and continued the march, unwilling to concede to fear or violence. Meredith survived the ordeal, and by the time the marchers made it to their final destination, he was able to join them. While the Meredith March included participants from all over, the three main organizations that spearheaded its continuance were SNCC, SCLC (with Dr. King as its president), and CORE (headed by Durham civil rights attorney Floyd B. McKissick since January). In Greenwood, Mississippi, Carmichael was arrested on trespassing charges, but after being released, he told the crowd of marchers that he had had enough of going to jail. In a passionate speech on the evening of June 16, he told the crowd: "The only way we gonna stop them white men from whuppin' us is to take over. What we gonna start sayin' now is Black Power." By the time his speech ended, Carmichael led the crowd in a call and response: "What do we want?" The crowd chanted "Black Power!" repeatedly.[48]

The phrase sparked controversy and debate about its meaning. Some civil rights leaders viewed it as irresponsible because it had a strong appeal to black nationalism while the mainstream civil rights movement operated under a decidedly integrationist framework. Others felt the term was too ambiguous and could therefore be left to interpretation. CORE national director Floyd B. McKissick, however, embraced Black Power because it represented the moment that African Americans rejected their status as

"Negroes" and demanded to be called "Black." McKissick also explained, "Whites could not subtract violence from black power." About a week after Carmichael invoked Black Power at the Mississippi rally, Wheeler traveled to Greece, Egypt, and Syria as a lecturer for the US State Department. Upon his return to the States, however, his health took a serious turn and he grew extremely ill. He did not make a full recovery until about early October. Wheeler's physicians believed he was suffering from exhaustion that stemmed from the stresses of work and his many civic responsibilities. Upon his doctor's orders, Wheeler took a break to recuperate and spent several weeks at a rest home in Capahosic, Virginia.[49]

Despite his declining health, Wheeler was well enough to give an address at the SRC's annual meeting in November in which he focused on Black Power and the challenges it posed to the civil rights movement. "When it all is totaled up," argued Wheeler, "1966 unfortunately will be remembered as the year of two imponderables—the Black Power slogan and the term White Backlash." The White Backlash, Wheeler explained, represented "poorly concealed racism," bolstered by a complete abandonment of the need to protect the citizenship rights of black Americans. He criticized and dismissed White Backlash as being false conservatism. "Genuine conservatism," continued Wheeler, "seeks to identify that which is worthwhile and preserve it." At the same time, conservatives "should support every honest effort toward the betterment and orderly development of our nation." He considered the language of Black Power to be fueling negative white attitudes, no matter what the intent. He argued that if Americans were to accept the popular explanation for what Black Power meant, they would recognize it as "greater political, economic, and cultural leverage for Negroes." That, noted Wheeler, was something he and the many organizations he affiliated himself with had worked to achieve for decades. Nevertheless, the Black Power slogan "generated discordant overtones," and he believed it was not a good idea to exchange one form of racism for another.[50]

Yet even if the Black Power slogan elicited wrongheadedness, Wheeler clarified, the underlying problems that contributed to its upsurge had been decades in the making. Therefore, those issues had to be fully understood and no longer ignored. "If we take the trouble to listen," Wheeler explained, "we can hear an urgent message in this slogan—a message of patience worn thin, of hopes too often shattered, of promises too long unfulfilled." In other words, the Black Power slogan could not be used as a scapegoat or as a rationale for racism. Wheeler's overall point to the SRC members was that neither Black Power nor White Backlash would move the country forward productively. They were opposite extremes that could distract from the larger economic struggle for civil rights. Moreover, Wheeler feared that the two "imponderables" would stall progress toward greater freedom and reverse hard-fought gains, similar to what happened to freedpeople after Reconstruction. Finally, Wheeler believed that the battle for freedom could not be won without interracial cooperation because it was also "about freeing the southern white man . . . freeing him from the shackles of bigotry and the enslaving hypnosis of the political demagogue."[51]

By this time, Wheeler had decided to resign as the SRC president to reduce his obligations so that he could improve his health. However, the new executive director, Paul Anthony, pleaded with him to continue on as president because "it would be extremely unfortunate to lose your leadership at this time," especially since "during the past year and a half, there have been a number of staff changes at the Council and it would be very unfortunate if it appeared to the public that there were more changes than would be desirable for a continued, stable operation as the Council is known by its friends and supporters." Anthony assured Wheeler that "we can see to it that you have called to your attention an absolute minimum of the affairs of the organization; particularly any of the details which would tend to interrupt you or require time of you." Wheeler agreed and stayed on as the organization's president through 1969.[52]

By September 1967, amid the ongoing urban renewal program, the city council annexed the Bacon Street "area for additional Negro housing in the city." The decision immediately received criticism from black Durham, most notably from Benjamin S. Ruffin, now the executive director of the UOCI. Ruffin and others criticized the city council for deciding to squeeze another public housing project into the black section of the city. "Historically," Ruffin explained, "the southeastern area of Durham has been set aside for Negroes. The Durham City Council . . . did not deviate from the history of the city by voting to place another public housing project in the southeastern section of the city which already comprises

75% of the city's Negro housing." Ruffin warned that these actions would potentially cause uprisings similar to the ones that had already taken place in other parts of the country, such as Detroit and Newark. In that an overwhelming majority of black Durham opposed the actions the city council had taken, leaders from several organizations, including the UOCI, the DCNA, and the NAACP came together to discuss what could be done. People such as Ruffin also continued to criticize the DHA and called on its executive director, Carvie S. Oldham, to be fired. Other critics of the Bacon Street Housing Project, namely Louis E. Austin, placed blame squarely on the shoulders of Mayor Wense Grabarek for not taking black concerns about housing seriously. "The greatest tragedy," Austin proclaimed, "that has resulted in the refusal of the City Council of Durham to listen to the earnest pleas of the leaders of its Negro citizens . . . is the stark loss of faith in Durham's white leadership. . . . There is now a widespread feeling among Negro citizens of intelligence here that for the most part the City Council is but a puppet organization with its control being manipulated by a source well hidden behind the scenes but whose identity is well-known to any and all Negroes of average intelligence in Durham. . . . It is the opinion of this newspaper that nothing has happened in Durham within the past 40 years or more to bring Negro citizens of all walks of life together, as the apparent determination on the part of the white power structure to ram the Bacon Street housing project down Negroes['] throats come hell or high water."[53]

The opposition to the Bacon Street Housing Project rallied black Durham. The protestors were not against public housing per se but wanted the city to integrate the city's housing more fully while spreading the development of these projects across the landscape, and not just in black areas. Despite the black community's stance on the Bacon Street Housing Project, however, the DHA moved forward with plans to build two hundred housing units on twenty acres of land adjacent to McDougald Terrace. Ruffin and other leaders opposed to the city council's actions made appeals to white organizations such as the Durham Council on Human Relations (DCHR), the Durham affiliate branch of the NCCHR, and the SRC. In a speech to the DCHR, Ruffin warned white city leaders that there would be increased tensions between black Durham and city leaders if the latter failed to address their concerns.

Ruffin strongly urged the DCHR to join the voices of dissent in the black community and challenged whites in the audience to become better informed about the plight of black people in Durham. By early October, despite some 35,000 or so black Durhamites being opposed to the measure, the city council voted in favor of building the Bacon Street Project. Black Durham saw the move as marginalizing their voice, a sign of the white power structure's ultimate disrespect toward them.[54]

As black Durham bemoaned the fact that the city had approved another public housing project in this area, the actions elicited closer inspection of the DHA more generally. In September 1967, too, a citizens advisory committee visited some of the city's housing projects to get a firsthand look at the conditions faced by blacks living in them. The grievances included: "lack of recreation, unfinished landscaping, poor ventilation during summer months, apartments not being painted and bad communication channels between tenants and the Housing Authority." More importantly, the citizens group called attention to the DHA's executive director, Carvie S. Oldham. Attorney H. M. Michaux Jr., a leader in the DCNA, represented black public housing residents, and at the meeting with the citizens group, "Oldham was questioned on his 'about face attitude' regarding tenant organization, by Atty. H. M. Michaux, Jr., to which he answered that he has been accused of many things during his directorship, but he stated that attempts during the past six years have been made to employ a social worker." In the ongoing Bacon Street Housing Project debate, black ministers throughout the city staged protests. By December 1967, past DCNA leaders and now city councilmen Shag Stewart and Caldwell E. Boulware (the longtime DCNA executive secretary) backed calls to fire Oldham. In March, resistance surfaced again to the DHA's plans to build an additional 2,500 public housing units, roughly 1,279 of them in southeast Durham. Guy Rankin, head of the newly formed East Durham Group, complained, "We don't understand how a Housing Authority Board would purposely put a minority group in one corner of the city and create a super ghetto." "Some people might be offended," Rankin said, "but, we see that Hope Valley and Forrest Hills or Crosdale [Croasdaile] [two of the wealthiest neighborhoods in Durham] don't have any of their fair share of the projects." Moreover, Rankin also expressed the black community's sentiments when he said, "Our feeling is that with

1279 units in southeast Durham, we certainly have our fair share and that North, South, East and West [Durham] should have equal distribution. I don't see how people can let this go on."[55]

Despite Wheeler's poor health, which posed a problem for him again during the latter half of 1967, he continued with his involvement in several progressive developments in Durham and across other parts of North Carolina. In the late 1960s, the NC Fund had begun to support independent spin-off agencies to help sidestep the political developments unfolding from the New Right. These were the challenges that Wheeler had warned would come during the implementation phase of the black freedom movement. In January 1967, as the White Backlash strengthened its resolve and conservative politicians targeted the War on Poverty, Wheeler helped start the statewide Low Income Housing Development Corporation (LIHDC) and became its president. As the NC Fund sought to "increase the supply of housing for low-income people," it received approval from the OEO to set-up a spin-off program for that purpose. According to LIHDC history, it was "organized to develop and assist local nonprofit housing sponsors. . . . [and] hopes to establish knowledgeable and sophisticated groups to operate housing programs on a self-sustaining basis in the future." The establishment of spin-off programs like the LIHDC became necessary as the NC Fund and its CAPs came under intense scrutiny by the state's Republicans, particularly US Congressman Jim Gardner and others who sought to block further OEO funding. They wanted to roll back the liberal policies of the Johnson administration's Great Society because they believed the NC Fund used government funds for political activities, which they believed to be outside the scope of the OEO. The LIHDC received its initial grant of $345,406 directly from OEO and approximately $41,875 from the NC Fund. When the LIHDC began, it operated in Durham, Greensboro, Salisbury, and Charlotte. By 1970, it had spread to about eighteen cities throughout the state.[56]

In February 1967, Wheeler helped lay the groundwork for the establishment of the North Carolina Voter Education Project (NCVEP). At the initial luncheon (which was also attended by VEP director Vernon E. Jordan) Wheeler gave an overview of the DCNA's experience and history in voter registration as the organization had "one of the highest percentages of registered Negroes voters in the State." Therefore, he strongly "supported the formation of a statewide [voter education] council." The NCCHR was one of the strongest SRC branches, and he believed that an additional SRC entity could prove just as effective. A few weeks after the meeting, Jordan wrote to Wheeler with optimism, saying, "Your presence at the meeting and the interest demonstrated there convinced me that a state-wide project there is more than a mere possibility." At another planning meeting in March, the NCVEP's thirty-one-member steering committee selected John Edwards as executive director. During the direct-action protest during the early 1960s, Edwards had been one of the student leaders. He later became the DCNA's chairman during the 1980s. In addition to the "small one-year operational grant" from the SRC, the NCVEP received a "six-month program development grant" from the NC Fund. The NCVEP used the grant for "workshops [which] were held on how to organize voter registration campaigns, how to get out the vote, election laws of North Carolina, community organization and voter registration, and the 1965 Voting Rights Act." The OB's Howard Fuller gave the keynote on "the Negro and politics." In October, the NCVEP staff along with representatives from UOCI, the Durham NAACP, and the DCNA traveled to Fayetteville, where they held similar workshops for the Fayetteville Public Housing Tenants' Organization.[57]

By April 1968, President Johnson announced to the American public that he would not seek another run for the presidency, largely due to the failures of the Vietnam War. Nothing could have prepared Wheeler, the black freedom movement, or the nation for what took place on April 4. On that day, Dr. Martin Luther King Jr. was assassinated by an unknown assassin's bullet. King had been in Memphis to support a black sanitation workers' strike, which underscored the remaining economic injustices. The date normally held another kind of significance for the Wheeler family as Wheeler's daughter, Julia Wheeler Taylor (now following in her father's footsteps as an officer at M&F Bank's Raleigh Branch), was to celebrate her thirty-first birthday. Wheeler had known King since the civil rights leader was a boy and then a young man coming of age as a student at Morehouse College, where Wheeler served on the board of trustees. Over the previous decade, Wheeler had had the opportunity to work with King on several projects related to black higher education in the South, and both King and his father served with Wheeler on the Morehouse College board of trustees at the time of the younger King's assassination. In the aftermath of his death, both the DCNA and SRC passed resolutions and sent condolences to Coretta Scott King, Dr. King's widow. The DCNA's resolution said King's "non-violent program made great contributions to the progress of Negroes and their efforts to achieve first-class citizenship," and "the nation has lost its champion of civil and human rights for common men." The DCNA also cautioned Durham's black community to "exemplify self-restraint and self-discipline which will be the greatest memorial to our fallen leaders." The SRC's resolution read in part: "This is the time for white Americans to forego lecturing black Americans against violating the non-violent philosophy to which Dr. King's life will stand as a memorial for all time. . . . Let white America acknowledge that black Americans, as Dr. King has proved, have equal moral personality as human beings and have the qualities of leadership and courage and dignity which all Americans need." At its next meeting, the Morehouse College board of trustees discussed starting a fund for King's children, and before ending the meeting, Wheeler challenged the board members to pledge their contributions to the fund right then and there; the board raised $107,000 before adjourning. King's death led to widespread uprisings in every major city across the United States. In Durham, a day after King's death, there was a silent protest march from Fayetteville Street to City Hall. However, in the ensuing days Durham fell victim to widespread arson, which forced local leaders to bring in the National Guard and institute a citywide curfew. King's death left a huge void in the civil rights movement, and it also reminded the entire country how far it had to go before it would be a truly free, prosperous, and open society.[58]

In 1969, former Vice President Richard M. Nixon began his first term as president of the United States. Nixon's election effectively ended what had been one of the most optimistic yet tumultuous decades in American history. In Wheeler's final year as the SRC president, Black Power consciousness made its way to the offices of the SRC in Atlanta, Georgia. The organization's black staff formed a grievance committee and looked to Wheeler to help their cause. In addition, black students took on their administrators at college campuses across the country. In Wheeler's hometown of Durham, a group of black students at Duke

University took over the Allen Administration Building to force the school to provide black studies programs and to increase the overall enrollment of black students at the university. In Atlanta, a group of students held Wheeler and other members of the Morehouse board of trustees hostage and demanded the school incorporate more courses that reflected black consciousness.

The story of urban renewal in Durham, like in so many other cities throughout the country, is a complicated and multilayered narrative that often leaves us with more questions than answers. The history of urban renewal is often boiled down to alleged culprits—including the black business elite—profiting at the expense of poorer citizens. While there is truth in this assessment, the narrative warrants a broadened perspective. If Wheeler promoted urban renewal for self-serving motives, that would mean he was victimizing the same community that had previously benefited from his battle for freedom. Such an assessment stands in stark contrast to the history in this book's previous chapters. It does not gel with Wheeler's record of achievement and commitment to seeking racial equality and economic justice for blacks, and it doesn't consider other factors that might explain the end results. It presumes Durham's black leadership were naïve or incapable of seeing through the veil of deceit, even though their previous actions on so many issues reflected thoroughness, careful analysis, and strategic planning. In the past, black leaders scrutinized every bond proposal that stood to have adverse effects on black Durham, and they did the same when it came to urban renewal. In the end, the outcome of urban renewal in Durham revealed the limitations and paradox of its black leadership, especially its black business leaders.[59]

If examined closely, the reasoning behind Wheeler's support for urban renewal is consistent and in line with his vision of New South prosperity. First, he remained adamant about the decade of the 1960s being the time for blacks to reenter the larger marketplace. In 1964, he "described the next order of business" for blacks this way: "The current wave of militancy can succeed only in removing the artificial barriers to our return to the marketplace." Going further, he noted that "Negro businessmen must help the Negro 'reenter the marketplace through pressure for maintenance of a free and open society by every means at our disposal, including some of the extraordinary ones in which all too few of us have participated in recent months." In other words, black business would advance if black businesspeople fought for racial and economic equality for black people. Second, Wheeler believed in equal housing and saw urban renewal as the best path to opening up the wider housing market to blacks in accordance with freedom of movement. Urban renewal had the added benefit of providing access by improving educational and employment opportunities available to blacks. He viewed urban renewal as being in the best interest of civil rights, black economic power, and New South prosperity.[60]

In the end, Wheeler and others mistakenly placed too much stock in these possibilities. However, he may have done so because he had witnessed change through years of continued agitation. As Wheeler explained in a *Business Week* article, "Some Negro businessmen have never known the thrill of seeing relationships change from a patronizing popularity to mutual understanding and respect."[61] Lastly, Wheeler believed that the direct action or "second phase" of blacks' battle for freedom had reached its twilight hour. They had entered a new day—the third or implementation phase of their efforts. This third, and perhaps final, phase of the black freedom movement was unchartered territory. In Wheeler's mind, this would be the most difficult area to penetrate because it would result in blacks truly becoming part of the larger American society. In many ways, then, urban renewal's failures represented the major challenges blacks faced at that juncture, challenges Wheeler and his fellow leaders well understood. Yet they were still unwelcomed strangers in their own home.

Conclusion

> The fight is far from over. Many, many objectives have not been achieved. Some are yet only barely sighted. Equality is still more an ideal than a fact. Until it is a fact, the crusade needs every ally it can get.
>
> John Hervey Wheeler, 1967

"On the wall behind John Wheeler's desk is a candid photograph of Wheeler and former President Johnson working together," according to a "Tar Heel of the Week" article in the *Raleigh News and Observer*. Wheeler approvingly called Johnson "quite a person" as the two had come to know and work closely with one another beginning in 1961. At M&F Bank, Wheeler also kept "personally autographed pictures on his office wall [of] Hubert Humphrey . . . John Kennedy, and Ralph Bunche." "And," noted another newspaper article, "Wheeler has never forgotten his first love: education." In the last decade of his life, Wheeler continued his activism and refused to relinquish most of his numerous responsibilities. In 1971, for example, he supported a bill to abolish the death penalty in North Carolina. "At this period in our history," the activist banker argued in a speech before the General Assembly's House Judiciary Committee, "little or no reason remains for us to continue the exercise of vengeance by man against man." Furthermore, he explained, the death penalty had become "recognized as a cruel and unusual penalty, inflicted for the most part against the poor, the black population and the uneducated."[1]

During this same time, Wheeler received many awards and accolades for his civil rights work. In 1967, his alma mater, Morehouse College, presented him with an honorary doctorate for his work as a member of its board of trustees. In 1970, Duke University, where former North Carolina governor Terry Sanford became president, also awarded him an honorary doctorate. That same year, he received the Frank Porter Graham Civil Liberties Award for his defense of freedom for all North Carolinians.

The next year, North Carolina Central University (formerly North Carolina College) bestowed upon him an honorary doctorate as well. In 1976, Morehouse College formally dedicated "John H. Wheeler Hall" as the school's Social Sciences and Business Administration Building. At the dedication ceremony, Wheeler told the audience, "The establishment of this new facility is many times more important as a tool for training young black leaders to take their appointed places in American life than the honor which Morehouse [has] bestowed upon me." Fittingly, several tennis courts flank Wheeler Hall, facilitating a sport that he loved and played until three years before his death. The institutions he had a hand in shaping continue to thrive. These include M&F Bank; NC Mutual; Morehouse College; the Atlanta University Center (AUC); the original building of the St. Joseph's AME Church, which has operated as the St. Joseph's Historic Foundation since 1975 and continues to preserve black Durham's history and serve as a cultural arts center; and the Stanford L. Warren Library, a branch of the Durham County Library System. In the 1970s, the DCNA changed its name to the Durham Committee on the Affairs of Black People, and although one could argue that it wields less political power than it once did, it continues as an important civil rights organization.[2]

Because of their father's activism and sacrifices, Wheeler's two children, Julia Wheeler Taylor and Warren Hervey Wheeler, had access to an increasingly integrated American society, and both became pioneers in their fields. Julia eventually followed in her father's footsteps and became M&F Bank's first woman president in 1983. Although she took a path similar to her father's, Julia made the decision early on to forge her own identity, regardless of her father's reputation in business. In 1955 she went to work for M&F Bank at its Raleigh Branch, where she temporarily replaced another woman employee on maternity leave for three months. Well before she decided on a career in banking, however, she recognized the limitations placed on the professional aspirations of black women at that time, traditional gender roles that limited her career options to nurse, teacher, or secretary. Much like her mother, Julia knew for sure that she did not want to become a teacher.[3]

While her father fought for employment opportunities for black Americans, there were limits on how far black women could advance in business, even at her father's bank. At one point, Julia served as acting branch manager at the Raleigh location, but it was made clear to her that she would have the position only until a "qualified man" could be hired as a permanent replacement. Julia eventually broke down some of those barriers because of her skills and abilities in finance. In her determination to break free from her father's shadow, she struck out on her own because she "knew she had to go somewhere and prove [herself] on [her] own." In 1961 she packed up her car and drove across country. Ending up in Los Angeles, Julia quickly managed to obtain three job offers and went to work for Bank of America as the secretary to a branch manager. While her father could not devote as much time to his children as their mother did, Julia remembered that he encouraged her to "do your best in whatever you do." Julia was quickly lured away from Bank of America when she landed a job with the Broadway Federal Savings and Loan Association. There, she witnessed firsthand women in positions of authority as officers, something that served as a serious awakening for her. Julia became an officer with the financial institution. Los Angeles provided her with a strong sense of fulfillment and accomplishment because she had enormous success. Julia returned to the Tar Heel State in 1965 and went back to M&F Bank's Raleigh Branch. She became assistant cashier in 1966 and vice president and manager a year later, the branch's senior vice president in 1978. After working at the bank for eighteen years, she became head of the institution, which made her the third generation to manage the bank that her maternal grandfather, Dr. Stanford L. Warren, had helped establish. Julia blazed a new path for black women in corporate America, while also continuing the legacies of the black women who had worked for decades at NC Mutual and M&F Bank. Between 1983 and 2000, when Julia retired from M&F Bank, she helped propel the institution into the twenty-first century, including online banking.[4]

Warren Hervey Wheeler took a more unconventional career path than his sister. Ever since 1957, when Julia took her younger brother along to her flying lessons, Warren Hervey was "sky struck." At age sixteen, he began taking flying lessons himself. After graduating from high school, he attended NC A&T for about a year and contemplated a career in electrical engineering; however, college interested Warren very little, and he left. He enrolled in the American Flyers School in Oklahoma City, and by age nineteen, he had a commercial pilot's license. In part because of his limited flying experience but also because airlines refused to hire black pilots at the time, Warren was unable to obtain employment with any of the major commercial airlines. To accumulate the required flying hours, he started a small flying school in Chapel Hill with financial assistance from his parents. Because of his father's political connections with then governor Terry Sanford, Warren had the opportunity to fly the governor across the state on chartered flights. With firsthand knowledge of Warren's flying ability, Sanford personally contacted Piedmont Airline's president, Tom Davis, who allowed Warren to take their pilot's examination in 1966. When he passed, the company hired him on full-time, making him, at twenty-two, one of the youngest pilots with the airline as well as its first black pilot. In 1969, Warren made an even bigger leap by starting his own business, Wheeler Flying Service, which he billed as a "charter, air cargo, and aircraft maintenance service." By the mid-1970s, Wheeler Flying Service had become Wheeler Airlines and carried about one thousand passengers a year. It specialized in flights to rural parts of eastern North Carolina, a void in larger airlines' service, and it scheduled flights between Charlotte and Durham, between Greenville and Charlotte, and to Newport News and Richmond, Virginia. While managing Wheeler Airlines with significant assistance from his mother, who took on a number of tasks including bookkeeping, Warren Hervey stayed on as a pilot with Piedmont Airlines. Over seventeen years, until it closed in 1986, Wheeler Airlines trained more than one hundred African American pilots for careers in aviation, and it made hiring and training minority pilots a priority.[5]

On July 6, 1978, John Hervey Wheeler died at his home in Durham after several years of health challenges. The following September, six hundred people gathered at the Raleigh Civic Center for a one-hundred-dollar-a-plate dinner honoring his life. Former Chapel Hill mayor Howard N. Lee, who at the time was secretary of North Carolina's Department of Natural Resources and Community Development, chaired the celebratory evening. In attendance were North Carolina governor James B. Hunt Jr., House Speaker Carl J. Stewart, State Senator Kenneth B. Royall, New York congressman Allard Lowenstein, former HUD secretary Robert C. Weaver, North Carolina Court of Appeals judge Richard

Erwin, State Senator Clarence E. Lightner, U.S. Attorney H. M. "Mickey" Michaux Jr., John W. Winters, and State Representative Henry E. Frye. The dinner marked Wheeler's lifelong accomplishments as a businessman, lawyer, political and civil rights activist, civic leader, and philanthropist, and it kick-started the John H. Wheeler Foundation, a scholarship fund that Lee hoped would grow to $5 million. In part because the Wheeler family was uncertain about the idea, Lee eventually gave it up and gave the $80,000 that had been raised to the North Carolina Central University Law School, where Wheeler had been among the first graduates. The John H. Wheeler Endowment and John H. Wheeler Scholarship Fund continue to financially support law students at the university, which has ranked among the top clinical law schools in the country. Lee believed honoring Wheeler was important because he "had really been a key to bridging the gap between the ethnic groups," and therefore "his life [needed to] be extended through reaching into future generations and helping those generations both financially and psychologically."[6]

Wheeler had been a mentor to a rising generation of black political leaders in North Carolina. Lee initially met Wheeler ten years earlier after Lee gave a speech at the state Democratic Convention; by that time, Wheeler was the state Democratic Party's treasurer. Reflecting back on his speech, Lee recalled saying something like "black power plus white power divided by green power would lead to people power." Wheeler seemed very impressed by the speech because it reflected his own philosophical outlook and emphasis on economic power; in the years that followed, Wheeler took Lee under his wing. When the state Democratic Party restructured itself after the 1968 Democratic National Convention in Chicago, Lee became the state Democratic Party's second vice chair, a move that he credited Wheeler with helping to "mastermind." Through the years, Lee continued to seek Wheeler's political advice on a range of issues. When Lee decided to run for lieutenant governor in 1976, he went straight to Wheeler since he was considered to be the "king-maker" for blacks seeking statewide political office. Although Wheeler felt Lee's plan to run for that particular office was premature because "North Carolina wasn't ready for a black lieutenant governor," he gave Lee his full support. Lee ultimately lost the Democratic nomination in a primary runoff, but since then he has held several political offices, including becoming a state senator during the 1990s. In 2003, he became the chairman of the North Carolina State Board of Education.[7]

Vernon E. Jordan Jr. also fondly recalled how Wheeler mentored him, "laid on hands," and opened up new leadership opportunities for him. Recognizing Jordan's leadership potential, Wheeler frequently sent the young civil rights leader to represent him as a stand-in on national commissions and boards. Wheeler provided Jordan with "an opportunity to meet people . . . but also to be a part of the discussion of issues at the national level that related to local problems." In his memoir *Vernon Can Read!* Jordan wrote that as their relationship grew, Wheeler became "an advisor and confidant" to him. "I was never with John Wheeler," noted Jordan, "without being instructed and inspired" by "lessons in leadership." In 1965, in keeping with his desire to see that qualified blacks received top-level management positions, Wheeler asked SRC's executive committee to consider Jordan for the executive director's post. In 1977, Wheeler handpicked Jordan to succeed him as the second board chairman of the AUC. He later became executive director of the United Negro College Fund (UNCF) and then the National Urban League (NUL). Jordan also enjoyed a successful business career in corporate America, serving on the board of directors at American Express. After the 1992 presidential election, he headed president-elect Bill Clinton's transition team, the first African American to hold such a position. Jordan called Wheeler and others North Carolina's "freedom fighters" and "courageous individuals in times when courage was in short supply in North Carolina and the South."[8]

In addition to Lee and Jordan, Wheeler became a mentor to several other young and ambitious black leaders, including Nathan Garrett, who Wheeler put on the board of directors at M&F Bank. Strikingly, Wheeler also mentored the black radical Benjamin S. Ruffin Jr., the former Operation Breakthrough (OB) community organizer. In the late 1960s and early 1970s, Ruffin became one of Wheeler's biggest critics and challenged his leadership of organizations such as the DCNA. Yet Ruffin received an important lesson from Wheeler that helped seal their relationship. When Ruffin "decided to take on the Durham Committee on Negro Affairs" and accused "the Committee of not being open enough" because it held meetings behind closed doors in matters that concerned the entire black community, he met with Wheeler to discuss the issue. Without hesitancy, Wheeler pointed out that at that moment, Ruffin had become a party to the kind of behind-the-scenes tactics he so despised. Wheeler taught Ruffin that it was always unwise to enter into controversial meetings where important decisions had to be made without caucusing supporters beforehand to ensure certain measures would pass. The meeting "blew [Ruffin's] mind." Wheeler later helped him in a development project called Unity Village.

Some blacks saw Wheeler's embrace of Ruffin as self-serving, as evidence he feared that the younger activist, who had large appeal with the black masses, would eclipse his own political leadership. This was especially true during the height of the black power movement, when, to avoid political showdowns, Wheeler refused to call yearly mass meetings to elect DCNA officers as the organization's constitution had stipulated.[9]

Whatever Wheeler's motives for taking Ruffin under his wing, he nurtured the young leader's potential and appointed Ruffin to the board of directors at M&F Bank. Once Jim Hunt Jr. became North Carolina's governor in 1977, Wheeler assisted Ruffin in obtaining a position as one of the governor's staff members. Ruffin became the director of the North Carolina Human Relations Council and then the governor's special assistant to minority affairs in 1978. Some black leaders saw Ruffin's appointment as Wheeler's move to have a "direct pipeline into the governor's office." In some ways, Ruffin's appointment tempered the younger man's bent toward militancy as he now worked from within the establishment to seek black inclusion in state government. Ruffin was later credited with increasing the number of African Americans in government, and he had a hand in increasing the number of black judges throughout the state from two to seventeen. After Ruffin's stint in the Hunt administration, he joined corporate America and went on to work for the NC Mutual. From there he joined RJR Nabisco as director of corporate affairs; he also served in that same capacity with R. J. Reynolds Tobacco. Like his mentor, Ruffin also became a leader in higher education. Most notably, Ruffin received an appointment to the Board of Governors of the UNC System in 1991. In 1998, he made history by becoming the board's first black chairman, bringing to fruition Wheeler's determination in earlier decades that blacks enjoy power sharing at integrated institutions. As the UNC System's board chairman, Ruffin was a very vocal advocate on behalf of historically black colleges and universities (HBCUs) operated by the state. Between 1998 and 2002, Ruffin helped steer a $3.5 billion bond deal toward "construction and renovations on UNC and community college campuses. This was the largest bond referendum in the history of American higher education." On July 16, 2018, another one of Wheeler's mentees, North Carolina congressman G. K. Butterfield of North Carolina's First District (which includes Durham) stood before his colleagues on the floor of the US House of Representatives and urged them to pass H.R. 3460. The bill that Butterfield introduced would name the US courthouse in Durham the John Hervey Wheeler United States Courthouse. The bill passed in a voice vote, and a formal dedication of the courthouse was planned for the fall of 2019. Amid controversies around the country surrounding public historical memory, the courthouse stands as testament to John Hervey Wheeler's struggle for racial and economic justice.[10]

Acknowledgments

Let me start by thanking Anne Dean Dotson, senior acquisitions editor, and the rest of the team at the University Press of Kentucky for making this a great process all around. I am also appreciative to the Civil Rights and the Struggle for Black Equality in the Twentieth Century series editors, Steven F. Lawson, Cynthia Griggs Fleming, and Hasan Kwame Jeffries. Additionally, I'd like to thank Kathleen Kearns and Susan Murray for their careful copyediting and the anonymous readers for providing extremely helpful feedback, which no doubt improved the manuscript significantly. Much appreciation also goes out to the *North Carolina Historical Review* and its editor, Anne Miller, for granting permission to include an earlier article I published in the journal.

The journey into the historical profession began at my alma mater, North Carolina Central University (NCCU), in Durham, North Carolina. These professors and mentors are part of my extended "eagle" family because they taught me to soar and always demonstrated a genuine commitment to their students. Thanks to Carlton Wilson, Jerry Gershenhorn, Freddie Parker, Jim Harper, Lydia Lindsey, Percy Murray, Henry Lewis Suggs, Baiyina Muhammad, and the late Renaldo Lawson (1943–2018). The late Sylvia M. Jacobs (1946–2013) introduced "her" students to the Association for the Study of African American Life and History (ASALH), and I am forever grateful to her for doing so. I share this alongside a great group of other colleagues and friends trained at the "sloping hills, the verdant green."

I am grateful to have been a part of such a rich and vibrant scholarly community at the University of North Carolina at Chapel Hill (UNC). Thanks to Jim Leloudis, Jerma Jackson, Crystal Feimster, Jacquelyn Dowd Hall, and Reginald Hildebrand for their invaluable expertise. I would also like to thank Heather Williams, W. Fitzhugh Brundage, Malinda Maynor Lowry, Harry Watson, Genna Rae McNeil, Joseph Glatthaar, Donald

Reid, Sarah Shields, John Sweet, and Theda Perdue. Thanks to colleagues who shared advice, laughter, and encouragement along the way. They include Will Griffin, Jennifer Dixon-McKnight, Chris Cameron, Josh Davis, Dwana Waugh, Tim Williams, Robert Ferguson, Hilary Green, Catherine Conner, Shannon Eaves, Brandon Byrd, Brad Proctor, Randy Browne, Warren Milteer, Evan Faulkenbury, and Cecelia Moore. I will always remain indebted to the Moore Undergraduate Research Apprentice Program (MURAP), especially James Coleman, Rosa Perelmuter, Henry Frierson, Karla Slocum, Caroline Tyson, Sandy Darity, Aman Nadhiri, and Kennetta Hammond Perry. Finally, thank you to Dr. Cookie Newsom of the Department of Diversity and Multicultural Affairs for exposing me to new ways of thinking about diversity in higher education.

To the Department of History at the University of Tennessee, Knoxville, because I have learned some very important lessons about academia from all of you, a heartfelt thank you! In particular, I would like to thank staff members Mary Beckley, Bernie Koprince, and Kim Harrison, as well as faculty members Shannen Dee Williams, Julie Reed, Tore Olsson, Luke Harlow, Monica Black, Ernie Freeberg, Kristen Block, Chris Magra, Bill Mercer, Bob Hutton, Pat Ruttenberg, Chad Black, Vejas Liulevicius, Jeff Norrell, and Charles Sanft. Thanks to the UT Humanities Center for awarding me a yearlong fellowship during the 2016–2017 academic year, which allowed me to make significant progress on the book manuscript. In particular, thanks to Tom Heffernan, Amy Alias, Joan Murray, and all of the Fellows. Thanks for unwavering support from Rickey L. Hall (University of Washington), formerly the vice chancellor of the Office for Diversity and Inclusion.

The broader field of history is filled with so many brilliant minds that have made such a positive impact on me personally and professionally. These scholars include Jarvis Hargrove, Tony Frazier, Sonja Woods, Takeia Anthony, D' Weston Haywood, A. J. Donaldson, LaKesha Laster, Starr Battle, Marcus Allen, Terry Moseley, Brian Robinson, Marcus Nevius, Maurice Hobson, Sowande' Mustakeem, Deirdre Cooper Owens, James Conway, Shirletta Kinchen, Daryl Scott, Gregory Mixon, Shennette Garett-Scott, Pero Dagbovie, Robert E. Weems Jr., Juliet E. K. Walker, Chad Williams, Thavolia Glymph, the late Raymond Gavins (1942–2016), Arwin Smallwood, Philip Rubio, John H. Morrow Jr., Tomiko

Brown-Nagin, LaShawn Harris, Kamal McClarin, Crystal Sanders, Gavin Wright, Charles McKinney Jr., Andre Johnson, Shannon King, Nishani Frazier, Sharita Jacobs, Eric Duke, K. T. Ewing, Reggie Ellis, Stefan Bradley, the late Leslie Brown (1954–2016), Randal Jelks, Clarence Lang, Sundiata Cha-Jua, Andrew Canady, Robert Smith, and Bill Link.

The relationship between the historian and archivist is an important one. I owe much gratitude to the incredible staff at the Atlanta University Center Robert W. Woodruff Library for making the John Hervey Wheeler Collection (JHWC) accessible to me for research well before the papers were fully processed. The library also gave me the RWWL Travel Award, which made it possible for me to complete significant follow-up research. A warm thanks goes to Karen Jefferson, Andrea Jackson (now executive director at the Black Metropolis Research Consortium), Kayin Shabazz, Stacy Jones, Melvin Collier, Tiffany Atwater, Amber Anderson, and Sarah Tanner for always providing me with a welcoming environment to conduct archival research. The Southern Historical Collection at UNC is an equally awesome place to do research, and I had the rare opportunity to pull my own research materials from the shelves while working there as a graduate student. I am especially grateful to Matt Turi, Laura Hart, Tim West, Rachel Canada, Biff Hollingsworth, Jason Tomberlin, and Holly Smith (now college archivist at Spelman College). The guiding influence behind most research projects on black Durham is none other than NCCU archivist André D. Vann, and the same is true for this book. I can't thank him enough because he first pointed me to the JHWC, shared research, answered countless queries, and revealed his vast knowledge about all things North Carolina. Lynn Richardson at the North Carolina Collection of the Durham County Library was always an excellent resource as well. The John Hope Franklin Research Center for African and African American History and Culture at Duke University awarded me a travel grant to conduct research at the Rubenstein Library, which proved immensely helpful. The staff at the Auburn Avenue Research Library in Atlanta, Georgia, found documents for me that informed an important part of my research at a very crucial moment in the process. I also received the Moody Research Grant from the Lyndon B. Johnson Memorial Library and Museum to examine the LBJ Presidential Papers in Austin, Texas.

To my family and friends, I appreciate all of you more than words can express, and this book is as much a testament to your love, support, and sacrifice as much as anything else. A special thanks to my uncle Keith Torrence for free room and board in Atlanta while conducting the bulk of this research on a graduate student budget, and to my cousin Dominique Cuthbertson for her research assistance. To my wife, Eboni, love is a powerful expression, and you've shown me that in ways you'll never understand. Through your love you've taught me about sacrifice, forgiveness, strength, commitment, trust, selflessness, kindness, perseverance, thoughtfulness, and compassion. I've become a better human being because of you. Thank you for being such a great friend to me even when I don't deserve it. To God be the Glory!

Notes

Introduction

1. John H. Wheeler, "A Negro Banker Speaks to the South," *Tarheel Banker* 24 (November 1945): 27.

2. "John H. Wheeler Resume," Wheeler Biographical File, Atlanta University Center Robert W. Woodruff Library (hereinafter "Wheeler Resume"); "Banker with a Mission: Successful Negro Bank President, Firm in Pushing for Both Negro Advancement and North Carolina Development, Wins an Influential Role throughout South and in the Nation," *Business Week*, May 16, 1964; "Wheeler: His Commitments Go Far beyond His Bank," *Carolina Financial Times* (Raleigh), February 9, 1976; "'The Battle for Freedom Begins Every Morning': John Hervey Wheeler, 1908–1978," *Whetstone* (3rd quarter 1978), North Carolina Mutual Life Insurance Company Archives, David M. Rubenstein Rare Book and Manuscript Library, Duke University, Durham, N.C. (hereinafter DMRRBML); "Reflections—John Hervey Wheeler: A Life of Service," Atlanta University Charter Day Convocation Program, October 13, 1978, Wheeler Biographical File, Atlanta University Center Robert W. Woodruff Library; Robert Penn Warren, *Who Speaks for the Negro?* (New York: Random House, 1965), 300–305; *Dictionary of North Carolina Biography*, s.v. "Wheeler, John Hervey"; *African American National Biography*, s.v. "Wheeler, John Hervey."

3. Juliet E. K. Walker, *The History of Black Business in America: Capitalism, Race, Entrepreneurship* (New York: Macmillan Library Reference USA, 1998), chap. 7; William Link, *North Carolina: Change and Tradition in a Southern State* (Wheeling, Ill.: Harlan Davidson, 2009), 338; E. Franklin Frazier, "Durham: Capital of the Black Middle Class," in *The New Negro: An Interpretation*, ed. Alain Locke (1924; New York: Johnson Reprint Corporation, 1968), 333–40; *Pittsburgh Courier*, December 24, 1927, October 26, 1929; David T. Beito and Linda Royster Beito, *T. R. M. Howard's Fight for Civil Rights and Economic Power* (Urbana: University of Illinois Press, 2009), xi.

4. "Wheeler Resume"; "Banker with a Mission"; "Wheeler: His Commitments Go Far beyond His Bank"; "The Battle for Freedom Begins Every Morning"; "Reflections—John Hervey Wheeler: A Life of Service"; Warren, *Who Speaks for the Negro?*, 300–305; *Dictionary of North Carolina Biography*, s.v. "Wheeler, John Hervey"; *African American National Biography*, s.v. "Wheeler, John Hervey."

5. "Wheeler Resume"; "Banker with a Mission"; "Wheeler: His Commitments Go Far beyond His Bank"; "The Battle for Freedom Begins Every Morning"; "Reflections—John Hervey Wheeler: A Life of Service"; Warren, *Who Speaks for the*

Negro?, 300–305; *Dictionary of North Carolina Biography,* s.v. "Wheeler, John Hervey"; *African American National Biography,* s.v. "Wheeler, John Hervey."

6. "Wheeler Resume"; "Banker with a Mission"; "Wheeler: His Commitments Go Far beyond His Bank"; "The Battle for Freedom Begins Every Morning"; "Reflections—John Hervey Wheeler: A Life of Service"; Warren, *Who Speaks for the Negro?*, 300–305; *Dictionary of North Carolina Biography,* s.v. "Wheeler, John Hervey"; *African American National Biography,* s.v. "Wheeler, John Hervey"; John H. Wheeler, "Civil Rights Groups—Their Impact upon the War on Poverty," *Law and Contemporary Problems* 31 (Winter 1966): 152–58.

7. "John Wheeler: Working Quietly for the Progress of Blacks," *Raleigh News and Observer,* March 15, 1970.

8. Wheeler was especially an active member of the Beta Phi Chapter of the Omega Psi Phi Fraternity, Incorporated in the Bull City.

1. From Slavery to Middle-Class Respectability

1. John H. Wheeler, "Kittrell College Faces Today's Challenge for Freedom and Character in Education," March 1, 1960, p. 3, John H. Wheeler Collection, Atlanta University Center Robert W. Woodruff Library (hereinafter cited as JHWC); "John H. Wheeler Delayed Birth Certificate," August 11, 1959; Arthur Bunyan Caldwell, ed., *History of the American Negro and His Institutions, Georgia Edition,* pt. 1 (A. B. Caldwell, 1917), 229–31; Mariah Stuart, *An Economic Detour: A History of Insurance in the Lives of American Negroes* (New York: W. Malliet, 1940), 226–27.

2. John L. Wheeler, *N.C. Mutual Bulletin,* July 12, 1948, JHWC; Dolores Janiewski, *Sisterhood Denied: Race, Gender, and Class in a New South Community* (Philadelphia: Temple University Press, 1985), 74.

3. R. McCants Andrews, *John Merrick: A Biographical Sketch,* electronic ed, (Durham: Seeman Printery, 1920), 158, 160, http://docsouth.unc.edu/nc/andrews/andrews.html#ill1; William K. Boyd, *The Story of Durham: City of the New South* (Durham: Duke University Press, 1925), 282–83, https://babel.hathitrust.org/cgi/pt?id=uc1.$b726899;view=1up;seq=2.

4. John H. Wheeler, "N.C. Mutual Life Insurance Company Founder's Day Address," October 20, 1972, pp. 1–2, JHWC.

5. Ibid.

6. Bennett H. Young, *A History of Jessamine County, Kentucky: From Its Earliest Settlement to 1898* (Louisville, KY: Courier-Journal Job Printing, 1898), 13, 62, 70–71, 79, 85–86, 92–93, 158–61, 234–35; Caldwell, *History of the American Negro, Georgia Edition,* 229; "John L. Wheeler Obituary," April 2, 1957; "Retired Officer of N.C. Mutual Dies in Atlanta," NC Mutual press release, April 1, 1957; "Resolution on the Death of J. L. Wheeler," NC Mutual, April 1, 1957, JHWC; *Carolina Times* (hereinafter cited as *CT*), April 6, 1957; William Jesse Kennedy Jr., "Taps for John L. Wheeler," April 1957, all in JHWC; John H. Wheeler, interview by August Meier, ca. 1960, Durham, N.C., notes, box 139, p. 2, August Meier Papers, Schomburg Center

for Research in Black Culture, New York; Stuart, *An Economic Detour*, 226–27; Herbert G. Gutman, *The Black Family in Slavery and Freedom* (New York: Vintage, 1976), chap. 6; Heather Andrea Williams, *Help Me to Find My People: The African American Search for Family Lost in Slavery* (Chapel Hill: University of North Carolina Press, 2012).

7. Richard D. Sears, *Camp Nelson, Kentucky: A Civil War History* (Lexington: University Press of Kentucky, 2002), xix, xxi, xxvi, xxxiii–xxxiv, xxxvi, xxx, xxxix, l; Richard D. Sears, "John G. Fee, Camp Nelson, and Kentucky Blacks, 1864–1865," *Register of the Kentucky Historical Society* 85 (Winter 1987): 29–45; Victor B. Howard, *The Evangelical War against Slavery and Caste: The Life and Times of John G. Fee* (Selinsgrove, Pa.: Susquehanna University Press, 1996), 150, 158; Marion B. Lucas, *A History of Blacks in Kentucky: From Slavery to Segregation, 1760–1891*, vol. 1 (Frankfort: Kentucky Historical Society, 1992), 151, 154–55, 160–63; George C. Wright, *Life behind a Veil: Blacks in Louisville, Kentucky, 1865–1930* (Baton Rouge: Louisiana State University Press, 1985), 17–18; Young, *A History of Jessamine County*, 185; Victor B. Howard, *Black Liberation in Kentucky: Emancipation and Freedom, 1861–1884* (Lexington: University Press of Kentucky, 1983), 45, 51; James C. Klotter and Freda C. Klotter, *A Concise History of Kentucky* (Lexington: University Press of Kentucky, 2008), 117; Wheeler, interview by August Meier, 2; "Biographical Sketch of Margaret Hervey Wheeler," JHWC.

8. Howard, *Black Liberation in Kentucky*, 167, 170; Klotter and Klotter, *A Concise History of Kentucky*, 120; Lucas, *A History of Blacks in Kentucky*, 230, 234, 255.

9. Caldwell, *History of American Negroes, Georgia Edition*, 229, 231.

10. Charles H. Wesley, *Richard Allen: Apostle of Freedom* (1935; Washington, D.C.: Associated Publishers, 1969); Stephen W. Angell and Anthony B. Pinn, eds., *Social Protest Thought in the African Methodist Episcopal Church, 1862–1939* (Knoxville: University of Tennessee Press, 2000); Richard S. Newman, *Freedom's Prophet: Bishop Richard Allen, the AME Church, and the Black Founding Fathers* (New York: New York University Press, 2008); Charles Spencer Smith, *A History of the African Methodist Episcopal Church; Being a Volume Supplemental to a History of the African Methodist Episcopal Church, by Daniel Alexander Payne, D.D., LL.D., Late One of Its Bishops Chronicling the Principal Events in the Advance of the African Methodist Episcopal Church from 1856 to 1922* (1922; New York: Johnson Reprint, 1968), 340–69; Frederick A. McGinnis, *A History and an Interpretation of Wilberforce University* (Blanchester, Ohio: Brown, 1941), 35–42; Richard R. Wright and John R. Hawkins, *Centennial Encyclopedia of the African Methodist Episcopal Church* (Philadelphia: Book Concern of the AME Church, 1916), 374; William A. Joiner, *A Half Century of Freedom of the Negro in Ohio* (Xenia, Ohio: Smith Adv. Co.), 45; Kevin N. Gaines, *Uplifting the Race: Black Leadership, Politics, and Culture in the Twentieth Century* (Chapel Hill: University of North Carolina Press, 1996), 21, chap. 3; James D. Anderson, *The Education of Blacks in the South, 1860–1935* (Chapel Hill: University of North Carolina Press, 1988), 130, 245, chap. 4. By 1900, the AME Church controlled several black colleges including Edward Waters College (Florida), Allen University (South Carolina), Paul Quinn College (Texas), Western University (Kansas),

Shorter College (Arkansas), Campbell College (Mississippi), Payne College (Alabama), Turner Normal College (Tennessee), Lampton College (Louisiana), Bethel College (Alabama), Payne Theological Seminary (Ohio), and Morris Brown College (Georgia). G. F. Richings, *Evidences of Progress among Colored People* (Philadelphia: George S. Ferguson Company, 1902), 49, 183, http://docsouth.unc.edu/church/richings/richings.html; Caldwell, *History of American Negroes, Georgia Edition,* 229, 231; McGinnis, *A History and an Interpretation of Wilberforce University,* 158, 161; Caldwell, *History of American Negroes, Georgia Edition,* 231; Charles H. Johnson to Elizabeth L. Jackson, December 2, 1897, JHWC; Elizabeth L. Jackson to John L. Wheeler, December 4, 1897, JHWC; Stuart, *An Economic Detour,* 226; "Retired Officer of North Carolina Mutual Dies in Atlanta," NC Mutual press release, April 1, 1957; "Resolution on the Death of J. L. Wheeler," NC Mutual, April 1, 1957, JHWC; *CT,* April 6, 1957; William Jesse Kennedy Jr., "Taps for John L. Wheeler," April 1957, JHWC.

11. Samuel Thomas Peace, *"Zeb's Black Baby," Vance County, North Carolina: A Short History* (Henderson, N.C.: Seeman Printery, 1955), 351–64; Mark Crawford, *Confederate Courage on Other Fields: Four Lesser Known Accounts of the War Between the States* (Jefferson, N.C.: McFarland, 2000), 135–56; "A Bill to Incorporate Kittrell Springs Female College," February 23, 1869, Session Records, General Assembly Record Group, State Archives of North Carolina, http://digital.ncdcr.gov/cdm/ref/collection/p16062coll19/id/1162; LeRoy M. Lee, "The Women in the Times: An Address Delivered at the Annual Commencement of Kittrell's Spring Female College," June 28, 1866, (microform), Davis Library, University of North Carolina at Chapel Hill; "Kittrell Springs Female College," *Raleigh Christian Advocate,* November 18, 1868, https://www.newspapers.com/clip/1529764/kittrell_springs_female/; John R. Hawkins, *The Educator: A Condensed Statement of the Department of Education of the African Methodist Episcopal Church, with One Hundred Illustrations* (Kittrell, N.C.: African Methodist Episcopal Church, 1906), 27–30; "Kittrell College Catalogue, 1918–1919," pp. 5–6, DMRRBML; *Christian Recorder,* August 19, 1886, http://www.accessible.com/accessible/print; *Christian Recorder,* May 19, 1880, http://www.accessible.com/accessible/print; Glenda Gilmore, *Gender and Jim Crow: Women and the Politics of White Supremacy in North Carolina, 1896–1920* (Chapel Hill: University of North Carolina Press, 1996), 244n11; *Christian Recorder,* December 31, 1885, http://www.accessible.com/accessible/print; "Kittrell Normal and Industrial Institute Fourth Annual Report, 1889–1890," p. 25, DMRRBML. There are variations on the spelling of Reverend R. W. H. Leak's last name in multiple sources on the AME Church, which alternate between spelling it with and without the "e" at the end. *Christian Recorder,* August 19, 1886; "Kittrell College Catalogue, 1918–1919," pp. 5–6, DMRRBML; *Christian Recorder,* March 12, 1891, http://www.accessible.com/accessible/print; "Kittrell Normal and Industrial Institute Fourth Annual Report, 1889–1890," p. 25, DMRRBML; Hawkins, *The Educator,* 27–30; Wheeler, "Kittrell College Faces Today's Challenge for Freedom and Character in Education," March 1, 1960, JHWC; Starr Lakena Battle, "Lest We Forget: The History of Kittrell College, Kittrell, North Carolina, 1886–1976" (master's thesis,

North Carolina Central University, 2011); Wright, *Centennial Encyclopedia of the African Methodist Episcopal Church,* 315; Smith, *A History of the African Methodist Episcopal Church,* 357–59.

12. *Kittrell Normal and Industrial Institute Sixth Annual Report, 1891–1892,* p. 11, DMRRBML; *Kittrell Normal and Industrial Institute Fourth Annual Report, 1889–1890,* p. 25, DMRRBML; Caldwell, *History of the American Negro, Georgia Edition,* 231.

13. Edwin Du Bois Shurter, ed., *The Complete Orations and Speeches of Henry W. Grady* (New York: Hinds, Noble, and Elredge, 1910), 12–13, 19; Talitha L. LeFlouria, *Chained in Silence: Black Women and Convict Labor in the New South* (Chapel Hill: University of North Carolina Press), 2015; George Tindall, *Emergence of the New South, 1913–1945* (Baton Rouge: Louisiana University Press, 1967); Edward L. Ayers, *Promise of the New South: Life after Reconstruction* (New York: Oxford University Press, 1993); C. Vann Woodward, *Origins of the New South, 1877–1913* (Baton Rouge: Louisiana University Press, 1951); Paul M. Gaston, *New South Creed: A Study in Southern Myth-Making* (Montgomery, AL: New South Books, 2002); Daniel S. Margolies, *Henry Watterson and the New South: The Politics of Empire, Free Trade, and Globalization* (Lexington: University Press of Kentucky, 2006); Gavin Wright, *Old South, New South: Revolutions in the Southern Economy since the Civil War* (Baton Rouge: Louisiana State University Press, 1996); Robert J. Norrell, *James Bowron: The Autobiography of a New South Industrialist* (Chapel Hill: University of North Carolina Press, 1991).

14. *The Hand-Book of Durham, North Carolina: A Brief and Accurate Description of a Prosperous and Growing Southern Manufacturing Town* (Durham: Educator Company, 1895), introduction, 3; Jean Bradley Anderson, *Durham County: A History of Durham County, North Carolina* (Durham: Duke University Press, 1990), 132–33; Boyd, *The Story of Durham,* 97, chap. 6.

15. *The Hand-Book of Durham,* 75; William Jess Kennedy Jr., *The North Carolina Mutual Story: A Symbol of Progress, 1898–1970* (Durham: North Carolina Mutual Life Insurance Company, 1970), 1–2.

16. Leslie Brown, *Upbuilding Black Durham: Gender, Class, and Black Community Development in the Jim Crow South* (Chapel Hill: University of North Carolina Press, 2008), 30–33; Boyd, *The Story of Durham,* 278–79; Anderson, *Durham County,* 155–56, 166.

17. Janette Thomas Greenwood, *Bittersweet Legacy: The Black and White "Better Classes" in Charlotte, 1850–1910,* 177, 197, chap. 5, 189; Helen G. Edmonds, *The Negro and Fusion Politics in North Carolina, 1894–1901* (Chapel Hill: University of North Carolina Press, 1951), chap. 10; Paul D. Escott, *Many Excellent People: Power and Privilege in North Carolina, 1850–1900* (Chapel Hill: University of North Carolina Press, 1985), 241, 247, 253–54. For more on the 1898 Wilmington Race Riot, see David S. Cecelski and Timothy B. Tyson, *Democracy Betrayed: The Wilmington Race Riot of 1898 and Its Legacy* (Chapel Hill: University of North Carolina Press, 1998); Leon H. Prather, *We Have Taken a City: The Wilmington Racial Massacre and Coup of 1896* (Rutherford, N.J.: Fairleigh Dickinson University Press, 1984); *1898*

Wilmington Race Riot Report (Raleigh: Research Branch, Office of Archives and History, N.C. Department of Cultural Resources, 2006); Gilmore, *Gender and Jim Crow,* 85–89; Eric Anderson, *Race and Politics in North Carolina, 1872–1901: The Black Second* (Baton Rouge: Louisiana State University Press, 1981), 254.

18. Lee A. Craig, *Josephus Daniels: His Life and Times* (Chapel Hill: University of North Carolina Press, 2013); *1898 Wilmington Race Report;* Peace, *"Zeb's Black Baby,"* 12–14. The Republican stronghold in Vance County was partly due to a larger political phenomenon known as the "Black Second," North Carolina's Second Congressional District fashioned in 1872 to maintain heavily Democratic white-majority voting districts in eastern North Carolina (Escott, *Many Excellent People,* 255).

19. Andrews, *John Merrick;* Kennedy, *The North Carolina Mutual Story;* Walter B. Weare, *Black Business in the New South: A Social History of the North Carolina Mutual Life Insurance Company* (Durham: Duke University Press, 1993), 21–22; Brown, *Upbuilding,* 117; Janiewski, *Sisterhood Denied;* Boyd, *The Story of Durham;* Anderson, *Durham County;* Andre D. Vann and Beverly Jones, *Durham's Hayti* (Charleston, S.C.: Arcadia, 1999); John Sibley Butler, *Entrepreneurship and Self-Help among Black Americans: A Reconsideration of Race and Economics,* rev. ed. (Albany: State University of New York Press, 2005); Archibald Rutledge, "They Call Him 'Co-Operation,'" *Mutual,* reprinted from the *Saturday Evening Post,* March 27, 1943, C. C. Spaulding Vertical File, Stanford L. Warren Library, Durham, N.C.; C. C. Spaulding, "Pioneer Insurancemen, Bankers Hailed"; "Business Tycoon Died on Date of 78th Birthday," *Carolinian,* August 9, 1952.

20. In Durham, these New South ideals emphasized the superficial—economic progress rather than racial exclusion, inequality, racial injustice, and discrimination. Washington, Du Bois, and E. Franklin Frazier wrote about New South prosperity as I've defined it. At the same time, New South ideals hinged on racial and class oppression, as Kevin Gaines argues; he notes that racial uplift ideology reinforced white supremacy and racial superiority indirectly, not challenging the boundaries of black citizenship but rather creating an "in-limbo" status for the black middle-class elite (Gaines, *Uplifting the Race,* introduction, chaps. 1–3).

21. Frank W. Cooley to J. L. Wheeler, May 30, 1906; Letter of Recommendation from Joseph P. Shorter, April 28, 1906; Letter of Recommendation from John A. Cotton, April 12, 1906, all in JHWC; Stuart, *An Economic Detour,* 227; "Retired Officer of N.C. Mutual Dies in Atlanta," NC Mutual press release, April 1, 1957, JHWC.

22. "Kittrell Commencement," *Christian Recorder,* June 12, 1890; Andrews, *John Merrick,* 135, 192; John H. Wheeler, "Kittrell College Faces Today's Challenge for Freedom and Character in Education," March 1, 1960, JHWC, 6; Kennedy, *The North Carolina Mutual Story,* 25, 189; Battle, "Lest We Forget," 27–28; *CT,* June 26, 1926, Pearson Papers, DMRRBML. For a list of graduates from Kittrell between 1890 and 1919, see "Kittrell College Catalogue, 1918–1919," 42–50; on S. L. Warren's class, see 44. Warren later became John Hervey's father-in-law. "The Kittrell Normal and Industrial Institute, 1891–1892," p. 11, DMRRBML, 11; Kennedy, *The North Carolina Mutual Story,* 32; Battle, "Lest We Forget," 19.

23. "Certificate of Membership and Subscription for Four Shares of the Capital Stock of the American Union Industrial Company issued to J. L. Wheeler," June 3, 1904, JHWC; "Agent's Certificate of the American Union Benefit Association," June 15, 1914, JHWC; *The Insurance Year Book* (New York: Spectator, 1904), 689; John H. Wheeler, "Kittrell College Faces Today's Challenge for Freedom and Character in Education," March 1, 1960, p. 6, JHWC; Recommendation from Joshua H. Jones, April 27, 1906; Recommendation from Charles H. Johnson, April 28, 1906; J. L. Wheeler, "N.C. Mutual Bulletin for the Southeastern District," July 12, 1948, all in JHWC.

24. J. M. Avery, D. B. Green, and A. R. Moore, *The Mutual Album* (Durham: N.C. Mutual, 1909); Andrews, *John Merrick,* 108, 87; Kennedy, *The North Carolina Mutual Story,* 24-30, 44–45, 39–40; Andrews, *John Merrick,* 108, 50–56, 91–92, 148–51; Weare, *Black Business,* 81–82, 3–4; Stuart, *An Economic Detour,* 195, 274–75, 285; Garrett-Scott, "To Do a Work That Would Be Very Far Reaching," 11n25.

25. Booker T. Washington, "Durham, North Carolina: A City of Negro Enterprise," *Independent* 70 (March 1911); Brown, *Upbuilding,* 12–14; John N. Ingham, "Building Businesses, Creating Communities: Residential Segregation and the Growth of African American Business in Southern Cities, 1880–1915," *Business History Review* 77 (Winter 2003): 660; W. E. B. Du Bois, "The Upbuilding of Black Durham," *World's Work* 23 (January 1912).

26. Boyd, *The Durham Story,* 277–95; Weare, *Black Business,* 53, 91; Brown, *Upbuilding,* 32–33; Caldwell, *History of the American Negro, Georgia Edition,* 231; Stuart, *An Economic Detour,* 227.

27. George Wayne Cox, "How Long Is Long Enough?," *Southwest Georgian* (Albany), June 7, 1941, NC Mutual Scrapbook, North Carolina Mutual Life Insurance Company Archives; Kennedy, *The North Carolina Mutual Story*, 31–32; Weare, *Black Business,* 89, 91; Caldwell, *History of the American Negro, Georgia Edition,* 231; Clifford M. Kuhn, Harlon E. Joye, and E. Bernard West, *Living Atlanta: An Oral History of the City, 1914–1948* (Athens and Atlanta: University of Georgia Press and the Atlanta Historical Society, 1990), 252, 152, 95, 100, 105; Caldwell, *History of the American Negro, Georgia Edition,* 231; Herman "Skip" Mason, *Going against the Wind: A Pictorial History of African-Americans in Atlanta* (Atlanta: Longstreet, 1992); Alexa Benson Henderson, *Atlanta Life Insurance Company: Guardian of Black Economic Dignity* (Athens: University of Georgia Press, 1990); Willard Gatewood, *Aristocrats of Color: The Black Elite, 1880–1920* (Bloomington: Indiana University Press, 1993); Stuart, *An Economic Detour,* 226–27; "Retired Officer of N.C. Mutual Dies in Atlanta," NC Mutual press release, April 1, 1957, JHWC; "Resolution on the Death of J. L. Wheeler," NC Mutual, April 1, 1957, JHWC; *CT,* April 6, 1957; William Jesse Kennedy Jr., "Taps for John L. Wheeler," April 1957, JHWC.

28. *Durham Morning Herald* (hereinafter cited as *DMH*), August 2, 1953; John Hervey Wheeler, interview by Robert Penn Warren (hereinafter cited as Wheeler interview), 1964, digital audio available through "Robert Penn Warren's *Who Speaks for the Negro?* An Archival Collection," http://whospeaks.library.vanderbilt.edu/interview/john-hervey-wheeler; Warren, *Who Speaks for the Negro?*, 300–305.

29. "Banker with a Mission: Successful Negro Bank President, Firm in Pushing for both Negro Advancement and North Carolina Development, Wins an Influential Role throughout South and in the Nation," *Business Week,* May 16, 1964.

30. Caldwell, *History of the American Negro, Georgia Edition,* 231; "John L. Wheeler Obituary," JHWC; *Atlanta Constitution,* May 19, 1922; *Atlanta Journal,* March 19, 1950.

31. Alton Hornsby Jr., *Black Power in Dixie: A Political History of African Americans in Atlanta* (Gainesville: University Press of Florida, 2009), 50; *Atlanta Constitution,* October 9, 1915.

32. *Atlanta Constitution,* October 9, 1915; Hornsby, *Black Power in Dixie;* Tera Hunter, *To 'Joy My Freedom: Southern Black Women's Lives and Labors after the Civil War* (Cambridge: Harvard University Press, 1997), 104–5; Tomiko Brown-Nagin, *Courage to Dissent: Atlanta and the Long History of the Civil Rights Movement* (Oxford: Oxford University Press, 2011), 60–61.

33. *Atlanta Constitution,* October 9, 1915; Hornsby, *Black Power in Dixie;* Hunter, *To 'Joy My Freedom,* 104–5; Brown-Nagin, *Courage to Dissent,* 60–61; Kenneth Robert Janken, *Walter White: Mr. NAACP* (Chapel Hill: University of North Carolina Press, 2006), 22–26; Benjamin E. Mays, *Born to Rebel: An Autobiography* (Athens: University of Georgia Press, [1971], 2003), 89; Kuhn, Joye, and West, *Living Atlanta,* 152–53.

34. Mays, *Born to Rebel,* 67–78, 75–83.

35. Wheeler interview.

36. Benjamin G. Brawley, *A History of Morehouse College* (College Park, Md.: McGrath, 1917), 9–10; Edward A. Jones, *A Candle in the Dark: A History of Morehouse College* (Valley Forge: Judson, 1967), 80–89, chaps. 4–5; Glenn Sisk, "Morehouse College," *Journal of Negro Education* 27 (Spring 1958): 201–8; Will W. Alexander, "Phylon Profile, XI: John Hope," 4–13; Ridgely Torrence, *The Story of John Hope* (New York: Macmillan, 1948), 228–30.

37. Wheeler to Kemper Harreld, July 1, 1957, JHWC; Jones, *A Candle in the Dark,* 93–95.

38. *Morehouse Tiger* 1 (1925); *Maroon Tiger* 2, no. 3 (January 1926); J. H. Wheeler, "From the Delphian Oracle: The Trend of Modern Art," *Maroon Tiger* 3, no. 1 (October 1927); J. H. Wheeler, "The College Man's Religion," *Maroon Tiger* 2, no. 4–5 (February-March 1927).

2. Black Business Activism in the Great Depression

1. *Pittsburgh Courier,* October 26, 1929. In addition to McDougald, the other sixteen men in the "second line of defense" were Edward R. Merrick, William Jesse Kennedy Jr., Dr. Clyde Donnell, Edward Decatur Pratt, L. W. Wilhoute, A. Moore Shearin, Rencher N. Harris, J. E. Ormes, Henry M. Michaux, Atlas Barbee, T. D. Parham, F. L. McCoy, M. Hugh Thompson, C. J. Gates, Louis E. Austin, and Alfonso Elder.

2. Ibid.

3. *Norfolk Journal and Guide,* November 16, 1929; "Richard L. McDougald Obituary," October 5, 1944, courtesy of NCCU archivist Andre D. Vann.

4. "Wheeler Resume"; *DMH,* August 2, 1953; *Carolina Financial Times* (Raleigh), February 9, 1976; *Maroon Tiger,* May-June 1929, 4; Selena Wheeler, interview by Brenda Williams, June 27, 1995, #V-0042, Southern Oral History Program (#4007), Southern Historical Collection, Wilson Library, University of North Carolina at Chapel Hill.

5. Frazier, "Durham: Capital of the Black Middle Class," 333–40; Janiewski, *Sisterhood Denied,* 67. Several decades later, Frazier would become more critical of black business and its role in helping black Americans reach social, political, and economic equality. E. Franklin Frazier, *Black Bourgeoise* (New York: Free Press, 1965).

6. Hugh Penn Brinton, "The Negro in Durham: A Study of Adjustment to Town Life" (Ph.D. diss., University of North Carolina at Chapel Hill, 1930), iii, 69–70, 80–88, 170.

7. Ibid., 172–73.

8. Ibid., 70, 80–88, 192; Wheeler, interview by August Meier, 3; Asa T. Spaulding, interview by Walter B. Weare, April 14, 1979, # C-OO13–2, Southern Oral History Program Collection (#4007), Southern Historical Collection, Wilson Library, University of North Carolina at Chapel Hill; *New York Age,* December 20, 1919; Charles R. Frazer, "Building a Negro Bank," 1956, p. 10, JHWC.

9. *Nashville Globe,* February 18, 1910; Walker, *The History of Black Business in America,* 187.

10. *Nashville Globe,* February 18, 1910; Harry T. Gatton, *Banking in North Carolina* (Raleigh: North Carolina Bankers Association, 1987), 59-61; Walter L. Fleming, *The Freedmen's Savings Bank: A Chapter in the Economic History of the Negro Race* (1927; Westport, Conn.: Negro Universities Press, 1970), 38; Robert C. Kenzer, *Enterprising Southerner: Black Economic Success in North Carolina, 1865–1915* (Charlottesville: University Press of Virginia, 1997); Robert C. Kenzer, "The Black Businessman in the Postwar South: North Carolina, 1865–1880," *Business History Review* (Spring 1989): 61–87.

11. *The Hand-Book of Durham,* 29–31; Howard E. Covington Jr., *Favored by Fortune: George W. Watts and the Hills of Durham* (Chapel Hill: University of North Carolina Press, 2004), 52–53; Robert F. Durden, *The Dukes of Durham, 1865–1929* (Durham: Duke University Press, 1975), 148-151; Boyd, *The Story of Durham,* 116–19, 288–99; *Durham Recorder,* February 5, 1907; Andrews, *John Merrick,* 50–55, http://docsouth.unc.edu/nc/andrews/andrews.html; Hans Dominique Lassiter, "A History of Mechanics and Farmers Bank, 1908–1969" (master's thesis, North Carolina Central University, 2000), 5–7; Kenzer, *Enterprising Southerner,* 80–85.

12. Gatton, *Banking in North Carolina; Raleigh Times,* February 19, 1907; *Raleigh News and Observer,* February 20, 1907; *Greensboro Daily News,* February 20, 1907; *Raleigh News and Observer,* February 24, 1907; *Greensboro Daily News,*

February 24, 1907; Andrews, *John Merrick,* 50–55; Lassiter, "A History of Mechanics and Farmers Bank" 5–7; Boyd, *The Story of Durham,* 288–89; Anderson, *Durham County,* 256–57; Weare, *Black Business,* 81; "Mechanics and Farmers Bank Enters 20th Successful Year," unidentified newspaper article, August 1908, Pearson Papers, DMRRBML; Walker, *The History of Black Business,* 190, 193.

13. *Raleigh Times,* August 4, 1908; *Charlotte News,* August 4, 1908; *Chatham Record* (Pittsboro), August 5, 1908; *Montgomerian* (Troy), August 6, 1908; *French Broad News* (Marshall), August 6, 1908; *Roanoke Beacon* (Plymouth), August 7, 1908; *Ansonian* (Wadesboro), August 11, 1908; "Negroes Open Bank: Owned, Lock, Stock and Barrel by Colored People—As a White Paper Sees Them," *Afro-American,* August 22, 1908; "Mechanics and Farmers Bank Enters 20th Successful Year," unidentified newspaper article, August 1928, Pearson Papers, DMRRBML; *Norfolk Journal and Guide,* August 11, 1928; Boyd, *The Durham Story,* 116–19; "Reports of the Condition of the State, Private and Savings Banks" (Raleigh: E. M. Uzzell and Company, State Printers and Binders, November 27, 1908, 23, November 16, 1909), 24.

14. Arnett G. Lindsay, "The Negro in Banking," *Journal of Negro History* 14 (April 1929), 188; Boyd, *The Story of Durham,* 291; Weare, *Black Business,* 43; Brown, *Upbuilding,* 115–16; Janiewski, *Sisterhood Denied,* 79; John N. Ingham and Lynne B. Feldman, *African-American Business Leaders: A Biographical Dictionary* (Westport, Conn.: Greenwood, 1994), 151–67; Pauli Murray, *Proud Shoes: The Story of an American Family* (New York: Harper and Brothers, 1956), 272; "Obituary of William Gaston Pearson," September 25, 1947, Pearson Papers, DMRRBML; "Chronological Summary of Specific W. G. Pearson Achievements," 44–46, Pearson Papers, DMRRBML; Andrews, *John Merrick,*; "The Royal Knights of King David Historical Sketch," 4, 10–17, Pearson Papers, DMRRBML; "Mechanics and Farmers Bank Enters 20th Successful Year," unidentified newspaper article, August 1928, Pearson Papers, DMRRBML; *Greensboro Daily News,* November 27, 1910; *Winston-Salem Journal,* September 20, 1918; *DMH,* September 20, 1918; *Charlotte Observer,* September 20, 1918; Weare, *Black Business,* 29; Brown, *Upbuilding,* 115–16; Anderson, *Durham County,* 221; *Raleigh Times,* January 5, 1910.

15. *DMH,* January 19, 1919; *DMH,* February 9, 1919; *DMH,* May 4, 1919; "Reports of the Condition of the State, Private and Savings Banks," October 21, 1913, 31; Kennedy, *The North Carolina Mutual Story,* 45; George W. Adams, "Wrong Report Out," *DMH,* March 26, 1914; *Roanoke-Chowan Times,* October 21, 1918; *Independent,* October 15, 1920; *Oxford Public Ledger,* October 19, 1920; *Greensboro Daily News,* November 27, 1910; *Winston-Salem Journal,* September 20, 1918; *DMH,* September 20, 1918; *Charlotte Observer,* September 20, 1918.

16. *DMH,* November 10, 1918; *DMH,* November 16, 1918; *DMH,* January 19, 1919; *DMH,* February 9, 1919, *DMH,* May 4, 1919; *DMH,* August 7, 1919; *Winston-Salem Journal,* August 8, 1919; *DMH,* August 30, 1919; *Greensboro Daily News,* January 15, 1920; *Raleigh News and Observer,* February 8, 1920; *DMH,* July 3, 1921; *DMH,* January 26, 1921; *DMH,* February 5, 1921, *DMH,* February 13, 1921; *DMH,* December 18, 1921.

17. *DMH,* October 30, 1921; *DMH,* January 15, 1922; *Norfolk Journal and Guide,* March 4, 1922; *DMH,* January 17, 1922; *DMH,* January 24, 1922; *DMH,* January 31, 1922; *DMH,* February 7, 1922; "Mechanics and Farmers Bank Enters 20th Successful Year," unidentified newspaper article, 1928, DMRRBML. The two banks combined their boards of directors and selected officers: Dr. Stanford L. Warren (board chairman) (executive committee); C. C. Spaulding (president) (executive committee); William "Bill" H. Wilson (cashier); Richard L. McDougald (active vice president) (executive committee); Dr. Aaron M. Moore (second vice president) (executive committee); Edward R. Merrick (third vice president) (executive committee); Dr. Clyde Donnell (fourth vice president) (executive committee); Dr. W. C. Strudwick (fifth vice president) (executive committee); Britton Pearce (sixth vice president); John M. Avery (trust officer) (executive committee); T. D. Parham (assistant cashier, formerly cashier of the Fraternal Bank and Trust Company); J. C. Scarborough (executive committee chairman); W. G. Pearson (executive committee); Dr. James E. Shepard (executive committee); and W. Gomez (executive committee).

18. Archibald Rutledge, "They Call Him 'Co-Operation,'" *The Mutual,* reprinted from *Saturday Evening Post,* March 27, 1943, C. C. Spaulding Vertical File, Stanford L. Warren Library, Durham, N.C.; C. C. Spaulding, "Pioneer Insurancemen, Bankers Hailed"; "Business Tycoon Died on Date of 78th Birthday," *Carolinian,* August 9, 1952; *DMH,* December 18, 1921.

19. *Union Herald* (Raleigh), August 3, 1922; Frazer, "Building a Negro Bank," 1–5; *Norfolk Journal and Guide,* January 20, 1923; *DMH,* December 31, 1922. The M&F Bank's Raleigh board of managers included Britton Pearce (acting vice president), A. W. Pegues, C. E. Lightner, John Love, and G. A. Edwards.

20. Frazer, "Building a Negro Bank," 5–7.

21. Ibid., 7–8; Gatton, *Banking in North Carolina,* 81.

22. *Pittsburgh Courier,* December 24, 1927; *Norfolk Journal and Guide,* August 11, 1928; *Baltimore Afro-American,* August 11, 1928; *Norfolk Journal and Guide,* December 29, 1928; *Baltimore Afro-American,* February 9, 1929; Lindsay, "The Negro in Banking," 188; *New York Age,* September 22, 1928.

23. Frazer, "Building a Negro Bank," 8–9; *Baltimore Afro-American,* February 9, 1929; Lindsay, "The Negro in Banking," 188.

24. Henderson, "Richard R. Wright," 54, 58–60; Walker, *The History of Black Business,* 312; *Norfolk Journal and Guide,* July 23, 1927; *Norfolk Journal and Guide,* August 6, 1927; *Pittsburgh Courier,* August 13, 1927; *Baltimore Afro-American,* September 22, 1928.

25. *DMH,* August 2, 1953

26. Henderson, "Richard R. Wright," 68; *DMH,* August 2, 1953; *New York Age,* December 20, 1919.

27. Weare, *Black Business,* 121–23; Kennedy, *The North Carolina Mutual Story;* "Obituary of R. L. McDougald," October 5, 1944; *Norfolk Journal and Guide,* October 7, 1944; Asa T. Spaulding, interview by Walter B. Weare; April 16, 1979, #C-0013-3, Southern Oral History Program Collection (#4007), Southern Histori-

cal Collection, Wilson Library, University of North Carolina at Chapel Hill; Weare, *Black Business,* 121–23; *Pittsburgh Courier,* October 26, 1929.

28. *Norfolk Journal and Guide,* December 20, 1930.

29. Walker, *The History of Black Business,* 191–93; Lila Ammons, "The Evolution of Black-Owned Banks in the United States between the 1880s and 1990s," *Journal of Black Studies* 26 (March 1996): 474; *Baltimore Afro-American,* August 9, 1930; *Pittsburgh Courier,* October 26, 1929.

30. Frazer, "Building a Negro Bank," 11; *Statesville Record and Landmark,* December 22, 1931.

31. Frazer, "Building a Negro Bank," 12; *Daily Times-News,* August 28, 1933.

32. Link, *North Carolina: Change and Tradition,* 338; Milton Ready, *The Tarheel State: A History of North Carolina* (Columbia: University of South Carolina Press, 2005), 324; Wheeler, "A Negro Banker," 26, 7; *Carolina Financial Times* (Raleigh), February 9, 1976; *Norfolk Journal and Guide,* March 18, 1933; *Baltimore Afro-American,* March 18, 1933; Henderson, "Richard R. Wright," 73; *CT,* November 20, 1937.

33. John H. Wheeler, "Keynote Address at the First Annual Housing and Urban Renewal Clinic at N.C. A&T," November 2–3, 1961, JHWC; Wheeler interview, 5; Nathan Garrett, interview by author, August 4, 2008, in author's possession; Nathan Garrett, *A Palette, Not a Portrait* (New York: IUniverse, Inc., 2010), 118.

34. Harry Joseph Walker, "Changes in Race Accommodations in a Southern Community" (Ph.D. diss., University of Chicago, 1945), 124, 190; Anderson, *Durham County,* 372; Weare, *Black Business,* 242–45.

35. Walker, "Changes in Race Accommodations," 189; "John Wheeler: Working Quietly for the Progress of Blacks," *Raleigh News and Observer,* March 15, 1970; Viola G. Turner, interview by Walter B. Weare, transcript, April 17, 1979, #C-0016, p. 33, Southern Oral History Program Collection (#4007), Southern Historical Collection, Wilson Library, University of North Carolina at Chapel Hill, http://docsouth.unc.edu/sohp/C-0016/C-0016.html.

36. Walker, "Changes in Race Accommodations," 189, 210.

37. Augustus M. Burns, "Graduate Education for Blacks in North Carolina, 1930–1951," *Journal of Southern History* 46 (May 1980), 195–96; Jerry B. Gershenhorn, "*Hocutt v. Wilson* and Race Relations in Durham, North Carolina, during the Early 1930s," *North Carolina Historical Review* 78 (July 2001); 293, 291–92, 295; *DMH,* March 18, 1933; *DMH,* March 17, 1933; *DMH,* March 19, 1933.

38. Burns, "Graduate Education for Black North Carolinians," 195–96; Gershenhorn, "*Hocutt v. Wilson,*" 275, 293; *DMH,* March 18, 1933; *DMH,* March 17, 1933; *DMH,* March 19, 1933.

39. Burns, "Graduate Education for Black North Carolinians," 195–96; Gershenhorn, "*Hocutt v. Wilson,*" 295; *DMH,* March 18, 1933; *DMH,* March 17, 1933; *DMH,* March 19, 1933.

40. *DMH,* March 18, 1933; *DMH,* March 17, 1933; *DMH,* March 19, 1933; Conrad Odell Pearson, interview by Walter B. Weare, transcript, April 18, 1979,

#H-0218, p. 18, Southern Oral History Program Collection (#4007), Southern Historical Collection, Wilson Library, University of North Carolina at Chapel Hill, http://dc.lib.unc.edu/cdm/compoundobject/collection/sohp/id/12022/rec/7 (hereinafter cited as Pearson interview); Ware, "Hocutt: Genesis of Brown," 227; Weare, *Black Business*, 232.

41. *Baltimore Afro-American*, August 8, 1931; Walker, "Changes in Race Accommodations," 158.

42. Pearson interview, 86–88; *CT*, November 23, 1929; "Durham NAACP Membership Report," August 11, 1930, February 16, 1931; William Pickens to J. T. Taylor, September 24, 1930; J. T. Taylor to W. T. Andrews, September 26, 1930; William Pickens to J. T. Taylor, October 3, 1930; William Pickens to J. T. Taylor, October 4, 1930; William Pickens to J. T. Taylor, October 9, 1930; Rev. R. M. Williams to J. H. Buchanan, October 14, 1930; William Pickens to J. H. Buchanan, October 14, 1930; William Pickens to J. T. Taylor, November 3, 1930; Robert W. Bagnall to J. T. Taylor, December 3, 1930; Robert W. Bagnall to J. T. Taylor, December 17, 1930; J. T. Taylor to Robert W. Bagnall, December 22, 1930; Robert W. Bagnall to J. T. Taylor, January 2, 1931; Robert W. Bagnall to J. T. Taylor, January 8, 1931; Robert W. Bagnall to J. T. Taylor, January 13, 1931, all in the NAACP Papers (microfilm), Duke University.

43. Pearson interview, 5, 16. In 1937, for example, Shepard had been able to hold dedication ceremonies for nine buildings on the campus of NCCN, built with funds from the state legislature and the Works Progress Administration (*CT*, December 4, 1937; *CT*, December 11, 1937).

44. *DMH*, March 22, 1933; Gershenhorn, "*Hocutt v. Wilson*," 296; Robert J. Cannon, "The Organization and Growth of Black Political Participation in Durham, North Carolina, 1933–1958" (Ph.D. diss., University of North Carolina at Chapel Hill, 1975); *DMH*, March 24, 1933.

45. *DMH*, March 25, 26, 1933.

46. *DMH*, March 29, 1933; Miles Mark Fisher to NAACP National Office, March 13, 1933, NAACP Papers; NAACP Department of Branches to Miles Mark Fisher, March 16, 1933; *DMH*, March 25, 1933; Kenneth W. Mack, *Representing the Race: The Creation of the Civil Rights Lawyer* (Cambridge: Harvard University Press, 2012), chap. 4; Alphonso Stewart Powe, "The Role of Negro Pressure Groups in Interracial Integration in Durham City, North Carolina" (Ph.D. diss., New York University, 1954), 119; Durham City School Board Meeting Minutes (hereinafter cited as DCSBMM), August 21, 1933.

47. *DMH*, March 29, 1933; Miles Mark Fisher to NAACP National Office, March 13, 1933, NAACP Papers; NAACP Department of Branches to Miles Mark Fisher, March 16, 1933; *DMH*, March 25, 1933.

48. *Atlanta Daily World*, December 10, 1944. Margery Janice Wheeler became a children's book author, illustrator, and teacher in the Newark, New Jersey, public school system. Wheeler, interview by August Meier, 8, 5; Mays, *Born to Rebel*, 139; Jelks, *Benjamin Elijah Mays*, 138; DCSBMM, September 12, 1934; DCSBMM, April 9, 1935.

49. Herbert Hoover, "Commencement Address at Howard University, June 10, 1932, http://www.presidency.ucsb.edu/ws/?pid=23123; Selena Wheeler, interview by Brenda Williams; Wheeler, interview by August Meier, 3; Dorothy Phelps Jones, *The End of An Era* (Durham: Brown Enterprises, 2001); Vann and Jones, *Durham's Hayti*, 20.

50. Beverly Washington Jones, *Stanford L. Warren Branch Library: 77 Years of Public Service* (Durham: Durham County Library, 1990), 67, 72, 74. Louis E. Austin to the Jury on Citation of Trustees (American Library Association), March 12, 1952, John Hervey Wheeler Vertical File, Stanford L. Warren Library.

51. Pearson interview; R. N. Harris to Louis E. Austin, June 19, 1962, Harris Papers, DMRRBML; Cannon, "The Organization and Growth of Black Political Participation," 9; "DCNA Executive Committee Year-End Report," August 1, 1936, J. S. Stewart Files, NCCU Archives; Walker, "Changes in Race Accommodations," 206–7; Powe, "The Role of Negro Pressure Groups," 56.

52. Pearson interview; R. N. Harris to Louis E. Austin, June 19, 1962, Harris Papers, DMRRBML; Cannon, "The Organization and Growth of Black Political Participation," 9; Walker, "Changes in Race Accommodations," 206–7; Powe, "The Role of Negro Pressure Groups," 56.

53. Spaulding, interview by Walter B. Weare; "DCNA 50 Anniversary Pamphlet," August 10, 1985.

54. "DCNA Executive Committee Year-End Report," August 1, 1936, 1; Earl E. Thorpe, "The Untold Story of the Durham Committee on the Affairs of Black People," Black History Month Lecture, February 2, 1981, Asa and Elna Spaulding Papers, DMRRBML; "DCNA Executive Committee Year-End Report," August 1, 1936, 1; Walker, "Changes in Race Accommodations," 208 (on NCCNA); see also NCCNA newspapers; NCCNA.

55. DCSBMM, July 6, September 24, 1936; *DMH,* December 30, 1936; Jerry B. Gershenhorn, "A Courageous Voice for Black Freedom: Louis Austin and the *Carolina Times* in Depression-Era North Carolina," *North Carolina Historical Review* 87 (January 2010) 72; *DMH,* December 30, 1936; DCSBMM, March 9, 1937; DCSBMM, May 9, 1938.

56. DCSBMM, July 7, 13, October 24, 1938.

57. *CT,* June 19, 1937; *CT,* August 28, 1937; Walker, "Changes in Race Accommodations," 213; Cannon, "The Organization and Growth of Black Political Participation," 52–53.

58. Walker, "Changes in Race Accommodations," 213; Cannon, "The Organization and Growth of Black Political Participation," 49–53. Well before the DCNA started, African Americans lobbied the city council to increase police protection and petitioned the leaders to hire black officers to handle the rising crime rate in Hayti. *DMH,* 1933; *CT,* June 3, 1938; *CT,* July 30, 1938.

59. *CT,* April 2, 1938; Walker, "Changes in Race Accommodation," 211–12.

60. *DMH,* April 13, 1941.

61. Pearson interview; Walker, "Changes in Race Accommodations," 208.

62. Pearson interview; Walker, "Changes in Race Accommodations," 208.

3. The Battle for Educational Equality in the Postwar New South

1. Wheeler, "A Negro Banker Speaks to the South," *Tarheel Banker,* November 1945, 7, 27.

2. Ibid.

3. Ibid., 26–27.

4. Ibid.

5. Southern Conference on Race Relations pamphlet, 3–4, Gordon Blaine Hancock Papers, DMRRBM.

6. Gordon Blaine Hancock to Wheeler, March 18, 1964, JHWC; Raymond Gavins, *The Perils and Prospects of Southern Black Leadership: Gordon Blaine Hancock, 1884–1970* (Durham: Duke University Press, 1977), 120–24.

7. Southern Conference on Race Relations pamphlet, 6.

8. Ibid., 6–7.

9. Ibid., 9; Gavins, *The Perils and Prospects of Southern Black Leadership,* 127, chaps. 5–6. For more on the SRC, see also Jacqueline Dowd Hall, *Revolt against Chivalry: Jesse Daniel Ames and the Women's Campaign against Lynching* (New York: Columbia University Press, 1979), chap. 9; Henry L. Suggs, *P. B. Young, Newspaperman: Race, Politics, and Journalism in the New South, 1910–1962* (Charlottesville: University Press of Virginia, 1988), chaps. 8–9; Julia Anne McDonough, "Men and Women of Good Will: A History of the Commission on Interracial Cooperation and the Southern Regional Council, 1919–1954" (Ph.D. diss., University of Virginia, 1993), chaps. 2–3; Paul Houser, "The Southern Regional Council" (master's thesis, University of North Carolina at Chapel Hill, 1950); Michael Dennis, *Luther P. Jackson and a Life for Civil Rights* (Gainesville: University Press of Florida, 2004), 90–96; "The Southern Regional Council," *Southern Frontier,* March 1944, 1, Guy Benton Johnson Papers (#3826), Southern Historical Collection, Wilson Library, University of North Carolina at Chapel Hill.

10. *CT,* January 13, 1940; Lassiter, "A History of Mechanics and Farmers Bank," 16–17; *CT,* February 3, 1940; *CT,* February 10, 1940.

11. *CT,* July 20, 1940; *Norfolk Journal and Guide,* July 20, 1940; *Norfolk Journal and Guide,* July 20, 1940.

12. *DMH,* May 3, 1942; *DMH,* December 5, 1942; *DMH,* December 10, 1942; *DMH,* December 19, 1942; *DMH,* December 18, 1942; *Norfolk Journal and Guide,* September 19, 1942; *Chicago Defender,* September 19, 1942; *CT,* March 6, 1943; *Norfolk Journal and Guide,* March 20, 1943; *Norfolk Journal and Guide,* October 2, 1943; *Pittsburgh Courier,* October 2, 1943; *Chicago Defender,* October 2, 1943.

13. *Norfolk Journal and Guide,* October 7, 1944; FBI Field Report, July 30, 1968; Vivian Rogers Patterson, interview by author, March 11, 2010, Southern Oral History Program (#4007), Southern Historical Collection, Wilson Library, University of North Carolina at Chapel Hill. In 1978, while still working at M&F Bank, Patterson graduated from the Stonier Graduate School of Banking, operated under the

auspices of the American Bankers Association at Rutgers University. Her thesis, "A Black Bank Revisited: An Update of 'Analysis of Operating Problems of a Bank Serving a Predominantly Negro Market' [1959]," focused on M&F Bank's survival during the civil rights movement and the extent to which it maintained its identity as a "black-owned" bank in the decade after the civil rights movement. Patterson returned to the question M&F Bank cashier Ilon Owen Funderburg had posed in his 1959 thesis at Stonier. Funderburg's "An Analysis of Operating Problems of a Bank Serving a Predominantly Negro Market" examined the extent to which M&F Bank had an exclusively black clientele and its ability to make steady profits despite stiff competition from the city's white-owned banks. The two analyses prove invaluable to understanding M&F Bank's history between 1945 and 1976.

14. Wheeler to Asa T. Spaulding, November 25, 1946, Asa and Elna Spaulding Papers, DMRRBML; Lassiter, "A History of the Mechanics and Farmers Bank," 21.

15. "Largest Negro Bank in World," *E.S.C. Quarterly* 7 (Winter 1949): 18, http://digital.ncdcr.gov/cdm/ref/collection/p249901coll22/id/452014; Article Draft, "Mechanics and Farmers, Durham, Largest Negro Bank in Nation," January 6, 1949; M. R. Dunnagan to Wheeler, January 6, 1949, both in JHWC; *DMH,* August 2, 1953; Lassiter, "A History of Mechanics and Farmers Bank," 28.

16. Durham Recreation Advisory Committee Meeting Minutes, April 3, 1946, JHWC; *DMH,* August 29, 1946; *DMH,* November 3, 1946; Durham Recreation Advisory Committee Meeting Minutes, January 29, 1947, JHWC; Wheeler to C. C. Spaulding, February 4, 1947, JHWC; Durham Recreation Advisory Committee Meeting Minutes, February 4, 1947, JHWC; Weare, *Black Business,* 197; Dedication of E. D. Mickle Recreation Building, February 26, 1955, JHWC. The RAC renamed the Fayetteville Street USO the W. D. Hill Recreation Center. Both Hill and Wheeler had been instrumental in getting the black USO facility for black soldiers. Hill had also been active in organizing recreational activities for black youth in the city.

17. Lewis Bowman and G. R. Boynton, "Coalitions as Party in a One-Party Southern Area: A Theoretical and Case Analysis," *Midwest Journal of Political Science* 8, no. 3 (August 1964): 278, 281–83, http://www.jstor.org/stable/2108956; Weare, *Black Business,* 261; Christina Greene, *Our Separate Ways: Women and the Black Freedom Movement in Durham, North Carolina* (Chapel Hill: University of North Carolina Press, 2005), 274, 23; Wheeler, "A Negro Banker Speaks to the South," 27; Philip F. Rubio, *A History of Affirmative Action, 1619–2000* (Jackson: University Press of Mississippi, 2001), 93; Philip F. Rubio, *There's Always Work at the Post Office: African American Postal Workers and the Fight for Jobs, Justice, and Equality* (Chapel Hill: University of North Carolina Press, 2010), 33; Robert R. Korstad and James L. Leloudis, *To Right These Wrongs: The North Carolina Fund and the Battle to End Poverty and Inequality in 1960s America* (Chapel Hill: University of North Carolina Press, 2010), 170; Wilbur Hobby, interview by William Finger, transcript, March 13, 1975, #E-0006, pp. 14–15, Southern Oral History Program Collection (#4007), Southern Historical Collection, Wilson Library, University of North Carolina at Chapel Hill, http://dc.lib.unc.edu/utils/getfile/collection/sohp/id/10868/filename/10910.pdf.

18. Bowman and Boynton, "Coalitions as Party in a One-Party Southern Area," 283; W. C. Dula and A. C. Simpson, *Durham and Her People: Combining History and Who's Who in Durham of 1949 and 1950* (Durham: Citizens Press, 1951), 143; Pearson interview, p. 60; Anderson, *Durham County*, 398; Brandon Winford, "The Struggle for Freedom Begins Every Morning: A History of the Durham Committee on Negro Affairs" (master's thesis, North Carolina Central University, 2007), 44–47.

19. DCSBMM, December 9, 1946, January 3, 1947.

20. *DMH,* March 28, 1947; Dula and Simpson, *Durham and Her People; DMH,* April 1, 1947; Wheeler to A. E. Burcham (city council member), March 31, 1947, Spaulding Papers, 1–2.

21. *DMH,* April 1, 1947

22. *Blue et al. v. Durham Public School District,* 95 F. Supp. 441 (1951), U.S. Dist. LEXIS 2611; *DMH,* January 23, 27, 1951; Kam Owen Carver, "The Role of the Durham Committee on the Affairs of Black People in the Pursuit of Equal Educational Opportunities, 1935–1954" (master's thesis, North Carolina Central University, 1992), 38–39.

23. Carver, "The Role of the Durham Committee on the Affairs of Black People," 38–39.

24. DCSBMM, October 1, 1947.

25. "North Carolina College Commencement Program," June 2, 1947, NCCU Archives, Durham, N.C.; Wheeler to E. L. Cannon Jr., June 3, 1947, JHWC; Wheeler to E. L. Cannon, June 14, 1947, JHWC; *Pittsburgh Courier,* July 12, 1947; *Norfolk Journal and Guide,* July 19, 1947; *Pittsburgh Courier,* January 24, 1948; *Baltimore Afro-American,* February 7, 1948; Sarah Caroline Thuesen, "Classes of Citizenship: The Culture and Politics of Black Public Education in North Carolina, 1919–1960" (Ph.D. diss., University of North Carolina at Chapel Hill, 2003), 275–76, 283–84; Sarah Caroline Thuesen, *Greater Than Equal: African American Struggles for Schools and Citizenship in North Carolina, 1919–1965* (Chapel Hill: University of North Carolina Press, 2013), 168–81; Mark V. Tushnet, *The NAACP's Legal Strategy against Segregated Education, 1925–1950* (Chapel Hill: University of North Carolina Press, 1987), 105–6.

26. *Baltimore Afro-American,* August 28, 1948; Thuesen, "Classes of Citizenship," 285–88; Thuesen, *Greater Than Equal,* 180.

27. Charles W. McKinney Jr., "Multiple Fronts: The Struggle for Black Educational and Political Equality in Wilson, North Carolina, 1941–1953," *North Carolina Historical Review* 88 (January 2011):15–21; Charles W. McKinney Jr., *Greater Freedom: The Evolution of the Civil Rights Struggle in Wilson, North Carolina* (Lanham, Md.: University Press of America, 2010), 38–42; *CT,* January 7, 28, 1950; Thuesen, *Greater Than Equal,* 190–91.

28. Genna Rae McNeil, *Groundwork: Charles Hamilton Houston and the Struggle for Civil Rights* (Philadelphia: University of Pennsylvania Press, 1983), 113–18, see also chap. 10; Richard Kluger, *Simple Justice: The History of* Brown v. Board of Education *and Black America's Struggle for Equality* (New York: Vintage, 1975); Tushnet, *The NAACP's Legal Strategy.*

29. *Blue et al. v. Durham Public School District et al.* 95 F. Supp. 441 (1951), U.S. Dist. LEXIS 2611; *DMH,* May 17, 1949; Greene, *Our Separate Ways,* 25.

30. *Blue et al. v. Durham Public School District et al.*, original summons, May 18, 1949, Durham County Library; "Before Brown, There Was Blue," *Herald-Sun,* December 13, 2011, http://www.heraldsun.com/view/full_story/16802777/article-Before-Brown—there-was-Blue; Notes on "Before Brown v. Board, There was Blue v. Durham," 60th Anniversary of Historic Case, Durham County Library, courtesy of Jerry B. Gershenhorn, December 19, 2011; Omega Curtis-Parker, phone interview by author, October 18, 2012. On the sixtieth anniversary of the case, many of the child plaintiffs—now retirement-age adults—were unaware that their names had even appeared as plaintiffs in the case. Other plaintiffs included W. A. Kenney Jr., by W. A. Kenney Sr., his father; Arthur Lee James, Raymond Edward James, Irene James, Richard James Jr., and Robert Jones James, by Richard James Sr., their father; Mildred Dawson, Jean Dawson, and Milton Dawson Jr., by Roberta B. Dawson, their mother; Dora Carrington, Emily Carrington, and Walton Carrington, by James Carrington, their father; Doris Rowland and Grace Rowland, by T. L. Rowland, their father; Elizabeth Harvey, by Oliver Harvey, her father; Mary Jane McCrae, by Aggie McCrae, her mother; Louie Pittman Jr., by Louie Pittman Sr., his guardian; Alfred Thompson, Martha Thompson, Niles Thompson Jr., and Ruth Thompson, by Niles Thompson Sr., their father; Cleveland Thomas Jr., and Janie Mae Thomas, by Cleveland Thomas Sr., their father; Annie Cobb, Jean Cobb, and Ruth Cobb, by C. C. Cobb, their father; Bennie Booker, by Benjamin B. Booker, her father; Doris Jean Curtis, Omega Curtis, and Cornelius Curtis, by J. L. Curtis, their father; Sarah Louise McNeil, John H. McNeil Jr., James McNeil, Charles Thomas McNeil, and Virginia McNeil, by John H. McNeil Sr., their father; Ella Docena Richmond and Raymond Richmond Jr., by Raymond Richmond Sr., their father; Helen Reid, by D. F. Reid, her father; Yvonne Lee Miller, by Felix Miller, her father.

31. "M. Hugh Thompson Obituary," William Jesse Kennedy Jr. Papers (#4925), Southern Historical Collection, Wilson Library, University of North Carolina at Chapel Hill, and the African American Resources Collection of North Carolina Central University (hereinafter cited as Kennedy Papers); Robinson O. Everett, interview by author, February 29, 2008, #U-0285, in the Southern Oral History Program Collection (#4007), Southern Historical Collection, Wilson Library, University of North Carolina at Chapel Hill; Dula and Simpson, *Durham and Her People,* 220. Houston's biographer Genna Rae McNeil points to racism encountered during and after World War I as a main reason why he went to law school. Between the 1930s and 1940s, Houston devised and engineered the NAACP's legal assault on education. Before working for the NAACP, Houston served as dean at Howard University's law school and trained a generation of civil rights lawyers, most notably Thurgood Marshall, James Nabrit, and Durham's own Conrad O. Pearson (McNeil, *Groundwork,* 45).

32. *DMH,* May 21, 1949.

33. Ibid.

34. Ibid.

35. *DMH,* May 20, 1949; *DMH,* 21, 1949; *Alston v. School Board of City of Norfolk* (1940), 112 F.2d 992, LexisNexis, see Oliver W. Hill as counsel for the case; *Corbin v. County School Board of Pulaski County* (1949), 177 F.2d 924, LexisNexis, see Oliver W. Hill, Spottswood Robinson III, and Martin A. Martin as counsel for the case; *Carter v. School Board of Arlington County, Va.* (1950), 182 F.2d 531, LexisNexis, see Robinson, Martin, and Hill as counsel for the case. During this time, Robinson became the southeastern regional director for the NAACP Legal Defense and Education Fund (LDF), an organization established in 1940 as a separate entity and NAACP offspring. Robinson became a lead attorney during the NAACP's *Brown* case alongside LDF chairman Thurgood Marshall. During the 1960s, the LDF became the primary legal arm for young civil rights activists (Kluger, *Simple Justice,* 221; Tushnet, *The NAACP's Legal Strategy,* 100; Gilbert Ware, "The NAACP-Inc. Fund Alliance: Its Strategy, Power, and Destruction," *Journal of Negro Education* 63 [Summer 1994]: 325; Jack Greenberg, *Crusaders in the Courts: Legal Battles of the Civil Rights Movement* [New York: Twelve Table Press, 2004], 17; "In Memoriam: Spottswood W. Robinson III, 1916–1998," *Journal of Blacks in Higher Education* 31 [Winter 1998–1999], 39). In later years, Wheeler and other Durham attorneys handled local cases funded by the LDF. *DMH,* May 29, 1949; *DMH,* June 7, 1949; *DMH,* June 9, 1949; *DMH,* July 31, 1949.

36. *Apocrisarius,* June 1950, North Carolina College Law School Phi Delta Pi Law Society, tenth anniversary ed., 23; Deborah J. Braswell, "A History of North Carolina Central University's Law School, 1939–1968" (master's thesis, North Carolina Central University, 1977), 19–21; *DMH,* October 8, 1950; *DMH,* October 31, 1950; Tushnet, *The NAACP's Legal Strategy,* 125–34; Kluger, *Simple Justice,* 282; Powe, "The Role of Negro Pressure Groups," 123–25; *CT,* June 17, 1950; *DMH,* June 9, 1950.

37. *CT,* June 24, 1950; *Blue et al. v. Durham Public School District et al.*, original summons, May 18, 1949, Durham County Library, 6–8.

38. *Blue et al. v. Durham Public School District et al.*, court transcript, vol. 1, June 26, 27, 1950, Durham County Library.

39. *DMH,* June 29, 1950; *Blue et al. v. Durham Public School District et al.*, court transcript, vol. 1, June 26, 27, 1950, vol. 2, June 28, 29, 1950.

40. *DMH,* June 30, 1950; *DMH,* July 1, 1950; *Blue et al. v. Durham Public School District et al.*, court transcript, vol. 1, June 26, 27, 1950; vol. 2, June 28, 29, 1950.

41. *Blue et al. v. Durham Public School District et al.*, court transcript, vol. 1, June 26, 27, 1950, vol. 2, June 28, 29, 1950; *Blue et. al. v. Durham Public School District,* 95 F. Supp. 441 (1951), U.S. Dist. LEXIS 2611; *DMH,* January 23, 1951; *DMH,* January 27, 1951.

42. Wilkerson, "The Negro School Movement in Virginia," 25; Tushnet, *The NAACP's Legal Strategy;* Kluger, *Simple Justice;* "Before Brown, There Was Blue," *Herald-Sun,* December 13, 2011.

43. *DS,* March 22, 1951; *DS,* April 8, 1951.

44. *DMH,* April 8, 1951.

45. Ibid.

46. "Wheeler Nominations Here Is Called 'Forward Step': Two Negro Leaders Claim Selection Would Advance Education Program of Entire City," unidentified newspaper clipping; Weare, *Black Business,* 278n245.

47. Tushnet, *The NAACP's Legal Strategy,* 21–22; *Brown v. Board of Education of Topeka,* 347 U.S. 483 (1954), from appendix section in Kluger, *Simple Justice,* 782; Thomas J. Pearsall to Curtis Briggs, September 13, 1954, Thomas Jenkins Pearsall Papers (#4300), Southern Historical Collection, Wilson Library, University of North Carolina at Chapel Hill (hereinafter cited as Pearsall Papers); Charles F. Carroll to County and City Superintendents, October 5, 1954, Pearsall Papers; "Petition of Harry McMullan, Attorney General of North Carolina, to Appear Amicus Curiae before the Supreme Court," September 9, 1954, Pearsall Papers.

48. Ralph Karpinos, "'With all Deliberate Speed': The *Brown v. Board of Education* Decision, North Carolina and the Durham City Schools, 1954–1963," typescript, 1972, Howard Papers, 3–5; *CT,* May 29, 1954; William H. Chafe, *Civilities and Civil Rights: Greensboro, North Carolina, and the Black Struggle for Freedom* (Oxford: Oxford University Press, 1980), 13, 42, 48; Davison M. Douglas, *Reading, Writing and Race: School Desegregation in Charlotte, North Carolina* (Chapel Hill: University of North Carolina Press, 1995), 27–28; Jack Michael McElreath, "The Cost of Opportunity: School Desegregation and Changing Race Relations in the Triangle since World War II" (Ph.D. diss., University of Pennsylvania, 2002), 130–31.

49. *CT,* May 29, 1954.

50. Ibid.

51. NCCHR Executive Committee Meeting Minutes, July 9, 1954, 2, 4, in the North Carolina Council on Human Relations Records (#4880), Southern Historical Collection, Wilson Library, University of North Carolina at Chapel Hill (hereinafter cited as NCCHR Records).

52. Guy B. Johnson to Wheeler, November 12, 1952, JHWC; Harry S. Jones (NCCHR executive secretary) to members of the nominating committee, December 4, 1961, NCCHR Records. Wheeler continued to serve on the executive committee when he resigned as treasurer. Nat R. Griswold (Arkansas Council on Human Relations) to Wheeler, January 19, 1960; Wheeler to Paul Rilling (SRC field director), February 10, 1960, JHWC.

53. Albert Coates and James C. N. Paul, *The School Segregation Decision: A Report to the Governor of North Carolina on the Decision of the Supreme Court of the United States on the 17th of May 1954* (Chapel Hill: UNC Institute of Government, 1954) 38–63; 65–86; 87–116; Douglass, *Reading, Writing and Race,* 27–28; McElreath, "The Cost of Opportunity," 130–31, 134; "Report of the Governor's Special Advisory Committee on Education," December 30, 1954, pp. 2, 5, Pearsall Papers; Chafe, *Civilities and Civil Rights,* 50; Karpinos, "With All Deliberate Speed," 6.

54. Wheeler, "New Farmers of America Convention Speech," September 30, 1954, JHWC; *Atlanta Daily World,* October 1, 1954.

55. Wheeler, "New Farmers of America Convention Speech," September 30, 1954, JHWC.

56. "Report of the Governor's Special Advisory Committee on Education," December 30, 1954, pp. 2–4, Pearsall Papers.

57. "Report to the Joint Committee on Education of the North Carolina Legislature," February 22, 1955, p. 1, NCCU Archives, Durham, N.C.; *CT,* February 26, 1955; *DMH,* February 23, 1955; "Can North Carolina Lead the Way?" *New South,* March 1955, 8; Greene, *Our Separate Ways,* 70; Wheeler, Morehouse College Founders Day Speech, 1955, JHWC.

58. "Report to the Joint Committee on Education of the North Carolina Legislature," 3–7, 10; *CT,* February 26, 1955; *DMH,* February 23, 1955; "Can North Carolina Lead the Way?," 8.

59. "Report to the Joint Committee on Education of the North Carolina Legislature," 7, 10; *CT,* February 26, 1955; *DMH,* February 23, 1955; "Can North Carolina Lead the Way?" 9, 12;

60. "Report to the Joint Committee on Education of the North Carolina Legislature," 7, 10; *CT,* February 26, 1955; *DMH,* February 23, 1955; "Can North Carolina Lead the Way?" 9, 12.

61. "Can North Carolina Lead the Way?," 9; Wheeler to Dr. George Mitchell, April 12, 1955, Southern Regional Council Papers, microfilm reel #145, Davis Library, University of North Carolina at Chapel Hill (hereinafter cited as SRC Papers).

62. Harry S. Jones to Program Planning Committee, April 12, 1955, SRC Papers; Dr. George Mitchell to Wheeler, April 27, 1955, SRC Papers.

63. "Pupil Assignment Act," pp. 1–3, Pearsall Papers; "Excerpts from Public School Laws of North Carolina, An Act to Provide for the Enrollment of Pupils in Public Schools," pp. 1–2, Pearsall Papers; "Report of the North Carolina Advisory Committee on Education," April 5, 1956, Pearsall Papers.

64. *Brown v. Board of Education of Topeka,* 349 U.S. 294 (1955); McKinney, *Greater Freedom,* 85; Karpinos, "With All Deliberate Speed," 5–6; Korstad and Leloudis, *To Right These Wrongs,* 34; Kluger, *Simple Justice,* 734.

65. DCSBMM, June 13, 20, 1955; Chris D. Howard, "Keep Your Eyes on the Prize: The Black Freedom Struggle for Civic Equality in Durham, North Carolina, 1954–1963" (honor's thesis, Duke University, 1983), 21; McElreath, "The Cost of Opportunity," 141; "Petition to the Durham School Board," July 11, 1955, Rencher Nicholas Harris Papers, 2, DMRRBM (hereinafter cited as Harris Papers); DCSBMM, July 11, 1955; M. Elaine Burgess, *Negro Leadership in a Southern City* (Chapel Hill: University of North Carolina Press, 1960), 124–25; Greene, *Our Separate Ways,* 70.

66. "Petition to the Durham School Board," July 11, 1955, pp. 1–2, Harris Papers; Burgess, *Negro Leadership in a Southern City,* 124–25; Greene, *Our Separate Ways,* 70.

67. "Petition to the Durham School Board," July 11, 1955, p. 5, Harris Papers; Greene, *Our Separate Ways,* 70; Burgess, *Negro Leadership in a Southern City,* 119, 125; Cannon, "The Organization and Growth of Black Political Participation," 88–89; DCSBMM, August 1, 1955.

68. Cannon, "The Organization and Growth of Black Political Participation," 88–89.

69. "Can North Carolina Have 'Voluntary' Segregation?" *New South,* September 1955, 7–8.

70. Roy Armstrong (admissions director at the University of North Carolina) to John Lewis Brandon, April 28, 1955, Leroy B. Frasier Sr. Papers (#4375-z), Southern Historical Collection, Wilson Library, University of North Carolina at Chapel Hill (hereinafter cited as Frasier Papers); L. B. Frasier to Bill Lofquist, July 19, 1955, Frasier Papers; *The Board of Trustees of the University of North Carolina, et al. v. Frasier,* 134 F. Supp. 589 (1955) U.S. Dist. LEXIS 2790, 1–3; *The Board of Trustees of the University of North Carolina, et al. v. Frasier* 350 U.S. 979 (1956), 1–2; Wheeler to Harold B. Wiley, November 11, 1955, JHWC; Wheeler to Thurgood Marshall, November 23, 1955, JHWC; Wheeler to George E. C. Hayes, November 23, 1955, JHWC.

71. F. D. Patterson to Wheeler, January 16, 1956; F. D. Patterson to Wheeler, January 31, 1956; Wheeler to Dr. F. D. Patterson, February 21, 1956; Wheeler to F. D. Patterson, March 6, 1956; Wheeler to F. D. Patterson, March 6, 1956, all in JHWC; *CT,* March 10, 1956.

72. "Report of the North Carolina Advisory Committee on Education," April 5, 1956, p. 6, Pearsall Papers.

73. Thomas to Wheeler, April 10, 1956. Wheeler to Thomas, April 12, 1956, JHWC.

74. "Report of the North Carolina Advisory Committee on Education," April 5, 1956, Pearsall Papers; Karpinos "With All Deliberate Speed," 13; Luther H. Hodges, *Businessman in the Statehouse: Six Years as Governor of North Carolina* (Chapel Hill: University of North Carolina Press, 1962), 93.

75. Hodges, *Businessman in the Statehouse,* 99; Karpinos, "With All Deliberate Speed,'" 13.

76. Karpinos, "With All Deliberate Speed," 13; "Memorandum from the DCNA's Education Committee to the North Carolina Advisory Committee to the United States Commission on Civil Rights," June 16, 1959, p. 2, William A. Clement Papers (#4024), Southern Historical Collection ,Wilson Library, University of North Carolina at Chapel Hill (hereinafter cited as Clement Papers); *McKissick v. Durham City Board of Education* 176 F. Supp. 3 (1959) U.S. Dist. LEXIS 2749, 4; DCSBMM, November 12, 1956; Burgess, *Negro Leadership in a Southern City,* 125; Greene, *Our Separate Ways,* 71.

77. "Penalties of Segregation," May 17, 1957, pp. 7–8, JHWC.

78. Ibid., 7–8, 10.

79. Ibid.

80. Wheeler to Joyner, May 20, 1957; Wheeler to Carlyle, May 20, 1957; Joyner to Wheeler, May 21, 1957; Carlyle to Wheeler, May 21, 1957, JHWC.

81. William Snider to Wheeler, June 28, 1957, JHWC; Wheeler to William Snider, July 2, 1957, JHWC.

82. William Snider to Wheeler, June 28, 1957, JHWC.

83. Chafe, *Civilities and Civil Rights,* 65; Douglass, *Reading, Writing, Race,* 44; "Penalties of Segregation," 7; Douglass, *Reading, Writing, Race,* 44–45.

4. Direct Action and the Search for "Freedom of Movement"

1. Douglas E. Moore to Wheeler, January 9, 1956, JHWC.

2. Wheeler, "Civil Rights Groups—Their Impact upon the War on Poverty," President's Address, SRC annual meeting, November 1965, JHWC; *New South,* 1965; *Law and Contemporary Problems* 31 (Winter 1966): 152–58, http://scholarship.law.duke.edu/lcp/vol31/iss1/11; "Banker with a Mission," *Business Week,* May 16, 1964.

3. *CT,* June 16, 1956; Osha Gray Davidson, *The Best of Enemies: Race and Redemption in the New South* (Chapel Hill: University of North Carolina Press, 1996), 88; 7–8; *DMH,* June 25, 1957; Burgess, *Negro Leadership in a Southern City,* 144; McElreath, "The Cost of Opportunity," 207.

4. *DS,* June 24, 1957; *DMH,* June 25, 1957; Jesse Boston, "The Lunch Counter Sit-In Demonstrations in Durham, North Carolina" (master's thesis, North Carolina Central University, 1975), 18–20; Greene, *Our Separate Ways,* 65–69; Davidson, *The Best of Enemies,* 88.

5. *Chicago Defender,* October 20–26, 1962.

6. Boston, "The Lunch Counter Sit-In Demonstrations in Durham, North Carolina," 19–20; 24–25; *CT,* June 29, 1957; *DMH,* June 25, 1957; *DS,* June 24, 1957.

7. *CT,* June 15, 1957; Davidson, *The Best of Enemies,* 88, 90; Greene, *Our Separate Ways,* 65–67.

8. *CT,* January 19, 1957; Anderson, *Durham County,* 432; *CT,* February 9, 1957; *CT,* March 16, 1957, *CT,* March 23, 1957; Burgess, *Negro Leadership in a Southern City,* 119–21; Weare, *Black Business,* 247.

9. *Atlanta Daily World,* April 3, 1957; "Obituary of John Leonidas Wheeler," April 2, 1957, JHWC; "Resolution made by the Directors, Officers and Employees of North Carolina Mutual Life Insurance Company," March 30, 1957, JHWC; *Baltimore Afro-American,* April 13, 1957; *Atlanta Daily World,* April 2, 1957.

10. DCNA Economic Committee Meeting Minutes, July 24, 1957, Floyd B. McKissick Papers (#4930), Southern Historical Collection, Wilson Library, University of North Carolina at Chapel Hill (hereinafter cited as McKissick Papers); "Annual Report of DCNA Economic Committee," January 12, 1958, McKissick Papers; Greene, *Our Separate Ways,* 67–68; *DMH,* July 18, 1957; *DS,* July 18, 1957; *CT,* July 20, 1957; Boston, "The Lunch Counter Sit-in Demonstrations in Durham, North Carolina," 21–22, 24; Greene, *Our Separate Ways,* 66–69.

11. Burgess, *Negro Leadership in a Southern City,* 144; Boston, "The Lunch Counter Sit-in Demonstrations in Durham, North Carolina," 24; Greene, *Our Separate Ways,* 67.

12. *CT,* July 20, 1957; *DS,* July 23, 1957.

13. *CT,* July 6, 1957; *CT,* July 13, 1957; *DS,* July 23, 1957; *CT,* July 20, 1957.

14. *DS,* July 18, 1957; *DMH,* July 19, 1957; *DS,* July 19, 1957; *CT,* July 20, 1957.

15. *DS,* July 18, 1957; *DMH,* July 19, 1957.

16. *DS,* July 18, 1957; *DMH,* July 19, 1957; *DS,* July 19, 1957; *CT,* July 20, 1957; *DS,* July 23, 1957; *DMH,* July 24, 1957; *CT,* July 27, 1957.

17. *CT,* July 27, 1957; Burgess, *Negro Leadership in a Southern City,* 143; Davidson, *The Best of Enemies,* 89.

18. "Resolution by the DCNA," October 17, 1957, Harris Papers.

19. "A Progress Report of the Economic Committee of the Durham Committee on Negro Affairs," October 12, 1956, 2; DCNA Economic Committee Meeting Minutes, November 15, 1956; DCNA Economic Committee Meeting Minutes, November 19, 1956; "Survey of Work done by the DCNA Economic Committee," December 6–8, 1956, all in McKissick Papers.

20. DCNA Economic Committee Meeting Minutes, July 24, 1957; "Annual Report of the DCNA Economic Committee," January 12, 1958; "Annual Report of the DCNA Economic Committee," January 18, 1959; "Report to Harry S. Jones," October 24, 1958; "Project Proposal for Merit Employment Survey," 1959; "Southeast Region Project Proposal: Merit Employment Survey," February 1959, all in McKissick Papers.

21. *CT,* February 6, 1960; Chafe, *Civilities and Civil Rights,* 71, 80–84; *DMH,* February 5, 1960; *CT,* February 13, 1960; *DMH, February* 6, 1960; *CT,* February 20, 1960.

22. Chafe, *Civilities and Civil Rights,* 86; *CT,* February 13, 1960; *DS,* February 8, 1960; *CT,* February 13, 1960; Boston, "The Lunch Counter Sit-In Demonstrations in Durham, North Carolina," 25; *DMH,* February 9, 1960; Anderson, *Durham County,* 438; Greene, *Our Separate Ways,* 76; Davidson, *The Best of Enemies,* 101; *DS,* February 9, 1960; Allan P. Sindler, *Negro Protest and Local Politics in Durham, N.C.* (New York: McGraw-Hill, 1965), 7–8; *DMH,* February 9, 1960; *Campus Echo,* February 26, 1960.

23. *DMH,* February 9, 1960; *DMH,* February 11, 1960; *CT,* February 20, 1960; *DMH,* February 13, 1960; Chafe, *Civilities and Civil Rights,* 86–87.

24. *DS,* February 12, *1960; DMH,* February 13, 1960; *CT,* February 13, 1960; *CT,* February 20, 1960; *CT,* February 13, 1960; *Campus Echo,* February 26, 1960; *CT,* February 20, 1960; *CT,* February 27, 1960.

25. *CT,* February 20, 1960.

26. Ibid.

27. Charles Payne, *I've Got the Light of Freedom: The Organizing Tradition and the Mississippi Freedom Struggle* (Los Angeles: University of California Press, 1995), 78.

28. Wheeler interview.

29. Martin Luther King Sr., *Daddy King: An Autobiography* (New York: Morrow, 1980); *Atlanta Daily World,* April 21, 1935; *CT,* December 22, 1956; Wheeler to MLK, October 1, 1958, JHWC; MLK to Wheeler, October 10, 1958, JHWC; William and Josephine Clement, interview by Walter and Juanita Weare, transcript,

June 19, 1986, #C-0031, pp. 52–53, Southern Oral History Program Collection (#4007), Southern Historical Collection, Wilson Library, University of North Carolina at Chapel Hill, http://docsouth.unc.edu/sohp/C-0031/C-0031.html.

30. Davidson, *The Best of Enemies,* 103; *DMH,* February 17, 1960; *CT,* February 20, 1960.

31. "Dr. Martin Luther King Jr. Speech at White Rock Baptist Church," February 16, 1960, Appendix B, in Boston, "The Lunch Counter Sit-In Demonstrations in Durham, North Carolina," 57–60; *CT,* February 20, 1960; *DMH,* February 17, 1960.

32. *CT,* February 13, 1960; *CT,* February 20, 1960; *CT,* February 27, 1960; *CT,* March 6, 1960.

33. Terry Sanford, interview by William H. Chafe, University of North Carolina at Greensboro, p. 5, http://library.uncg.edu/dp/crg/oralHistItem.aspx?i=67.

34. Floyd McKissick, interview by Chris D. Howard, March 3, 29, 1983, interview notes; "Report of the President, J. H. Wheeler to Stockholders for the Year Ending December 31, 1960 at its Annual Meeting," January 9, 1961, JHWC.

35. Watts Hill Jr. to Wheeler, March 17, 1960, pp. 2–3, JHWC; Boston, "The Lunch Counter Sit-In Demonstrations in Durham, North Carolina" includes excerpts from Hill's letter to Wheeler, pp. 29–30. Boston more than likely obtained the letter from Wheeler, but the source requested that Hill's name be withheld. Chafe, *Civilities and Civil Rights,* 71; Greene, *Our Separate Ways,* 76, 78.

36. Hill to Wheeler, March 17, 1960, JHWC; Sindler, *Negro Protest,* 9; Greene, *Our Separate Ways,* 78.

37. Hill to Wheeler, March 17, 1960, JHWC.

38. Ibid.

39. John Drescher, *Triumph of Good Will: How Terry Sanford Beat a Champion of Segregation and Reshaped the South* (Jackson: University Press of Mississippi, 2000); Hill to Wheeler, March 17, 1960, JHWC.

40. Hill to Wheeler, March 17, 1960, JHWC.

41. Ibid.

42. *CT,* January 23, 1960; *CT,* February 6, 1960; *CT,* February 12, 1960; "Wheeler Speaks on African Trip," *Campus Echo,* February 26, 1960.

43. Sindler, *Negro Protest,* 10–11; Clayborne Carson, *In Struggle: SNCC and the Black Awakening of the 1960s* (Cambridge: Harvard University Press, 1981), 19–21; Barbara Ransby, *Ella Baker and the Black Freedom Movement: A Radical Democratic Vision* (Chapel Hill: University of North Carolina Press, 2003), 239–41; McElreath, "The Cost of Opportunity," 229.

44. Hill to Wheeler, April 19, 1960, JHWC.

45. Ibid.; Wheeler to Terry Sanford, June 22, 1960; "List of Donors to Terry Sanford's Campaign (Mostly top businessmen from Durham, especially from N.C. Mutual)," June 22, 1960; Asa Spaulding to Wheeler, June 21, 22, 1960, all in Asa and Elna Spaulding Papers, DMRRBML.

46. Sindler, *Negro Protest,* 11–12; Howard, "Keep Your Eyes on the Prize," 37–38; Greene, *Our Separate Ways,* 81; McElreath, "The Cost of Opportunity," 231;

Howard E. Covington Jr. and Marion A. Ellis, *Terry Sanford: Politics, Progress, and Outrageous Ambitions* (Durham: Duke University Press, 1999), 231, 235–36, 239; Korstad and Leloudis, *To Right These Wrongs,* 41, 43.

47. Vivian McCoy, interview by Chris D. Howard, April 1, 1983, interview notes, p. 6, Chris D. Howard Papers, DMRRBML; *DMH,* May 19, 1963; McElreath, "The Cost of Opportunity," 308; *DMH,* May 18, 1963; Sindler, *Negro Protest,* 14; Howard, "Keep Your Eyes on the Prize," 103; 107–8; Greene, *Our Separate Ways,* 91; *DMH,* May 19, 1963.

48. *DMH,* May 20, 1963; "Opening Remarks of Mayor Grabarek, Durham's Interim Committee Press Conference," June 4, 1963, p. 3, Vice Presidential Office Files of George E. Reedy Pertaining to PCEEO, Lyndon B. Johnson Papers; Howard, "Keep Your Eyes on the Prize," 108–9; Robert P. Althauser, "The Durham Committee on Negro Affairs: 1962–1963," Confidential Report to the Voter Education Project, in the possession of Evan Faulkenbury, SUNY Courtland, May 1964.

49. *DMH,* May 21, 1963; *DS,* May 21, 1963; "Outline of Objectives from the NAACP-CORE Negotiation Committee and Negro Citizens of Durham Community to R. Wensell Grabarek," May 24, 1963, p. 1, Watts Hill Jr. Papers (#5162), Southern Historical Collection, Wilson Library, University of North Carolina at Chapel Hill (hereinafter cited as Watts Hill Jr., Papers); Howard, "Keep Your Eyes on the Prize," 114–15.

50. *DMH,* May 21, 1963; *DMH,* May 21, 1963; *DS,* May 21, 1963; "Opening Remarks of Mayor Grabarek, Durham's Interim Committee Press Conference," June 4, 1963, Vice Presidential Office Files of George E. Reedy Pertaining to PCEEO, box 28, Lyndon B. Johnson Papers, 3; McElreath, "The Cost of Opportunity," 308–9.

51. *DS,* May 20, 1963; *DMH,* May 21, 1963; *DMH,* May 22, 1963; "Opening Remarks of Mayor Grabarek, Durham's Interim Committee Press Conference," June 4, 1963, p. 3, Vice Presidential Office Files of George E. Reedy Pertaining to PCEEO, box 28, Lyndon B. Johnson Papers; *DS,* May 22, 1963; McElreath, "The Cost of Opportunity," 310; Howard, "Keep Your Eyes on the Prize," 123.

52. *DS,* May 22, 1963; Howard, "Keep Your Eyes on the Prize," 125; *DMH,* May 23, 1963; Greene, *Our Separate Ways,* 94.

53. *DMH,* May 23, 1963; *DMH,* May 21, 1963; *DS,* May 23, 1963; Sindler, *Negro Protest,* 17; Howard, "Keep Your Eyes on the Prize," 123–24; Greene, *Our Separate Ways,* 94; *DMH,* May 24, 1963.

54. "Interim Committee at Work: Subgroups to Begin Discussions Today," unidentified newspaper article, May 25, 1963; *DS,* May 25, 1963; Howard, "Keep Your Eyes on the Prize," 125; "Telegram to President John F. Kennedy from R. Wensell Grabarek and George Watts Carr Jr.," June 4, 1963, Vice Presidential Office Files of George E. Reedy Pertaining to PCEEO, box 28, Lyndon B. Johnson Papers; *CT,* June 1, 1963; *CT,* June 22, 1963; Vivian McCoy, interview by Chris D. Howard, April 1, 1983, interview notes, April 1, 1983, p. 6, Howard Papers, DMRRBML; R. Wense Grabarek, interview #24 by Chris D. Howard, April 1, 1983, interview notes, April 1, 1983, Howard Papers, DMRRBML; Joycelyn McKissick, interview #27 by Chris D. Howard, interview notes, Howard Papers, DMRRBML; Watts Carr Jr., interview by

Chris D. Howard, March 25, 1983, interview notes, p. 4, Howard Papers, DMRRBML; Howard, "Eyes on the Prize," 124; Greene, *Our Separate Ways,* 94.

55. "Durham's Interim Committee Report of the Subcommittee on Hotels, Motels, and Restaurants," pp. 16–18, Vice Presidential Office Files of George E. Reedy Pertaining to PCEEO, June 4, 1963, box 28, Lyndon B. Johnson Papers; "Final Report: Hotels, Motels and Restaurants Subcommittee," June 27, 1963, Watts Hill Jr. Papers; *CT,* June 22, 1963; *New York Times,* June 5, 1963; "Durham's Interim Committee Report of the Subcommittee on Fair Employment Practices," pp. 10–15, Vice Presidential Office Files of George E. Reedy Pertaining to PCEEO, box 28, Lyndon B. Johnson Papers; "Final Report: Fair Employment Practices Subcommittee," June 1963, folder 197, Watts Hill Jr. Papers.

56. "Durham's Interim Committee Report of the Subcommittee on Fair Employment Practices," pp. 10–15, Vice Presidential Office Files of George E. Reedy Pertaining to PCEEO, box 28, Lyndon B. Johnson Papers; "Final Report: Fair Employment Practices Subcommittee," June 1963, Watts Hill Jr. Papers; Vivian McCoy, interview by Chris D. Howard, April 1, 1983, interview notes, p. 7, Howard Papers, DMRRBML.

57. Wheeler to George E. Reedy, June 7, 1973, Vice Presidential Files of George E. Reedy Pertaining to PCEEO, Lyndon B. Johnson Papers; unsent Western Union telegram from Lyndon B. Johnson to R. Wensell Grabarek, June 7, 1963, Vice Presidential Files of George E. Reedy Pertaining to PCEEO, Lyndon B. Johnson Papers; Memo from George E. Reedy to Lyndon B. Johnson, June 10, 1963, Vice Presidential Files of George E. Reedy Pertaining to PCEEO, Lyndon B. Johnson Papers; *CT,* June 1, 1963; *CT,* June 8, 1963; *CT,* June 22, 1963; Howard, "Keep Your Eyes on the Prize," 128–29.

5. Equal Employment, Voting Rights, and Public Policy at the National Level

1. Wheeler to Sanford, April 29, 1961, McKissick Papers; Terry Sanford, "Inaugural Address," January 5, 1961, in *Messages, Addresses, and Public Papers of Terry Sanford, Governor of North Carolina, 1961–1965,* ed. Memory F. Mitchell (Raleigh: Council of State, State of North Carolina, 1966), 3, 6, 8; also quoted in Robert R. Korstad and James L. Leloudis, *To Right these Wrongs,* 36–45; Covington and Ellis, *Terry Sanford: Politics,* chaps. 10–11; Drescher, *Triumph of Goodwill,* chap. 3.

2. Wheeler to Sanford, April 29, 1961; Covington and Ellis, *Terry Sanford: Politics,* chaps. 10–11; Drescher, *Triumph of Goodwill,* chap. 3.

3. Chafe, *Civilities and Civil Rights,* 103; Wheeler to Sanford, April 29, 1961, McKissick Papers.

4. Wheeler to Sanford, April 29, 1961, McKissick Papers.

5. Ibid.

6. See Robert Samuel Smith, *Race, Labor, and Civil Rights:* Griggs versus Duke Power *and the Struggle for Equal Employment Opportunity* (Baton Rouge: Louisiana

State University Press, 2002); Robert Belton, *The Crusade for Equality in the Workplace: The* Griggs v. Duke Power *Story,* ed. Stephen L. Wasby (Lawrence: University Press of Kansas, 2014); Alfred W. Blumrosen, "The Legacy of *Griggs:* Social Progress and Subjective Judgments," *Chicago-Kent Law Review* 63 (April 1987): 1–42; Eleanor Holmes Norton, "The End of the Griggs Economy: Doctrinal Adjustment for the New American Workplace," *Yale Law and Review* 8, no. 2 (1990): 197–204; Timothy J. Minchin, *Hiring the Black Worker: The Radical Integration of the Southern Textile Industry, 1960–1980* (Chapel Hill: University of North Carolina Press, 1999); Timothy J. Minchin, *The Color of Work: The Struggle for Civil Rights in the Southern Paper Industry* (Chapel Hill: University of North Carolina Press, 2001); Timothy J. Minchin, *Fighting against the Odds: A History of Southern Labor since World War II* (Gainesville: University Press of Florida, 2005); Timothy J. Minchin, *From Rights to Economics: The Ongoing Struggle for Black Equality in the U.S. South* (Gainesville: University Press of Florida, 2007); David Hamilton Golland, *Constructing Affirmative Action: The Struggle for Equal Employment Opportunity* (Lexington: University Press of Kentucky, 2011); Thomas J. Sugrue, "Affirmative Action from Below: Civil Rights, the Building Trades, and the Politics of Racial Equality in the Urban North, 1945–1969," *Journal of American History* 91 (June 2004): 145–73; William P. Jones, *The March on Washington: Jobs, Freedom, and the Forgotten History of Civil Rights.* (New York: Norton, 2013); Judson MacLaury, *To Advance their Opportunities: Federal Policies toward African American Workers from World War I to the Civil Rights Act of 1964* (Knoxville: Newfound Press, University of Tennessee Libraries, 2008); Construction Industry Joint Conference, Joint Committee on Equal Employment Opportunity, August 9, 1963; Speech Given by Vice President Lyndon B. Johnson, Mexican American Education Conference Committee at the Statler Hilton Hotel, Los Angeles, California, August 9, 1963; Program of the Regional Conference of Community Leaders on Equal Employment Opportunity, August 9, 1963; Speech Given by Vice President Johnson, Regional Conference on Equal Employment Opportunity, McGregor Memorial Conference Center, Detroit, Michigan, August 15, 1963, all in JHWC; "John Wheeler: Working Quietly for the Progress of Blacks," *Raleigh News and Observer,* March 15, 1970; Belton, *The Crusade for Equality in the Workplace,* 6–8, 32–38, chap. 3; Smith, *Race, Labor, and Civil Rights,* chap. 4.

7. White House Press Release, March 6, 1961, JHWC; Executive Order #10925, March 6, 1961, Vice Presidential Office Files of George E. Reedy, Lyndon B. Johnson Papers, Lyndon B. Johnson Presidential Library and Museum (hereinafter cited as Reedy files); Christopher Howland Pyle, "The Politics of Civil Rights: The President's Committee on Equal Employment Opportunity, 1961–1962" (master's thesis, Columbia University, 1966), 19, 98–100, 149–55; MacLaury, *To Advance Their Opportunities,* 177; "The First Nine Months: Report of the President's Committee on Equal Employment Opportunity," January 15, 1962, JHWC.

8. William H. Chafe, *The Unfinished Journey: American since World War II,* 7th ed. (New York: Oxford University Press, 2011), 5; MacLaury, *To Advance Their Opportunities,* 89, 93–94; Jones, *March on Washington,* 1–3, 30–39; Golland, *Constructing Affirmative Action,* 11–12.

9. Jones, *March on Washington,* 1–3, 30–39; Harvard Sitkoff, *The Struggle for Black Equality, 1954–1992* (New York: Hill and Wang, 2008), 12; Smith, *Race, Labor, and Civil Rights,* 15–16; Golland, *Constructing Affirmative Action,* 11–12; Rubio, *A History of Affirmative Action*, 108–9; Glenda Gilmore, *Defying Dixie: The Radical Roots of Civil Rights, 1919–1950* (New York: Norton, 2008), 359–60; Gershenhorn, "Double V in North Carolina," 160; MacLaury, *To Advance Their Opportunities,* 94–117.

10. Pyle, "The Politics of Civil Rights," 2–3; Wheeler to Vice President Richard M. Nixon, March 7, 1958, JHWC.

11. Pyle, "The Politics of Civil Rights," 3; David Niven, *The Politics of Injustice: The Kennedys, the Freedom Rides, and the Electoral Consequences of a Moral Compromise* (Knoxville: University of Tennessee Press, 2003), 14.

12. Southern Regional Council, *The Federal Executive and Civil Rights* (Atlanta: Southern Regional Council, 1961), iv, 28, 15; "Voter Education Project Press Release," January 1962, JHWC; Pat Watters and Reese Cleghorn, *Climbing Jacob's Ladder: The Arrival of Negroes in Southern Politics* (New York: Harcourt, Brace and World, 1967), 44–46; Stephen Currier to Wheeler, July 21, 1961; Taconic Meeting Agenda, July 28, 1961, both in JHWC; SRC Memorandum from Leslie Dunbar to SRC executive committee members, July 31, 1961, p. 1, Marion A. Wright Papers (#3830), Southern Historical Collection, Wilson Library, University of North Carolina at Chapel Hill (hereinafter cited as Wright Papers); Leslie W. Dunbar and Peggy Dunbar, interview by Jacquelyn Dowd Hall, Bob Hall, and Helen Bresler, December 18, 1978, #G-00075, interview transcript, http://docsouth.unc.edu/sohp/G-0075/G-0075.html, pp. 30–31, Southern Oral History Program (#4007), Southern Historical Collection, Wilson Library, University of North Carolina at Chapel Hill (hereinafter cited as Dunbar interview); Wheeler's Notes from Taconic Foundation Meeting, August 1961, JHWC.

13. Pyle, "The Politics of Civil Rights," 149–55; MacLaury, *To Advance Their Opportunities,* 177.

14. Executive Order #10925, March 6, 1961, Executive Order Folder, Reedy Files; Pyle, "The Politics of Civil Rights," 14, Appendix B, 149.

15. Western Union telegram from Bert L. Bennett to Lyndon B. Johnson, March 22, 1961; Wheeler to Bennett, April 8, 1961; Bennett to Wheeler, April 12, 1961; Sen. Sam J. Ervin to Bennett, March 23, 1961; Vice President Lyndon B. Johnson to Bennett, March 24, 1961; Sen. Ervin to Wheeler, April 12, 1961; Bennett to Wheeler and John S. Stewart, March 5, 1963; George B. Autry to Wheeler, October 24, 1963, all in JHWC; Wheeler to Gov. Sanford, June 22, 1960; List of Donors to Terry Sanford's gubernatorial campaign, June 22, 1960, Spaulding Papers, DMRRBML; Asa T. Spaulding to Wheeler with campaign contributions, June 21, 22, 1960, all in Spaulding Papers, DMRRBML; Watts Hill Jr. to Wheeler, April 19, 1960, JHWC; Wheeler to Gov. Sanford, April 29, 1961, 14–15, McKissick Papers; Wheeler interview, June 1964, digital audio available through "Robert Penn Warren's *Who Speaks for the Negro? An Archival Collection,* http://whospeaks.library.vanderbilt.edu/interview/john-hervey-wheeler; Warren, *Who Speaks for the Negro?,* 300–305.

16. *Dictionary of North Carolina Biography,* s.v. "Larkins, John R."; Jeffrey J. Crow, Paul D. Escott, and Flora J. Hatley, *A History of African Americans in North Carolina,* rev. ed. (Raleigh: Office of Archives and History, North Carolina Department of Cultural Resources, 2002), 136; Larkins to Wheeler, March 30, 1961; Larkins to Bennett, February 8, 1961, both in JHWC.

17. Larkins to Wheeler, February 8, 1961; Larkins to Wheeler, May 30, 1961; Wheeler to Bennett, November 20, 1961; Wheeler to Frank A. Reeves, June 1, 1961; Bennett to Larkins, Wheeler, and John S. Stewart, May 22, 1961; Larkins to Bennett, May 9, 1961; Dr. Sam E. Duncan to Wheeler, June 20, 1961; James C. Brooks to Wheeler, June 20, 1961; Wheeler to Governor Sanford, September 7, 1961; Governor Sanford to Wheeler, September 20, 1961, all in JHWC.

18. *DMH,* July 13, 1959; For a comprehensive assessment of the DCNA's Economic Committee's activities, see the Durham Committee on Negro Affairs files, folders 7568a–7568f, 7569, 7570 a, 7568a–7570a, McKissick Papers; MacLaury, *To Advance Their Opportunities,* 178, 181–83.

19. *DMH,* April 10, 1961; *Raleigh News and Observer,* April 10, 1961; *Norfolk Journal and Guide,* April 29, 1961; Wheeler to Dr. Sam E. Duncan, May 5, 1961, JHWC; Wheeler to Asa T. Spaulding, April 18, 1961, Asa T. and Elna Spaulding Papers, DMRRBML.

20. Dunbar interview.

21. Wheeler to Robert F. Kennedy, March 7, 1961; Wheeler to Vice President Lyndon B. Johnson, March 8, 1961, both in JHWC.

22. Dunbar interview, 26; Nick Bryant, *The Bystander: John F. Kennedy and the Struggle for Black Equality* (New York: Basic, 2006), chap. 16; John Lewis, *Walking against the Wind: A Memoir of the Movement,* with Michael D'Orso (New York: Simon and Schuster, 1998), chaps. 7–9; Pyle, "The Politics of Civil Rights," 77–79, 101; MacLaury, *To Advance Their Opportunities,* 175, 192, 200–201, 245. That spring, the Congress of Racial Equality (CORE) organized a group of white and black activists to travel throughout the South on Greyhound buses to test enforcement of laws banning segregated interstate buses; while at bus terminals in various cities, the "Freedom Riders" attempted to desegregate waiting rooms. In a bus terminal in Rock Hill, South Carolina, not far from Charlotte, North Carolina (where Wheeler opened an M&F Bank branch a year later), John Lewis was severely beaten. In Anniston, Alabama, their bus was set ablaze, forcing Kennedy to move beyond his inclination to work behind the scenes. Civil rights activists became distrustful of the new administration because of its hesitancy about protecting the Freedom Riders (Raymond Arsenault, *Freedom Riders: 1961 and the Struggle for Racial Justice* [Oxford: Oxford University Press, 2006]; Sitkoff, *The Struggle for Black Equality*).

23. Wheeler to John Seigenthaler, March 22, 1961; Sen. Jordan to Wheeler, May 12, 1961; Sen. Ervin to Wheeler, May 13, 1961, all in JHWC; Covington, *Henry Frye,* 83–84, 81, 64, 82, 144; Wheeler to Sen. Jordan, May 23, 1961; Wheeler to Sen. Ervin, May 23, 1961; Wheeler to Frank A. Reeves, March 23, 1961, all in JHWC; Wheeler to Sen. Jordan, March 3, 1961; Wheeler to John Seigenthaler, March 22, 1961; Wheeler to Sen. Ervin, March 23, 1961; Wheeler to Sen. Jordan, March 23,

1961; Wheeler to John Seigenthaler, September 13, 1961; Wheeler to Sen. Ervin, March 3, 1961, all in JHWC; see also the William H. Murdock Papers, North Carolina Collection, Durham County Library (Main); Bennett to Wheeler, November 27, 1961; Wheeler to John Reilly, May 29, 1962; Clive W. Palmer to Joseph C. Biggers, November 22, 1961; Joseph C. Biggers to John Seigenthaler, May 30, 1961; Joseph C. Biggers to Robert F. Kennedy, May 30, 1961; Joseph C. Biggers to E. H. Burroughs, May 30, 1961, all in JHWC; *Baltimore Afro-American,* December 1, 1962. In 1969, Frye became the first black North Carolina legislator elected in the twentieth century. He served until 1982. When Frye decided to establish the Greensboro National Bank in the 1970s, he received counsel and advice from John Wheeler. Frye also later became the first black justice on the North Carolina Supreme Court and went on to become the court's first black chief justice; Covington notes that "Despite Wheeler's unenthusiastic reception, the two men remained in touch. Wheeler was impressed enough with Frye to put him forward as his candidate when Attorney General Robert F. Kennedy was looking for an African American to appoint to the U.S. attorney's office in the latter part of 1962."

24. Wheeler Sen. Ervin, May 3, 1961; Wheeler to Sen. Jordan, May 3, 1961; Bennett to Wheeler, October 22, 1962; Bennett to Louis E. Martin, January 21, 1963; Bennett to Wheeler, November 11, 1961, all in JHWC.

25. Wheeler to Hugh Cannon, November 15, 1961; Wheeler to Louis E. Martin, October 17, 1962, both in JHWC.

26. Western Union Telegram from Wheeler to Robert F. Kennedy, November 7, 1962, JHWC; Wheeler to Louis E. Martin, October 17, 1962, both in JHWC; Howard E. Covington Jr., *Henry Frye: North Carolina's First African American Chief Justice* (Jefferson, N.C.: McFarland, 2013), 82; *Baltimore Afro-American,* December 1, 1962; Wheeler to John Reilly, May 29, 1962; Wheeler to Louis Martin, October 23, 1962; Joseph C. Biggers to James J. P. McShane, October 24, 1962; Joseph C. Biggers Personal Data Sheet; Memorandum from Wheeler about J. C. Biggers's application; Joseph C. Biggers to Henry Hall Wilson, April 10, 1963, all in JHWC.

27. Pyle, "The Politics of Civil Rights," 22–39, 46.

28. Wheeler to Arthur Goldberg, December 6, 1961, JHWC; Pyle, "The Politics of Civil Rights," 65; *Plans for Progress: Atlanta Survey,* 1, SRC, January 1963, Reedy Files, 1.

29. Pyle, "The Politics of Civil Rights," 68–74, 83–85; "Report of Theodore W. Kheel to Vice President Johnson on the Structure and Operations of the President's Committee on Equal Employment Opportunity," 1962, Reedy Files; MacLaury, *To Advance Their Opportunities,* 190–91, 211.

30. "Report of Theodore W. Kheel to Vice President Johnson on the Structure and Operations of the President's Committee on Equal Employment Opportunity," 1962, p. 44, Reedy Files; "Transcript of Proceedings," PCEEO, August 22, 1962, pp. 36, 338–39, Reedy Files; *Plans for Progress: Atlanta Survey,* pp. 1, 506, SRC, January 1963, Civil Service Commission Folder, Reedy Files; MacLaury, *To Advance Their Opportunities,* 212–13.

31. Memorandum from Hobart Taylor Jr. to Lyndon B. Johnson, February 19, 1963, 4, Reedy Files; MacLaury, *To Advance Their Opportunities,* 211; Note exchange between Wheeler and a PCEEO colleague, 1963, JHWC; MacLaury, *To Advance Their Opportunities,* 212–13. For more on the Southern Regional Council during the 1960s, see Steven P. Miller, "Whither Southern Liberalism in the Post–Civil Rights Era? The Southern Regional Council and its Peers, 1965–1972," *Georgia Historical Quarterly* 90 (Winter 2006): 547–68. Minchin, *From Rights to Economics,* chap. 3.

32. Wheeler to Governor Sanford, April 29, McKissick Papers.

33. NCCHR Memorandum, "A Brief Survey of the Possible Impact of Human Relations on North Carolina's Plans for Growth and Future Development," to Gov. Sanford, 1961, McKissick Papers.

34. Bennett to Wheeler, May 25, 1961; Carolyn Patricia Martin to Wheeler, May 12, 1961; Wheeler to Frank Reeves, 1961, all in JHWC.

35. Wheeler to Frank Reeves, May 22, 1961; Wheeler to Bert L. Bennett, May 22, 1961; Clarestene T. Stewart to Bureau of Internal Revenue, November 10, 1959; Eugenia V. Blair to Clarestene T. Stewart, November 13, 1959; Clarestene T. Stewart to Wheeler, August 7, 1961; Margaret M. Llewellyn to Clarestene T. Stewart, August 10, 1960; Margaret M. Llewellyn to Clarestene T. Stewart, March 24, 1961; Bennett to Wheeler, May 25, 1961; David L. Stephens to Wheeler, September 8, 1961, all in JHWC.

36. Alonzo Eubanks to Wheeler, July 20, 1961; Wheeler to John G. Field, July 25, 1961; John G. Field to John H. Wheeler, August 4, 1961, all in JHWC.

37. Wheeler to Governor Sanford, December 28, 1962; Wheeler to Governor Sanford, December 28, 1962; Wheeler to Adj. General Claude T. Bowers, December 28, 1962; Wheeler to Adj. General Claude T. Bowers, January 3, 1963, p. 1; Wheeler to Governor Sanford, December 28, 1962; Wheeler to Adj. General Claude T. Bowers, December 28, 1962; Wheeler to Adj. General Claude T. Bowers, January 3, 1963, p. 1; Merit System Council Meeting Minutes regarding the Hearing of Appeal of Mr. Alonzo Reid, July 29, 1963, p. 1; Wheeler to Arthur Chapin (Special Assistant to the U.S. Employment Service Secretary in the Department of Labor), September 3, 1963; Fred Stovall Royster (Chairman of the Merit System Council) to Reid, August 1, 1963, all in JHWC.

38. Alonzo S. Reid to Wheeler, November 21, 1963; Alonzo S. Reid to Wheeler, November 21, 1963; Alonzo S. Reid to Jack Howard, 1963; Jack Howard to Wheeler, October 15, 1963; Jack Howard to Alonzo S. Reid, October 1963, all in JHWC.

39. Wheeler to Arthur Chapin, September 3, 1963, JHWC.

40. *CT,* October 17, 1964; Wheeler interview.

41. *Baltimore Afro-American,* July 22, 1961; Larkins to Bennett, July 17, 1961; "Notes on Meeting of Sub-Committee on Communication with Governor Sanford," September 21, 1961, both in JHWC; Covington and Ellis, *Terry Sanford: Politics,* 277.

42. "Vocational Training Opportunities in North Carolina," North Carolina Good Neighbor Council, September 1963, p. 1, JHWC, 1; Korstad and Leloudis, *To Right These Wrongs,* 54–55, 70–72; Mitchell, *Messages, Addresses, and Public Papers of Terry Sanford: Politics,* 743; Crow, Escott, and Hatley, *A History of African*

Americans in North Carolina, 203–4; Terry Sanford, *But What About the People?* (New York: Harper and Row, 1966), 141–14; Gov. Terry Sanford, "Emancipation Day Speech," January 18, 1963, https://www.youtube.com/watch?v=wiXhP7tgFLg, as qtd. in Korstad and Leloudis, *To Right These Wrongs,* 54.

43. Korstad and Leloudis, *To Right These Wrongs,* 81–82; Sanford, "Emancipation Day Speech"; Covington and Ellis, *Terry Sanford: Politics,* 311.

44. Stephen Currier to Wheeler, July 21, 1961; "Taconic Meeting Agenda," July 28, 1961; Wheeler to Stephen Currier, July 31, 1961, all in JHWC; SRC Memorandum from Dunbar to Executive Committee, July 31, 1961, p. 1, Wright Papers.

45. SRC Memorandum from Dunbar to Executive Committee, July 31, 1961, p. 1, Wright Papers; Dunbar interview.

46. Memorandum Notes from the Taconic Conference, July 18, 1961, JHWC.

47. SRC Memorandum from Dunbar to Executive Committee, July 31, 1961, 2, Wright Papers; Dunbar interview; Dunbar to SRC Executive Committee, September 13, 1961, Wright Papers; Dunbar to James Farmer, Roy Wilkins, Whitney M. Young Jr., Wyatt T. Walker, Charles McDew, and Timothy L. Jenkins, September 13, 1961, Wright Papers.

48. Memorandum Notes from the Taconic Conference, July 18, 1961, JHWC; Dunbar interview; Dunbar to James Farmer et al., September 13, 1961, p. 3, Wright Papers.

49. Covington and Ellis, *Terry Sanford: Politics,* 279–80; "Transcript of President's Remarks at the University of North Carolina's Convocation," *New York Times,* October 13, 1961; Invitation from UNC to Wheeler to attend President John F. Kennedy's University Day Address, October 12, 1961, JHWC.

50. Dunbar to Joseph Haas (SRC legal counsel), October 27, 1961, JHWC; Manning Marable, *Malcolm X: A Life of Reinvention* (New York: Viking, 2011), 160–61; Louis E. Lomax, "The Negro Revolt against 'The Negro Leaders,'" *Harper's Magazine* 220, no. 1321 (June 1960), 48; Louis Lomax, "Script for Radio Broadcast on WRAI," October 17, 1961, p. 3, JHWC. Lomax began by saying: "I came upon a good story, a scoop. For the good of the race because some people said if I broke the story then I'd muddy the water and the thing wouldn't come to pass. I kept quiet. I've been quiet about the story for the better part of three months now and I'm by no means the only reporter, Negro or White, in the United States who knows the story that I am going to share on this commentary."

51. Roy Wilkins to Dunbar, October 17, 1961, pp. 1–2; Dunbar to Joseph Haas, October 27, 1961, p. 1; Dunbar to Stephen Currier, November 1961, pp. 1–2, all in JHWC.

52. Voter Education Project News Release, January 1962, Wheeler Collection. On the history of the Voter Education Project, see Watters and Cleghorn, *Climbing Jacob's Ladder;* Evan Faulkenbury, "Poll Power: The Voter Education Project and the Financing of the Civil Rights Movement, 1961–1992" (Ph.D. diss., University of North Carolina at Chapel Hill, 2016).

53. *Important Notice!!! Are You Registered?, No!: Attention, Citizen, This is Your Last Call for Registration,* Flyers for DCNA Voter Registration Drive,

May 1962, both in SRC Papers; *DS,* May 14, 1962; *DMH,* May 15, 1962; *DMH,* May 27, 1962.

54. Vernon E. Jordan Jr., interview by author, March 9, 2010. According to Jordan, Wheeler "mentored me and often sent me to represent him on the national commissions on which he sat. He would be an advisor and confidant to me for many years, and he was a blessing in my life." Vernon E. Jordan Jr. and Annette Gordon-Reed, *Vernon Can Read: A Memoir* (New York: Public Affairs, 2001), 177; "John Wheeler: Working Quietly for the Progress of Blacks," *Raleigh News and Observer,* March 15, 1970.

55. Wheeler also became vice chairman of the National Citizens Committee for Community Relations, a national body appointed by the president to facilitate the implementation of the Civil Rights Act of 1964 in communities across the country. "Remarks by Attorney General Robert F. Kennedy to the National Citizens' Committee for Community Relations," August 18, 1964, JHWC; *CT,* August 22, September 5, 1964.

6. Urban Renewal and the Prospects of a Free and Open Society

1. Rubye Gattis, comments at the premiere screening of *Change Comes Knocking: The Story of the NC Fund,* March 25, 2008, UNC–Chapel Hill, http://www.law.unc.edu/centers/poverty/events/archive20072008/; Greene, *Our Separate Ways,* 117; Korstad and Leloudis, *To Right These Wrongs,* 189, 195.

2. Vann and Jones, *Durham's Hayti,* chap. 5; Rebecca Kathleen Blackmon, "When the Bulldozers Came: A Historical Analysis of Urban Renewal and Community Action in a New South City" (honor's thesis, University of North Carolina at Chapel Hill, 1996); Anderson, *Durham County,* 407; Reginald Mitchener, interview by Glenn Hinson, November 15, 1976, December 7, 1976, February 7, 1979, May 23, 1979, #H-0212–1, Southern Oral History Program (#4007), Southern Historical Collection, Wilson Library, University of North Carolina at Chapel Hill; *CT,* September 25, 1965.

3. Weare, *Black Business,* 243–44; Keech, *The Impact of Negro Voting* (Chicago: Rand McNally, 1968), 27, 31.

4. Vivian Rogers Patterson, interview by author, March 11, 2010, Southern Oral History Program (#4007), Southern Historical Collection, Wilson Library, University of North Carolina at Chapel Hill; Howard N. Lee, interview by author, February 29, 2008, #U-0298, Southern Oral History Program (#4007), Southern Historical Collection, Wilson Library, University of North Carolina at Chapel Hill.

5. Howard N. Lee, interview.

6. Digital Scholarship Lab, "Renewing Inequality," *American Panorama,* ed. Robert K. Nelson and Edward L. Ayers, https://dsl.richmond.edu/panorama/renewal/#view=0/0/1&viz=cartogram.

7. Wheeler, "Keynote Address at the First Annual Housing and Urban Renewal Clinic at N.C. A&T," November 2–3, 1961, in JHWC; John F. Bauman, "Housing

Act of 1949," in *Encyclopedia of American Urban History,* ed. David R. Goldfield (Thousand Oaks: Sage, 2007), 357–59, Anderson, *Durham County,* 499, 411; "Obituary of J. J. "Babe" Henderson Sr.," March 1, 1998, in author's possession.

8. Anderson, *Durham County,* 499–11; John Hervey Wheeler, "Keynote Address at the First Annual Housing and Urban Renewal Clinic at N.C. A&T," November 2–3, 1961.

9. *Where Shall We Go From Here? Report of the Commission on Race and Housing* (Berkeley: University of California Press, 1958), 64–65.

10. Spencer M. Overton to Wheeler, December 6, 1958; Wheeler to James M. Dabbs, January 20, 1959; Dabbs to Wheeler, January 6, 1959; Wheeler, "Speech to the Cleveland Association of Real Estate Brokers," May 19, 1969, all in JHWC.

11. *DMH,* July 6, 1958; "The Housing Act of 1954 and Implications for Minorities," lecture presented before the Seventh Annual Human Relations Institute, sponsored by the Dayton Urban League, February 21, 1955, p. 1, Spaulding Papers, DMRRBML; Bauman, "Housing Act of 1954," in *Encyclopedia of American Urban History,* ed. David R. Goldfield (Thousand Oaks: Sage, 2007), 359–60; *Outlook for Durham* (Durham: City Planning Department, spring 1957); *CT,* February 15, 1958; *CT,* April 5, 1958.

12. *DMH,* July 6, 1958; Anderson, *Durham County,* 406–7; *CT,* January 3, 1959.

13. Wheeler to Asa Spaulding, October 8, 1959; Asa Spaulding to Val J. Washington, October 8, 1959; Robinson O. Everett to Asa Spaulding, January 5, 1960, Spaulding Papers, DMRRBML; *CT,* September 5, 1959.

14. "Renewal Committee Has Serious Job," unidentified newspaper article, Spaulding Papers, DMRRBML; *DMH,* December 18, 1958; *DMH,* January 15, 1959; *DS,* October 15, 1959; *DMH,* October 31, 1959; *DMH,* November 14, 1959; *DMH,* October 22, 1959; "Land Utilization and Marketability Study, Hayti–Elizabeth Area Project 1," June 7, 1961; W. Fitzhugh Brundage, *A Southern Past: A Clash of Race and Memory* (Cambridge: Belknap Press of Harvard University Press, 2005), 232.

15. "Renewal Committee Has Serious Job," unidentified newspaper article, Spaulding Papers, DMRRBML; *DMH,* December 18, 1958; *DMH,* January 15, 1959; *DS,* October 15, 1959; *DMH,* October 31, 1959; *DMH,* November 14, 1959; *DMH,* October 22, 1959; "Land Utilization and Marketability Study, Hayti–Elizabeth Area Project 1," June 7, 1961

16. *CT,* January 7, 1961; *CT,* June 17, 1961; *CT,* June 24, 1961; *CT,* July 22, 1961; *CT,* July 29, 1961; *CT,* August 19, 1961; *CT,* August 19, 1961; *CT,* September 9, 1961; *CT,* December 2, 1961; *CT,* August 25, 1962; *CT,* September 15, 1962.

17. *DMH,* June 15, 1961; *CT,* January 7, 1961; *CT,* June 17, 1961; *CT,* June 24, 1961; *CT,* July 22, 1961; *CT,* July 29, 1961; *CT,* August 19, 1961; *CT,* September 9, 1961; *CT,* December 2, 1961; *CT,* August 25, 1962; *CT,* September 15, 1962.

18. *CT,* January 7, 1961; *CT,* June 17, 1961; *CT,* June 24, 1961; *CT,* July 22, 1961; *CT,* July 29, 1961; *CT,* August 19, 1961; *CT,* September 9, 1961; *CT,* December 2, 1961; *CT,* August 25, 1962; *CT,* September 15, 1962.

19. *North Carolina's Research Triangle Park: An Investment in the Future,* John Wilson Productions, video DVD, 2008, https://vimeo.com/11199745.

20. Hodges, *Businessman in the Statehouse*, chap. 9; Howard E. Covington Jr., *Favored by Fortune: George W. Watts and the Hills of Durham* (Chapel Hill: University of North Carolina at Chapel Hill Library, 2004), 263–74; William M. Rohe, *The Research Triangle: From Tobacco Road to Global Prominence* (Philadelphia: University of Pennsylvania Press, 2011), 61–83; *North Carolina's Research Triangle Park: An Investment in the Future;* Albert N. Link and John T. Scott, "The Growth of Research Triangle Park," *Small Business Economics* 20 (2003): 167–75.

21. *North Carolina's Research Triangle Park: An Investment in the Future*; Rohe, *The Research Triangle Park*, 67–70.

22. Korstad and Leloudis, *To Right These Wrongs,* 193.

23. *CT,* September 15, 1962; *CT,* September 22, 1962; *DMH,* October 7, 1962; *CT,* October 6, 1962. By December 1961, the approval of the final location of the proposed East-West Expressway by the federal urban renewal officials in Atlanta was announced. The State Highway Department determined the exact path the East-West Expressway would take through the Hayti–Elizabeth Street Urban Renewal Area but had to get the approval because it was in an urban renewal area. This approval announcement meant the DRC could move forward with the city's urban renewal program, acquire property, and begin clearance in the urban renewal area within the first project. *DMH,* December 5, 1961.

24. Http://blogs.lib.unc.edu/shc/index.php/2010/05/02/video-of-governor-terry-sanfords-emancipation-speech-to-the-north-carolina-press-association/; Korstad and Leloudis, *To Right These Wrongs,* 81.

25. Korstad and Leloudis, *To Right These Wrongs,* 59–65; George Esser, *My Years at the North Carolina Fund, 1963–1970: An Oral History,* with Rah Bickley (Research Triangle Park: George Esser, 2007), 15–19.

26. Esser, *My Years at the North Carolina Fund,* 28, 36–39; Korstad and Leloudis, *To Right These Wrongs,* 82–83; "Statement by Governor Terry Sanford," September 30, 1963, North Carolina Fund Records (#4710), Southern Historical Collection, Wilson Library, University of North Carolina at Chapel Hill (hereinafter cited as NC Fund Records); Korstad and Leloudis, *To Right These Wrongs,* 82.

27. "Articles of Incorporation of the North Carolina Fund," July 18, 1963, NC Fund Records; North Carolina Fund Meeting Minutes, July 26, 1963, NC Fund Records; Esser, *My Years at the North Carolina Fund,* 43–46; Korstad and Leloudis, *To Right These Wrongs,* 83–85, 87.

28. North Carolina Fund Meeting Minutes, September 12–13, 1963, NC Fund Records; Korstad and Leloudis, *To Right These Wrongs,* 89; Western Union telegram from Asa T. Spaulding to Wheeler, March 1, 1962, Asa and Elna Spaulding Papers, DMRRBML. An invitation to attend the dedication ceremony for the M&F Bank Charlotte Branch to be held on March 4, 1962, Asa and Elna Spaulding Papers, DMRRBML; Asa T. Spaulding to A. E. Spears (vice president, M&F Bank Charlotte Branch), March 9, 1963, Asa and Elna Spaulding Papers, DMRRBML; Dedication

Ceremony Program (held at Johnson C. Smith University Church), March 4, 1962, Asa and Elna Spaulding Papers, DMRRBML.

29. Nathan Garrett, interview by Brandon Winford, August 4, 2008.

30. Lyndon B. Johnson, "State of the Union Address," January 8, 1964, http://www.pbs.org/wgbh/americanexperience/features/primary-resources/lbj-union64/.

31. "Banker with a Mission," *Business Week,* May 16, 1964.

32. LBJ to Wheeler, October 11, 1960, JHWC; "President Lyndon B. Johnson's Remarks at the University of Michigan," May 22, 1964, http://www.lbjlib.utexas.edu/johnson/archives.hom/speeches.hom/640522.as; http://www.americanrhetoric.com/speeches/lbjthegreatsociety.htm;http://www.pbs.org/wgbh/americanexperience/features/primary-resources/lbj-michigan/; Esser, *My Years at the North Carolina Fund,* 81–83.

33. SRC Annual Meeting Minutes, January 29–30, 1964, folder SRC 1964, JHWC; Wheeler to Bertha Hamilton, March 25, 1964, JHWC; SRC Annual Meeting Minutes, January 29–30, 1964, Wheeler Papers, 8; John Wheeler, "Poverty and Segregation in the South: New Concepts, Old Truths," *New South,* November 1964, 4, 9; Miller, "Whither Southern Liberalism in the Post-Civil Rights Era?"

34. Leslie Dunbar to Arthur Hollis Edens, March 27, 1964; Leslie Dunbar to Martin Luther King Jr., January 5, 1964; Wheeler to John Stewart (administrative officer to Hubert Humphrey), December 28, 1964; Leslie Dunbar to Billy Moyer (special assistant to President Johnson), December 7, 1964; John T. Duffner (executive assistant to the deputy attorney general) to Wheeler, 1966, all in JHWC.

35. Moreland Griffith Smith to Wheeler, January 12, 1966; Moreland Griffith Smith to Robert C. Weaver, January 14, 1966; Wheeler to Robert C. Weaver, February 14, 1966; Robert C. Weaver to Wheeler, February 21, 1966; Moreland Griffin Smith (director of SRC's Urban Planning Project) to Wheeler, April 12, 1966; Sargent Shriver (director of the Office of Economic Opportunity) to Wheeler, May 3, 1965; Bill Moyers (special assistant to the president) to Wheeler, March 15, 1965; John W. Macy Jr. (chairman of the US Civil Service Commission) to Wheeler, March 25, 1965; Baton Bryant to Wheeler, March 15, 1965, all in JHWC.

36. Hasan Kwame Jeffries, *Bloody Lowndes: Civil Rights and Black Power in Alabama's Black Belt* (New York: New York University Press, 2009), 43–45; Maurice Isserman and Michael Kazin, *America Divided: The Civil War of the 1960s* (New York: Oxford University Press, 2012), 126–31; Watters and Cleghorn, *Climbing Jacob's Ladder,* 26–27, 45–50; Leslie Dunbar to Lee C. White, August 16, 1965, p. 1, JHWC.

37. Leslie Dunbar to Lee C. White, 1–2.

38. *CT,* February 10, 1962; *CT,* July 7, 1962; *CT,* April 20, 1963; *CT,* August 3, 1963; Brundage, *The Southern Past,* 218; Anderson, *Durham County,* 408.

39. *CT,* July 7, 1962; *CT,* April 20, 1963; *CT,* August 3, 1963.

40. *CT,* August 10, 1963; *CT,* August 17, 1963; *CT,* September 4, 1963.

41. *CT,* August 24, 1963; *CT,* March 7, 1964.

42. Gerald C. Horne, *The Fire This Time: The Watts Uprising and the 1960s* (New York: Da Capo, 1997), 3; 53–60; Peniel Joseph, *Waiting 'Til the Midnight Hour: A*

Narrative History of Black Power in America (New York: Henry Holt, 2006), 121–22; Isserman and Kazin, *America Divided,* 131–33; Greene, *Our Separate Ways,* 105–6, 109–13; Korstad and Leloudis, *To Right These Wrongs,* 186–87; Ross Rocklin, "Durham Housing in the 1960s: A Story of Discrimination and the Fight for Tenants Rights," Public Policy Paper, Terry Sanford Institute of Public Policy, Duke University, May 2003, 20–21; *CT,* December 10, 1966; *Thorpe v. Housing Authority of the City of Durham,* 386 U.S. 670; *Housing Authority of the City of Durham v. Joyce C. Thorpe,* 271 N.C. 468; *CT,* August 28, 1965.

43. Wheeler, "Civil Rights Groups—Their Impact upon the War on Poverty," 152–58.

44. *CT,* September 25, 1965.

45. *CT,* October 9, 1965; *CT,* December 25, 1965; *CT,* January 15, 1966; *CT,* February 12, 1966; *CT,* February 12, 1966.

46. *CT,* February 26, 1966; *CT,* July 2, 1966; Greene, *Our Separate Ways,* 124–26.

47. *CT,* December 10, 1966; *CT,* December 10, 1966; *Thorpe v. Housing Authority of the City of Durham,* 386 U.S. 670; *Housing Authority of the City of Durham v. Joyce C. Thorpe,* 271 N.C. 468.

48. Moreland Griffith Smith to Wheeler, January 12, 1966, 152–58; Moreland Griffith Smith to Robert C. Weaver, January 14, 1966; Wheeler to Robert C. Weaver, February 14, 1966; Robert C. Weaver to Wheeler, February 21, 1966; Moreland Griffin to Wheeler, April 12, 1966, all in JHWC; *Eyes on the Prize: The Time Has Come, 1964–1966, Episode 7* (Alexandria, Va.: PBS video, 1987); John Hope Franklin and Evelyn Brooks Higginbotham, *From Slavery to Freedom: A History of African Americans,* 9th ed. (New York: McGraw-Hill, 2011), 557–59; Joseph, *Waiting 'Till the Midnight Hour,* 141–42; Harold Cruse, *The Crisis of the Negro Intellectual: A Historical Analysis of the Failure of Black Leadership* (New York: Quill, 1984), 544–46; Jeffries, *Bloody Lowndes,* 187–92.

49. *Eyes on the Prize: The Time Has Come, 1964–1966,* episode 7; Franklin and Higginbotham, *From Slavery to Freedom,* 557–59; Vivian Patterson to Milton A. Gilbert, August 8, 1966; Vivian Patterson to Mildred Johnson, August 8, 1966; Mildred Johnson to Vivian Patterson, August 16, 1966; Paul Anthony to Wheeler, November 28, 1966, all in JHWC; Dr. Charles Watts (Lincoln Hospital), interview, 1968 FBI Field Reports, U.S. Department of Justice; W. L. Cook (NCM executive), interview, 1968 FBI Field Reports, U.S. Department of Justice; Dr. Irwin A. Brody (Neurologist at Duke Hospital), interview, 1968 FBI Field Reports, U.S. Department of Justice; Dr. Alton Mayberry (psychiatrist), interview, 1968 FBI Field Reports, U.S. Department of Justice.

50. Wheeler, "Of Conflict, Growth and Progress," *New South* 22 (Winter 1967): 2–9; Miller, "Whither Southern Liberalism?," 355–57.

51. Wheeler, "Of Conflict, Growth and Progress," 2–9; Miller, "Whither Southern Liberalism?" 355–57; Paul Anthony to Wheeler, November 28, 1966, JHWC.

52. Paul Anthony to Wheeler, November 28, 1966, JHWC.

53. *CT,* September 9, 1967; *CT,* September 16, 1967; *CT,* September 30, 1967; *CT,* October 7, 1967; *CT,* October 14, 1967; *CT,* October 21, 1967; *CT,* October 28, 1967; *CT,* November 25, 1967; *CT,* December 16, 1967.

54. *CT,* September 9, 1967; *CT,* September 16, 1967; *CT,* September 30, 1967; *CT,* October 7, 1967; *CT,* October 14, 1967; *CT,* October 21, 1967; *CT,* October 28, 1967; *CT,* November 25, 1967; *CT,* December 16, 1967.

55. *CT,* September 9, 1967.

56. *CT,* October 14, 1967; Esser, *My Years at the North Carolina Fund,* 266–75.

57. Minutes of the North Carolina Voter Education Meeting, February 27, 1967, JHWC; Vernon E Jordan (VEP director) to Wheeler, March 11, 1967, JHWC; "First Annual Report of the North Carolina Voter Education Project," December 31, 1967, JHWC.

58. *CT,* March 30, 1968; "A Resolution Pertaining to the Death of Dr. Martin Luther King Jr. by the Durham Committee on Negro Affairs, Durham, North Carolina," JHWC; Minutes of the SRC Executive Committee Meeting, April 6, 1968, JHWC; Miller, "Whither Southern Liberalism?," 557–58; Julius A. Locket, interview, 1968 FBI Field Reports, U.S. Department of Justice.

59. Brundage, *The Southern Past,* 219, chap. 6.

60. "Banker with a Mission," *Business Week,* May 16, 1964; Wheeler interview, "Robert Penn Warren's *Who Speaks for the Negro?:* An Archival Collection," http://whospeaks.library.vanderbilt.edu/.

61. "Banker with a Mission," *Business Week,* May 16, 1964.

Conclusion

1. "The Tar Heel of the Week—John Wheeler: Working Quietly for the Progress of Blacks," *Raleigh News and Observer,* March 15, 1970; "Wheeler: His Commitments Go Far beyond His Bank," *Carolina Financial Times,* February 9, 1976; "To End Capital Punishment: Death Penalty Bill Supported" in the local and state section, April 9, 1971, *DMH,* JHWC.

2. Wheeler to Sanford, June 9, 1970; citation by Terry Sanford, June 1, 1970; Terry Sanford to Wheeler, March 16, 1970, all in Terry Sanford Papers, DMRRBML; "Morehouse Dedicates John H. Wheeler Hall," 1976.

3. John Hervey lost his mother on December 29, 1976, three days before his sixty-eighth birthday ("Obituary of Margaret Hervey Wheeler," January 2, 1976, Kennedy Papers). His wife, Selena Warren Wheeler, died on July 18, 2014, at the age of 102. "Tar Heel of the Week: A Family Banking Tradition Gets a Woman's Touch," *Raleigh News and Observer,* April 6, 1986; http://paulimurrayproject.org/durhamstories/bwswomen/juliataylo.html; http://paulimurrayproject.org/durhamstories/bwswomen/JuliaTaylor.mp3.

4. "Tar Heel of the Week: A Family Banking Tradition Gets a Woman's Touch," *Raleigh News and Observer,* April 6, 1986; http://paulimurrayproject

.org/durhamstories/bwswomen/juliataylo.html; http://paulimurrayproject.org/durhamstories/bwswomen/JuliaTaylor.mp3.

5. "Aviation: Wheeling Wheeler," *Time,* July 21, 1975; Martin Weston, "First Black Airline Gets off the Ground," *Ebony,* April 1976; "You Can Get There From Here," *Raleigh News and Observer,* December 8, 1974; "Black Pilot Can Fly You Anywhere," unidentified newspaper article, 1976; "Wheeler Airlines to Add Plane, Expand Service," *Herald Sun,* 1974; Betty Kaplan Gubert, Miriam Sawyer, and Caroline M. Fannin, "Warren H. Wheeler," in *Distinguished African Americans in Aviation and Space Science* (Westport, Conn.: Oryx, 2002), 289–91; "Wheeler Airlines: An American First," *Tar Heel Junior Historian* 43, no. 1 (Fall 2003), http://avstop.com/history/F03.wheeler.airlines.pdf.

6. "Establish Foundation for John H. Wheeler," *Oracle,* Fall 1979, 13; "600 Attend Fund Raiser Honoring John Wheeler," *Raleigh News and Observer,* October 2, 1978; Howard Lee, interview by author, February 29, 2008, #U-0298, Southern Oral History Program Collection (#4007), Southern Historical Collection, Wilson Library, University of North Carolina at Chapel Hill; Vernon Jordan Jr., interview by author, March 9, 2010, Southern Oral History Program; "Establish Foundation for John H. Wheeler," *Oracle,* Fall 1979, 13; "600 Attend Fund Raiser Honoring John Wheeler," *Raleigh News and Observer,* October 2, 1978; Howard Lee, interview by author; Vernon Jordan, interview by author; "Establish Foundation for John H. Wheeler," *Oracle,* Fall 1979, 13; "600 Attend Fund Raiser Honoring John Wheeler," *Raleigh News and Observer,* October 2, 1978; *Of Counsel: The Magazine of North Carolina Central University School of Law,* http://law.nccu.edu/wordpress/img/uploads/2010/09/ofCounsel_Spring2010.pdf.; Howard Lee, interview by author.

7. Howard Lee, interview by author; *Paths toward Freedom: A Biographical History of Blacks and Indians in North Carolina by Blacks and Indians*; "The Tar Heel of the Week: Lee Brings Moderate Approach to Resources Post," *Raleigh News and Observer,* 1977.

8. Vernon Jordan, interview by author, March 9, 2010, in the Southern Oral History Program; Vernon Jordan Jr., *Vernon Can Read!,* 77; Sermon given by Vernon E. Jordan Jr. at Watts Street Baptist Church, Durham, North Carolina, January 17, 2010, pp. 1–2, in author's possession; John Hervey Wheeler FBI Files, 1968; Speech by Vernon E. Jordan Jr. at Watts Street Baptist Church in Durham, North Carolina, January 17, 2010, speech in author's possession.

9. Nathan Garrett, interview by author, August 4, 2008.

10. Jo-Ann Robinson, "An Interpretive Biography of Benjamin S. Ruffin, the First African American Chair of the UNC Board of Governors: How Life Experience Informs Practice" (Ph.D. diss., North Carolina State University, 2009); "A Joint Resolution Honoring the Life and Memory of Benjamin Sylvester 'Ben' Ruffin, Jr.," North Carolina General Assembly 2007 Session, http://www.ncleg.net/sessions/2007/bills/senate/pdf/s1183v1.pdf; "Benjamin Ruffin Posthumously Honored," https://www.northcarolina.edu/news/2007/11/benjamin-ruffin-posthumously-honored; "Benjamin Ruffin Moves to Advisory Relationship Honored for Service to with RJR," RJ Reynolds Press Release, February 11, 1999; William V. "Bill" Bell, "Ben Ruffin:

A Tribute," December 13, 2006, http://www.indyweek.com/indyweek/ben-ruffin-a-tribute/Content?oid=1200059; "Ben Ruffin, Former UNC and RJR Executive, Dies in Winston-Salem," *Business Journal,* December 7, 2006; http://www.bizjournals.com/triad/stories/2006/12/04/daily28.html; "Benjamin S. Ruffin to Speak at UNCG Commencement May 19," UNCG press release, May 13, 2002, http://www.uncg.edu/iss/ruffin.html; "Butterfield Introduces Bill to Rename Durham Federal Courthouse after John Hervey Wheeler," press release, August 1, 2017; "Is Jesse Helms Blocking Honor for Black Wall Street Leader?," *Herald Sun,* August 4, 2017; CSPAN-U.S. Cable, US House of Representatives, July 16, 2018.

Bibliography

Primary Sources

Manuscript and Special Collections

Atlanta, Georgia

Atlanta University Center Robert W. Woodruff Library
- Dennard Cleveland Papers
- John Hope Papers
- Thomas D. Jarrett Papers
- John Hervey Wheeler Collection
- John Hervey Wheeler Vertical File

Auburn Avenue Research Library on African American Culture and History

Morehouse College Archives

Stuart A. Rose Manuscript, Archives, and Rare Book Library
- Leslie Dunbar Papers

Austin, Texas

Lyndon B. Johnson Presidential Library and Museum
- Lyndon B. Johnson Papers
  - Vice Presidential Office Files of George E. Reedy

Chapel Hill, North Carolina

Wilson Library, University of North Carolina
- North Carolina Collection
- Southern Historical Collection
  - Jesse Daniel Ames Papers (#3686)
  - William A. Clement Papers (#4024)
  - James McBride Dabbs Papers (#3816)
  - Leroy B. Frasier, Sr. Papers (#4375-z)
  - George Watts Hill, Jr. Papers (#5162)
  - Guy Benton Johnson Papers (#3826)
  - William Jesse Kennedy, Jr. Papers (#4925)

Floyd B. McKissick Papers (#4930)
North Carolina Commission on Interracial Cooperation Records (#3823)
North Carolina Council on Human Relations Records (#4880)
North Carolina Fund Records (#4710)
Thomas Jenkins Pearsall Papers (#4300)
Raymond Milner Wheeler Papers (#4366)
Marion A. Wright Papers (#3830)

Charlotte, North Carolina

J. Murrey Atkins Library Special Collections, UNC-Charlotte
Kelly M. Alexander Sr. Papers

Durham, North Carolina

David M. Rubenstein Rare Book & Manuscript Library, Duke University
Gordon Blaine Hancock Papers
Rencher Nicholas Harris Papers
Wilbur Hobby Papers
Chris D. Howard Papers
Benjamin Muse Papers
North Carolina Mutual Life Insurance Company Archives
William Gaston Pearson Papers
Terry Sanford Papers
Asa T. and Elna Spaulding Papers
Charles Clinton Spaulding Papers
Durham Public Schools, Main Administrative Building
Durham City School Board Meeting Minutes
North Carolina Central University Archives
North Carolina Collection, Durham County Library (Main)
Durham City Schools Administrative Files
Durham City Schools Legal Files
Durham Historic Photographic Archives
Durham Urban Renewal Records
William H. Murdock Papers
James E. Shepard Memorial Library, North Carolina Central University
John S. "Shag" Stewart Papers
Stanford L. Warren Branch, Durham County Library
Clippings File

New York, New York

Schomburg Center for Research in Black Culture
August Meier Papers

Washington, DC

Library of Congress
  Hugh H. and Mabel Smythe Papers

Microfilm Collections

Southern Regional Council Papers
NAACP Papers

Oral Histories

Southern Oral History Program Collection (#4007), Southern Historical Collection, Wilson Library, University of North Carolina at Chapel Hill
  Atwater, Ann
  Clement, William A., and Josephine Dobbs Clement
  Dunbar, Leslie
  Everett, Robinson O. Interview by author. February 29, 2008.
  Frasier, Ralph. Interview by author. June 7 and 8, 2010.
  Fuller, Howard.
  Garrett, Nathan N.
  Hobby, Wilbur.
  Jordan, Vernon E., Jr. Interview by author. March 9, 2010.
  Lee, Howard N. Interview by author. February 28, 2008.
  McKissick, Floyd B., Sr.
  Michaux, H. M. "Mickey," Jr.
  Mitchener, Reginald.
  Patterson, Vivian Rogers. Interview by author. March 11, 2010.
  Pearson, Conrad O.
  Spaulding, Asa T.
  Turner, Viola G.
  Wheeler, Selena Lucille Warren.

Interviews in Author's Possession

Allison, F. V. "Pete," II. Interview by author. January 20, 2006.
Anderson, Jean Bradley. Interview by author. 2006.
Davis, Eddie. Phone interview by author. October 24, 2012.
Fitts, Howard M., Sr. Interview by author. March 13, 2006.
Garrett, Nathan N. Interview by author. August 4, 2008.
Parker, Omega Curtis. Phone interview by author. October 18, 2012.

Miscellaneous interviews

Louie B. Nunn Center for Oral History, University of Kentucky Libraries
Wheeler, John Hervey. Interview by Robert Penn Warren. 1964, Robert Penn Warren Civil Rights Oral History Project. This interview is available digitally from the Nunn Center: https://kentuckyoralhistory.org/ark:/16417/xt7dnc5sb84p. It is also available digitally in the Robert Penn Warren digital archival collection.

Robert Penn Warren's *Who Speaks for the Negro?* An Archival Collection, Robert Penn Warren Center for the Humanities, Vanderbilt University
Wheeler, John Hervey. Interview by Robert Penn Warren, 1964. This interview is available digitally from the Robert Penn Warren digital archival collection: https://whospeaks.library.vanderbilt.edu/interview/john-hervey-wheeler.

Secondary Sources

Books

Anderson, Eric. *Race and Politics in North Carolina, 1872–1901: The Black Second.* Baton Rouge: Louisiana State University Press, 1981.

Anderson, James D. *The Education of Blacks in the South, 1860–1935.* Chapel Hill: University of North Carolina Press, 1988.

Anderson, Jean Bradley. *Durham County: A History of Durham County, North Carolina.* Durham: Duke University Press, 1990.

Andrews, Robert McCants. *John Merrick: A Biographical Sketch.* Durham: Seeman Printery, 1920. http://docsouth.unc.edu/nc/andrews/andrews.html.

Angell, Stephen W., and Anthony B. Pinn, eds. *Social Protest Thought in the African Methodist Episcopal Church, 1862–1939.* Knoxville: University of Tennessee Press, 2000.

Arsenault, Raymond. *Freedom Riders: 1961 and the Struggle for Racial Justice.* Oxford: Oxford University Press, 2006.

Asch, Chris Myers. *The Senator and the Sharecropper: The Freedom Struggles of James O. Eastland and Fannie Lou Hamer.* New York: New Press. 2008.

Ayers, Edward L. *Promise of the New South: Life after Reconstruction.* New York: Oxford University Press, 1993.

Baradaran, Mehrsa. *The Color of Money: Black Banks and the Racial Wealth Gap.* Cambridge: Belknap Press of Harvard University Press, 2017.

Batchelor, John E. *Race and Education in North Carolina: From Segregation to Desegregation.* Baton Rouge: Louisiana State University Press, 2015.

Beito, David T., and Linda Royster Beito. *Black Maverick: T. R. M. Howard's Fight for Civil Rights and Economic Power.* Urbana: University of Illinois Press, 2009.

Belton, Robert. *The Crusade for Equality in the Workplace: The* Griggs v. Duke Power *Story.* Edited by Stephen L. Wasby. Lawrence: University Press of Kansas, 2014.

Boyd, William K. *The Story of Durham: City of the New South.* Durham: Duke University Press, 1925.

Branch, Taylor. *Parting the Waters: America in the King Years, 1954–1963.* New York: Simon and Schuster, 1988.

Brawley, Benjamin G. *A History of Morehouse College.* College Park, Md.: McGrath, 1917.

Brown, Leslie. *Upbuilding Black Durham: Gender, Class, and Black Community Development in the Jim Crow South.* Chapel Hill: University of North Carolina Press, 2008.

Brown-Nagin, Tomiko. *Courage to Dissent: Atlanta and the Long History of the Civil Rights Movement.* Oxford: Oxford University Press, 2011.

Brundage, W. Fitzhugh, ed. *Booker T. Washington and Black Progress: Up from Slavery 100 Years Later.* Gainesville: University Press of Florida, 2003.

———. *The Southern Past: A Clash of Race and Memory.* Cambridge: Belknap Press of Harvard University Press, 2005.

———, ed. *Where These Memories Grow: History, Memory, and Southern Identity.* Chapel Hill: University of North Carolina Press, 2000.

Bryant, Nick. *The Bystander: John F. Kennedy and the Struggle for Black Equality.* New York: Basic Books, 2006.

Burgess, M. Elaine. *Negro Leadership in a Southern City.* Chapel Hill: University of North Carolina Press, 1960.

Butler, John Sibley. *Entrepreneurship and Self-Help among Black Americans: A Reconsideration of Race and Economics.* Rev. ed. Albany: State University of New York Press, 2005.

Caldwell, A. B., ed. *History of American Negro and His Institutions, Georgia Edition.* Atlanta: Caldwell, 1917.

———, ed. *History of the American Negro and His Institutions, North Carolina Edition.* Atlanta: Caldwell, 1917.

Carson, Clayborne. *In Struggle: SNCC and the Black Awakening of the 1960s.* Cambridge: Harvard University Press, 1981.

Cecelski, David S. *Along Freedom Road: Hyde County, North Carolina, and the Fate of Black Schools in the South.* Chapel Hill: University of North Carolina Press, 1994.

Cecelski, David S., and Timothy B. Tyson. *Democracy Betrayed: The Wilmington Race Riot of 1898 and Its Legacy.* Chapel Hill: University of North Carolina Press, 1998.

Chafe, William H. *Civilities and Civil Rights: Greensboro, North Carolina, and the Black Struggle for Freedom.* Oxford: Oxford University Press, 1980.

———. *The Unfinished Journey: American since World War II.* 7th ed. New York: Oxford University Press, 2011.

Coates, Albert, and James C. N. Paul. *The School Segregation Decision: A Report to the Governor of North Carolina on the Decision of the Supreme Court of the United States on the 17th of May 1954.* Chapel Hill: Institute of Government, 1954.

Collier-Thomas, Bettye, and V. P. Franklin, eds. *Sisters in the Struggle: African American Women in the Civil Rights–Black Power Movement.* New York: New York University Press, 2001.

Covington, Howard E., Jr. *Favored by Fortune: George W. Watts and the Hills of Durham.* Chapel Hill: University of North Carolina Press, 2004.

———. *Henry Frye: North Carolina's First African American Chief Justice.* Jefferson, N.C.: McFarland, 2013.

Covington, Howard E., Jr., and Marion A. Ellis. *Terry Sanford: Politics, Progress, and Outrageous Ambitions.* Durham: Duke University Press, 1999.

Craig, Lee A. *Josephus Daniels: His Life and Times.* Chapel Hill: University of North Carolina Press, 2013.

Crawford, Mark. *Confederate Courage on Other Fields: Four Lesser Known Accounts of the War Between the States.* Jefferson, N.C.: McFarland, 2000.

Crosby, Emilye, ed. *Civil Rights History from the Ground Up: Local Struggles, A National Movement.* Athens: University of Georgia Press, 2011.

Crow, Jeffrey, Paul D. Escott, and Flora J. Hatley. *A History of African Americans in North Carolina.* Rev. ed. Raleigh: N.C.: Office of Archives and History, North Carolina Department of Cultural Resources, 2002.

Cruse, Harold. *The Crisis of the Negro Intellectual: A Historical Analysis of the Failure of Black Leadership.* New York: Quill, 1984.

Davidson, Osha Gray. *The Best of Enemies: Race and Redemption in the New South.* Chapel Hill: University of North Carolina Press, 1996.

Dennis, Michael. *Luther P. Jackson and a Life for Civil Rights.* Gainesville: University Press of Florida, 2004.

Dickerson, Dennis C. *African American Preachers and Politics: The Careys of Chicago.* Jackson: University Press of Mississippi, 2010.

———. *Militant Mediator: Whitney M. Young, Jr.* Lexington: University Press of Kentucky, 1998.

Dittmer, John. *Local People: The Struggle for Civil Rights in Mississippi.* Urbana: University of Illinois Press, 1994.

Douglas, Davison M. *Reading, Writing, Race: School Desegregation in Charlotte, North Carolina.* Chapel Hill: University of North Carolina Press, 1995.

Drescher, John. *Triumph of Good Will: How Terry Sanford Beat a Champion of Segregation and Reshaped the South.* Jackson: University Press of Mississippi, 2000.

Du Bois, W. E. B. *The Autobiography of W. E. B. Du Bois: A Soliloquy on Viewing My Life from the Last Decade of Its First Century.* New York: Oxford University Press, 2007.

Dula, William A., and A. C. Simpson. *Durham and Her People: Combining History and Who's Who in Durham of 1949 and 1950.* Durham: Citizens Press, 1951.

Durden, Robert F. *The Dukes of Durham, 1865–1929.* Durham: Duke University Press, 1975.

Edmonds, Helen G. *The Negro and Fusion Politics in North Carolina, 1894–1901.* Chapel Hill: University of North Carolina Press, 1951.

Escott, Paul D. *Many Excellent People: Power and Privilege in North Carolina, 1850–1900.* Chapel Hill: University of North Carolina Press, 1985.

Esser, George. *My Years at the North Carolina Fund, 1963–1970: An Oral History.* With Rah Bickley. Research Triangle Park: George Esser, 2007.

Ezra, Michael, ed. *The Economic Civil Rights Movement: African Americans and the Struggle for Economic Power.* New York: Routledge, 2013.

Faulkenbury, Evan. *Poll Power: The Voter Education Project and the Movement for the Ballot in the American South.* Chapel Hill: University of North Carolina Press, 2019.

Fee, John G. *Autobiography of John G. Fee.* Chicago: National Christian Association, 1891.

Fergus, Devin. *Liberalism, Black Power, and the Making of American Politics, 1965–1980.* Athens: University of Georgia Press, 2009.

Ferguson, Karen. *Top Down: The Ford Foundation, Black Power, and the Reinvention of Racial Liberalism.* Philadelphia: University of Pennsylvania Press, 2013.

Fleming, Walter L. *The Freedmen's Savings Bank: A Chapter in the Economic History of the Negro Race.* 1927; Westport, Conn.: Negro Universities Press, 1970.

Franklin, John Hope, and Evelyn Brooks Higginbotham. *From Slavery to Freedom: A History of African Americans.* 9th ed. New York: McGraw-Hill, 2011.

Frazier, E. Franklin. *Black Bourgeoisie.* New York: Free Press, 1965.

Gaines, Kevin. *Uplifting the Race: Black Leadership, Politics, and Culture in the Twentieth Century.* Chapel Hill: University of North Carolina Press, 1996.

Garrett-Scott, Shennette. *Banking on Freedom: Black Women in U.S. Finance before the New Deal.* New York: Columbia University Press, 2019.

Garrow, David. *Bearing the Cross: Martin Luther King, Jr., and the Southern Christian Leadership Conference.* New York: Perennial Classics, 2004.

Gaston, *New South Creed: A Study in Southern Myth-Making.* Montgomery, Ala.: New South Books, 2002.

Gates, Henry Louis, Jr., and Evelyn Brooks Higginbotham, eds. *African American National Biography.* Oxford: Oxford University Press, 2008.

Gatewood, Willard. *Aristocrats of Color: The Black Elite, 1880–1920.* Bloomington: Indiana University Press, 1993.

Gatton, Harry T. *Banking in North Carolina.* Raleigh: North Carolina Bankers Association, 1987.

Gavins, Raymond. *The Perils and Prospects of Southern Black Leadership: Gordon Blaine Hancock, 1884–1970.* Durham: Duke University Press, 1977.

Gershenhorn, Jerry B. *Louis Austin and the Carolina Times: A Life in the Long Black Freedom Struggle.* Chapel Hill: University of North Carolina Press, 2018.

Gill, Tiffany M. *Beauty Shop Politics: African American Women's Activism in the Beauty Industry.* Urbana: University of Illinois Press, 2010.

Gilmore, Glenda. *Defying Dixie: The Radical Roots of Civil Rights, 1919–1950.* New York: Norton, 2008.

———. *Gender and Jim Crow: Women and the Politics of White Supremacy in North Carolina, 1896–1920.* Chapel Hill: University of North Carolina Press, 1996.

Golland, David Hamilton. *Constructing Affirmative Action: The Struggle for Equal Employment Opportunity.* Lexington: University Press of Kentucky, 2011.

Greenberg, Jack. *Crusaders in the Courts: Legal Battles of the Civil Rights Movement.* New York: Twelve Tables Press, 2004.

Greene, Christina. *Our Separate Ways: Women and the Black Freedom Movement in Durham, North Carolina.* Chapel Hill: University of North Carolina Press, 2005.

Greenwood, Janette Thomas. *Bittersweet Legacy: The Black and White "Better Classes" in Charlotte, 1850–1910.* Chapel Hill: University of North Carolina Press, 1994.

Gubert, Betty Kaplan, Miriam Sawyer, and Caroline M. Fannin. *Distinguished African Americans in Aviation and Space Science.* Westport, Conn.: Oryx, 2002.

Gutman, Herbert. *The Black Family in Slavery and Freedom.* New York: Vintage, 1976.

Hall, Jacqueline Dowd. *Revolt against Chivalry: Jesse Daniel Ames and the Women's Campaign against Lynching.* New York: Columbia University Press, 1979.

The Hand-Book of Durham, North Carolina: A Brief and Accurate Descriptions of a Prosperous and Growing Southern Manufacturing Town. Durham: Educator Company, 1895.

Harlan, Louis R. *Booker T. Washington: The Wizard of Tuskegee, 1901–1915.* Oxford: Oxford University Press, 1986.

———. *The Making of a Black Leader.* Oxford: Oxford University Press, 1972,

Harris, Abram L. *The Negro as Capitalist: A Study of Banking and Business among Negroes.* Gloucester, Mass.: Peter Smith, 1968.

Harrison, Lowell H., and James C. Klotter. *A New History of Kentucky.* Lexington: University Press of Kentucky, 1997.

Hartshorn, W. N. *An Era of Progress and Promise: The Religious, Moral, and Educational Development of the American Negro since His Emancipation.* Boston: Priscilla, 1910. http://digital.ncdcr.gov/cdm4/document.php?CISOROOT=/p249901coll37&CISOPTR=4602&CISOSHOW=444.

Hassan, Amina. *Loren Miller: Civil Rights Attorney and Journalist.* Norman: Oklahoma University Press, 2015.

Hawkins, John R. *The Educator: A Condensed Statement of the Department of Education of the African Methodist Episcopal Church.* AME Church, 1906.

Henderson, Alexa Benson. *Atlanta Life Insurance Company: Guardian of Black Economic Dignity.* Tuscaloosa: University of Alabama Press, 1990.

Hill, Laura Warren, and Julia Rabig, eds. *The Business of Black Power: Community Development, Capitalism, and Corporate Responsibility in Postwar America.* Rochester, N.Y.: University of Rochester Press, 2012.

Hobson, Maurice. *The Legend of the Black Mecca: Politics and Class in the Making of Modern Atlanta.* Chapel Hill: University of North Carolina Press, 2017.

Hodges, Luther H. *Businessman in the Statehouse: Six Years as Governor of North Carolina.* Chapel Hill: University of North Carolina Press, 1962.

Holt, Thomas C., and Elsa Barkley Brown. *Major Problems in African-American History.* Vol. 2: *From Freedom to "Freedom Now," 1865–1990s.* Boston: Houghton Mifflin, 2000.

Hopkins, James Franklin. *A History of the Hemp Industry in Kentucky.* Lexington: University of Kentucky Press, 1951.

Horne, Gerald C. *The Fire This Time: The Watts Uprising and the 1960s*. New York: Da Capo, 1997.
Hornsby, Alton, Jr. *Black Power in Dixie: A Political History of African Americans in Atlanta*. Gainesville: University Press of Florida, 2009.
Howard, Victor B. *Black Liberation in Kentucky: Emancipation and Freedom, 1862–1884*. Lexington: University Press of Kentucky, 1983.
———. *The Evangelical War against Slavery and Caste: The Life and Times of John G. Fee*. Selinsgrove, PA: Susquehanna University Press, 1996.
Hunter, Tera. *To 'Joy My Freedom: Southern Black Women's Lives and Labors after the Civil War*. Cambridge: Harvard University Press, 1997.
Ingham, John N., and Lynne B. Feldman. *African-American Business Leaders: A Biographical Dictionary*. Westport, Conn.: Greenwood, 1994.
Isserman, Maurice, and Michael Kazin. *America Divided: The Civil War of the 1960s*. New York: Oxford University Press, 2012.
Jalloh, Alusine, and Toyin Falola, eds. *Black Business and Economic Power*. Rochester, N.Y.: University of Rochester Press, 2002.
Janiewski, Dolores. *Sisterhood Denied: Race, Gender, and Class in a New South Community*. Philadelphia: Temple University Press, 1985.
Janken, Kenneth R. *Walter White: Mr. NAACP*. Chapel Hill: University of North Carolina Press, 2006.
———. *The Wilmington Ten: Violence, Injustice, and the Rise of Black Politics in the 1970s*. Chapel Hill: University of North Carolina Press, 2015.
Jeffries, Hasan Kwame. *Bloody Lowndes: Civil Rights and Black Power in Alabama's Black Belt*. New York: New York University Press, 2009.
Jelks, Randal. *Benjamin Elijah Mays, Schoolmaster of the Movement: A Biography*. Chapel Hill: University of North Carolina Press, 2012.
Jenkins, Carol, and Elizabeth Gardner Hines. *Black Titan: A. G. Gaston and the Making of a Black American Millionaire*. New York: One World, 2004.
Joiner, William A. *A Half Century of Freedom of the Negro in Ohio*. Xenia, Ohio: Smith Adv. Co., 1915.
Jones, Beverly Washington. *Stanford L. Warren Branch Library: 77 Years of Public Service*. Durham: Durham County Library, 1990.
Jones, Dorothy Phelps. *The End of an Era*. Durham: Brown Enterprises, 2001.
Jones, Edward A. *A Candle in the Dark: A History of Morehouse College*. Valley Forge, Pa.: Judson, 1967.
Jones, William P. *The March on Washington: Jobs, Freedom, and the Forgotten History of Civil Rights*. New York: Norton, 2013.
Jordan, Vernon E., Jr. *Vernon Can Read: A Memoir*. With Annette Gordon-Reed. New York: Public Affairs, 2001.
Joseph, Peniel. *Waiting 'Til the Midnight Hour: A Narrative History of Black Power in America*. New York: Henry Holt, 2006.
Kaiser Index to Black Resources 1948–1986. Vol. 5. Brooklyn, N.Y.: Carlson, 1992.
Keech, William R. *The Impact of Negro Voting*. Chicago: Rand McNally, 1968.
Kennedy, William Jesse, Jr. *The North Carolina Mutual Story: A Symbol of Progress, 1898–1970*. Durham: North Carolina Mutual Life Insurance Company, 1970.

Kenzer, Robert C. *Enterprising Southerner: Black Economic Success in North Carolina, 1865–1915.* Charlottesville: University Press of Virginia, 1997.

King, Martin Luther, Sr. *Daddy King: An Autobiography.* New York: Morrow, 1980.

Klotter, James C., and Freda C. Klotter. *A Concise History of Kentucky.* Lexington: University Press of Kentucky, 2008.

Kluger, Richard. *Simple Justice: The History of* Brown v. Board of Education *and Black America's Struggle for Equality.* New York: Vintage, 1975.

Korstad, Robert R. *Civil Rights Unionism: Tobacco Workers and the Struggle for Democracy in the Mid-Twentieth-Century South.* Chapel Hill: University of North Carolina Press, 2003.

Korstad, Robert R., and James L. Leloudis. *To Right These Wrongs: The North Carolina Fund and the Battle to End Poverty and Inequality in 1960s America.* Chapel Hill: University of North Carolina Press, 2010.

Kuhn, Clifford M., Harlon E. Joye, and E. Bernard West. *Living Atlanta: An Oral History of the City, 1914–1948.* Athens and Atlanta: University of Georgia Press and the Atlanta Historical Society, 1990.

Lee, Chana Kai. *For Freedom's Sake: The Life of Fannie Lou Hamer.* Urbana: University of Illinois Press, 1999.

LeFlouria, Talitha L. *Chained in Silence: Black Women and Convict Labor in the New South.* Chapel Hill: University of North Carolina Press, 2015.

Lewis, David Levering. *W. E. B. Du Bois: Biography of a Race, 1868–1919.* New York: Henry Holt, 1993.

Lewis, John. *Walking against the Wind: A Memoir of the Movement.* With Michael D'Orso. New York: Simon and Schuster, 1998.

Link, William. *North Carolina: Change and Tradition in a Southern State.* Wheeling, Ill.: Harlan Davidson, 2009.

Litwicki, Ellen M. *America's Public Holidays, 1865–1920.* Washington, D.C.: Smithsonian Institution Press, 2000.

Locke, Alain, ed. *The New Negro: An Interpretation.* New York: Johnson Reprint Corporation, 1968.

Lucas, Marion B. *A History of Blacks in Kentucky: From Slavery to Segregation, 1760–1891.* Vol. 1. Frankfort: Kentucky Historical Society, 1992.

Mack, Kenneth W. *The Creation of the Civil Rights Lawyer.* Cambridge: Harvard University Press, 2012.

MacKinnon, Aran S. *The Making of South Africa: Culture and Politics.* Upper Saddle River, N.J.: Pearson Prentice Hall, 2004.

MacLaury, Judson. *To Advance Their Opportunities: Federal Policies toward African American Workers from World War I to the Civil Rights Act of 1964.* Knoxville: Newfound Press, University of Tennessee Libraries, 2008.

Mandela, Nelson. *Long Walk to Freedom: The Autobiography of Nelson Mandela.* Boston: Little, Brown, 1994.

Marable, Manning. *Malcolm X: A Life of Reinvention.* New York: Viking, 2011.

Margolies, Daniel S. *Henry Watterson and the New South: The Politics of Empire, Free Trade, and Globalization.* Lexington: University Press of Kentucky, 2006.

Marlowe, Gertrude Woodruff. *A Right Worthy Grand Mission: Maggie Lena Walker and the Quest for Black Economic Empowerment.* Washington, D.C.: Howard University Press, 2003.

Mason, Herman "Skip." *Going against the Wind: A Pictorial History of African-Americans in Atlanta.* Atlanta: Longstreet, 1992.

Mays, Benjamin E. Mays. *Born to Rebel: An Autobiography.* Athens: University of Georgia Press, 2003.

McGinnis, Frederick A. *A History and an Interpretation of Wilberforce University.* Wilberforce, Ohio: Brown, 1941.

McKinney, Charles W., Jr. *Greater Freedom: The Evolution of the Civil Rights Struggle in Wilson, North Carolina.* Lanham, Md.: University Press of America, 2010.

McNeil, Genna Rae. *Groundwork: Charles Hamilton Houston and the Struggle for Civil Rights.* Philadelphia: University of Pennsylvania Press, 1983.

Miller, Albert George. *Elevating the Race: Theophilus G. Stewart, Black Theology, and the Making of an African American Civil Society, 1865–1924.* Knoxville: University of Tennessee Press, 2003.

Minchin, Timothy J. *The Color of Work: The Struggle for Civil Rights in the Southern Paper Industry.* Chapel Hill: University of North Carolina Press, 2001.

———. *Fighting against the Odds: A History of Southern Labor since World War II.* Gainesville: University Press of Florida, 2005.

———. *From Rights to Economics: The Ongoing Struggle for Black Equality in the U.S. South.* Gainesville: University Press of Florida, 2007.

———. *Hiring the Black Worker: The Radical Integration of the Southern Textile Industry, 1960–1980.* Chapel Hill: University of North Carolina Press, 1999.

Mitchell, Memory F., ed. *Messages, Addresses, and Public Papers of Terry Sanford, Governor of North Carolina, 1961–1965.* Raleigh: Council of State, State of North Carolina, 1966.

Murray, Pauli. *Proud Shoes: The Story of an American Family.* New York: Harper and Brothers, 1956.

———. *Song in a Weary Throat: Memoir of an American Pilgrimage.* New York: Liveright, 2018.

Nembhard, Jessica Gordon. *Collective Courage: A History of African American Cooperative Economic Though and Practice.* University Park: Pennsylvania State University Press, 2014.

Newman, Richard S. *Freedom's Prophet: Bishop Richard Allen, the AME Church, and the Black Founding Fathers.* New York: New York University Press, 2008.

Newman, Robert J., and Joel Nathan Rosen. *Black Baseball, Black Business: Race Enterprise and the Fate of the Segregated Dollar.* Jackson: University Press of Mississippi, 2014.

Niven, David. *The Politics of Injustice: The Kennedys, the Freedom Rides, and the Electoral Consequences of a Moral Compromise.* Knoxville: University of Tennessee Press, 2003.

Norrell, Robert J. *James Bowron: The Autobiography of a New South Industrialist.* Chapel Hill: University of North Carolina Press, 1991.

———. *Reaping the Whirlwind. The Civil Rights Movement in Tuskegee.* Chapel Hill: University of North Carolina Press, 1998.

———. *Up from History: The Life of Booker T. Washington.* Cambridge: Belknap Press of Harvard University Press, 2009.

Paths toward Freedom: A Biographical History of Blacks and Indians in North Carolina by Blacks and Indians. Raleigh: Center for Urban Affairs, North Carolina State University, 1976.

Perdue, Theda. *Race and the Atlanta Cotton States Exposition of 1895.* Athens: University of Georgia Press, 2010.

Prather, Leon H. *We Have Taken a City: The Wilmington Racial Massacre and Coup of 1896.* Rutherford, N.J.: Fairleigh Dickinson University Press, 1984.

Pak, Susie J. *Gentlemen Bankers: The World of J. P. Morgan.* Cambridge: Harvard University Press, 2013.

Payne, Charles. *I've Got the Light of Freedom: The Organizing Tradition and the Mississippi Freedom Struggle.* Los Angeles: University of California Press, 1995.

Peace, Thomas. *"Zeb's Black Baby": Vance County, North Carolina: A Short History.* Durham, N.C.: Seeman Printery, 1955.

Ramage, James A., and Andrea S. Watkins. *Kentucky Rising: Democracy, Slavery, and Culture from the Early Republic to the Civil War.* Lexington: University Press of Kentucky, 2011.

Ransby, Barbara. *Ella Baker and the Black Freedom Movement: A Radical Democratic Vision.* Chapel Hill: University of North Carolina Press, 2003.

Ready, Milton. *The Tarheel State: A History of North Carolina.* Columbia: University of South Carolina Press, 2005.

Richings, G. F. *Evidence of Progress among Colored People.* Chapel Hill: Academic Library, University of North Carolina at Chapel Hill, 1902.

Rohe, William M. *The Research Triangle: From Tobacco Road to Global Prominence.* Philadelphia: University of Pennsylvania Press, 2011.

Rosen, Richard, and Joseph Mosnier. *Julius Chambers: A Life in the Legal Struggle for Civil Rights.* Chapel Hill: University of North Carolina Press, 2016.

Rubio, Philip F. *A History of Affirmative Action, 1619–2000* (Jackson: University Press of Mississippi, 2001).

———. *There's Always Work at the Post Office: African American Postal Workers and the Fight for Jobs, Justice, and Equality.* Chapel Hill: University of North Carolina Press, 2010.

Rummel, Jack. *African-American Social Leaders and Activists.* New York: Facts on File, 2003.

Sanders, Crystal R. *A Chance for Change: Head Start and Mississippi's Black Freedom Struggle.* Chapel Hill: University of North Carolina Press, 2016.

Sanford, Terry. *But What about the People?* New York: Harper and Row, 1966.

Scarborough, William Sanders. *The Autobiography of William Sanders Scarborough: An American Journey from Slavery to Scholarship.* Detroit: Wayne State University Press, 2005.

Sears, Richard D. *Camp Nelson, Kentucky: A Civil War History.* Lexington: University Press of Kentucky, 2002.

Shaw, Stephanie. *What a Woman Ought to Be and to Do: Black Professional Women Workers during the Jim Crow Era.* Chicago: University of Chicago Press, 1996.

Sindler, Allan P. *Negro Protest and Local Politics in Durham, N.C.* New York: McGraw-Hill, 1965.

Sitkoff, Harvard. *The Struggle for Black Equality, 1954–1992.* New York: HarperCollins, 1993.

Smith, Charles Spencer. *A History of the African Methodist Episcopal Church; Being a Volume Supplemental to a History of the African Methodist Episcopal Church, by Daniel Alexander Payne, D.D., LL.D., Late One of Its Bishops Chronicling the Principal Events in the Advance of the African Methodist Episcopal Church from 1856 to 1922.* 1922. Reprint, New York: Johnson Reprint, 1968.

Smith, Robert Samuel. *Race, Labor, and Civil Rights:* Griggs versus Duke Power *and the Struggle for Equal Employment Opportunity.* Baton Rouge: Louisiana State University Press, 2002.

Steward, Theophilus G. *Fifty Years in the Gospel Ministry, from 1864 to 1914: Twenty-Seven Years in the Pastorate: Sixteen Years' Active Service as Chaplain in the U.S. Army: Seven Years Professor in Wilberforce University: Two Trips to Europe: A Trip to Mexico: in Two Parts, with Appropriate Illustrations.* Chapel Hill: Academic Affairs, University of North Carolina, 2001.

Stuart, Mariah S. *An Economic Detour: A History of Insurance in the Lives of American Negroes.* New York: W. Malliet, 1940.

Suggs, Henry Lewis. *P. B. Young, Newspaperman: Race, Politics, and Journalism in the New South, 1910–1962.* Charlottesville: University Press of Virginia, 1988.

Sullivan, Patricia. *Days of Hope: Race and Democracy in the New Deal Era.* Chapel Hill: University of North Carolina Press, 1996.

———. *Lift Every Voice and Sing: The NAACP and the Making of the Civil Rights Movement.* New York: New Press, 2009.

Talbert, Horace. *The Sons of Allen: Together with a Sketch of the Rise and Progress of Wilberforce University, Wilberforce, Ohio.* Xenia, Ohio: Aldine, 1906.

Thomas, Karen Kruse. *Deluxe Jim Crow: Civil Rights and American Health Policy, 1935–1954.* Athens: University of Georgia Press, 2011.

Thuesen, Sarah Caroline. *Greater Than Equal: African American Struggles for Schools and Citizenship in North Carolina, 1919–1965.* Chapel Hill: University of North Carolina Press, 2013.

Tindall, George. *Emergence of the New South, 1913–1945.* Baton Rouge: Louisiana State University Press, 1967.

Torrence, Ridgely. *The Story of John Hope.* New York: Macmillan, 1948.

Tushnet, Mark V. *The NAACP's Legal Strategy against Segregated Education, 1925–1950.* Chapel Hill: University of North Carolina Press, 1987.

Tyson, Timothy B. *Radio Free Dixie: Robert F. Williams and the Roots of Black Power.* Chapel Hill: University of North Carolina Press, 1999.

Vann, Andre D., and Beverly Washington Jones. *Durham's Hayti*. Charleston, S.C.: Arcadia, 1999.

Walker, Juliet E. K. ed. *Encyclopedia of African American Business History*. Westport, Conn.: Greenwood, 1999.

———. *The History of Black Business in America: Capitalism, Race, Entrepreneurship*. New York: Macmillan Library Reference USA, 1998.

Ward, Brian. *The 1960s: A Documentary Reader*. Malden, Mass.: Wiley-Blackwell, 2010.

Warren, Robert Penn. *Who Speaks for the Negro?* New York: Random House, 1965.

Washington, Booker T. *Up from Slavery*. Oxford: Oxford University Press, 1995.

Watters, Pat, and Reese Cleghorn. *Climbing Jacob's Ladder: The Arrival of Negroes in Southern Politics*. New York: Harcourt, Brace and World, 1967.

Weare, Walter B. *Black Business in the New South: A Social History of the North Carolina Mutual Life Insurance Company*. Durham: Duke University Press, 1993.

Weems, Robert, Jr. *Black Business in the Black Metropolis: The Chicago Metropolitan Assurance Company, 1925–1985*. Bloomington: Indiana University Press, 1996.

———. *Business in Black and White: American Presidents and Black Entrepreneurship in the Twentieth Century*. New York: New York University Press, 2009.

———. *Desegregating the Dollar: African American Consumerism in the Twentieth Century*. New York: New York University Press, 1998.

Weems, Robert, Jr., and Jason P. Chambers, eds. *Building the Black Metropolis: African American Entrepreneurship in Chicago*. Urbana: University of Illinois Press, 2017.

Wesley, Charles H. *Richard Allen: Apostle of Freedom*. Washington, D.C.: Associated Publishers, 1969.

Williams, Heather Andrea. *Help Me to Find My People: The African American Search for Family Lost in Slavery*. Chapel Hill: University of North Carolina Press, 2012.

———. *Self-Taught: African American Education in Slavery and Freedom*. Chapel Hill: University of North Carolina Press, 2005.

Woodward, C. Vann. *Origins of the New South, 1877–1913*. Baton Rouge: Louisiana University Press, 1951.

Wright, Gavin. *Old South, New South: Revolutions in the Southern Economy since the Civil War*. Baton Rouge: Louisiana State University Press, 1996.

———. *Sharing the Prize: The Economics of the Civil Rights Revolution in the American South*. Cambridge: Belknap Press of Harvard University Press, 2013.

Wright, George C. *Life behind a Veil: Blacks in Louisville, Kentucky, 1865–1930*. Baton Rouge: Louisiana State University Press, 1985.

Wright, Richard R., and John R. Hawkins. *Centennial Encyclopedia of the African Methodist Episcopal Church*. Philadelphia: Book Concern of the AME Church, 1916.

Young, Bennett H. *A History of Jessamine County, Kentucky from Its Earliest Settlement to 1898*. Louisville, Ky.: Courier-Journal Job Printing Co., 1898.

Articles

Alexander, Will W. "Phylon Profile, XI: John Hope." *Phylon* 8, no. 1 (1947): 4–13.

Ammons, Lila. "The Evolution of Black-Owned Banks in the United States between the 1880s and 1990s." *Journal of Black Studies* 26, no. 4 (March 1996): 467–89.

Blumrosen, Alfred W. "The Legacy of *Griggs:* Social Progress and Subjective Judgments." *Chicago-Kent Law Review* 63 (April 1987): 1–42.

Bowman, Lewis, and G. R. Boynton. "Coalitions as Party in a One-Party Southern Area: A Theoretical and Case Analysis." *Midwest Journal of Political Science* 8, no. 3 (August 1964): 277–97. http://www.jstor.org/stable/2108956.

Burns, Augustus M. "Graduate Education for Blacks in North Carolina, 1930–1951." *Journal of Southern History* 46, no. 2 (May 1980): 195–218.

Cha-Jua, Sundiata, and Clarence Lang. "The 'Long Movement' as Vampire: Temporal and Spatial Fallacies in Recent Black Freedom Studies." *Journal of African American History* 92 (Spring 2007): 265–88.

Du Bois, W. E. B. "The Upbuilding of Black Durham." *World's Work* 23 (January 1912).

Garrett-Scott, Shennette. "A Historiography of African American Business." (2009) *Business and Economic History Online* 7 (2009): 1–33.

———. "To Do a Work That Would Be Very Far Reaching: Minnie Geddings Cox, the Mississippi Life Insurance Company, and the Challenges of Black Women's Business Leadership in the Early Twentieth-Century United States." *Enterprise and Society* 17 (September 2016): 473–514.

Gershenhorn, Jerry B. "A Courageous Voice for Black Freedom: Louis Austin and the *Carolina Times* in Depression-Era North Carolina." *North Carolina Historical Review* 87 (January 2010): 57–92.

———. "Double V in North Carolina: The *Carolina Times* and the Struggle for Racial Equality during World War II." *Journalism History* 32, no. 3 (Fall 2006): 156–67.

———. "*Hocutt v. Wilson* and Race Relations in Durham, North Carolina, during the 1930s." *North Carolina Historical Review* 78 (July 2001): 275–308.

Hall, Jacquelyn Dowd. "The Long Civil Rights Movement and the Political Uses of the Past." *Journal of American History* 91, no. 4 (March 2005): 1233–66. http://www.historycooperative.org/cgi-bin/printpage.cgi.

Henderson, Alexa Benson. "Richard R. Wright and the National Negro Bankers Association: Early Organizing Efforts among Black Bankers, 1924–1942." *Pennsylvania Magazine of History and Biography* 117, no. 1–2 (January-April 1993): 51–81.

"In Memoriam: Spottswood W. Robinson III, 1916–1998." *Journal of Blacks in Higher Education,* no. 31 (Winter 1998–1999): 39.

Ingham, John N. "Building Businesses, Creating Communities: Residential Segregation and the Growth of African American Business in Southern Cities, 1880–1915." *Business History Review* 77, no. 4 (Winter 2003): 639–65.

Kenzer, Robert C. "The Black Businessman in the Postwar South: North Carolina, 1865–1880." *Business History Review* (Spring 1989): 61–87.

Korstad, Robert R., and James L. Leloudis. "Citizen Soldiers: The North Carolina Volunteers and the War on Poverty." *Law and Contemporary Problems* 62, no. 4 (1999): 177–97.

Lindsay, Arnett G. "The Negro in Banking." *Journal of Negro History* 14, no. 2 (April 1929): 156–201.

Link, Albert N., and John T. Scott. "The Growth of Research Triangle Park." *Small Business Economics* 20 (2003): 167–75.

Lomax, Louis E. "The Negro Revolt against 'The Negro Leaders.'" *Harper's Magazine* 220, no. 1321 (June 1960): 41–48.

McKinney, Charles W., Jr. "Multiple Fronts: The Struggle for Black Educational and Political Equality in Wilson, North Carolina, 1941–1953." *North Carolina Historical Review* 88, no. 1 (January 2011): 1–39.

Miller, Steven P. "Whither Southern Liberalism in the Post–Civil Rights Era? The Southern Regional Council and Its Peers, 1965–1972." *Georgia Historical Quarterly* 90 (Winter 2006): 547–68.

Norton, Eleanor Holmes. "The End of the Griggs Economy: Doctrinal Adjustment for the New American Workplace." *Yale Law and Review* 8, no. 2 (1990): 197–204.

Sanders, Crystal R. "Blue Water, Black Beach: The North Carolina Teachers Association and Hammocks Beach in the Age of Jim Crow." *North Carolina Historical Review* 92 (April 2015): 145–64.

———. "North Carolina Justice on Display: Governor Bob Scott and the 1968 Benson Affair." *Journal of Southern History* 79 (August 2013): 659–80.

Sears, Richard D. "John G. Fee, Camp Nelson, and Kentucky Blacks, 1864–1865." *Register of the Kentucky Historical Society* 85 (Winter 1987): 29–45.

Sisk, Glenn. "Morehouse College." *Journal of Negro Education* 27 (Spring 1958): 201–8.

Sugrue, Thomas J. "Affirmative Action from Below: Civil Rights, the Building Trades, and the Politics of Racial Equality in the Urban North, 1945–1969." *Journal of American History* 91 (June 2004): 145–73.

Ware, Gilbert. "The NAACP-Inc. Fund Alliance: Its Strategy, Power, and Destruction." *Journal of Negro Education* 63, no. 3 (Summer 1994): 323–35.

Washington, Booker T. "Durham, North Carolina: A City of Negro Enterprises." *Independent* 70 (March 1911): 642–50.

Wheeler, John Hervey. "Apartheid Implemented by Education in South Africa." *Journal of Negro Education* 30, no. 3 (Summer 1961): 241–50.

———. "Civil Rights Groups—Their Impact upon the War on Poverty." *Law and Contemporary Problems* 31 (Winter 1966): 152–58. http://scholarship.law.duke.edu/lcp/vol31/iss1/11.

———. "A Negro Banker Speaks to the South." *Tarheel Banker*, November 1945.

Wilkerson, Doxey. "The Negro School Movement in Virginia: From 'Equalization' to 'Integration.'" *Journal of Negro Education* 29, no. 1 (Winter 1960): 17–29.

Winford, Brandon K. "'The Bright Sunshine of a New Day': John Hervey Wheeler, Black Business, and Civil Rights in North Carolina, 1929–1964." *North Carolina Historical Review* 93 (July 2016): 235–78.

Dissertations, Theses, and Papers

Battle, Starr Lakena. "Lest We Forget: The History of Kittrell College, Kittrell, North Carolina, 1886–1976." Master's thesis, North Carolina Central University, 2011.

Blackmon, Rebecca Kathleen. "When the Bulldozer's Came: A Historical Analysis of Urban Renewal and Community Action in a New South City." Honor's thesis, University of North Carolina at Chapel Hill, 1996.

Boston, Jesse. "The Lunch Counter Sit-In Demonstrations in Durham, North Carolina." Master's thesis, North Carolina Central University, 1975.

Bowman, Robert Louis. "Negro Politics in Four Southern Counties." Ph.D. diss, University of North Carolina at Chapel Hill, 1964.

Braswell, Deborah J. "A History of North Carolina Central University's Law School, 1939–1968," Master's thesis, North Carolina Central University, 1977.

Brinton, Hugh Penn. "The Negro in Durham: A Study of Adjustment to Town Life." Ph.D. diss., University of North Carolina at Chapel Hill, 1930.

Cannon, Robert Joseph. "The Organization and Growth of Black Political Participation in Durham, North Carolina, 1933–1958." Ph.D. diss., University of North Carolina at Chapel Hill, 1975.

Carver, Kam Owen. "The Role of the Durham Committee on the Affairs of Black People in the Pursuit of Equal Educational Opportunities, 1935–1954." Master's thesis, North Carolina Central University, 1992.

Cole, Olivia W. "Rencher Nicholas Harris: A Quarter of a Century of Negro Leadership." Master's thesis, North Carolina Central University, 1967.

Ellis, Ann Wells. "The Commission on Interracial Cooperation, 1919–1944, Its Activities and Results." Ph.D. diss., Georgia State University, 1975.

Faulkenbury, Evan. "Poll Power: The Voter Education Project and the Financing of the Civil Rights Movement, 1961–1992." Ph.D. diss., University of North Carolina at Chapel Hill, 2016.

Foy, Marjorie Anne Elvin. "Durham in Black and White: School Desegregation in Durham, North Carolina, 1954–1963." Master's thesis, University of North Carolina at Greensboro, 1991.

Funderburg, I. Owen. "An Analysis of Operating Problems of a Bank Serving a Predominantly Negro Market." Master's thesis, Rutgers University, 1959.

Houser, Paul. "The Southern Regional Council." Master's thesis, University of North Carolina at Chapel Hill, 1950.

Howard, Chris D. "Keep Your Eyes on the Prize: The Black Freedom Struggle for Civic Equality in Durham, North Carolina, 1954–1963." Honors' thesis, Duke University, 1983.

Karpinos, Ralph. "'With All Deliberate Speed': The *Brown v. Board of Education* Decision, North Carolina and the Durham City Schools, 1954–1963." Typescript, 1972, Chris D. Howard Papers, DMRRBML.

Lassiter, Hans Dominique. "A History of Mechanics and Farmers Bank, 1908–1969." Master's thesis, North Carolina Central University, 2000.

McDonough, Julia Anne. "Men and Women of Good Will: A History of the Commission on Interracial Cooperation and the Southern Regional Council, 1919–1954." Ph.D. diss. University of Virginia, 1993.

McElreath, Jack Michael. "The Cost of Opportunity: School Desegregation and Changing Race Relations in the Triangle since World War II." Ph.D. diss., University of Pennsylvania, 2002.

Mosley, Terry. "'Let's Keep the Big Boys Honest': Wilbur Hobby, the Life of a North Carolina Labor Leader 1925–1992." Master's thesis, North Carolina Central University, 2006.

Patterson, Vivian Rogers. "A Black Bank Revisited: An Update of 'Analysis of Operating Problems of a Bank Serving a Predominantly Negro Market' [1959]." Master's thesis, Rutgers University, 1978.

Powe, Alphonso Stewart. "The Role of Negro Pressure Groups in Interracial Integration in Durham City, North Carolina." Ph.D. diss., New York University, 1954.

Pyle, Christopher Howland. "The Politics of Civil Rights: The President's Committee on Equal Employment Opportunity, 1961–1962." Master's thesis, Columbia University, 1966.

Rice, David H. "Urban Renewal in Durham: A Case Study of a Referendum." Master's thesis, University of North Carolina at Chapel Hill, 1966.

Robinson, Jo-Ann. "An Interpretive Biography of Benjamin S. Ruffin, the First African American Chair of the UNC Board of Governors: How Life Experience Informs Practice." Ph.D. Diss., North Carolina State University, 2009.

Thuesen, Sarah Caroline. "Classes of Citizenship: The Culture and Politics of Black Public Education in North Carolina, 1919–1960." Ph.D. diss., University of North Carolina at Chapel Hill, 2003.

Walker, Harry Joseph. "Changes in Race Accommodations in a Southern Community." Ph.D. diss., University of Chicago, 1945.

Winford, Brandon. "'The Battle for Freedom Begins Every Morning': John Hervey Wheeler, Civil Rights, and New South Prosperity." Ph.D. diss., University of North Carolina at Chapel Hill, 2014.

———. "The Struggle for Freedom Begins Every Morning: A History of the Durham Committee on Negro Affairs." Master's thesis, North Carolina Central University, 2007.

Web Sources

To Secure These Rights: The Report of the President's Committee on Civil Rights. October 1947. http://www.trumanlibrary.org/civilrights/srights1.htm.

Reports

Althauser, Robert P. "The Durham Committee on Negro Affairs: 1962–1963." Confidential Report to the Voter Education Project. May 1964.

1898 Wilmington Race Riot Report. Raleigh: Research Branch, Office of Archives and History, N.C. Department of Cultural Resources, 2006.

The Federal Executive and Civil Rights. Atlanta, Ga.: Southern Regional Council, 1961.

Index

Page numbers in italics refer to illustrations.

Civil Rights and the Struggle for Black Equality in the Twentieth Century

Series Editors

Steven F. Lawson, Rutgers University
Cynthia Griggs Fleming, University of Tennessee
Hasan Kwame Jeffries, Ohio State University

Freedom's Main Line: The Journey of Reconciliation and the Freedom Rides
Derek Charles Catsam

Gateway to Equality: Black Women and the Struggle for Economic Justice in St. Louis
Keona K. Ervin

The Chicago Freedom Movement: Martin Luther King Jr. and Civil Rights Activism in the North
edited by Mary Lou Finley, Bernard LaFayette Jr., James R. Ralph Jr., and Pam Smith

The Struggle Is Eternal: Gloria Richardson and Black Liberation
Joseph R. Fitzgerald

Subversive Southerner: Anne Braden and the Struggle for Racial Justice in the Cold War South
Catherine Fosl

Constructing Affirmative Action: The Struggle for Equal Employment Opportunity
David Hamilton Golland

An Unseen Light: Black Struggles for Freedom in Memphis, Tennessee
edited by Aram Goudsouzian and Charles W. McKinney Jr.

River of Hope: Black Politics and the Memphis Freedom Movement, 1865–1954
Elizabeth Gritter

The Dream Is Lost: Voting Rights and the Politics of Race in Richmond, Virginia
Julian Maxwell Hayter

Sidelined: How American Sports Challenged the Black Freedom Struggle
Simon Henderson

Becoming King: Martin Luther King Jr. and the Making of a National Leader
Troy Jackson

Civil Rights in the Gateway to the South: Louisville, Kentucky, 1945–1980
Tracy E. K'Meyer

In Peace and Freedom: My Journey in Selma
Bernard LaFayette Jr. and Kathryn Lee Johnson

Democracy Rising: South Carolina and the Fight for Black Equality since 1865
Peter F. Lau

Civil Rights Crossroads: Nation, Community, and the Black Freedom Struggle
Steven F. Lawson

Selma to Saigon: The Civil Rights Movement and the Vietnam War
Daniel S. Lucks

In Remembrance of Emmett Till: Regional Stories and Media Responses to the Black Freedom Struggle
Darryl Mace

Freedom Rights: New Perspectives on the Civil Rights Movement
edited by Danielle L. McGuire and John Dittmer

This Little Light of Mine: The Life of Fannie Lou Hamer
Kay Mills

After the Dream: Black and White Southerners since 1965
Timothy J. Minchin and John A. Salmond

Faith in Black Power: Religion, Race, and Resistance in Cairo, Illinois
Kerry Pimblott

Fighting Jim Crow in the County of Kings: The Congress of Racial Equality in Brooklyn
Brian Purnell

Roy Wilkins: The Quiet Revolutionary and the NAACP
Yvonne Ryan

James and Esther Cooper Jackson: Love and Courage in the Black Freedom Movement
Sara Rzeszutek

Thunder of Freedom: Black Leadership and the Transformation of 1960s Mississippi
Sue [Lorenzi] Sojourner with Cheryl Reitan

For a Voice and the Vote: My Journey with the Mississippi Freedom Democratic Party
Lisa Anderson Todd

Pittsburgh and the Urban League Movement: A Century of Social Service and Activism
Joe William Trotter Jr.

John Hervey Wheeler, Black Banking, and the Economic Struggle for Civil Rights
Brandon K. Winford

Art for Equality: The NAACP's Cultural Campaign for Civil Rights
Jenny Woodley

For Jobs and Freedom: Race and Labor in America since 1865
Robert H. Zieger

Made in the USA
Middletown, DE
03 June 2023

31989738R00210

CORE COMMUNICATION

A Guide to Organizational Assessment, Planning and Improvement

Brent D. Ruben, Ph.D.
and Stacy M. Smulowitz, ABC

IABC INTERNATIONAL ASSOCIATION OF BUSINESS COMMUNICATORS

One Hallidie Plaza, Suite 600 / San Francisco, CA 94102, USA